# Feminist Criticism:

*Essays on Theory, Poetry and Prose*

edited by

## CHERYL L. BROWN

and

## KAREN OLSON

The Scarecrow Press, Inc.
Metuchen, N.J. & London
1978

**Library of Congress Cataloging in Publication Data**

Main entry under title:

Feminist criticism.

    Includes indexes.
    1.  American literature--Women authors--History and criticism--Addresses, essays, lectures.
2.  Feminism and literature--Addresses, essays, lectures.  3.  Criticism--Addresses, essays, lectures.  4.  English literature--Women authors--History and criticism--Addresses, essays, lectures.
I.  Brown, Cheryl L., 1951-    II.  Olson, Karen.
PS147.F4      810'.9'9287      78-8473
ISBN 0-8108-1143-X

To
MOTHERTIME
whose pendulum
is beginning
to swing

# TABLE OF CONTENTS

# Table of Contents

# ACKNOWLEDGMENTS

Quotations of poetry by Diane Wakoski are reprinted by permission of Simon & Schuster, Inc. , from The Motorcycle Betrayal Poems (New York, 1971), copyright © 1971 by Diane Wakoski. Material of Margaret Atwood's is reprinted by permission of Simon & Schuster, Inc. , from Surfacing (New York, 1973), copyright © 1973 by Margaret Atwood.

Certain lines of Emily Dickinson's poetry are reprinted by permission of the publishers and the Trustees of Amherst College from The Poems of Emily Dickinson, ed. Thomas H. Johnson (Cambridge, Mass. : Belknap Press of Harvard University Press, 1958), copyright © 1951, 1955 by the President and Fellows of Harvard College. Certain other lines of poetry are reprinted by permission of the publisher from The Complete Poems of Emily Dickinson, ed. Thomas H. Johnson (Boston: Little, Brown, n. d.), copyright 1929 and 1935 by Martha Dickinson Bianchi; copyright © renewed 1957 and 1963 by Mary L. Hampson. Certain portions of Dickinson's letters are reprinted by permission of the publisher from The Letters of Emily Dickinson, ed. Thomas H. Johnson and Theodora Ward (Cambridge, Mass. : Belknap Press of Harvard University Press, 1958; 3 vols.), copyright © 1958 by the President and Fellows of Harvard College.

Some quotations from H. D. 's poetry are reprinted by permission of the publishers from H. D. (Hilda Doolittle), Hermetic Definition (New York: New Directions Publishing Corporation, 1972; Cheadle, England: Carcanet Press); copyright © 1958, 1959, 1961, 1969, 1972 by Norman Holmes Pearson.

Quotations from Plath's poetry are reprinted by permission of Harper & Row, Publishers, Inc. , and Olwyn Hughes, from Ariel by Sylvia Plath, copyright © 1965 by Ted Hughes; from Crossing the Water by Sylvia Plath, copyright © 1971 by Ted Hughes; and from Winter Trees by Sylvia Plath, copyright © 1972. Material from The Bell Jar by Sylvia Plath, copyright © 1971 by Harper & Row, Publishers, Inc. , is reprinted by permission of Harper & Row and Faber and Faber Limited. Poetry from The Colossus and Other Poems by Sylvia Plath, copyright © 1967 by Ted Hughes, is reprinted by permission of Olwyn Hughes and Alfred A. Knopf, Inc.

Lines of poetry by Anne Sexton are reprinted by permission of the publisher, Houghton Mifflin Company, and the Sterling Lord Agency, Inc. , from To Bedlam and Part Way Back, copyright © 1960 by Anne Sexton; All My Pretty Ones, copyright © 1961, 1962 by Anne Sexton; Live or Die, copyright © 1966 by Anne Sexton; Love Poems, copyright © 1967, 1968, 1969 by Anne Sexton; Transformations, copyright © 1971 by Anne Sexton; The Book of Folly, copyright © 1972 by Anne Sexton; The Death Notebooks, copyright 1974 by Anne Sexton; The Awful Rowing Toward God, copyright 1975 by Loning Conant, Jr. , Executor of the Estate of Anne Sexton; and 45 Mercy Street, copyright © 1976 by Linda Gray Sexton and Loring Conant, Jr.

# PREFACE

"Sir, a woman's preaching is like a dog's walking on his hinder legs. It is not done well; but
you are surprized to find it done at all."

Samuel Johnson--July 31, 1763

It should not surprise anyone that women write well about
themselves and other women and that what they write strikes
some readers as annoying and superfluous preaching; however, in the spring of 1975, what did surprise us was that
what women critics were writing about women's literature
was not being published in respectable numbers and not readily accessible to concerned students and teachers. As a
consequence, we decided to collect feminist criticism already in print and to supplement those articles with others
that had not yet been published. Our work resulted in this
anthology--one we hope will give women writers their just
recognition and give students and teachers a classroom text
from which to begin their studies. We also hope that the
anthology will raise a few consciousnesses along the way because we all could benefit from becoming more sensitive to
the women's movement, more sensitive to literature, and
more sensitive to ourselves as the movement and literature
affect our daily lives.

When we discussed how to introduce the anthology, we wanted
to avoid arguing its worth solely as a book by and about
women writers. Certainly, giving exposure to women writers is important, and the writers we expose are good; however, they are good not because of or in spite of the fact
they are women. They all can hold their own in academic
circles. We prefer to offer the book simply as a valuable
collection of literary essays regardless of who contributed
to it and what those contributors chose to write on.

We envision the anthology as a classroom text for both English and Women's Studies courses and for any course in criticism taught in either department. The theoretical section
discusses the methodology of feminist criticism, and the
practical sections apply those principles to poetry and prose.

In the practical sections, we attempted to include articles on
those women's works that are frequently taught, and we tried
to assure some breadth in the chronology and in the questions
asked.    We hope the articles spark stimulating discussion.
We would like to see new questions asked and new answers
found.

This anthology is indebted to the faculty and staff of the Department of English and to the Student Research Allocations
Committee at the University of New Mexico.    We would also
like to extend a special thanks to Maureen Kelly for proof-
reading and to the contributors for making this venture pleasurable and productive.    Without the help of these people, the
anthology would not have been possible.

Cheryl L.  Brown and Karen Olson
May 1977

Margret Andersen

## FEMINISM AS A CRITERION
## OF THE LITERARY CRITIC*

The literary critic who first used feminism as a criterion was, to my knowledge, Christine de Pisan. Born in 1364, she also was the first woman ever to live, as a widow and with her children, on the money she earned with her pen. This outspoken feminist cannot so easily be frowned upon: in France, she is the first critic to speak of Dante. Her quarrel however--she was involved in the first querelle des femmes--was not with Dante but rather with Jehan de Meun, author of the later part of the Roman de la Rose. In her "Ode au Dieu d'Amour" she says of him:

> And Jehan de Meun in le Roman de la Rose,
> What a long story! What a difficult work!
> Clear and obscure thoughts
> Has he put there ...

To her, the Roman de la Rose is a textbook on the art of deceiving and seducing women, "a book on the art of great deception/ .../ to deceive many a virgin/ is its aim."[1] In "Playdoyer pour les femmes," Christine de Pisan objects in defence of women to the unfair description of the feminine character given by such writers as Jehan de Meun:

> Thus women are often ill-spoken of
> by many people and quite unjustly
> It's word of mouth and also often written
> ...
> Let gentlemanly preachers talk
> I say ...
> That woman's nature is most generous.

*Reprinted by permission of the author and publisher from Atlantis: A Women's Studies Journal 1, 1 (fall 1975), 3-13.

The author of la Cité des Dames (1405) is convinced that
woman has as many qualities as man, that lack of physical
strength does not imply lack of intelligence; but that as long
as woman is kept out of all serious discussions, she cannot
develop an independent mind.  Of course, there are exceptions, and in le Dittié sur Jeanne D'Arc (1429), Christine de
Pisan writes enthusiastically about Joan's exceptional achievements:

> Hé!  What honour for the feminine
> Sex!
> ...
> By a woman is assured and regained
> What a hundred thousand men could not
> win ...
> ...
> A young girl of fifteen years!
> Is this not something against nature?

From Christine de Pisan on, feminist criticism tries to
make its voice heard.

In Protection for Women (1589), Jane Anger speaks
of the necessity of feminist criticism as male critics "suppose that there is not one amongst us who can or dare reprove their slanders."[2]  Not only does she reprove the
slanders of misogynous writers, she lashes out at male writers in general for their conceit, false rhetoric, lack of substance: "The desire that every man has to show his true
vein in writing is unspeakable, and their minds are so carried away with the manner, as no care at all is had of the
matter.  They run so into rhetoric as often times they over-
run the bounds of their wits and go they know not whither"
(p. 24).

Anne Finch (1661-1720), who published her first volume of poetry anonymously, wrote about the woman writer
facing her prejudiced critics and being forced to become a
writer in hiding.  She, by the way, also points out a need
for what we call Women's Studies:

> Did I my lines intend for publick view
> How many censures wou'd their faults persue
> Some wou'd, because such words they do affect,
> Cry they're insipid, empty, uncorrect.
> And many have attain'd, dull and untaught
> The name of Witt, only by finding fault.

True judges might condemn their want of witt,
And all might say, they're by a woman writt.
Alas! a woman that attempts the pen,
Such an intruder on the rights of men,
Such a presumptuous creature, is esteem'd,
The fault can by no vertue be redeem'd.
They tell us, we mistake our sex and way;
Good breeding, fassion, dancing, dressing, play
Are the accomplishments we should desire;
To write or read, or think, or to enquire
Wou'd cloud our beauty, and exhaust our time,
And interrupt the conquests of our prime;
Whilst the dull mannage, of a servile house,
Is held by some, our utmost art, and use. [3]

Mme. de Staël, the French critic forced into hiding
by Napoleon, notes in De la Littérature (1880) "the changes
wrought in literature" by women. [4] She sees romanticism
not only as a gift of the North, but also as having developed
under the influence of women. She remarks that Shakespeare
could treat his women protagonists in any way he wanted,
and thus points out that social conventions, of which Shakespeare was free, later forced writers to create women characters corresponding to society's view of women: "The customs of the English regarding women were not yet formed
in Shakespeare's time; political disorder had precluded social
conventions. The position of women in tragedies was thus
left entirely to the will of the author; so Shakespeare, in
speaking of women, sometimes used the noblest language that
love could inspire and at others words in the worst and most
vulgar taste" (p. 198). Again, a female critic and a feminist who looks at women with objectivity and great interest.
One chapter of Mme. de Staël's book deals with the question
of "Women Who Cultivate Literature." Here she speaks of
the reluctance with which the public bestows its approval upon
a female writer and of man reducing woman "to the most absurd mediocrity." Thus any creative woman becomes "an
unusual woman. Say no more" (p. 235).

Do critics lose their objectivity when their feminism
becomes a criterion? When we read Virginia Woolf's essay
on "The Lives of the Obscure" we know that this is not so.
She tells the story of Laetitia Pinkerton who "so imbued with
the old traditions of her sex ... wrote, as ladies talk, to
give pleasure.... Thus Laetitia is in the great tradition of
English women of letters." [5] Virginia Woolf presents Mrs.
Pinkerton with quite some irony and certainly with all necessary objectivity.

It is evident from this brief survey that a tradition of feminist critique exists. With the greater accessibility to education, for women, with the greater rise of feminism in the twentieth century, such criticism has become more widely represented, more universally known. England has Virginia Woolf; France, Simone de Beauvoir. And North America? The writings of Diane Trilling, Margaret Lawrence, Kate Millett, Florence Howe, Margaret Atwood, and--last not least-- Mary Ellmann shall provide the substance for our analysis of feminist critique in North America.

What really is feminist criticism? What are its flaws, its temptations, its qualities? Is it in any way valid, or maybe even necessary?

Often, this sort of criticism is a retort to what Mary Ellmann so wittingly calls "phallic criticism," to a criticism that Virginia Woolf, for instance, feared greatly:

> I will here sum up my impressions before publishing
> A Room of One's Own. It is a little ominous that
> Morgan won't review it. It makes me suspect that
> there is a shrill feminine tone in it which my inti-
> mate friends will dislike. I forecast, then, that
> I shall get no criticism, except of the evasive
> jocular kind, from Lytton, Roger and Morgan. (He
> wrote yesterday, 3 Dec., and said he very much
> liked it); that the press will be kind and talk of its
> charm and sprightliness; also I shall be attacked
> for a feminist and hinted at for a Sapphist; Sybil
> will ask me to luncheon; I shall get good many
> letters from young women. I am afraid it will
> not be taken seriously. Mrs. Woolf is so accom-
> plished a writer that all she says makes easy read-
> ing ... this very feminine logic ... a book to be
> put in the hands of girls. 6

The rebuttal of "phallic criticism" can sometimes be extremely funny and Mary Ellmann's Thinking about Women has often made me laugh out loud. According to her, "books by women are treated as though they themselves were women, and criticism embarks, at its happiest, upon an intellectual measuring of bust and hips," almost as though "women wrote with breasts instead of pens."7 And, of course, "there must always be two literatures like two public toilets, one for Men and one for Women" (p. 30).

Ellmann suggests that men's books could be discussed

in similar terms and parodies the first paragraph of a review of Françoise Sagan's la Chamade in which Stanley Kauffmann writes: "Poor old Françoise Sagan. Just one more old-fashioned old-timer, bypassed in the rush for the latest literary vogue and for youth. Superficially, her career in America resembles the lifespan of those medieval beauties who flowered at 14, were deflowered at 15, were old at 30 and crones at 40." Ellmann submits: "Poor old François Sagan.... Superficially, his career in America resembles the life-span of those medieval troubadours who masturbated at 14, copulated at 15, were impotent at 30 and prostate cases at 40" (p. 30).

However, Ellmann herself says no to this "emulative project" which "would be diverting for a book season or two if it were possible to convince conventional journals to print" such amusing exercices de style (p. 30). One could try them out in composition classes, of course, but who, really, wants to imitate what is distasteful? And gallows humour suggests, after all, that one is about to be executed which, as far as woman's fate is concerned, is no longer quite true.

There is quite definitely a destructive element in feminist criticism. Many a teacher of literature has been fearful to accept Simone de Beauvoir's The Second Sex or Kate Millett's Sexual Politics because of their criticism of D. H. Lawrence, fearful maybe even to read their analyses, as they would endanger their views of a much cherished writer. I myself explored the reasons for this fear in an essay on feminist criticism included in Mother Was Not a Person. 8 It is never easy to introduce fundamental changes into one's Weltanschauung. Events in political or private life may lead or force one to accept such changes, but there is a scarcity of people who will accept them voluntarily or who will actively search for possibilities of change. Consequently, it is not easy to become a feminist. It is even frightening, for the understanding of the feminist cause means changes in all domains of life, political and private.

Indeed it is sometimes quite painful to be a feminist. When I could not see Hamlet anymore without giving much of my attention to Ophelia and to the cavalier way in which she is treated by both her father and her lover; when I became annoyed with myself for still humming the German folksong (written by Goethe) "Sah ein Knab' ein Röslein steh'n," which tells the story of a beautiful but helpless maiden who cannot defend herself successfully against the male aggressor; when Camus suddenly was no longer flawless in my eyes because of

his failure to see woman other than in her relationship to
man, I had to realize that something quite grave had happened.

It became evident that a new way of thinking had in-
vaded me totally.  So far, I had objected to certain attitudes
of relatives, colleagues, friends, foes; I had seen discrimination and sexism in education, law, customs, public life, ad-
vertising, etc.  But now, I was beginning to discover it also
in works of art that I used to cherish.  The critic in me
was taking into account a new dimension--my feminine con-
sciousness--and the musée imaginaire, which used to be my
ultimate refuge, was not safe anymore, was in need of reno-
vation, as everything it housed became subject to my feminist
critique.

In a way, of course, this painful process led to a
rejuvenation of my mind, my eyes, my ears, my feelings.
It led to the discovery of new friends, in my everyday reality as well as in what goes beyond it.  This then is the constructive side of feminist criticism.

Let me give you an example: I had always been somewhat reluctant to read with any serious interest the works of
Colette.  (Both for my M. A. and my Ph. D. theses, I attacked
such literary male giants as Proust and Claudel.)  Somehow,
in my snobbism, I did not like the titles of Colette's novels:
Gigi, Claudine ..., Chéri, etc.  I had thought of their author
as a facile and therefore popular woman novelist.  Recently,
Colette became one of the writers I have newly discovered
for myself.

Undoubtedly, some will reject the idea of consciousness-raising in the field of literary criticism and will belittle
the idea, as the feminist cause is belittled in so many fields.
Of course, impartial and impassionate criticism is what we
all have stood for, in the past.  But let us not forget that
much of the impartial criticism has often been passionately
biased.  We have accepted critics of pronounced religious
(Pierre-Henri Simon) or political (George Lukacs) convictions.
Why not accept a feminist outlook which will contribute to
the elucidation of other aspects of literary works?

I certainly do not want to read women writers only,
nor do I want to limit my enjoyment of the visual arts to
the works of women artists only.  Nevertheless, a compensatory program of study and reflection seems in order.  A
woman discovers herself more easily in the company and with

the help of other women. It is not only helpful but also necessary for me to become acquainted with what I have ignored
for so long. I must become more familiar with the female
artist and the female thinker, before I can try to build for
myself a new imaginary museum in which both men and women will hold their place. What I am proposing is an en-
richment and not an impoverishment of knowledge.

Quite often there is a slightly "personal touch" apparent
in writings by women critics or teachers of literature and
this has puzzled me. Florence Howe, for instance, frequently
refers to her Jewish background. But she herself explains
why this must be so, as she believes that "the connections
between feminism and literature are deep and abiding" and
begin "in our consciousness about our lives."[9] In her pres-
idential address, on "Literacy and Literature," delivered at
the 88th Annual Convention of the MLA, in Chicago, on December 27th, 1973, Howe reflects on the connection between
literature and life. "Literature," she says, "in its most
ancient and in its most modern forms, illuminates lives,
teaches us what is possible, how to hope and aspire."[10] If
we can agree to accept her hypothesis that the teacher of
literature touches "directly the lives of people in the process
of growing up, of deciding how to live, what work to seek,
and with what purpose"[11]; if we can furthermore agree to
see the teaching and the criticism of literature as having
some similitude, then we can, perhaps, conceive of a slightly
personalized criticism as a respectable activity.

Adrienne Rich has defined what the new feminist approach means to the literary critic: "Re-vision," she calls
it, "the act of looking back, of seeing with fresh eyes, of
entering an old text from a new critical direction--is for us
more than a chapter in cultural history: it is an act of
survival."[12]

The term "survival" is well known to the Canadian reader, as Margaret Atwood has published a thematic guide to
Canadian literature under the same title. As a critic, Atwood,
whose works can be called feminist, does not distinguish
between writings of women and writings of men. Survival
is about Canadian literature. Speaking of Canadians and
their literature, Atwood says,

> What a lost person needs is a map of the territory,
> with his own position marked on it so he can see
> where he is in relation to everything else. Litera-
> ture is not only a mirror; it is also a map, a

geography of the mind. Our literature is one such map, if we can learn to read it as our literature, as the product of who and where we have been. We need such a map desperately, we need to know about here, because here is where we live. For the members of a country or of a culture, shared knowledge of their place, their here, is not a luxury but a necessity. Without that knowledge we will not survive. [13]

Speaking of women and of the significance of the discovery of "their" literature we could rewrite the paragraph without much difficulty:

What a lost woman needs is a map of the territory, with her own position marked on it, so she can see where she is in relation to everything else. Literature is not only a mirror; it is also a map, if we can learn to read it as our literature, as the product of who and where we have been. We need such a map desperately, we need to know about here, because here is where we live. For the members of a sex or a culture, shared knowledge of their place, their here, is not a luxury but a necessity. Without that knowledge we will not survive.

Black studies, Canadian studies, women's studies have much in common.

It is my belief that feminist critique is zeitbedingt. It is helping women to recognize themselves, to find their position on a territory which used to be exclusively male, to surface, to survive. It is helping men to do away with "phallic criticism." Women critics now tend to counter "phallic criticism" with a criticism marked by woman's pride in her sex. In her foreword to The School of Femininity, Margaret Lawrence defines her book as following a definite pattern of thought, namely "that women for the first time in history upon a large scale are saying their particular say about themselves, about men, and about life as it treats them separately and together with men." [14] It is high time for literary criticism to take this phenomenon into account.

I do not propose that there be two distinct branches of criticism: one by, for, and on men--the other by, for, and on women. But we, both men and women, must stop treating books by women "as though they themselves were

women. " "Phallic criticism" has served and is still serving
to perpetuate the myth of the artistic (and other) inferiority
of women; consequently, "vulvate criticism" seems, at the
present time, justified as a weapon to combat this myth.

If Walpole could permit himself to call Mary Wollstonecraft a "hyena in petticoats," if Southey could call Charlotte
Brontë "a day-dreamer," and if R. W. Chambers could write
that "poor Margery Kempe is to be classed with those hotels
that Baedeker describes as 'variously judged,'"[15] then it is
perfectly legitimate that Mary Ellmann should call Robert
Frost a "camping type" (p. 14) and that Kate Millett should
refer to Norman Mailer as to a "would-be-Irish-buffoon."[16]
As long as the words "feminine" and "woman writer" are
used as pejorative qualifications such combat is as necessary
as any querelle des anciens et des modernes. Feminism and
feminist critique will not simply "go away"; the "fad," as
many hopefully call feminism, will not fade out. Les anciens
et les modernes will have to arrive at an understanding, in
order to allow the streams of male and female consciousness
to converge into a river of simply human, heterosexual consciousness.

## REFERENCES

1. All quotations from C. de Pisan are my own translations
from Oeuvres Poétiques de Christine de Pisan,
Maurice Roy, ed. (Paris: Firmin Didot, 1886).
2. In Joan Goulianos, ed. , By a Woman Writt (Baltimore:
Penguin Books, 1974), p. 25.
3. In Goulianos, op. cit. , pp. 71-72.
4. Mme. de Staël on Politics, Literature, and National Character, translated, edited and with an introduction
by Morroe Berger (New York: Doubleday, 1964),
p. 158.
5. Virginia Woolf, The Common Reader, First Series (London: Hogarth Press, 1957), p. 161.
6. Leonard Woolf, ed. , A Writer's Diary: Being Extracts
from the Diary of Virginia Woolf (London: Hogarth
Press, 1959), p. 148.
7. (New York: Harcourt Brace Jovanovich, 1968), pp. 29
and 35. Further references will be noted in the
text.
8. Compiled by M. Andersen (Montreal: Content Publishing
and Black Rose, 1972), pp. 88-89.
9. In Images of Women in Fiction, Susan Koppelman Cornil-

lon, ed. (Bowling Green, Ohio: Bowling Green
University Popular Press, 1972), pp. 253-277.
10. PMLA, 89(May 1974), 433.
11. Ibid.
12. In Florence Howe, op. cit. , p. 440.
13. (Toronto: Anansi, 1972), pp. 18-19.
14. (Toronto: Nelson, 1936), p. xii.
15. In Goulianos, op. cit. , p. xv.
16. Sexual Politics (New York: Avon Books, 1971), p. 325.

Annis Pratt

## THE NEW FEMINIST CRITICISM*

A good deal of the fiction by and about women centers
upon the heroine's entanglement with patriarchal norms which
historically have enforced the forfeiture of the female self
by law. "Man and wife are one person," goes a 1632 in-
tepretation of the Common Law, "but understand in what
manner. When a small brook or little river incorporateth
with Rhodanus, Humber or the Thames, the poor rivulet
looseth its name, it is carried and recarried with the new
associate, it beareth no sway, it possesseth nothing during
coverture. A woman as soon as she is married, is called
covert, in Latin, nupta, that is veiled, as it were, clouded
and overshadowed, she has lost her streame.... To a married woman, her new self is her superior, her companion,
her master."[1] Is it a fear of losing one's psychic "streame,"
one's unique identity as a human being, that is working deep
in the bone of Clarissa Harlowe, Sue Bridehead, Maggie Tul-
liver, Mrs. Ramsay, Anna Wulf and their American sisters,
and can a comprehension of this malaise help or hinder our
understanding of the literature by and about women?

It is hardly surprising that there is emerging a new
feminist criticism to approach such questions. Its pitfalls
are so immediately obvious that it seems imperative to consider as dispassionately as possible a typical field that such
criticism might survey, the strictures it should impose upon
itself and its principal modes of attack. In fiction the field
would range from feminist literature narrowly defined as
works in which the author's explicit intention is to expose

---

*Reprinted by permission of the author and publisher from
College English 32 (May 1971), 872-8. Copyright © 1971 by
the National Council of Teachers of English. This article is
a revision of the author's paper read at the MLA workshop
on Feminist Literature and Feminine Consciousness, December 1970.

some aspect of sexism, to feminine literature broadly defined
as by and about women.  At the narrow end of the spectrum
we have novels, for example, which probe into woman's situation in the same manner that Steinbeck examined the plight
of the dust bowl farmers in The Grapes of Wrath; at the
broader end we have Moll Flanders, Clarissa Harlowe, The
Mill on the Floss, and, more recently, Ship of Fools.  The
first task for the new feminist critic will be one of identification, the searching out and listing of feminist and feminine
works.  Identifying explicitly feminist fiction for bibliographical purposes is not a difficult matter when it comes to such
works as Grant Allen's The Woman Who Did (1895) or Willa
Cather's O Pioneers! (1913); there are also, however, a
good number of lesser known works such as David Phillips's
Susan Lenox:  Her Fall and Rise (1917) and Margaret Culkin
Banning's The Dowry (1954), which are specifically concerned
with the resistance encountered by the woman who, to use
Simone de Beauvoir's term, attempts to transcend.

    The searching out and listing of feminist fiction has
been begun by Joseph Blotner and, less systematically, by
Lucinda Cisler; a thorough bibliographical effort, perhaps
cooperative, is needed to bring together information now
scattered in any number of separate sources. [2]  A book-
length study is also needed which will do for women's literature in the period 1720-1970 what William York Tindall's
Forces in Modern British Literature, 1885-1956 did for his
period:  a full-length scholarly and historical survey accom-
panied by descriptive bibliography.

    The bringing of feminist fiction to the light of day
will involve two critical skills:  the textual analysis necessary
to determine which works are novelistically successful, and
the contextual analysis which considers the relevance of a
group of works, even if artistically flawed, as a reflection
of the situation of women.  The new feminist critic should
be a "new critic" (in the aesthetic rather than the political
sense) in judging the formal aspects of individual texts; she
should be "feminist" in going beyond formalism to consider
literature as it reveals men and women in relationship to
each other within a socio-economic context, that web of role
expectations in which women are enmeshed.  That she should
be a "new" rather than an "old feminist" will become clear
a little later.

    Ann Snitow's analysis of the cellular family in the
fiction of Ivy Compton-Burnett (Aphra, Autumn 1970) is an
example of the mixture of textual and contextual criticism

that needs to be done. Book-length studies are needed on
such broader questions as the links tying such novelists as
Willa Cather, Theodore Dreiser, Ellen Glasgow and Edith
Wharton (and such poets as Edna St. Vincent Millay, Sara
Teasdale and Elinor Wylie) to the progressive movement,
which might in turn explain the upsurge of explicitly feminist
fiction written between 1890 and 1930. "The effects of the
growing women's movement are apparent in the literature
of the time," writes Herbert Marder of England in the nineteenth century--"many important writers were influenced by
feminist ideas, and a significant part of the social criticism
in Victorian novels has to do with the grievances of women."[3]
Similarly, the whole range of the sentimental novel needs
to be re-examined from a new feminist perspective.[4]

Immediately to one side of explicit feminist fiction,
and often overlapping it, there is a literature by avowed
feminists which can only be described as deliberately oblique
on the woman question. Larzer Ziff has described how Constance Cary Harrison, Gertrude Atherton and their sisters
at the turn of the century, in order "to give themselves
more freedom ... dealt with a heroine who had two successive marriages. The first was the crucial one, and the dependence upon men was attacked as the marriage's inadequacies were detailed."[5] By this subterfuge Harrison's Bachelor
Maid (1894) passed through the portals of gentility while Sister Carrie, Jude the Obscure, George Moore's Esther Waters
and Mrs. Gaskell's Ruth were met by storms of patriarchal
abuse.

Critics thus need to examine the relationship between
oblique approaches to feminism and the economic demands
of the fiction market in the same way that they have brought
interesting insights to the works of the Victorian novelists
through analysis of the prerequisites of serial publication.
The contextual critic must pass by the chimeras of "intentional fallacy" and aesthetic distaste for economics when
analyzing an author's use of a marketable fictional convention as a deflecting mask for feminism. Such craftswomen
as Sarah Orne Jewett, Mary Wilkins Freeman and Kate Chopin, during the same period that Harrison guided Bachelor
Maid through the presses, managed to publish carefully
wrought stories about gentle separatists, the confinement of
spinsterhood and the indelicacies of race mixing by passing
as local colorists. Here the new feminist critic must consider certain fictional conventions as politico-economic strategies without for a moment suspending her critical judgement.

As we move toward the broader range of feminist
fiction we will find novels written by persons with known
sentiments about the woman question but who approach it
obliquely because of novelistic considerations. The same
person who when writing expository prose will present her
feminism directly may, because of fictional prerequisites,
deflect her message through the conventions of plot, character, imagery and thematic structure so that its effect is
dramatic rather than polemical. Herbert Marder has remarked of Virginia Woolf that "Her desire to play the [fem-
inist] moralist was in conflict with her artistic conscience,"
a conflict that created the tensional energy upon which her
novels were built. Marder requires us to take her feminism
in the broad sense of an "intense awareness of her identity
as a woman ... [and] its meaning," he rightly concludes,
"should not be restricted to the advocacy of women's rights"
(Feminism & Art, p. 2).

Similarly, Doris Lessing's The Golden Notebook has
been taken to be a model of what the author, in some dismay,
described to Florence Howe as "a work of latter-day feminism" although her intention in writing it was to create a
careful fictional construction centering upon "a complex of
ideas which could be described as left--and which were born
with the French Revolution."6  The question of woman's
freedom in The Golden Notebook requires both textual analysis
of the intricate and ironic juxtapositions which form the tensional structure of the novel and a contextual analysis which
goes beyond the question of the emancipation of women to
the quest of men and women for liberty since 1789.   Here,
as in Lessing's Children of Violence novels, Katherine Anne
Porter's Ship of Fools and, to a slightly lesser extent, Dorothy Richardson's Pilgrimage, we are dealing with a fiction
which includes a brilliant exploration of woman's existential
situation within a carefully orchestrated treatment of other
and broader human conflicts and relationships--a genre which
I would define as encyclopedic feminism.

At the broadest range of the spectrum we have these
novels which are unintentionally if implicitly feminist and of
concern because of their place in the literature of women.
Here the new feminist critic is likely to encounter the kind
of abuse that Hazel Mews met at the hands of the London
Times Literary Supplement reviewer of her Frail Vessels
(1969).   The problem was that the reviewer's definition of
feminist fiction was too narrow: a feminist, he felt, would
be a dogmatic preacher; any novelist worth her salt would
be too keen an artist to write a "feminist novel"; and even

if there were such a thing it would be flawed by "a continual
desire to instruct, a constant deliberate admixture of ethical,
moral, political, sociological or religious powder [which]
will produce a texture so gritty as to be unreadable [sic].
The powder will be spat out with the jam, and the book forgotten."[7] He then accuses Mews of desecrating Jane Austen,
Fanny Burney, and Mme. de Scudéry by imputing "political
influence" to their works. We can expect such reactions as
we turn to those brilliant works of implicit feminism which
mark the history of the novel: our definitions of feminist
fiction must be broad enough and our critical tools fine enough
so that it will be clear that it is such accusers and not ourselves who are parochial.

Unfortunately there are critics who have set forth to
survey the field of feminine and feminist fiction who are
themselves equipped with too stereotyped an understanding
of feminism. Two of them, who make very peculiar bedfel-
lows, have seriously misjudged the texts of novels because
of a myopic misunderstanding of their contexts: Leslie Fiedler in Love and Death in the American Novel (1962) and
Josephine Lurie Jessup in The Faith of Our Feminists (1950).
In his chapter on "Richardson and the Tragedy of Seduction"
Fiedler argues that Clarissa Harlowe is based on a ritual
combat between "Seducer" and "Pure Maiden" and attributes
to this plot the germination of the entire range of sentimental
and popular fiction of the next two hundred years. "From
Charlotte Temple to the latest daytime serial on radio or
TV," he insists, "the legend of a moral struggle ending in
the moral dominance of women informs the literature which
makes the mass mind of America. In this country the only
class war is between the sexes!"[8]

One could hardly disagree with this pioneering analysis
of sexual politics did not the blame for "Virginity" and "Morality" tend to fall in Fiedler's criticism squarely upon the
female side of the argument. Although elsewhere in the book
he traces the putting of woman on a pedestal of purity to the
courtly code, thus defining it as a male projection, the implication for the sentimental and popular fiction which he
analyzes is that it is largely a female weapon. Clarissa's
problem is certainly that she takes refuge within her physical
virginity, but her situation is complicated in that she uses
it to resist not only her seducer but also her potential husband. Her cry to Lovelace, "I have no patience, sir, to be
thus constrained. Must I never be at liberty to follow my
own judgement? Be the consequence what it may, I will
not be thus constrained" (Modern Library, 1950, p. 205),

is one of rejection not only of his extra-marital suit but of
the constraints of marriage itself.    Clarissa's "heroic feminism" consists much less in any moral-physical prudery
than in a human integrity which cries out against being en-
slaved against her will--whether within marriage or out of
it.    Here she is in accord with the heroines of Jane Austen
and Fanny Burney whose refusal to marry without affection
was shockingly out of step with the marital practices of their
times.    To Clarissa, Elizabeth Bennet, and Evelina "virginity" connotes a form of negative emancipation in the freedom
to reject the forfeiture of the self to partriarchal demands--
by suicide, if necessary.

    Josephine Jessup, like Fiedler, assumes that a fem-
inist fiction manifests the "moral" superiority of women over
men and depicts them engaged in a battle of the sexes which
must be resolved either in marriage or female separatism.
Taking as her models Edith Wharton, Ellen Glasgow and
Willa Cather, craftswomen whom Fiedler did not mention in
his book, Jessup attributes to them explicitly stereotyped
"old feminist" intentionality:    "and the spirit of her whom
these writers zealously served--Athena, the spirit of woman
disjunct and triumphant in her separateness--shows forth in
the body of their novels."[9]   I am not objecting here to "old"
or separatist feminism (which Caroline Bird rather narrowly
defined as out to "prove that women can be like men, if
necessary by remaining single")[10] as a possible position to
take personally but as a distorting critical perspective.    Although Jessup points out some aspects of her three novelists'
work that are startlingly relevant to the feminism of which
they were all aware, she tends to misjudge them because
of her stereotypical definition of the genre.

    Edith Wharton's Lily Bart (of The House of Mirth),
for example, comes out of Jessup's battle of the sexes as
a prototypical triumphant woman and Lawrence Selden as her
"ideal foil," the antithesis creating of the work a "model
feminist vehicle."    She misses the point that Lily's situation
is the result of the same socio-economic expectations as
Clarissa's and that they make of her a tragic rather than an
heroic figure.    Her feminism consists in the negative emancipation derived from her consciousness of the sexist nature
of her destiny and her courage to go down to her death resisting it.    Lawrence Selden, like Newland Archer in Edith
Wharton's other feminist masterpiece, The Age of Innocence,
is shown up as weak not in relation to the heroine but in relation to his own tragic flaw, his ineffectual feminism.    Both
heroes give mouth service to the emancipation of women

while complying despite themselves with patriarchal norms, and it is the inauthenticity of their feminism which provides the structural irony of the works. These novels are indeed "feminist vehicles," but in an Aristotelian or tragic rather than an Athenian or triumphant sense.

In considering the stereotypes imposed by fiction upon women as well as the stereotypes imposed by critics upon feminine fiction, we come to a mode of attack which has engaged the attention of such critics as Mary Ellmann in her exposé of "phallic criticism" in Thinking About Women (1968), Kate Millett in Sexual Politics (1970) and a number of other students of "the image of woman in literature." The example of Josephine Lurie Jessup will warn us away, I should hope, from becoming stereotypical in our own right. It is difficult not to feel about Molly Bloom on her chamberpot what Eldridge Cleaver must feel about Jack Benny's Rochester, but a good critic will not withdraw her attention from a work which is resonant and craftsmanlike even if it is chauvinistic. If the critical palate is soured by the evaluation of the works of Durrell, Burgess, Faulkner, Nabokov, Bellow, etc., it would seem better to turn one's attention from attack to defense, from examples of distorted images of women to examples of healthier representation. [11]

New feminist critics engaged in the tasks of bibliographical, textual, and contextual criticism may notice that the heroines they study manifest interestingly parallel characteristics during their psychic development. It is startling to realize that volumes have been written about the development of the male psyche as if it, in itself, defined the human soul. If there is a "myth of the hero" there must also be a "myth of the heroine," a female as well as a male Bildungsroman, parallel, perhaps, but by no means identical. Carefully avoiding the hazards of stereotyping, we must study the relationship, for example, between Alexandra's love of the land in Willa Cather's O Pioneers!, Martha Quest's and Anna Wulf's similar passion for parts of the veldt in Doris Lessing's fiction and the relationship between Sarah Orne Jewett's heroines and the trees and gardens with which they often identify. We might also consider the relationship between the naturism of such heroines and certain hallucinatory passages in which they discover a "muse" or "other"-- not a female sprite but a virile earth-god or male figure. Heathcliff, Maud Bodkin has noted, may be Catherine's Beatrice.

The heroines of fiction (as well as of poetry and drama)

can be described as passing through the immanent phases of
adolescent naturism, sexual initiation, marriage and childbirth in a quest for a transcendence which is sometimes separatist, sometimes androgynous, and sometimes visionary.
We will thus find it helpful to develop a fourth and archetypal
mode of new feminist criticism which will describe the psycho-
mythological development of the female individual in literature. [12]

It is when we consider the fact that woman's development takes place over and against the sexual "other," maleness as externalized into a recalcitrant field of action which
cannot be escaped by separatism, that we realize her complex
polarity.  Maleness is inescapable precisely because it is as
much a psychic feature of the woman as femaleness is of the
man.  Although the forms of socio-sexual classification in
culture--men do this and women do that--can be seen as
externally imposed upon the individual, this avoids the fact
that it is impossible to separate the male and the female
within the human psyche.

It is this internal androgyneity of the self that generates, when repressed, the distorted sexual relationships
that characterize the unexamined life--misogyny, man-hating,
sadism, masochism, etc.--and, conversely, it generates such
externalized misunderstandings or exaggerations as the worship of male gods and heroes on the part of woman and of
earth-mothers or sex goddesses and "pure women" on the
part of man.  The novel of a mature relationship between
the sexes has been rare both in British and American literature because it is so unusual for a man and a woman to enjoy
sexual androgyneity, that delightful interchange of the aggressive and the gentle, the adventurous and the nurturing facul-
ties residing in each personality.  This sexual reciprocity
which occurs, as Simone de Beauvoir describes it, when two
transcendencies meet face to face, is so rarely lived or described in a western civilization devoted alternately to the
epic-patriarchal and to the worship of "eternal womanhood"
that it might become the norm (if utopian) which the new
feminist critic seeks in fiction.

We can expect the outcry of our colleagues against
the idea of a new feminist criticism to be immediate and
scathing.  The mere term will provoke the petulance not
only of those in our profession who resent critical attentions
paid to the humanity of women, but also of those who feel
that the discipline will be sullied by contextual analysis.  The
quest for a feminist literature is a humanistic one, nonethe-

less, devoted to the cleansing of misconceptions held by both men and women in our culture.  It should not be allocated to token female employees kept from incorporating it into regular courses, nor should it be taught in sexually segregated classrooms.  Colleges which pretend to a liberal arts curriculum will have to devote attention to feminist literature not only for the scholarly reason that it has been neglected but because of the pedagogical imperative that no institution which calls its curriculum humanist can be justified in ignoring it.

## REFERENCES

1. The Lawes Resolutions of Womens Rights; or The Lawes Provision for Women (London, 1632), quoted in Eleanor Flexner, Century of Struggle (Cambridge, Mass.:  Belknap Press, 1968), pp. 7-8.
2. See Joseph Blotner, The Modern American Political Novel (Austin:  University of Texas Press, 1966), pp. 164-190; Lucinda Cisler, Women:  A Bibliography (New York:  private printing, 1970); Sheila Tobias, Female Studies No. 1, and Florence Howe Female Studies No. 2 (Pittsburgh:  Know, Inc. , 1970).
3. Herbert Marder, Feminism & Art:  A Study of Virginia Woolf (Chicago:  University of Chicago Press, 1968), p. 7.
4. See Fred Pattee's The Feminine Fifties; Larzer Ziff's The American 1890s; B. G. McCarthey's The Female Pen:  Women Writers and Their Contribution to the English Novel, 1621-1744; and Hazel Mews' Frail Vessels:  Women's Role in Women's Novels from Fanny Burney to George Eliot.
5. Larzer Ziff, The American 1890s (New York:  Viking Press, 1961), p. 279.
6. Florence Howe, "Talk with Doris Lessing:  Excerpts from an Interview," Nation, 6 March 1967, p. 312.
7. Anon. , "Clever Ladies," TLS, 3 December 1970, p. 278.
8. Leslie Fiedler, Love and Death in the American Novel (New York:  World Pub. Co. , 1962), p. 62.
9. Josephine Lurie Jessup, The Faith of Our Feminists (New York:  R. Smith, 1950), p. 13.
10. Caroline Bird, Born Female (New York:  David McKay, 1968), p. 161.
11. The editors of the Fall 1970 issue of Women:  A Journal of Liberation, for example, carefully juxtapose a section on "The Men Who Wrote About Us" (stereo-

typical criticism) with one on "Discovering Our Sister Authors. "

12.    Approaches have been made in W. D. Howells' Heroines of Fiction, Patricia Thompson's The Victorian Heroine: A Changing Ideal and also in Gerarda von Middendorf's The Hero in the Feminine Novel.

Lillian S. Robinson

## DWELLING IN DECENCIES:
## RADICAL CRITICISM AND
## THE FEMINIST PERSPECTIVE*

I reached the point of thinking you were right,
and that your culture was the true one.... By
a hair, I missed becoming one of you.
--The Schoolboys of Barbiana, Letter to a Teacher

Feminist criticism, as its name implies, is criticism
with a Cause, engaged criticism. But the critical model presented to us today is merely engaged to be married. It is
about to contract what can only be a mésalliance with bourgeois modes of thought and the critical categories they inform. To be effective, feminist criticism cannot become
simply bourgeois criticism in drag. It must be ideological
and moral criticism; it must be revolutionary.

Having begun thus bluntly, I feel tempted to retreat
somewhat, to equivocate and speak optimistically of "steps
in the right direction." Literary theory has existed so long
without a self-conscious female component that I hesitate to
find fault when one is forthcoming. Nonetheless, I am convinced that established criticism cannot provide the intellectual
means to advance in what will prove to be right directions.

Even criticism that calls itself radical frequently falls

*Reprinted by permission of the author and publisher from
College English 32 (May 1971), 879-89. Copyright © 1971 by
the National Council of Teachers of English. A version of
this essay was presented at the MLA Workshop on Feminist
Literature and Feminine Consciousness, December 1970. The
author is grateful to Annis Pratt, Katherine Ellis of Columbia
University, and Lise Vogel of Boston University for their
help.

into masculine habits of expression:  the human antecedent
takes the pronoun "he" and the human generalization is sexually particularized as "Man" or "mankind."   The existence
of these terms may be a lexical accident, their survival an
anachronism.   But their continued use by professed radicals
reflects a grave failure of consciousness.   Those who recognize the class and racial bias of traditional literary study
have paid, at best, only perfunctory notice to its sex bias.
If radical critics are sexist, however, that does not mean
feminists can ignore what they tell us about literature and
criticism.   Rather, we must construct a method that applies
radical insights about culture and politics, but does so in
the context of a coherent feminist analysis.

       To some extent, the terms of this discussion recapi-
tulate debates within the American women's movement.   The
questions I pose about our discipline reflect a larger question about ourselves:  can women be liberated in our present
political economy, or is more fundamental change required?
For those of us who choose a radical response to this question, there is a more pressing problem.   I am referring to
the tension between "feminists," narrowly defined as those
who believe that the basic social conflict is between the sexes
and that all men benefit from male supremacy, and so-called
"politicos," who believe that the fundamental conflict is between classes and that sexism is a part of that struggle.
This is not merely a sectarian quarrel, and I bring it up in
a literary discussion because much of my present argument
depends on the definition of "feminism."   In this paper, I
characterize as feminist women's consciousness of being "the
other" in a male-dominated system.   Within the limits of
literature, at least, women's exclusion is clearly shared by
all non-white and working-class men.   "High" culture is a
male domain, but not all men may participate in it.   Recognition of these facts does not make my approach less feminist.   It does suggest the critical direction I think we should
pursue.


                              II


       My earlier unsupported allusion to bourgeois ideology
probably had two immediate effects:  it made me a marked
woman and it turned off part of my audience.   I hope this
response is not irrevocable, for my use of the term is quite
precise and is meant as neither random invective nor (red)
flag-waving.   None of us is to blame for our exposure to
certain training, including a conditioned revulsion to the rhet-

oric of class warfare.   We are at fault only if we insist--in the face of all evidence--that the realm of the mind is above that struggle, that it is some abstract Agora where ideas duel gracefully among themselves, all unconscious of whose interests they serve.

What happens then is that we perceive history--literary history above all--as the consecutive predominance of certain ideas, schools and values, independent of the conditions or the people that produced them.   Marx and Engels observed that it had not occurred to the philosophers who were their contemporaries "to inquire into the connections of German philosophy with German reality, the relation of their criticism to their own material surroundings."[1]  Similarly, the members of our profession have chosen to ignore the class origins of literary categories and standards.   This is something that women, in particular, cannot afford to do.

I have called certain categories of thought "bourgeois," choosing a term that usually has connotations of class rather than sex divisions.   As I have said, I think that cultural criticism helps us to clarify what "class analysis" has to do with feminism.   When I characterize an idea as bourgeois, I am doing so in the traditional Marxist sense:

> The ideas of the ruling class are in every epoch the ruling ideas: i. e. the class which is the ruling material force of society is at the same time its ruling intellectual force.   The class which has the means of material production at its disposal has control at the same time over the means of mental production, so that thereby, generally speaking, the ideas of those who lack the means of mental production are subject to it.   The ruling ideas are nothing more than the ideal expression of the dominant material relationships, the dominant material relationships grasped as ideas [Marx and Engels, p. 39].

Italian adolescents have expressed the same view somewhat more colorfully: "How could a young gentleman argue with his own shadow, spit on himself and on his own distorted culture while using the very words of that culture?"[2]   Both these arguments involve observations about the nature of the dominant ideology and the difficulty of formulating a critique from within its sphere of influence.   (Others have demonstrated the application of this analysis to literary criticism rigorously and at length; I trust I do not have to rehearse the

radical arguments before discussing how they relate to a
feminist perspective. )

    Feminist theory may avoid the class question, but it
is quite explicit as to women's sense of being culturally disinherited.  It may seem that I needlessly polarize the issue
by insisting on the relations between material and ideological
power.  Aren't there many bourgeois women, after all?  Well,
no.  The wives and daughters of the ruling class do not
somehow mystically partake in someone else's relation to
the means of production:

> The category [woman] seems to cut across all clas-
> ses; one speaks of working-class women, middle-
> class women, etc.  The status of women is clearly
> inferior to that of men, but analysis of this condi-
> tion usually falls into discussing socialization, psy-
> chology, interpersonal relations, or the role of
> marriage as a social institution.  Are these, how-
> ever, the primary factors?  In arguing that the
> roots of the secondary status of women are in fact
> economic it can be shown that women as a group
> do indeed have a definite relation to the means of
> production and that this is different from that of
> men.  The personal and psychological factors then
> follow from this special relation to production, and
> a change in the latter will be a necessary (but not
> sufficient) condition for changing the former. [3]

The essential female relation to the means of production is
embodied in women's traditional tasks in the home, housework, child-rearing, even supervision of housework and serving as hostess.  We are used to borrowing sociological vocabulary and speaking of women's "rôle," but it is useful,
first, to comprehend it materially.  And it is vital to do so
if we are to understand that vast body of literature in which
female characters acquire, question, accept, or modify their
"rôles," the social definition of woman.

    Just above, I used a Marxist source because I think
it very cogently summarizes one side of a vexed economic
question.  But I first encountered a proposal to "capitalize"
household duties in a less doctrinaire setting, the writings
of Virginia Woolf.  Addressing a man of the ruling class,
Virginia Woolf says, "you should provide a wage to be paid
by the State to those whose profession is marriage and moth-
hood. "[4]  In suggesting this, with a sense of futility but not
of irony, Virginia Woolf recognizes the psychological effects

of economic conditions; payment of a regular salary to unpaid
women workers is, she states, "the most effective way in
which we can ensure that the large and very honourable class
of married women shall have a mind and a will of their own."
She also translates into material terms the feeling of "other-
ness" typical even of women who are "of" the bourgeoisie.
For instance, she explains her repetition of the phrase "educated man's daughter" to designate such a woman:

> Our ideology is still so inveterately anthropocentric
> that it has been necessary to coin this clumsy
> term ... to describe the class whose fathers have
> been educated at public schools and universities.
> Obviously, if the term 'bourgeois' fits her brother,
> it is grossly incorrect to use it of one who differs
> so profoundly in the two prime characteristics of
> the bourgeoisie--capital and environment. [5]

So when I speak of the bourgeoisie and its intellectual productions, I feel I am doing so as a feminist, referring to a
group from which women are by and large excluded and in
whose interest that exclusion is justified.

## III

Annis Pratt has outlined how "feminist" critics can
make use of bibliographical, textual, contextual, and archetypal modes. My response has been to say that feminism
is necessarily alienated from those modes--at least as we
have come to understand them. It remains for me to suggest something to put in their place.

As women, we should be aware of how idealization
serves oppression. Throughout much of our literature, fan-
ciful constructs of the ideal female, her character and psychology, have obscured the limitations suffered by actual
women. Worse, they have encouraged expectations and behavior that only strengthen the real oppression. Feminist
critics are not likely to ape male poets in sentimentalizing
the female spirit. But there is a kind of idealism to which
we become susceptible when we explore the question of feminine consciousness. For we, too, have a tendency to ignore
its material basis.

I grant that I am making a kind of play on words,
but it is not intended to blur the distinction between "idealization" and "idealism." In literature, to idealize means to

ignore, perhaps to "transcend," reality. The philosophical
tendency called "idealism" means to ignore material conditions. Whereas the former is more or less the opposite
of realism, the latter is the opposite of materialism.[6] I
see no point in reopening all the books that give us a view
of "feminine consciousness" unless we have a firm grasp of
what anybody's consciousness is: "The production ... of
consciousness is at first directly interwoven with the material
activity and the material intercourse of men [sic], the language of real life.... Life is not determined by consciousness, but consciousness by life" (Marx and Engels, pp. 13-
14, 15). Perhaps this sounds more like an assertion that
works through repetition of key phrases than an argument.
In another place, Marx reiterates the idea and fills in some
of what may appear to be rhetorical gaps:

> In the social production of their life, men [sic,
> again] enter into definite relations that are indispen-
> sable and independent of their will, relations of
> production which correspond to a definite stage of
> development of their material productive forces.
> The sum total of these relations of production con-
> stitutes the economic structure of society, the real
> foundation, on which rises a legal and political
> superstructure and to which correspond definite
> forms of social consciousness. The mode of pro-
> duction of material life conditions the social, po-
> litical and intellectual life process in general. It
> is not the consciousness of men [sic, dammit]
> that determines their being, but, on the contrary,
> their social being that determines their conscious-
> ness.[7]

How would feminist criticism based on this view of
consciousness differ from what Annis Pratt calls "contextual"
criticism? For one thing, she speaks of contextual analysis
as considering "the relevance of a group of works, even if
artistically flawed, as a reflection of the situation of women
.... [The critic] should be 'feminist' in going beyond formalism to consider literature as it reveals men and women
in relationship to each other within a socio-economic context,
that web of role expectations in which women are enmeshed."
I think I understand what "context" might mean when freed
of sociological terminology, but I cannot deduce what kind
of literary criticism it might inspire. The only examples
with which we are provided have to do with the exigencies
of the literary marketplace, not the full material situation
of author or characters. Beyond this, we are apparently

being asked to regard the book as an historical artifact revealing its "context" and at the same time a product of a
context that we should somehow "take into account" as we
read.

        I think that writers themselves give us a better idea
of how to proceed.   Novelists and playwrights, even when
they mystify womanhood, usually consider it almost a matter
of course to relate their characters' psychological circumstances to their material situation.   And even when the "resolution" is a highly suspect one, we are frequently made
to see how it is materially conditioned.   Many books about
women concentrate on the moral and social "choices" they
make; their authors almost always show us how little material scope for choosing they really have.   As you can see,
this is more than just telling us how much money someone
has or can get--although writers, when speaking of women,
are astonishingly explicit about these facts.   It is rather a
matter of relating them to someone's sense of herself and
to what happens in her life.   It also means understanding
the extent to which sexual identity itself is a material fact.
(What Annis Pratt calls "archetypal" feminist criticism,
dealing as it does with myths of female life-history, either
applies here or is futile.)

        To be specific, what is it that Becky Sharp wants
and how does she come to want it?   What really happens to
Eugénie Grandet?   What if either of them were a man in
the same circumstances?   Those are obvious examples, perhaps, but I need not rely only on them.   I could give you
instead Isabel Archer, Anne Eliot, Lily Bart, Cranford's
Miss Matty Jenkyns, or Constance Chatterley.   None of these
is a feminist heroine nor a "simple" case of economic determinism.   None of their creators was--to understate the
case--a Marxist.   But all of them have given us information
that we have not as yet learned to interpret.


                                IV


        I have not taken up Annis Pratt's four categories in
their original order, because the mode she calls "contextual"
was the only one I thought might be feminist at all.   The
others are much more firmly entrenched in standard lit-crit
assumptions, and it is harder for me to see how they can
be useful to us.   I hasten to repeat that it is not something
"old-fashioned" or stuffy about traditional criticism that I
object to, but rather its use in the service of ruling-class

interests.   It should be clear, for instance, that sexual stereotypes serve somebody's interest; they are not the result
of what some writer "happens" to believe because of a particularly noble (or vicious) mother or because of mythic
Motherhood.   Similarly, a prevailing ideology about sexual
love--something that literature certainly promotes--has a
great deal to do with basic social relationships and institutions.   It is no accident that certain groups benefit from
their existence and that others are oppressed by them.   I
have mentioned two central aspects of Western literature.
They are there, whatever critical posture we choose to adopt.
But criticism does determine the way they function in our
lives.   These two are also specifically sexual ideas; current
critical fashions devote great attention to more general themes
like "Man's" isolation, alienation, and individualism.   It has
clearly been convenient for the operation of our society for
us to believe in and teach these themes as "universals."
To say nothing of the greatest bourgeois theme of all, the
myth of pluralism, with its consequent rejection of ideological
commitment as "too simple" to embrace the (necessarily
complex) truth.

        These last observations are an oblique introduction to
my remarks on archetypal criticism, which deserves more
than the testy parentheses of the preceding section.   As I
understand it, archetypal criticism is the application to literature of Jungian psychology.   It seems to me that nothing
could be more harmful to a coherent and fruitful reading of
"the literature of women" than Jungianism with its liturgical
pronouncements about The Masculine and The Feminine--not
to mention The Universal and The Innate.   That such criticism has very real and very negative social effects seems
to me undeniable.   But its implications for women are particularly sinister.   If we find that heroines "manifest interestingly parallel characteristics during their psychic development," this does not mean that we should perpetrate general-
izations about the female psyche as specious as those of the
male psyche.   Of course it is infuriating that the male psyche
has been treated "as if it, itself, defined the human soul."
But it is also infuriating that the human soul has been defined so oppressively, and we should not correct only the
lesser injustice.   There are, indeed, parallel characteristics
in the lives of fictional women.   We should not make a mythic
fetish of these, but consider why they exist.   To what extent
do they coincide with the social reality of women's lives?
Where they do not, did their authors wish this development
upon them?   To what end did they impose it?   What are the
social effects of literary conventions dealing with women?

I think these are important questions, but they are far from the realm of psychic archetypes.

The bibliographical question, too, has been incorrectly posed, for it assumes what it attempts to prove: that our principal focus should be neglected works that can in some way or other be classified as "feminist." This is only one of the tasks of a feminist critic, particularly when she is also a critic of culture and society. I agree that feminist writings and the "literature of women" as a whole must be reexamined. But to limit ourselves to that area is to imply that feminists have nothing to add to analyses of the "male" literature that makes up the great body of "our" literary tradition. I think we have a significant contribution to make to the radical criticism of that tradition--a contribution that is not encompassed by merely saying "ugh!" and turning away.

It is true that the literary mistreatment of women has been compounded by the critical mistreatment of women's literature. Mary Ellmann points out some of the ramifications of this in Thinking About Women: assumptions about "feminine style," sexual analogy, treating women's books as if they were women. Carol Ohmann's essay, "Emily Brontë in the Hands of Male Critics," is a history of one such case. It incisively documents the critical habits of more than a century with regard to Wuthering Heights, a novel whose "sex" was unknown for the first years of its life. Women authors generally and those, in particular, who are "only" concerned with female psychology, are treated with a most destructive combination of condescension and neglect.

Sometimes it is worse than that. I have recently read through Fred Lewis Pattee's The Feminine Fifties (New York: Appleton-Century, 1940), a book that is listed in one of Annis Pratt's footnotes and that she apparently considers a step in the right direction. It is a general history of American literature in the decade before the Civil War and the adjective is supposed to describe the decade itself. Alluding to the fashion of alliterative designations for periods, the author says:

> There are at least ten 'f' words that describe
> phases of the decade: fervid, fevered, furious,
> fatuous, fertile, feeling, florid, furbelowed, fighting,
> funny.... To find a single adjective that would
> combine them all--can it be done? Would not
> such a word be a veritable world in itself? Un-

> questionably.   That I have found this word, how-
> ever, my title reveals [p. 3].

Pattee concludes the first chapter with an even more vicious
observation.   He says it was "a feminine period undoubtedly.
Thomas Cholmondely, of London, to whom Thoreau in 1857
sent a copy of the second edition of Leaves of Grass, could
sum up the poems and the poet with this startling verdict:
'I find reality and beauty, mixed with not a little violence
and coarseness--both of which are to me effeminate.' Not
only did this characterize the early Whitman and his work,
but the decade as well ..." (p. 11).   This history devotes
considerably more space than most to women writers and
the feminist movement.   But the results are what you might
expect from someone who accepts and appears to delight in
sexual stereotypes, who puts women's rights between inverted
commas, and who cannot usefully distinguish between what
is female, feminine, feminist, and effeminate.   Had it merely
neglected women, Pattee's book would have been just a ram-
bling and inoffensive piece of writing.   Its emphasis on the
"feminine," however, makes it dangerous.

   A book that Annis Pratt castigates for its "old feminist" stereotyping is Josephine Lurie Jessup's The Faith of
Our Feminists (New York:   Richard R. Smith, 1950).   I
think this "study" of Edith Wharton, Ellen Glasgow, and Willa
Cather is worse than stereotyped.   It is both anti-feminist
and thoroughly reactionary.   Jessup's thesis is based on the
identification of feminism with any form of female independence, however short of separatism it may come; her bias
is implicit in her opening remark that "straightaway woman
discovered her limitation she set about denying it" (p. 9).
Pursuing a theological metaphor throughout, she regards
feminism as the cult of Athena and thus can describe it
triumphantly as "a faith which waned during the lifetime of
its most distinguished adherents" (p. 117).   Her own theology
is less clear.   She stresses but fails to analyze the relations
of each of the three writers to the Episcopal Church and remarks almost inconsequentially at the end of her book that
the trouble with present-day American literature is that "we
lack Dante's inscription [sic] 'In His will is our peace'" (p.
118).

   Her politics are clearer, and they are the reason
why I give any attention at all to this eccentric volume.   For
Jessup's views are a vulgarization of bourgeois values of a
sort not normally admitted in books of criticism.   She believes in "spiritual triumphs" and in an author's "paying

tribute" to the opposite sex. She makes many novels feminist victories by showing how someone's death or destruction was a "moral" defeat for the (often unidentified) enemy.
And she appears to resent these imagined triumphs.  At the
same time, she thinks that male writers have done better by
the female sex because they have idealized it.  Similarly
(and I suppose paradoxically), she claims that women writers
have given male characters dignity: "Even at its bitterest,
feminist fiction never describes the human male as the end-
product of slum situations, or a creature peculiarly given
to incest and inversion, or yet merely a fighting-and-lusting
animal" (p. 88).  It is as if she thinks writers who describe
it are responsible for the depravity that results from social
conditions; treating people with dignity would thus consist in
imagining more privileged moral types.  Jessup generally
has trouble with "social conditions."  She believes Dreiser
"the realist" is saying the same thing as Wolfe "the romantic," which is that "man, good as an individual, somehow
[sic] absorbs and spreads contamination through group living"
(p. 87).  Ironically, she seems to have chosen her subject
because, for these three novelists, "life defines itself less
often as a conflict between the individual and society than as
a struggle between the sexes" (p. 88).  Besides, male writers are distressing because their social comment is so dif-
fuse: "The feminist, for her part, has just one complaint.
She disapproves of sexuality [sic]" (p. 117).  Perhaps I am
over-emphasizing these two stupid books.  But they are what
you find when you go looking for studies of the literature of
women.  They may be the nadir, but they certainly provide
reason enough for feminists to turn to our own literature.

Most literature, however, is not our own, and that
is why I do not think there is a bibliographical problem.  For
much of what we have to do involves the rethinking of familiar
material:  "Is one to extol or to expose?  This is a question
of attitude.  What attitude is wanted?  I would say both."[8]
My citation is ironic in some measure; we shouldn't need
Chairman Mao to tell us that feminist politics can expose
something essential about the literature of and by men.  "Exposure" does not mean simply repeated revelation of sexism.
I have heard even self-proclaimed feminists speak as if Kate
Millett's Sexual Politics were definitive and exhaustive.  Millett has made a beginning by discussing political implications
of the language and themes of literature.  Her method is
suggestive, not prescriptive, and there are other ways to
unmask sexist bias and place it in historical perspective.

There are also questions that will occur to us and not

to other critics. I think, for instance, of Ulysses, which
makes Annis Pratt flinch as a feminist while, as a critic,
she acknowledges its literary worth. For the moment, let
us set aside the question of "literary worth" in works that
are ideologically repellent. Instead, let us think of how to
approach the novel not as a feminist one moment and as a
critic the next, but as a feminist critic. Annis Pratt says
she responds to Molly Bloom on the chamber pot as a black
militant must to stereotypes of Negro servants.[9] The solution is not to ignore it and go on to something else. On
the contrary, I believe only a feminist knows what Molly
Bloom is really about and can ask the questions that will
demonstrate the real functioning of sexual myth in Joyce's
novel.

A simpler example is the Nausicaa episode, which
proceeds through representation of the thoughts of Gerty Mac-
Dowell and Leopold Bloom. As Tindall describes it, "For
Gerty's part ... [Joyce] wickedly chose the style of a cheap
Victorian 'novelette'--what he called 'a namby-pamby jammy
marmalady drawersy ... style with effects of incense, mari-
olatry, masturbation, stewed cockles.' The ultimate indecency of the chapter is not Bloom's action but this style,
which, embodying and presenting Gerty, is Gerty."[10] We
should recall that in this chapter whose symbol is "Virgin"
and in which Bloom reflects on the "womanly woman," Gerty-
Nausicaa is also Milly, Mary, and Molly. What is the function of Joyce's stylistic parody--and the venom behind it?
(And what are the politics of Joyce's relationship to the kind
of prose he imitates? To the women who read and wrote
it? It is interesting that Hawthorne made specific reference
to Maria Cummins' The Lamplighter, one of Joyce's sources
for the Nausicaa style, when he inveighed against the "d--d
mob of scribbling women." Was Joyce, too, just pissed off
at the competition? Or is there an idea--even an ideology--
in the background?)

What is the significance of the literary equipment with
which Joyce provides Gerty and Molly, on the one hand, Bloom
and Stephen on the other? What does Tindall intend when he
says that Joyce employs the parodic style "wickedly" and
that it is an "indecency"? What does it mean for women in
general, and those of the lower classes in particular, to
realize fiction as Gerty does? Why is this "trash" the literature they are fed? Is there a way of reading and identifying with books that women typically adopt in our society?
How come? If her style "is" Gerty, how has that come
about? What is the significance of her lapses from it? Why

are her fantasies more contemptible than anyone else's? These are not rhetorical questions and there are many more we might profitably ask. The answers to some of them would lead to a better understanding of this section of Ulysses and of the novel as a whole. Others will turn us away from the book to issues concerning the sociology of literature. What has criticism to say about the real Gerty MacDowells? What are the effects on them and on society of escapist fiction and its characteristic style? And, always, cui bono--who profits?


## V

I have left the hardest issue, the question of style, until last. Throughout Annis Pratt's essay, there is an emphasis on textual criteria that are somehow independent of ideology. Thus, she can speak of some feminist works as being historically useful, although "artistically flawed"; and of the critic who considers context "without for a moment suspending her textual judgment"; and of works "which are resonant and craftsmanlike, if [male] chauvinistic examples of the fictional art." I shall spare all of us the ritual invective against the New Criticism. But I do not believe we have hitherto had objective standards by which to judge literary art, and the application of a feminist perspective will not mean adding ideology to a value-free discipline. (Thinking About Women shows one aspect of "textual analysis," the phallic approach to writings by and about women.) I do not suggest that we elevate anachronism into criticism, demanding that the writers of the past meet present-day expectations of political awareness, but rather that we consider what relation form has to moral and ideological content.

Along with spurious objectivity, I wish to discard the notion of critical "disinterestedness" that is one of Matthew Arnold's legacies to our profession. It is clear that to Arnold a disinterested approach does not mean a dispassionate one, but one that treats ideas in their "proper" intellectual sphere and does not attempt to involve them in the realm of practical political action. As I said before, I do not believe there is a separate domain of ideas, and I think that it is dangerous to behave as if there were. But Arnold hardly intended a separation of the critical faculty from standards of moral judgment. Nor did he think that "style" is independent of ideology, otherwise what does it mean to deflate jingoist pretensions by repeating "Wragg is in custody"? Crit-

icism has progressed so far into formalism that we have forgotten not so much that art has content but that content has
content.

I have been using the word "morality" as if it still
meant something in intellectual circles.   In reality, it is
one of those platitudinous babies that are always being thrown
out with the bath water.   For, when we recognized that there
was no moral permanence, we apparently decided that there
was no basis for moral judgments.   We failed to acknowledge
that morality is political and has material causes.   Moral
certainty itself began to look a bit naive, whatever its nature.
When I read W. D. Howells' Heroines of Fiction last week,
I was appropriately amused by its approach to moral questions.   In the introductory chapter, Howells describes the
hallmarks of nineteenth-century literature as "voluntary
naturalness, instructed singularity." Defoe is an earlier
writer who has these qualities, but does not share Howells'
modern morality: "He was, frankly, of the day before we
began to dwell in decencies, before women began to read
novels so much that the novel had to change its subject, or
so limit its discussion that it came to the same thing . . . .
Because of his matter, and not because of his manner or
motive, his heroines must remain under lock and key and
cannot be so much as raised in mixed companies."[11]   Of
course, Howells is an easy target for those claiming more
sophisticated sexual standards.   Poor deluded soul, he thought
he knew what "goodness" was, in writing and in behavior,
and he thought that they were the same thing.   The decencies
in which I should like to dwell are quite different from
Howells' unexamined categories.   But maybe there was
something worth rescuing from his tub-load of assumptions--
before they all went down the drain.

It was Sartre, I think, who asked whether it would
be possible to write a "good" anti-Semitic novel in the wake
of Nazi genocide.   Someone replied that Céline has done
precisely that.   I imagine we would all counter by asking,
"What do you mean 'good'?" A radical kind of textual criticism might well be able to answer that question.   It could
usefully study the way the texture of sentences, choice of
metaphors, patterns of exposition and narrative relate to
ideology.   I call such an approach radical and insist that
feminism is part of it because up to now we have been very
narrow in defining what we mean by the "content" that "form"
is supposed to convey.   In my education, for instance, much
attention was devoted to such concepts as Metaphysical Wit,
but curiosity was never directed to the social conditions that

informed the making of those conceits. I never inquired
how they functioned off the page. Radical criticism of texts
would obviously be more meaningful than a standard that
simply said, "This is acceptable, that is not" without showing
how this and that worked. It would thus actively demonstrate
that ideology need not be dogma, that it can provide critical
tools to broaden our present vision.

Communist Party critics of the '30s are frequently
sneered at for praising authors of whom "no one today has
heard," while attacking those whose reputations have grown
since then. Their detractors act as if the voice of the people had spoken and rejected the Communist position, when
what happened was the enthronement of an opposing critical
fashion. Radical criticism should be able to do more than
point out a "correct line" on sex or class. Applying our
analysis to texts will determine, as dogma would not, what
it means to keep saying, "That is a sexist book--but it's
great literature."

* * *

I began by referring to a mésalliance between "feminism" and established critical modes. It might be amusing
to extend the conceit to speak of oppressive relationships,
bourgeois mind-fuck and foredoomed offspring. A more
exact simile, however, would be the shotgun wedding. Some
people are trying to make an honest woman out of the feminist critic, to claim that every "worthwhile" department
should stock one. I am not terribly interested in whether
feminism becomes a respectable part of academic criticism;
I am very much concerned that feminist critics become a
useful part of the women's movement. Old feminism concentrated on what Marxists call superstructure and Mr. Nixon
might call a piece of the action; that is, on legal and human
rights within unaltered institutions. New feminism is about
fundamentally transforming institutions. In our struggle for
liberation, Marx's note about philosophers may apply to critics as well: that up to now they have only interpreted the
world and the real point is to change it.

REFERENCES

1. Karl Marx and Frederick Engels, The German Ideology,
    1845-46 (New York: New World International, 1967),
    p. 6.

2. The Schoolboys of Barbiana, Letter to a Teacher (New
    York:  Random House, 1970), p. 90.
3. Margaret Benston, "The Political Economy of Women's
    Liberation," reprinted from Monthly Review, Sep-
    tember 1969 (Boston:  New England Free Press,
    1969), p. 13.
4. Virginia Woolf, Three Guineas (1938) (New York:  Har-
    court, Brace and World, 1963), pp. 110-111.
5. Ibid. , p. 146, note 2.  In the first sentence, I take it
    she means "androcentric," not "anthropocentric."
6. I qualify this because I'm not happy with the notion of
    "opposites" applied to literary styles.  There is
    no single way of avoiding idealization; realism, to
    be sure, is one way, but so are many kinds of
    distortions.
7. Karl Marx, "Preface to A Contribution to The Critique
    of Political Economy" (1859), in Karl Marx and
    Frederick Engels, Selected Works in One Volume
    (New York:  International, 1968), p. 182.
8. Mao Tse-tung, "Talks at the Yenan Forum on Litera-
    ture and Art" (1942), in Mao Tse-tung on Litera-
    ture and Art (Peking:  Foreign Languages Press,
    1967), p. 3.
9. Actually, the stereotype she uses is Jack Benny's Ro-
    chester, who is far from obsequious and seems to
    me to follow, rather, the old dramatic convention
    of the clever servant.  But we might well ask what
    the uses of that convention were to class (and even
    slave) societies.
10. William York Tindall, A Reader's Guide to James Joyce
    (New York:  Farrar, Straus and Cudahy, 1959),
    p. 193.
11. William Dean Howells, Heroines of Fiction, Volume 1
    (New York and London:  Harper and Brothers,
    1901), pp. 2-3.

Annette Kolodny

## SOME NOTES ON DEFINING
## A "FEMINIST LITERARY CRITICISM"*

As yet, no one has formulated any exacting definition
of the term "feminist criticism." When applied to the study
of literature, it is used in a variety of contexts to cover a
variety of activities, including (1) any criticism written by
a woman, no matter what the subject; (2) any criticism written by a woman about a man's book which treats that book
from a "political" or "feminist" perspective; and (3) any criticism written by a woman about a woman's book or about
female authors in general. The kinds of investigations included under these last two general headings have allowed us
to better define the portrayal of and attitudes toward female
characters in a variety of authors and, where appropriate,
helped us to expose the ways in which sexist bias and/or
stereotyped formulations of women's roles in society become
codified in literary texts. Those scholars and critics concerned with female authors in general have, in some cases,
embarked on a still more ambitious quest. Taking their cue
from Virginia Woolf's fond hope that women would, someday,
develop a literary style of their own, shaped "out of their
own needs for their own uses," these critics have looked to
the recent outpouring of women's materials in order to see
if they might discern there some unique "feminine mode" or,
as Virginia Woolf had assumed, the emergence of a feminine
style expressive of a unique female "mind."[1]

The major assumption behind this kind of criticism,
of course, is the assumption that there is something unique
about women's writing. But just wherein that alleged uniqueness lies has, to date, been only crudely approximated, labelled variously as the product of woman's unique biology, her

*Reprinted by permission of the author and publisher from
Critical Inquiry 2 (autumn 1975), 75-92. Copyright © 1975
by the University of Chicago Press.

"feminine consciousness," or her peculiar relationship to a
social order in the face of which she is always something
"alien" or "other"; sometimes the three are compounded, in
unclear and often confusing ways.   As a result, those studies
which purport to label a unique "mode" or "style" and to
suggest, also, some deep underlying source, often fail to
clarify precisely what that source might be.

    The suggestion of yet deeper layers of explanation,
quite understandably, is tantalizing, but the very vagueness
of the critical terminology employed may unnecessarily be
involving the feminist critic in unintended, extraneous, or
even unanswerable questions.   I am particularly concerned
that, because the idea of the woman who is an artist is still
new to the larger academic community (if indeed it has been
accepted at all) and because other groups within the women's
movement are still vitally debating the relationship between
biology and social roles, we will unwittingly allow ourselves
to be saddled with the potentially fruitless debate over the
relative merits of nature versus nurture.   Were we to address
the argument at all, it should be only to admit the possibility
of biological determinants behind certain apparent literary
continuities (the flying imagery in Kate Chopin's The Awakening and, again, in Erica Jong's Fear of Flying, for example)
and, further, to point out that there would have to be corresponding (or even identical?) biological determinants for
men as well.   To begin our criticism by looking for even the
possibility of such underlying factors, however, would leave
us in danger of discovering what might not be there--since
the form of the question necessarily predisposes the outcome
of the inquiry.

    More importantly, I think we need to make clear that
what women have so far expressed in literature is what they
have been able to express, as a result of the complex interplay between innate biological determinants, personal and
individual talents and opportunities, and the larger effects of
socialization, which, in some cases, may govern the limits
of expression or even of perception and experience itself.
What is permitted now may not have been in the past--as
witness the universal damnation and silencing which greeted
Kate Chopin's exploration of female sexuality in The Awakening (1899) compared with the best-seller status accorded
Sandra Hochman's Walking Papers in 1971, and Erica Jong's
success with Fear of Flying (1973).

    Whatever the biological potentials, then, they are always
mediated by and given expression through cultural overlay,

with the two (biology and culture) acting as mutually inter-
dependent systems, each affecting the other. Moreover, as
every society and social group has its commonly accepted
rules of discourse--rules which frequently vary for men and
women--these, too, will influence the parameters of what
may or may not be spoken or revealed and, in some cases,
extend even to claims upon what is admitted as TRUE or
meaning-filled. The question of style, or of formal literary
conventions, then, becomes intricately involved with the recognition that, as a society alters its definitions of what is
appropriate or acceptable, so, too, it alters what its artists
may express and how they may reveal themselves. With
regard to literature specifically, this gets translated into
the interplay between inherited tradition and conscious, even
idiosyncratic, artistic choice--and this last, the incidence
of conscious artistic choice, simply must not be slighted
when we study what and how women use language.

Hopefully, the problem is simply one of terminology
and, hence, available to clarification; in which case it would
be our responsibility to develop a critical vocabulary difficult
to misread. In continuing to use phrases like "feminine
mode," "feminine style," or "feminine consciousness"--phrases
which, in many cases, could prove quite fruitful--we would
be obliged to define what we see as their components and,
just as important, the relationship between those components.
(I argue this point so strenuously because, in insisting that
Erica Jong reveal the autobiographical underpinnings of her
novel, magazine reviewers and T. V. talk-show hosts demonstrated the potentially dangerous corollary which too easily
follows upon any overemphasis on biological determinants.
The demand that the book finally be admitted as autobiography
was, implicitly, an admission by these gentlemen that they
could or would not easily accept the notion of females performing conscious and intentional creative acts. Thus, by
attributing its narrative to "autobiography," the inherently
sexist view might be maintained that women's productions
are attributable to something less than fully conscious artistic
invention. )

Still, if we continue to pursue the question of women's
style, as I think we should, we find a highly suggestive meth-
odological beginning in Josephine Donovan's fine essay, "Feminist Style Criticism." In it, she subjects the work of several women writers to close stylistic analysis and gives
every indication that, should this approach be pursued on a
far larger scale than her own modest article permits, it
just might "lead us to make further conclusions about 'fem-

inine style. '   "Would we continue to find recurring traits?"
she asks, and, "If we did, could we reach conclusions about
the female mind?"   But, while agreeing that "such an approach
is worth further exploration," one must also be aware that
the very phrasing of the questions suggests that she has, all
along, been looking for those "recurring traits" and that her
reading has, in a sense, been thus directed.   As a result,
even tentatively voiced as it is, Ms. Donovan's observation
that women novelists are unique for having developed "to a
high degree" what she calls a "'tropismic' level of aware-
ness--that is, the awareness of the underlife or the inner
mind of the world's reality"--comes across as an overly
hasty pronouncement, generalizing on the basis of too few
examples.   In addition, the source of that imputed "tropismic"
awareness--biological determinism, socialization, or conscious
artistic choice--is only vaguely hinted at, leaving one with
the uncomfortable sense that, in spite of her attempts to
curb the tendency, Donovan has pretty much accepted Woolf's
and Dorothy Richardson's suggestions "that there is such a
thing as female consciousness and that women writers must
evolve a style appropriate to that consciousness."[2]  Her unacknowledged commitment to that underlying premise, with
its inherent confusions and obfuscations, finally causes the
analysis to fall victim to its own good intentions.

No one, however, could quibble with the real value
of those intentions.   For, standing behind the Donovan article,
as it gives impetus to so much else usually labelled as
"feminist criticism," is an abiding commitment to discover
what, if anything, makes women's writing different from men's.
It strikes me that at least one aspect of the pursuit will
finally prove chimerical; for, if we insist on discovering
something we can clearly label as a "feminine mode," then
we are honor-bound, also, to delineate its counterpart, the
"masculine mode."   With the exception of Virginia Woolf's
few brief remarks, scattered throughout A Room of One's
Own, no one who has studied the rich variety of male writing has yet dared such a summation; and I should like to
think that a similar confinement could not be possible for
the richness and variety of women's writing.   But it is
precisely that richness and variety which will escape us if
we practice a criticism based on assumptions, sometimes
even unacknowledged assumptions, instead of beginning with
questions.   In other words, before we can ask how women's
writing is different or unique, we must first ask is it?

Neurologically, Woolf's assertion that "the nerves that
feed the brain ... differ in men and women"[3] cannot be ac-

cepted; but if she intended her comment metaphorically, as
most feminist critics have decided to read it, then she was
quite accurately (if overdramatically) pointing to the fact that
women's experience of the world differs from men's--a fact
we no longer even debate.  That women often write out of
that different and sometimes "other" perspective of experience has by now become virtually a truism in feminist critical circles.  What we have not fully acknowledged is that
the variations among individual women may be as great as
those between women and men--and, in some cases perhaps,
the variations may be greater within the same sex than that
between two particular writers of different sexes.

My point, then, is that we need to do more than merely
qualify all our assumptions about the uniqueness of women's
consciousness, experience of the world, and resultant literary
production; we must throw such assumptions out altogether
and begin not with assumptions (acknowledged or not) but
with questions.  How then will we go about discovering what
is different or unique about women's literary expression (if,
indeed, there is something different about it)?  As I indicated
above, by not starting with that as our premise.  Instead,
we must begin by treating each author and each separate
work by each author as itself unique and individual.  Then,
slowly, we may over the course of time and much reading
discover what kinds of things recur and, more important
still, if things recur.

All of these precautions notwithstanding, having spent
the last four years intensively reading and teaching a fair
sampling of contemporary United States and Canadian women
writers, I would be less than honest if I suggested that I
had not already begun to be able to catalogue clearly demonstrable repetitions of particular thematic concerns, image
patterns, and stylistic devices among these authors.  Even
the most cursory survey of such repetitions will illustrate
just how inescapable they are.

Among other things, contemporary women writers
repeatedly invest their female characters with "reflexive
perceptions," a habit of mind that, itself, becomes a repeated stylistic device, as character after character is depicted discovering herself or finding some part of herself in
activities she has not planned or in situations she cannot
fully comprehend.  "I was surprised to find my feet moving,"
says Margaret Atwood's heroine, Marian, and in that statement (as in many others like it) Atwood clues us in, grammatically, to the amputated self-perception which is so much

the subject of her novel.   In fact, Atwood's first novel, The Edible Woman (Toronto, 1969), provides probably the most dramatic example of how the use of this particular device can both explore and reveal a character's internal and sub-conscious dilemmas.   Seated at a table in a cocktail lounge with her fiancé and another couple, Marian successively finds herself bored and then totally cut off from the conversation (a comparison of hunting experiences by the two men) and, finally, appalled at the brutality being revealed.   But still she sits there silently, until, as she tells us:

> ... I noticed with mild curiosity that a large drop of something wet had materialized on the table near my hand.   I poked it with my finger and smudged it around a little before I realized with horror that it was a tear.   I must be crying then!   Something inside me started to dash about in dithering mazes of panic.... [4]

While no single sentence here utilizes a complete formal re-flexive construction, all, taken together, combine to convey the message that Marian found herself crying--without in any way understanding or even being aware of the fact.

As Esther Greenwood explains her predicament, in Sylvia Plath's novel, The Bell Jar, there is an almost total disjunction between what she observes, how she feels about it, and what was actually going on around her: "I felt very still and very empty, the way the eye of a tornado must feel, moving dully along in the middle of the surrounding hullabaloo."[5]   That same amputation of Self from Self, then, determines the very imagery and syntax of Plath's sentence and, in Atwood, expands out to govern the narrative pattern itself.   With part two of The Edible Woman, Marian moves out of the first-person and into a third-person narration. It is at once a reminder of just how out of touch with her-self she has become and, simultaneously, a linguistic nota-tion that the movement from an "I" to a "her" perspective makes two separate people of the observer and the observed. As Marian takes on the standard female role of an object in the story, so, too, the narrative grammatically "objecti-fies" her in and through the third person.   It is a split which follows logically upon her own earlier sense of disjunction and adumbrates, through the narrative structure, the char-acter's own grammatically "reflexive" habit of self-percep-tion.

Still another phenomenon I keep coming across in wo-

men's writing is what I have labelled, for want of a better
term, "inversion"--and it works in a number of complex
ways.  On the one hand, the stereotyped, traditional literary
images of women--as, for example, the loving "Mom," the
"bitch," the Sex Goddess--are being turned around in women's
fiction, either for comic purposes, to explore their inherent
absurdity, or, in other instances, to reveal their hidden
reality, though in new ways, not previously apprehended.  On
the other hand, there is a tendency to "invert" even more
generalized traditional images and conventionalized iconograph-
ic associations so that they come to connote their opposites.
In Plath's work, where these "inversion" devices have been
given a great deal of attention by critics, we note that Dodo
Conway, who, in another age's literary iconography, would
have appeared as an ideal "Mom" figure, is here parodied
by means of that same "pregnant-Madonna" figure which had
once been regarded as virtually sacrosanct:

> A serene, almost religious smile lit up the woman's
> face.  Her head tilted happily back, like a sparrow
> egg perched on a duck egg, she smiled into the sun.

And shortly thereafter, of course, we discover that Dodo
Conway "was also a Catholic."[6]  More obvious in Plath's
work, as more than one critic has noted, is the presentation
of babies, traditionally a symbol of woman's fulfillment and
new life, as instruments and harbingers of death.  Similarly,
as we read the novels of Kate Chopin or Sandra Hochman,
the short stories of Tillie Olsen, or the poetry of Atwood,
we seem to discover almost a conspiracy to overthrow all
the nice, comfortable patterns and associations of a previous
(and, for the most part, male-dominated) literary tradition.
In these writers' pages, love is revealed as violence and
romance as fraud; suicide and death are imaged as comforting
and attractive, while loneliness and isolation become, for
their heroines, means to self-knowledge and contentment.

Extrapolated to thematic concerns, the "inversion"
pattern may even structure the plot, by denying our conventional expectations for a happy ending and substituting for it
an ending which is conventionally unhappy, but which, in
terms of the particular work, pleases or satisfies nonetheless.  The beginning of this kind of inversion, in women's
writing on this continent, at least, might be traced to Kate
Chopin's The Awakening.  There, the heroine, Edna Pointel-
lier, feels herself "like some new-born creature" at the
very moment she is about to commit suicide; and, as she
swims further out into the water, in the closing paragraphs,

she thinks of it as "the bluegrass meadow that she had tra-
versed when a little child, believing that it had no beginning
and no end. "[7]  The imagery here, like the story line, is
utilized to deny the conventional wisdom that swimming toward
one's death is necessarily a dreary defeat or some kind of
sinful or depressing termination.

In our own century, all kinds of inversion devices
were put to work--and given probably their fullest play to
date--in Djuna Barnes' difficult and sometimes perplexing 1936
novel, Nightwood.  It is not a novel written to explore the
world of perverts, as some of its earliest critics insisted,
but instead a novel which explores the psyches of those who
inhabit and perceive what is to the "normal" reader an inverted version of his own highly conventionalized sexual and
social reality.  The characters come alive most fully at
night, prowling the streets of European cities, and harbor
within their gendered bodies an inverted (or opposing) sexual
identity.  The most conventionally "feminine" character in
the novel, for example, is the male doctor, Dr. Mighty-
Grain-Of-Salt O'Conner, who, when alone in the privacy of
his bedroom, dons a flannel nightdress and wishes he could
be boiling potatoes for some husky husband about to return
home after a day's labor.

If the critical silence which has plagued this novel is
any evidence, then, ironically, Nightwood is a novel which
probably places its readers in precisely that situation in
which the main characters of more recent women's fiction
find themselves: that is, embroiled in the hopeless task of
trying to decode or decipher a strange and incomprehensible
reality.  More and more, women writers are presenting us
with female protagonists who experience the world as an
immense hieroglyph, needing to be deciphered--but offering
little in the way of clues or coherent patterns.  In Margaret
Atwood's latest novel, Surfacing (1972), there are the ancient
Indian glyphs which her unnamed "Surfacer" feels she must
decipher if she is to discover her father's whereabouts, or,
possibly, discover some secret message about herself; in
Edith Wharton's novels, the vast complex and involuted social
codes stand as obstacles which must be properly deciphered
and manipulated if Lily Bart is to survive (which she doesn't)
or Ellen Olenska act upon her love for Archer Newland (which
she isn't permitted to do).  Similarly, Joan Didion's Maria,
in Play It as It Lays (1970), is hopelessly trapped within
games whose rules she can't figure out and within roles whose
lines were written for her by others; the combined gambling
and movie-land metaphors which structure our experience of

Maria's dilemma show us a woman capable of figuring correctly the odds on a roll of the dice and capable of learning
the lines in a T.V. script, but, nonetheless, trapped within
the double-pun of role and roll and unable to manipulate or
in any way affect either. And it is precisely this inability
to perceive accurately and act effectively which makes of
Maria the consummate "inversion" device. For, at the
heart of this novel built on puns is the cleverest pun of all:
Maria, the "model," cannot "act." Pulling off what Sheryl
Snaper Perey has suggested is virtually a formal literary
exercise, Joan Didion has taken the classic Existential hero
and, through inversion, created his female counterpart. [8]
Only the female "model" is denied the ability to act authen-
tically--denied even the illusion of acting or making meaningful gestures. Her "real-world" relationships all, in one way
or another, dissolve in the course of the novel. And her
movie and T.V. roles reflect people totally dissimilar from
herself or characters in whom she cannot recognize herself.
But none provide her with the ability to really "act well,"
just as in her personal relationships she seems unable to
act meaningfully or effectively. The only apparent triumph
for Maria, and again it inverts the triumph of a Meursault,
is that she knows "what 'nothing' means."[9]

Appropriately the "model" (as she once literally was,
before becoming an actress) for the only possible Existential
heroine our society could produce, Maria reveals what has
become the most compelling fear in women's fiction today:
the fear of being fixed in false images or trapped in inau-
thentic roles. Hardly a theme peculiar to women in our
modern, postindustrial technocracy, the problem is nevertheless imaged in notably different--but recognizable--ways
in women's writing. Hence, Sylvia Plath's character, Esther
Greenwood, feels compelled to toss her New York wardrobe
"piece by piece" from off her hotel roof and out into "the
dark heart of New York" on her last night there. [10] The
empty suitcase she then carries with her on the train home
in a sense emblematizes her complete rejection of the Ladies
Day experience and the falsified images it tries to sell its
readers. What makes that rejection intrinsically "feminine,"
of course, is the fact that clothing is the means through
which the gesture is effected, serving, if you will, as a
kind of "objective correlative" for what is finally internal
(emotional or intellectual) activity. [11]

Making a similar use of clothing imagery, Diane Wakoski complains of not being able "to wear that pink dress
tonight" because doing so would, in effect, transform her into

a person she no longer wishes to be.    Immediately marking
the dress's importance with her title ("The Pink Dress"),
she then proceeds to explore its symbolic significance and
explains that it must be abandoned because "It betrayed all
that was strong in me."    To change her sense of Self, she
chooses another costume--"The leather boots" of the motorcyclist, in which she hopes to "stomp through the world/ and
remind everyone/ of the silver and gold and diamonds/ from
fairy tales/ glittering in their lives."    And the metamorphosis
(as so many women are taught to believe) is to be achieved
by means of changing one's external covering.    However,
Wakoski is never that simplistic--and, while she utilizes
the cliché, she finally demands that we perceive its shortcomings.    She cannot don the motorcyclist's costume either,
because, as the poem finally reveals, her "one favorite im-
age/ --the motorcyclist riding along the highway/ indepen-
dent/ alone" is not hers at all but the man's to whom the
poem is addressed. [12]

        When Margaret Atwood's heroine, Marian, runs away
from her own engagement party in order to escape being
fixed in celluloid images as Peter, her fiancé, attempts to
"shoot" her with a camera, the act culminates a series of
events in which Marian has donned images which are not
her own--beginning, significantly enough, with her purchasing
a dress for the party.    The saleslady who, earlier, had
assured her that the red-sequined dress she was trying on
is "'you, dear,'" only confirmed how literally we perceive
the old phrase that clothes become a woman.    No wonder,
then, that after having been pressured into buying a dress
"she didn't think ... was really her," having her hair done
in a style she doesn't care for, and allowing her friend to
choose her accessories for her, Marian complains that her
body seems "somehow no longer quite her own."[13]

        Granted that many of our male writers are similarly
exploring the distorted realities and amputated self-percep-
tions of their male characters, or examining the kinds of
entrapments and false images foisted upon us in contemporary
North America, the challenge to the feminist critic is not
only to analyze how and if the female experience of these
situations is qualitatively different, and hence differently
imaged and structured into a different kind of literary language, but also simultaneously to insist that we tread very
carefully before asserting that the sometimes grotesque or
apparently outré perceptions of reality granted us by women
writers and their female characters are a distortion of any
kind.    We may not enjoy or approve the world they show us--

but this should not give reviewers license simply to reject the validity of the subject matter altogether because it "makes one wonder, for the moment, with a little sick feeling, if all women are like this one, and that isn't a pleasant reflection"; nor should it permit them to write off a new and perhaps unnerving style as merely some neurotic authoress' "epic suicide note to the world," or to degrade an experiment in narrative format as an "exercise in literary pathology"; and, certainly, no legitimate critic should resort to dismissal by name calling, as when David Gleicher wrote off Atwood as a "female chauvinist" because he did not approve her presentation of Anna in Surfacing. [14] To cavalierly label Kate Chopin's Edna as immoral, or Joan Didion's Maria as mad, or Alix Kates Shulman's Sasha Davis as scatterbrained, or Sandra Hochman's Diana Balooka as masochistic, as a number of critics and reviewers have done, is to ignore the possibility that the worlds they inhabit may in fact be real, or true, and for them the only worlds available and, further, to deny the possibility that their apparently "odd" or unusual responses may in fact be justifiable and even necessary. To the feminist critic, then, goes the task of insisting that what may appear as impossibly freaky or neurotic at first reading is, in reality, the tentative process of discovering--in literary terms--what the world looks and feels like to that segment of the population which is taught the "only one way ... to control her future" is to "choose her man."[15] It is an appeal to precisely this recognition of a real and true "other" reality for women which undoubtedly prompted Sandra Hochman to have her heroine exclaim, "Out of my womanhood is my madness woven."[16] At once a self-conscious assertion that other realities ought to be available, such statements must also be read as an appeal to the reader to understand how inevitably a character's sex has denied her access to such possibilities and, instead, woven for her a reality which is at the same time unacceptable and inescapable.

Again, my point is not that women's fiction doesn't often explore the same kinds of paranoia, anxiety, and fear of entrapment which structures so much of the fiction written by men--obviously it does; but simply to acknowledge this without also understanding how and why women's fiction images these experiences differently and why a number of women writers show a decided preference for certain image patterns and often-repeated sentence construction is to miss the essential point that, insofar as women experience these problems in different ways from men, their language will mirror both the similarities and the differences. A man's sense of entrapment on the job and a woman's in the home may both finally share the same psy-

chiatric label, but the language of literature, if it is honest,
will reveal to us the building blocks, the minute-by-minute
experience of what it feels like to be trapped in those very
different settings.

One more example, and I think my point will be made:
the struggle to create a form, a means of articulation, is
a struggle shared by every artist, male or female, in every
medium.  But it is a struggle, apparently, with qualitatively
different components for a woman--or so Diane Wakoski seems
to suggest in her poem, "I Have Had to Learn to Live with
My Face." In it, learning to live with a face so homely that
"no one could love it" becomes an act of creation, as the
"lumpy, unformed, ... piece of dough" is carved into a
mind, a face, "a shape with arms & legs," until, finally,
a "person" is created "from a presence." And although she
invites the reader, male or female, to "reflect on your life/
and see your own sculpture at work," we realize that the
process has been a particularly self-conscious one for Wakoski because she is a woman and has, from the outset,
been confronted by the implicit need to create a beautiful
surface, to become, like the models in the fashion maga-
zines, one of "those people/ With elegant noses and rich
lips." For Wakoski, betrayed from the start by her homely
features, the abstract problem of form and the highly personal
(and here painful) process of articulating a viable Self are
imaged to reveal a new and unexpected intimacy:

> ... reality is
> learning to live with what you're born with,
> noble to have been anything but defeated,
> that pride and anger and silence will hold us above beauty,
> though we bend down often with so much anguish for
> a little beauty[. ][17]

A good feminist criticism, therefore, must first acknowledge that men's and women's writing in our culture will
inevitably share some common ground.  Acknowledging that,
the feminist critic may then go on to explore the ways in
which this common ground is differently imaged in women's
writing and also note the turf which they do not share.  And
after appreciating the variety and variance of women's ex-
perience--as we have always done with men's--we must then
begin exploring and analyzing the variety of literary devices
through which different women are finding effective voices.
As a consequence of this activity, we may even find ourselves better able to understand and to encourage women
writers' continued experiments in language--in stylistic de-

vices, genre forms, and image making--experiments which inevitably expand everyone's abilities to know and to express themselves.

The evidence so briefly surveyed here (and many more examples which I'm certain have already occurred to the reader) strongly suggests that there are demonstrable and identifiable repetitions of such things as thematic concerns, stylistic devices, and image patterns among a number of women writers; admittedly, many of these are also shared by contemporary male writers, but usually without the central emphasis, and always without the peculiarly "feminine" situational connotations they hold in women's writing--the use of clothing as iconography, for example. And, while not all women writers exhibit all of the stylistic devices and image patterns delineated here in all their work, all of those whom I have read do at least exhibit some of them. Whether this constitutes something we might want to label a "feminine mode," or even some proof of Virginia Woolf's contention that the creative power of women "differs greatly from the creative power of men,"[18] is, however, a wholly different question--and one that, as Josephine Donovan correctly suggests, can only be pursued after many more years and after much more material has become available. And, while the increased quantity of material so lately becoming available to us, with all its similarities and recurrences, may indeed signal the beginning of that tradition of women writers for which Virginia Woolf had longed, the limitations of that beginning must also be recognized.

What we are seeing in the recent upsurge of women's writing are unquestionably self-conscious experiments in forging a new literary language appropriate to the world inhabited by women--but, for the most part, it has so far been the small and rather limited world of a select cross-section of middle-to-upper-class educated women. To enjoy their literary productions as artifacts in isolation, then, is to forget that much of what is published comes from a particular socioeconomic, political, and psychological orientation and reveals, often enough, a fairly self-conscious relationship to the larger implications of the women's movement. And, however interesting this perspective may be, it is still a limited one--and so, necessarily, is the language forged out of it. To begin postulating any theories whatever, on the basis of this material, concerning any kind of unique feminine style or universal mode of expression would be absurd--as absurd, for example, as assuming that Virginia Woolf or Sandra Hochman

speak to, for, or about the world of the Welfare Mom in
Harlem, or that the Welfare Mom, if she could, would compose a literary language similar to either of theirs. The
critical search for common denominators in style or subject
matter among women writers will, of course, continue--as
it properly should; what it must avoid, however, is both
the tendency to become prescriptive, suggesting what women
ought to write, on the basis of what they have written, and
the tendency to set up authorities. After all, if the anthologies of feminist writings offer us repeated outcries against
those men who would claim to speak authoritatively for and
about women, it follows that any handy group of current
women writers ought not to be granted the privilege of speaking for and about all women either.

The overriding task of an intellectually vigorous feminist criticism as I see it, therefore, must be to school itself in rigorous methods for analyzing style and image and
then without preconception or preconceived conclusions to
apply those methodologies to individual works. Only then
will we be able to train our students, and our colleagues,
to read women writers properly, with greater appreciation
for their individual aims and particular achievements (goals
which I am convinced must structure any legitimate literary
criticism, regardless of its subject). The result will be a
healthy new questioning of all the old clichés and assump-
tions--as, for example, the tendency to agree with Hawthorne's condemnation of that "damned mob of scribbling
women," or to dismiss Edith Wharton as only a lesser Henry
James. The domestic novels of the "feminine fifties" are
even now being reread and reexamined, with results not unlike Hawthorne's own reversal (once he began reading, that
is). Confessing to his publisher, George Ticknor, that "I
have since been reading 'Ruth Hall'; and I must say that I
enjoyed it a good deal," he then asked Ticknor to communicate to that book's author, Fanny Fern, "how much I admire
her."[19] Similarly, an unbiased reading of Edith Wharton's
work should convince any reader that she was attempting a
quite different picture of human society than ever James
dreamed of, and that she must therefore be judged in light
of what she attempted, and not in terms of what a famous
contemporary declared his aims to be.

In accord with this, one vital goal of feminist scholarship must be the rediscovery and unearthing of texts by
women which have, for one reason or another, been either
lost or ignored. The fine start already made here suggests
that, soon enough, our discipline will be forced to rethink

the assumptions behind the "accepted canon" of "major authors." Many of us are already adding names and titles to our course lists which, five or ten years ago, we had never heard. Probably the most valuable and long-lasting achievement of feminist scholarship and feminist criticism, however, will be their insistence that we give the same kind of critical attention to women writers that we have always accorded our male writers. Persuasively arguing the urgency of this change of heart, Margret Andersen, professor of French literature at the University of Guelph, has pointed out the following anomaly in her essay, "Feminist Criticism":

> Henri Peyre speaks in his excellent study, French
> Novelists of Today, of the 'striking flowering of
> French feminine fiction.' ... Peyre adds that
> 'easily half of the talents in French fiction and
> short story, since 1930 or so, have been women.'
> However, only one of the 12 chapters of Peyre's
> book deals with the writings of women, altogether
> 30-40 pages. Fourteen of these pages furthermore
> deal with Simone de Beauvoir only, which does not
> leave much space for other authors. We must con-
> clude that Peyre needs only 15 pages to deal with
> 'half the talents' since 1930, the female half, and
> that the male half of the talents is dealt with much
> more fairly.[20]

To this kind of critical discrimination (and the pun is intended), feminist criticism must give the lie.

This does not mean that, in revealing its shortcomings, we are also obliged to dismiss the previous decades of male literary scholarship and criticism entirely in order to begin anew. But it does imply that we will have to reconsider that scholarship with at least a suspicious eye. For insofar as our literature (and by "our," I mean the English-language literature of North America, to which I have confined most of my critical remarks here) is, and has been, a literature largely of male making and of male concerns, in which even the best drawn of women are women drawn through men's eyes, it has, necessarily, given rise to a somewhat lopsided analytic framework. In unquestioningly accepting that literature as its given, excluding women's materials from analysis and investigation, a largely male-dominated academic establishment has, for the last seventy-five years or so, treated men's writing as though it were the model for all writing. In other words, the various theories on the craft of fiction, and the formalist and struc-

turalist models that have been based on this closed tradition,
but which have been offered up as "universals" of fictive form
or even (under the influence of the psycholinguists) as emana-
tions of yet deeper structures within human cognitive processes,
may in fact prove to be less than universal and certainly less
than fully human.

At this point, it is too early to guess how, or even if,
women's writing will challenge these models.  But we must at
least entertain the possibility that once more women begin finding authentic voices and structures for their literary expression,
they may produce texts which cannot be easily accommodated
within the definitions of what we used to think of as familiar and
comprehensible forms.  Monique Wittig's Les Guérillères
(Paris, 1969), which most critics have now agreed to call a
novel, puzzled many when it first appeared here in translation;[21]
and, more recently, Kate Millett's Flying (1974) confused critics both within and without the women's movement by refusing
to fit easily into either "autobiography" or "confession."[22]  It
is even conceivable that women will pick up and revitalize forms
to which we had not previously accorded full literary stature--
the autobiography or confession, for example.

In spite of all these exciting possibilities, however, a
too self-consciously "feminist" literary criticism would be
shortsighted if it summarily rejected all the inherited tools of
critical analysis simply because they had been based, for the
most part, on the examination of men's texts and men's language.
Let us, rather, use what we can from the past, embracing that
which is, in fact, illuminating and persuasive; let us refine or
add to, in order to perfect, those tools; and where the previous
critical methods are found wanting, let us there expend our energies in inventing new questions and new methods of analysis.

But, for a while at least, a useful feminist literary criticism will have a few other tasks as well.  It will be obliged to
separate political ideologies from aesthetic judgments, and
feminist critics must protect themselves and newly emerging
women authors from being treated as writers of polemic for
the movement and from being judged according to the clarity of
any political stance espoused.  In the same vein, feminist critics must themselves be wary of reading literature as though it
were polemic and hence treating it as they would a manifesto
or political tract; and they must also be wary of writing criticism which ends up as polemic.  If, when using literary materials to make what is essentially a political point, we find ourselves virtually rewriting a text, ignoring certain aspects of plot
or characterization, or oversimplifying the action to fit our

"political" thesis, then we are neither practicing an honest criticism nor saying anything useful about the nature of art (or about the art of political persuasion, for that matter). Nevertheless, feminist criticism must continue, for some time, to be avowedly "political"--in the largest sense of that term. And, as such, the honest feminist critic will not be able to help bringing to her reading the attitudes and ideologies of a raised feminine consciousness, an awareness which, depending on how it is used, could limit her ability to deal with literature in its own context, or, more happily, open up to her new ways of understanding, analyzing, and talking about the kinds of phenomena that motivate certain kinds of literary expression.

But it is precisely this same raised consciousness which will also pose the most difficult task for the feminist critic, challenging her to find better ways of appraising and talking about authors whose attitudes toward women or whose espousals of certain conventional attitudes she finds repugnant. Norman Mailer's name, of course, comes first to mind; granted that, in recent years, he has unwittingly argued himself into a ridiculous position as a "prisoner of sex" and a self-styled champion of male chauvinism, I'm not certain that we therefore want to stop teaching or reading The Naked and the Dead, which, however little attention it pays to its female characters, is still probably the finest novel to come out of World War II. Disappointing though it is, art and politics may not always coincide in ways we would like.

At the outset, we must accept the fact that the language of literature is a language dedicated to unearthing the underlying patterns of and forming connections in our world. If we do not approve the patterns we have inherited from our literary past--as appears to be the complaint behind Mary Anne Ferguson's anthology, Images of Women in Literature[23]-- then, as critics, we must help and encourage our young authors to forge new connections and find new relations. But we cannot forget that the images of Nature-as-Woman or Woman-as-Muse once held their own kinds of truths and worked forcefully within our shared cultural psyches; as such, they will always be with us--an inheritance from our past, not to be annihilated or forgotten, but, with a new consciousness of their less attractive implications, to be transcended, superseded, or even subsumed into something else. Hopefully, into patterns and images more satisfying to all of us, whatever our sex or sexuality.

Finally, having considered our various aims and meth-

ods, I would like to address myself to the question of "tone."
Raised as we have been on generations of critical one-upman-
ship, with many of our mentors delighting in the subtle put-
down or in contentious nastiness,[24] we need not ourselves
follow in that style; indeed, it is a style which stands as
anathema to the very idealism of the women's movement as
a whole.  Let us therefore openly admit that our enterprise
is a new one, its methods and parameters necessarily vague
and ill-defined, and that, consequently, those of us engaged
in the enterprise, with all its experimentation, will occasionally commit errors of judgment, make mistakes, and hopefully,
grow and change along with the enterprise we are in the
process of creating.  And, as all good, honest, and indepen-
dent-minded critics should, we will often want to disagree
with one another, correct what we feel to have been another's
mistake, or refine another's point of view.  All of which is
in the nature of the critical vocation.  But if we also keep
in mind that, basically, we share similar goals--that is,
the reenfranchising of women writers into the mainstream of
our academic curriculum through fairer, non-sex-biased,
and more judicious appraisals of their work--then perhaps
we can address and respond to one another's critical works
with a similar fairness and judiciousness, and disagree without rancor and without personal anger.  For, in truth, our
enterprise is communal to the extent that it is cumulative
and aggregative, and, simultaneously, individual to the extent
that each critical work is authored and unique.  In short,
what I am proposing is a kind of communal frame of mind
which encourages debate and dialogue among individuals--
but among individuals who are, first and foremost, committed to the validity of the shared effort.

Granted, none of this is as easy as it sounds.  While
we remain within the established hierarchies of academia,
competing for rank, salary, and tenure, and until we can
effect some fundamental changes in the nature of that establishment, we will be the victims of contradictory cue systems:  the feminist call to community and sisterhood, and
the academic establishment's call to personal self-assertion
and point-scoring (often at the expense of colleagues around
us).  I have no easy solutions as to how we can mediate
between the two and still maintain our sanity; I only know
we can and must develop not only new critical methodologies
but new and different critical voices as well.

To end where I began, then, it becomes clearer and
clearer why no one has yet formulated any exacting definition of "feminist criticism"--and why perhaps no one should

even try.  My own remarks, at best, have been only a com-
pilation of notes, intended to suggest possibilities for further
investigation and to share what I could of my own thoughts
and observations to date.  As such, they should be taken as
Elizabeth Long took Sheila Rowbotham's recent investigation
into women in history:  as an "initial exploration of an un-
mapped field."[25]  I have neither definitive conclusions to
put forth nor guides to offer, only the sense of participating
in a valuable and vigorous enterprise.

Furthermore, the term "feminist criticism" may itself prove self-defeating since, as I've suggested earlier,
the very critical goals it encompasses should finally reach
way beyond the gender denomination.  Largely agreeing with
Margret Andersen that there ought not "be two different
branches of criticism, one by, for and on men, the other
by, for and on women,"[26] I am nevertheless persuaded that
feminist criticism will, for a time, remain a quite separate
and necessarily compensatory kind of activity, attempting to
make up for all that has previously been omitted, lost, or
ignored, and practiced for the most part by women.  Not
merely because women, more than men, need to celebrate
their newly discovered right to expression and validation in
the arts, but more so because the kind of rigorous stylistic
and linguistic analysis called for here will depend on an
awareness of and sensitivity to the many layers of female
experience and its consequent verbal expression.  The male
critic, only recently exposed (if at all) to women's language
(written or otherwise), could not possibly begin to analyze
it adequately; the best of our women critics and scholars
will hardly be adequate to the enormous task--but at least
they will begin from a necessarily more informed base.
Were this kind of activity to remain in the hands of women
forever, however, or were women forced to practice a separate "feminist criticism" for too many more years to come,
the whole purpose of our endeavor would be lost--and such
a situation would only indicate how unwilling or unable the
rest of the discipline had been to take advantage of what we
had offered.  It would be a sad comment on humanist studies
in general were feminist criticism not permitted to so enlarge
the boundaries of all literary criticism that we finally achieved
a fully "humane" literary criticism.

## REFERENCES

1.  Virginia Woolf, <u>A Room of One's Own</u> (Harmondsworth,

Middlesex, England, 1945; reprinted 1972), p. 77
(first publ. 1928). See also Suzanne Juhasz, "The
Feminine Mode in Contemporary Poetry by Women"
(paper delivered at the American Studies Association
Conference, San Francisco, October 20, 1973); and
Josephine Donovan, "Feminist Style Criticism,"
Images of Women in Fiction: Feminist Perspectives,
ed. Susan Koppelman Cornillon (Bowling Green,
Ohio, 1972), p. 341.

2.   Donovan, pp. 352, 344.
3.   Woolf, p. 78.
4.   Margaret Atwood, The Edible Woman (Toronto, 1969),
       pp. 72, 70.
5.   Sylvia Plath, The Bell Jar (London, 1963), p. 3.
6.   Ibid. , p. 122.
7.   Kate Chopin, The Awakening and Other Stories, ed.
       Lewis Leary (New York, 1970), p. 340.
8.   See Sheryl Snaper Perey, "Play It as It Lays, by Joan
       Didion" (unpublished paper, written for Women's
       Studies 224, University of British Columbia, Van-
       couver, Spring 1974).
9.   Joan Didion, Play It as It Lays (New York, 1970, 1971),
       p. 213.
10.  Plath, p. 117.
11.  The symbolic use of clothing in women's writing is
       more fully explored in Teresa Higgins, "The Role
       of Clothes in The Edible Woman, 'The Pink Dress,'
       and The Bell Jar" (unpublished paper, written for
       English 485, University of British Columbia, Van-
       couver, April 18, 1973).
12.  Diane Wakoski, "The Pink Dress," in The Motorcycle
       Betrayal Poems (New York, 1971), pp. 157-60.
13.  Atwood, pp. 208, 218.
14.  Frances Porcher, untitled review of The Awakening by
       Kate Chopin, Reedy's Mirror (May 4, 1899), p. 6;
       Nicholas A. Samstag, untitled review of Play It
       as It Lays by Joan Didion, Saturday Review (Au-
       gust 15, 1970), p. 27; David Gleicher, "Female
       Chauvinism," review of Surfacing by Margaret
       Atwood, New Leader (September 3, 1973), pp. 18-19.
15.  Alix Kates Shulman, Memoirs of an Ex-Prom Queen
       (New York, 1972), p. 72.
16.  Sandra Hochman, Walking Papers (New York, 1971,
       1972), p. 209.
17.  Diane Wakoski, "I Have Had to Learn to Live with My
       Face," The Motorcycle Betrayal Poems (New York,
       1971), pp. 11-15.

18. Woolf, p. 87.
19. For a summary of the success of women novelists in
    the United States during the 1850s, and the context
    of Hawthorne's remarks, see James D. Hart, The
    Popular Book: A History of America's Literary
    Taste (New York, 1950; reprinted Berkeley, 1963),
    pp. 92-97. Typical of the attempt to reevaluate
    and make available previously unknown works by
    women writers is the fine little collection by Lee
    R. Edwards and Arlyn Diamond, eds., American
    Voices, American Women (New York, 1973); I
    particularly wish to thank Professor Diamond for
    bringing some of these writers to my attention
    and for her helpful remarks on an earlier draft
    of this essay.
20. Mother Was Not a Person, comp. by Margret Andersen
    (Montreal, 1972), p. 89; a revised version of the
    essay appears in this anthology.
21. The first English-language edition available here was
    Monique Wittig, Les Guérillères, translated by
    David Le Vay (London, 1971).
22. See, for example, Elinor Langer, "Confessing," Ms.
    (December 1974), pp. 69-71, 108.
23. See Mary Anne Ferguson, ed., Images of Women in
    Literature (Boston, 1973), for a survey of some
    of the stereotyped literary formulations of women;
    her introduction, pp. 1-29, is particularly helpful.
24. I do not mean to imply, of course, that all our male
    teachers engage in this kind of bloodletting, only
    to point out how pervasive a style it has been among
    some. An unfortunate, but pertinent, example of
    the worst of this style was Charles Shapiro's
    "Heroic Chauvinism," a review of Martha Stephens'
    The Question of Flannery O'Connor (Baton Rouge,
    1973), which appeared in Novel (Fall, 1974), pp.
    78-80; there Mr. Shapiro took out after "that cruel
    new breed, FEMINIST critics," and described us
    as a band of "literary ladies" who, vulture-like,
    might be "spotted hovering over the corpse" of a
    newly buried female author, or still engaged in
    "crunch[ing] and spit[ting] out ... Doris Lessing's
    bones ... before starting a new meal." Obviously,
    such gratuitous nastiness serves no critical func-
    tion whatsoever.
25. Elizabeth Long, "A Changing Women's World," a review
    of Sheila Rowbotham, Hidden from History (New
    York, 1975), in The New York Times Book Review

(March 16, 1975), p. 12.
26.    Andersen, p. 90.

Pamela Di Pesa

## THE IMPERIOUS MUSE:
## SOME OBSERVATIONS ON
## WOMEN, NATURE, AND THE POETIC TRADITION

Women poets, like women painters and composers, have long been considered anomalous. To a great degree, the difficulty women encountered in becoming poets was a result of adverse social circumstances and cultural norms that prevented them from entering freely into the public--and therefore into the poetic--arena. Even today, social equality between the sexes is far from a fact in the West, and many of our social institutions continue to foster the image of women as either supporters or imitators of men's work. No one interested in the relationship of poetry to society can afford to ignore the social repression of women.

However, there is another way to look at the problem of women as poets: why there were so few of them, and why many of the women who did write poetry offered so little competition to their male counterparts. For behind the social institutions that are of primary importance in shaping women's behavior lie the cultural images generated by those institutions. And once an image has taken root in the public imagination, it may become autonomous, freed from the institutions and situations that created it. Even when these latter have undergone radical change, the image may continue to exercise its power.[1]

The muse is just such an autonomous symbol.[2] As an idealized image of divine inspiration, the muse was once an integral part of a total cultural "set." But long after the belief in divine influence on the poet had disappeared, the muse lived on as a symbol of whatever forces inspired or moved him. For the Romantics, the muse may have undergone a transformation, appearing as Keats's Psyche or Wordsworth's "natural presences," but her basic identity remained unchanged. Today, we may still discern her presence behind the unknown influences, the "givens," poets speak about. (Valéry's ligne donnée comes immediately to mind.) Literally dead, the muse is alive metaphorically; she continues to affect the unconscious attitudes, if not the conscious thoughts, of actual and would-be poets.

As long as our idea of a poet implies inspiration, the muse will continue to be significant. It is easy to understand why she has had such a long-standing association with the Western poetic tradition. But the muse as a symbol is one thing; the particular figuration of this symbol as a woman is another. And it is understanding the reasons for the female muse that presents some difficulty. As we shall see, it was not by accident that the idea of inspiration was personified as a woman. To a predominantly male poetic tradition, that personification made good psychological sense. Given the fact that there have been comparatively few women poets, we may legitimately assume that there was never much pressure exerted on the muse to change her gender. Perhaps there simply have not been enough women poets to support a male muse.

Nevertheless, there is reason to believe that a male muse was never a likely invention, no matter how many women might have become poets. For a male muse does not make the same kind of psychological sense for women as a female muse does for men. It is significant that we cannot imagine a male muse without difficulty or amusement: what we are really saying when we admit that it is difficult to imagine a male muse is that it is difficult to imagine a female poet. The significance of the female muse, which was generally positive for male poets, must have been generally negative for female poets. Rather than functioning as a symbol of inspiration, the muse must have acted as a continual reminder to women of the prohibitions and prejudices of the literary tradition itself.

We cannot, of course, conclude that the negative significance of the muse acted as an absolute deterrent to women wanting to write poetry. But we can conclude that those women who did write poetry were doing so outside the scope of the traditional metaphor, in a conceptually impoverished situation. If it is true, as Otto Rank has said, that the self-labeling and self-training of an artist are essential to the creative process, then women poets have always labored with a serious handicap. [3]  The vocabulary available to a man seeking to define himself as a poet simply was not available to a woman.

One way to understand the nature of this vocabulary is to look at the ways in which poets have defined themselves, or, more specifically, at the "others" against which they have defined themselves. Here the formulations of Harold Bloom in his recent books are particularly useful. [4] Although he is discussing the difficulties experienced by male poets in relation to a male poetic tradition, Bloom's remarks by implication can lead us to a greater understanding of what the problems for women poets would be.

According to Bloom, the major "other" with which a poet as poet must contend is the poetic tradition. The poet's relation to this tradition is unavoidably ambivalent, governed as it is by conflicting senses of indebtedness and rebellion. The poet owes his consciousness as a poet to his predecessors, yet he must find a way to surmount this indebtedness and create on his own. Those poets who persist in the struggle with tradition, who are not overwhelmed by their forebears, are the ones Bloom calls "strong."

However, Bloom notes that before a strong poet can begin to come to terms with the tradition, he must first have dealt with another antagonist, nature. To a strong poet, nature is not as serious an obstacle as the tradition; nevertheless, it is a challenge that must be overcome if he is going to write poetry. Insofar as it stands for that which is essentially different from poetry and offers serious competition to it, nature represents an "other." It encompasses all those processes and phenomena that are eternal, unchanging, and unaffected by human effort: not only the life-impulses of sexuality and reproduction, but death as well. For in their own ways, both life and death threaten to eclipse poetry by making it appear insignificant. Formidable as this competition may seem to be, the strong poet soon recognizes that nature is not a primary antagonist for the very reason that it is not poetry. His real contest will be with those who are competing on his own ground: other poets.

Bloom never discusses in detail the means by which a poet conquers nature. But in developing his theory, he clearly relies on the Freudian concept of repression, assuming that the poet must sublimate the natural desires of the unconscious if he is to write poetry. The desire for primal pleasure must be repressed, and its objects sought indirectly, if it is not to overwhelm the poet. Nature, in the form of his own libidinal impulses, is thus a threat to the poet until he learns to deal with it by sublimation. [5]

A modification of Freud's theory was offered by Freud's disciple, Rank. For Rank, the artist is someone who seeks less to re-create in sublimated form the original objects of his desire than to transcend them. Not being content with the version of immortality offered to him by biological reproduction, the artist.pursues the unique immortality offered to him by art. His feelings for the opposite sex are necessarily ambivalent: he desires woman, but at the same time he regards her demands with hostility, since they represent an impingement of life upon art.

How, then, does the artist deal with this ambivalence? Rank's answer is that he represses his negative feelings, camouflaging them in an idealized image of woman--the muse. As a transmuted sexual object, woman-as-muse is stripped of most of her threatening connotations. What used to be a hindrance to the artist is now a help. [6] He has dealt with the apparent opposition between life and art by using the former in the service of the latter; he has overcome his first antagonist, nature, by drawing it, in the person of woman, into the second field of battle. Rather than distracting the artist in his struggle with tradition, the image of woman enters the contest as a kind of mediator, helping the artist in the same way that she has helped his predecessors--by providing him with poetic progeny.

Needless to say, both Freud's and Rank's theories are far from satisfactory as explanations of the complex motivations involved in artistic creation. [7] Furthermore, both theories maintain a fairly rigid dichotomy between art and life, and assume that whatever has been created in the realm of art has been created with energy taken from the realm of life. And Rank, in particular, takes it for granted that woman automatically represents nature to the artist (although admittedly this over-simplification has a great deal of historical precedent behind it). Reductive as they are, the theories of Freud and Rank nevertheless help to explain the two observations with which we began: that the muse has been a singularly powerful symbol for Western poets, and that many of those poets have been able to dispense fairly easily with nature as a minor obstacle. But surely one of the chief reasons that strong poets have seen nature as less of a problem than the poetic tradition is that the possibility of personifying nature as a female was always open to them.

If we are correct in assuming that the muse was born as a projection of the poet's ambivalence toward nature and woman, then we ought to be able to find in her idealized image traces of both positive and negative attitudes. 8   Indeed, a rapid survey of some of the mythological aspects of the muse confirms this expectation.   The muses of classical mythology represented the sources, both natural and poetic, of the poet's inspiration, and as such they suggested the dual emotions of desire and fear.

Primarily, the muses were associated with poetic inspiration.   As daughters of Zeus and Mnemosyne, they knew all things, the mysteries of past, present, and future. Their particular function was to praise the creation of Zeus in song, to offer a continual reminder of his power.   Their name, in fact, derives from the Greek word "Μουσα," meaning "to think" or "to remember."   Unlike the Olympian gods, the muses had no well-defined personalities, but acted chiefly as representatives of the cosmic knowledge the poet needed for his own work.   Thus, their connection to the springs of poetic inspiration seems at least partly derived from their association by parentage with the springs of life.   Mnemosyne's parents, Ouranos and Gaea, were the primordial gods of heaven and earth; through them as well, the muses were linked to an original creation-memory.   This association was maintained into the Roman era, when poets identified them with the Italian Camenae, prophetic nymphs of springs and goddesses of birth.

The key to the symbolic significance of the muses lies in their simultaneous embodiment of three principles: creation, memory, and prophecy.   They were the symbolic facilitators of poetry exactly because poetic creation--which has still not lost its link with prophecy--depends on a knowledge of origins.   For the poet, the muses were not only the witnesses of cosmic creation, but also the witnesses of poetic creation from its inception.   With their knowledge of poetic history, the muses could help the poet achieve continuity with the past.   Thus it is that at every important turning-point in his work, wherever he might be oppressed by a sense of aloneness before his yet unwritten poetry, the poet invoked their help.   Indeed, the muses were good to those who remembered them.   But the poet who forgot them, or who, like Thamyris in the myth, entered into competition with them, might find himself blinded and deprived of his poetic abilities.   (As punishment, the muses made Thamyris forget how to play the harp.)   The poet had to remember his debts to nature and to the poetic tradition, both of which the muses represented, or he would be punished by the loss of memory.

Other, more remote, details of mythology also suggest that behind the image of the muse as a fruitful source lies the shadow of paralysis and blockage. Hippocrene, one of the fountains over which the muses presided, had been opened by a kick from Pegasus' hoof. Pegasus, in turn, had sprung from the blood of the Medusa after she was killed by Perseus. When alive, the Medusa turned all who looked at her to stone, but Perseus avoided this fate by looking at her reflection in his shield. Metaphorically, his act signifies the necessity of dealing indirectly with the Medusa of nature in order to avoid being paralyzed by it. It is the muse who provides poets with this indirect means of communication, offering them an image of nature at once powerful and controlled by man. With the muse as their shield, poets insure that the springs of inspiration will flow unimpeded.

But what are the implications for women of this alliance between the muse and nature? All the answers to this question point to the fact that the woman poet is at a serious disadvantage in the struggle between art and life. First of all, if she feels ambivalent toward her role as a woman, she cannot project her ambivalence onto the opposite sex as easily as a man can. For it is women, not men, who have traditionally been the symbols of the natural impulses that must be repressed. Men, of course, are also fighting their own natures if they try to "transcend" life, but this fact is less easily recognized. They are not thought to be the earthbound creatures that women are.

For the woman poet, then, man "ought" to stand simply for life, but his symbolic meaning is much more complex than that. It can easily be seen that man represents for the woman poet not only sexuality and the reproductive instinct (everything that would tie her to physical responsibilities), but also nearly everything with which she must contend in the world of poetry.

Without a symbolic figure to receive some of her ambivalence, the woman poet is more likely than the man to direct all of it inward. Internalizing one's ambivalence in this way is much more problematic than projecting it onto another, for the simple reason that one is both the generator and the recipient of the ambivalence. Since the woman poet is primarily fighting what seems to be her own nature, she stands a good chance of losing the battle. She is the Medusa who will paralyze her own efforts.

Thus, the benefits that accrue to the male poet as a
result of externalizing his desires and fears cannot be enjoyed
by the female poet. Far from finding in the polarization of
art and life a solution, however artificial, to her conflict,
she finds only a greater problem. She seems to be much
too close to one pole, and is angry at finding herself there.
Yet there appears to be no way of breaking her bond with
nature. The resulting frustration and confusion might lead
to a case of arrested development in which she is unable to
break out of the repetitive motions of internal conflict. Thus,
she is doomed to fight the battle with nature over and over
again, never approaching the major battle with poetic tradition that lies ahead.

One conclusion we might draw, then, is that what is
often a minor battle for male poets is a major battle for
female poets, exactly because in fighting nature they seem
to be fighting their own natures. There have been very few
women who have attained the status of "strong" poets: poets
who have been able to get past nature and confront the poetic
tradition. And we should not overlook the fact that two who
come immediately to mind, Sappho and Emily Dickinson, did
not accept or live by the traditional definition of their "female nature." (Although Sappho and Emily Dickinson were
by no means the only women poets who effected the poetic
tradition, their cases may be taken as representative insofar
as they suggest that, for women, giving a strong answer to
nature has been a necessary prelude to making a strong stand
in poetry.)

The second conclusion we might draw is that women
who succeed in repressing nature and confronting the poetic
tradition are not thought to be--and are not in fact--doing
the same thing as men in a similar position. Repression
for women is not seen in the same light as repression for
men. In the mythology of the sexes that we have inherited,
men are thought to be more capable than women of sublimating
the chaotic impulses of the unconscious. They are comfortable
with institutional structures and cultural forms; women, on
the other hand, were not meant to stray so far from nature. [9]
Thus, women who do succeed in manipulating forms to write
poetry are considered to be doing something unnatural--or
at least something more unnatural than what men who write
are doing. The male poet is engaging in healthy and necessary repression, but the female poet is engaging in a neurotic
avoidance of her natural role.

Confronting the poetic tradition quite obviously has a

different significance for women than it does for men.  Since
the tradition is made up almost entirely of members of the
opposite sex, the female poet cannot relate to it in the same
way a male poet does.   For him, the problem in facing the
poetic tradition is that he feels too dependent on it, too identified with the productions of previous poets.   He must discover how to equalize his relationship with his predecessors.
And it is the muse who helps him to make this discovery,
to establish himself as a poet among his peers.   The female
poet, however, faces the tradition without benefit of a filial
relationship and without benefit of a muse.   There are too
few poetic "mothers" for the female poet, whereas for the
male poet there are too many "fathers."   And there is for
the female poet no connecting link in the form of a muse,
no symbolic mediator asserting her continuity with the past. [10]

When a woman looks back at the poetic tradition, she
is for all practical purposes an amnesiac.   Her history is
not embodied there, and the past that she sees seems too
foreign to be accepted as her own.   She has no past, and
without a past, it is very difficult to create a future.   She
is isolated from the poetic tradition when she tries to confront it as a poet.   (This may not be the case at all when
she confronts it as a reader, but that is a very different
sort of activity.)   Her isolation is not the productive isolation poets sometimes need in order to create; it is the sterile isolation in which the tradition does not speak to her, and
thus, she cannot speak to it.   Deprived of the dialogue with
the past that is necessary for poetic growth, the female poet
risks falling into a state of intellectual immobility.

We may legitimately wonder why women do not overlook the fact that the poetic tradition is a male tradition, and
see it as just as much theirs as men do.   There seems to
be no logical reason why an act of imagination could not surmount the many symbolic obstacles facing the woman poet,
just as an act of will can surmount the practical obstacles.
But perhaps some of the reasons that women find it difficult
to identify with the poetic tradition are that they see it as a
body of work to which their own sex has contributed comparatively little, that they consider a great deal of the poetry
written by men to have been written indirectly at their expense, and that they have so successfully internalized the
image of themselves as mediating, muse-like figures that
they cannot imagine themselves in the role of creators.

A few women poets, like Sappho and Dickinson, were
able to capitalize on the anomalous position they occupied in

relation to tradition and to go off in directions of their own.
But, as we noted earlier, some of their exemplary poetic
freedom seems to have hinged on their independence from
the stereotypes of womanhood.  Whether, having rejected
these stereotypes, they then found themselves in a position
similar to that of male poets--namely, needing a muse--is
difficult to say.  Even more difficult would be the discovery
of who their muses were, if they had any.  Perhaps, as
history has assumed, Sappho's muse was a woman, and, as
Harold Bloom has suggested, Dickinson's was death. [11]  But
clearly the ways taken by Sappho and Dickinson are not going
to be taken by every woman poet.  Who, then, will facilitate
writing for women?

Perhaps the only answer is "no one."  A personal
muse, whether male or female, depends too closely on the
bifurcation of nature and culture.  We might solve the problem of the female muse by reversing all of the traditional
alignments so that men would represent natural creation and
women would represent artistic creation.  But such a re-
alignment, aside from being improbable, would only create
a second problem--the problem of the male muse.  The solution seems to lie in the reordering of the relations of the
sexes to the spheres of nature and culture, so that both sexes
would feel themselves to belong equally to both spheres.  Nature would cease to be a greater obstacle for women than it
is for men, and the poetic tradition (to which more women
will have contributed) would be an equally great obstacle for
them both.  The necessity for repression and the desire for
immortality will not disappear, but they will eventually be
approached by way of different metaphors.

## REFERENCES

1.  Two essays that explore the persistence of unfavorable
     images of women writers are Cynthia Ozick's "Wo-
     men and Creativity:  The Demise of the Dancing
     Dog" and Elaine Showalter's "Women Writers and the
     Double Standard."  Both appear in Vivian Gornick
     and Barbara K. Moran, eds. , Woman in Sexist
     Society (New York:  Basic Books, 1971).
2.  I will be using "muse" and "muses" interchangeably in
     this essay, on the assumption that the particular
     attributes of each of the nine classical muses have
     not been relevant to poets.  For them, "the muses"
     has the same symbolic significance as "the muse."

3. In "Life and Creation," from Rank's Art and Artist (New York: Knopf, 1932). "Life and Creation" is reprinted in William Phillips, ed. , Art and Psychoanalysis (New York: World Pub. Co. , 1963), pp. 306-333.

4. The theory that I am condensing here is set forth in detail in The Anxiety of Influence (New York: Oxford University Press, 1973). Further elaborations and applications appear in A Map of Misreading (New York: Oxford University Press, 1975).

5. Freud's theory of repression is presented in several places and in different contexts. Most relevant to our subject, however, is his discussion of "Creative Writers and Day-Dreaming," in The Complete Psychological Works of Sigmund Freud, vol. 9, ed. James Strachey (London: Hogarth Press, 1959).

6. "Life and Creation," in Phillips, op. cit.

7. Freud himself recognized that his theory was unable to explain the uniqueness of literary creation: he introduced his conjectures in the above-mentioned paper as "the beginnings of an explanation of the creative work of writers." He was chiefly interested in pointing out how, in respect to psychodynamics, literary creation resembles other civilized activities; he did not try to account for its particularity.

8. Bloom, in The Anxiety of Influence, pp. 59-65, discusses the symbolic ambiguity of the muse, but attributes it not so much to a transference of the poet's ambivalence toward primal impulses as to the primal nature of the poetic "scene" itself, in which the muse inevitably plays a part. The poet knows that the muse "has whored with many before him," and the longer he dwells with her, the smaller he becomes in comparison with the others.

9. This mythology has spawned several sub-mythologies, one of which is based on the idea that the work of women writers is inferior in its manipulation of forms--is rawer, less mediated by structure, than the work of men. Various ramifications of this judgment are explored in the Ozick and Showalter essays cited above.

10. The point is made by Bloom in A Map of Misreading, p. 33, that the death of the muse as a symbol of literary continuity will certainly come when women have created a poetic tradition of their own.

11. A Map of Misreading, p. 186.

Barbara J. Williams

## A ROOM OF HER OWN:
## EMILY DICKINSON AS WOMAN ARTIST

Many people don't like Emily Dickinson. As a friend
admitted to me, "She's so feminine. You know. All that
talk of burrs on hems, and pinning trinkets on gowns. She's
feminine in the worst way--in a pre-adolescent, naive way.
Perfect for a high school anthology, but she hardly holds up
as a serious, mature artist."

But for all the talk of gowns and trinkets, she also
writes with even greater frequency of vests and guns. In
fact, she seems as comfortable with her "boyhood" as with
her girlhood, with sexual aggression as well as sexual passivity, for she assumes either pose with equal facility. She
signed at least one letter as "Brother Emily" (L 367)[1], called
herself a "Bachelor" (L 204), referred to herself as "Uncle
Emily" (L 315) to her nephews on many occasions. She frequently "bearded" her pronouns, as she once expressed it
(L 1026). And her use of scientific and legal terms far
surpasses her use of domestic images. Clearly, the label
"feminine" when applied to art needs further definition, or
at least description.

Probably we can easily agree on what it is not. It
is not art produced for women. Nor is it art that is produced by women, necessarily. Just because an artist is a
woman does not mean all her experiences--and expressions
thereof--are female. As one modern artist has suggested,
menstruation is female, but picking up a pencil is not.[2]
Furthermore, I think all will agree that it is futile to play
the parlor game of trying to guess the sex of an artist simply
by looking at his/her--its?--work. After all, male artists
can paint flowers, too.

And yet, would anyone think that a man had written
Emily Dickinson's poetry? I contend that, in this instance
at least, Emily Dickinson's femaleness--literally--is the source
of the vitality of her poetry. Her experience as a woman was

the informing force that shaped her work, the fact of her
existence that gave her work its continuity--and its power.


Emily Dickinson criticism typically tends to overlook the
cultural context in which the poet lived, and with some justi-
fication, since Emily Dickinson became a recluse in her mature years.   Too often her withdrawal is sensationally explained as the result of an unfortunate love affair (the details
of which vary), as though writing poetry came to her only as
an afterthought.   In a more positive theory, her reclusiveness
can be taken as a move to preserve and nurture a fragile
genius.   But her slamming the door on the world was also
a dramatic gesture of dissent.   Born in the very patriarchal
nineteenth century, Emily Dickinson resoundingly rejected
the priorities of her age.   The fact that so few of her poems
deal with the current events of the day--for example, in only
one poem does she indirectly allude to the Civil War--is an
indication of what she thought about the world outside.

Nevertheless, living in the Gilded Age did leave its
trace on Emily Dickinson's poetry in one very important set
of metaphors.   Even though she was born of a genteel family,
she was economically dependent and therefore physically dependent on others for survival.   In an age when a person's
worth was measured by his bank roll, Emily felt her poverty
keenly.   In her letters she often feigned a disdainful disregard for the economic growing pains that convulsed the nation
throughout the period, but at the same time she demonstrated
a rare and subtle awareness that her economic (and political)
impotence was the birthright of her sex.   For example, when
the country was in the throes of the Panic of 1873, she flip-
pantly compared the ensuing political finger-pointing to a
hair-pulling contest and offered the only assistance she would
be able to give as a woman:

> I should feel it my duty to lay my 'net' on the na-
> tional altar, would it appease finance, but as Jay
> Cooke can't wear it, I suppose it won't.   I believe
> he opened the scare.   M[attie] says D[id] pulled
> her hair, and D[id] says M[attie] pulled her hair,
> but the issue at court will be, which pulled the
> preliminary hair [L 401].

She went on to concede that the crash did not affect her anyway: "I am not yet 'thrown out of employment,' nor ever
receiving 'wages' find them materially 'reduced,' ..." (L 401);
"Owning but little Stock in the 'Gold of Ophir' I am not sub-

ject to large Reverses--" (L 395).

In her poetry, she reiterates obsessively that she is
poor, that she is a "beggar," a word she uses thirty-nine
times in her poetry. [3]  This sense of economic inferiority
is the source of one of Emily Dickinson's major themes:
wealth and how to acquire it.    Notably, this wealth is never
calculated in dollars and cents, but in jewels and precious
metals, currencies of exchange uncommon in this country.
Because they are exotic and remote--un-American--they are
more attractive to Emily.

In fact, Emily often joked about her very unpatriotic
tendencies:

> Why cant I be a Delegate to the Great Whig Con-
> vention?--dont I know all about Daniel Webster,
> and the Tariff and the Law?   Then, Susie I would
> see you, during a pause in the session--but I dont
> like this country at all, and I shant stay here any
> longer!  "Delenda est" America, Massachusetts
> and all! [L 94].

Although Emily read The Springfield Republican (along with
five other newspapers) faithfully every day, she never took
its news very seriously and mocked those who did:

> Who writes those funny accidents, where railroads
> meet each other unexpectedly, and gentlemen in
> factories get their heads cut off quite informally?
> The author, too, relates them in such a sprightly
> way, that they are quite attractive.   Vinnie [Emily's
> sister] was disappointed to-night, that there were
> not more accidents-- ... [L 133].

When visitors gathered at the Dickinsons, she complained
that the conversation always revolved around the standardized
subjects of the day:  " ... the bond and the free, the 'poor
in this world's goods,' and the 'almighty dollar,['] and 'what
in the world they are after' ... " (L 128).   On another
occasion, Emily related to her cousin, "Austin and I were
talking the other Night about the Extension of Consciousness,
after Death and Mother told Vinnie, afterward, she thought
it was 'very improper'" (L 650).

In an age when introspection was considered a breach
in etiquette, Emily Dickinson became a "pathetic Crusoe"
(L 685) through her poetry, seeking wealth and status in dis-

tant lands, usually mythical or tropical, transcending in both
time and temperature the sterile, cold literalness of nineteenth-century New England.　Her attitude was like that of
the little runaway boy she had heard about.　When asked
where he was going, he replied "'Vermond or Asia'" (L 685).
Distance and delight were correlate in Emily Dickinson's
poetic scheme of things.


But the lode that became Emily's richest source of metaphor
ran deeper than the cultural stratum of the period in which
she lived.　It lay in the fact that she was born a woman, and
a poet, and she perceived that the two distinctions represented
a conflict of interests.　To be a woman--a vocation and an
art, quite literally, in the nineteenth century--meant that
one had to deny self; to be a poet, as Emily Dickinson defined it, meant a lifetime of spiritual exploration to the end
of self-discovery.　If, as Thomas H. Johnson has observed,
Emily Dickinson "lived by paradoxes,"[4] this dilemma was
the most fundamental to her development as a poet.　As a
growing child, "when I was a Boy" (P 986) as she was fond
of saying, Emily Dickinson was reared in the Calvinistic
tradition that held the individual morally responsible for controlling and shaping her/his life.　The highest of premiums
was placed on self-improvement, and she learned to live by
that premium.　Then as a grown woman, she was expected
to disenfranchise her selfhood.　She discovered that her worth
was not to be determined by her own efforts; it was to be
defined by destiny.　As Simone de Beauvoir has explained,
to be a woman is to deny the most basic of human instincts--
Existence.　And it is a dilemma peculiar to womankind:

> The young man's journey into existence is made
> relatively easy by the fact that there is no contra-
> diction between his vocation as human being and
> as male; and this advantage is indicated even in
> childhood.　Through self-assertion in independence
> and liberty, he acquires his social value and con-
> currently his prestige as male. . . .

> But for the young woman, on the contrary, there
> is a contradiction between her status as a real
> human being and her vocation as a female.　And
> just here is to be found the reason why adolescence
> is for a woman so difficult and decisive a moment.
> Up to this time she has been an autonomous indivi-
> dual: now she must renounce her sovereignty. [5]

The vibrant, intelligent Emily did not give up her throne voluntarily; it was pulled out from under her. Appreciated for her intelligence and talents as a girl, the aspiring poet watched her uniqueness devalued as she approached maturity. The father who had once given her open access to his library inexplicably shifted his priorities for her when she became a young adult. Her "talent" was better placed elsewhere--in the kitchen, perhaps--as the servant of old who had buried his coin instead of investing it wisely:

> I got down before father this morning, and spent a few moments profitably with the South Sea rose [Melville's Typee]. Father detecting me, advised wiser employment, and read at devotions the chapter of the gentleman with one talent. I think he thought my conscience would adjust the gender [L 285].

Squire Dickinson's respective attentions to her and her brother Austin provided a gauge against which she measured her sudden depreciation. As dearly as she loved her brother, Emily could not help but resent his position of favor. Often her envy passed under the guise of humor. In the following excerpt, notice how she has translated Austin's situation into terms of power: "crown," "sceptre," "Lord," "Jove," "Kings." Her final pun is as telling as it is clever:

> Suppose 'Topknot' should come down, and speak to his brothers, and sisters, or bind up the broken hearts of divers deserted friends, suppose he should doff his crown, and lay down his lofty sceptre, and once more a patient child receive reproof, and correction, salute the insulted rod, and how to the common Lord!
>
> An affection of nin[e]teen years for the most ungrateful of brothers jogs now and then at my elbow, and calls for paper and pen. Permit me to tie your shoe, to run like a dog behind you. I can bark, see here! Bow wow! Now if that is'nt fine I don't know! Permit me to be a stick, to show how I will not beat you, a stone, how I will not fling, musquito, I will not sting. Permit me to be a fowl, which Bettie shall dress for dinner, a bantam, a fine, fat hen. I will crow in my grave if you will, Chanticleer being still, tho' sleeping. Herein I 'deign to condescend to stoop so low,' what a high hill between me, and thee, a hill, upon

> my word, it is a <u>mountain</u>, I dare not climb.   Let's
> call it 'Alp,' or '<u>Ande</u>,' or yet the 'Ascension
> Mount. '   I have it!--you shall be 'Jove' a sitting
> on great 'Olympus,' a whittling the lightnings out,
> and hurling at your relations.   Oh, 'Jupiter'!   fie!
> for shame!   <u>Kings</u> sometimes have fathers and
> mothers.   Father and I are going to have a Cattle
> Show Wednesday.   School masters and Monkeys
> half price.   I guess you had better 'come down'
> [L 37].

As this excerpt also indicates, Emily Dickinson first became obsessed with the notion of size at this crucial period in her life. Her status suddenly shrunk, she began to think of herself as "small" and "low" in relation to the giants who populated the world around her. In her poetry, she consistently identifies with flies, gnats, and the more homely variety of birds. Her desire to grow in size takes the form of the many food and famine metaphors in her poetry:

> It would have starved a Gnat--
> To live so small as I--
> And yet I was a living Child--
> With Food's necessity
>
> . . .
>
> Nor like the Gnat--had I--
> The privileges to fly
> And seek a Dinner for Myself
> How mightier He--than I--
>
> . . . [P 612][6]

In her attempt to achieve size and acclaim heights, Emily found, in Simone de Beauvoir's words,

> the sphere to which [a woman] belongs is everywhere
> enclosed, limited, dominated by the male universe:
> high as she may raise herself, far as she may ven-
> ture, there will always be a ceiling over her head,
> walls that will block her way. [7]

Emily must have had a keen awareness of spiritual--and possibly physical, considering her reclusiveness--entombment, which takes the form of her many prison images throughout her canon. She often called herself the "Prisoner of Chillon" and other famous captives in her letters (e. g. , L 27). Her poems are replete with images of bondage, e. g. fetters, dun-

geons, and sentences of condemnation. Furthermore, she
consistently laments that what makes incarceration so difficult
to bear is that the prisoner had once been free:

> . . .
>
> Can the Lark resume the Shell--
> Easier--for the Sky--
> Wouldn't Bonds hurt more
> Than Yesterday?
>
> Wouldn't Dungeons sorer grate
> On the Man--free--
> Just long enough to taste--
> Then--doomed new--
>
> God of the Manacle
> As of the Free--
> Take not my Liberty
> Away from Me-- [P 728]

The barrier that Emily Dickinson faced as a maturing
woman and aspiring poet was not simply a contemporary (nor
temporary) obstruction.  It was as old as patriarchy itself:
the higher evaluation, and therefore the higher expectation,
of the manchild.  In the words of Virginia Woolf,

> Let us suppose that a father from the highest mo-
> tives did not wish his daughter to leave home and
> become writer, painter or scholar....  There was
> an enormous body of masculine opinion to the ef-
> fect that nothing could be expected of women intel-
> lectually.  Even if her father did not read out loud
> these opinions, any girl could read them for her-
> self; and the reading, even in the nineteenth cen-
> tury, must have lowered her vitality, and told pro-
> foundly upon her work. 8

In the nineteenth century, a display of intelligence in
a woman was not only unexpected but actually thought unbe-
coming in a "lady."  Emily often gives evidence in her letters that she was aware of this precept.  "'Burnharm' must
think Fanny a scholastic female," she once wrote to her
cousin.  "I wouldn't be in her place!  If she feels delicate
about it, she can tell him the books are for a friend in the
East Indies" (L 225; see also L 22).  When Austin complained
that he did not understand her difficult style, she was immediately suspicious.  Her tone is playful, but notice once
again her concern with size and her fear of being unable to

keep up with Austin, who obviously had a head start:

> I feel quite like retiring, in presence of one so
> grand, and casting my small lot among small birds,
> and fishes--you say you don't comprehend them,
> you want a simpler style. <u>Gratitude</u> indeed for all
> my fine philosophy! I strove to be exalted thinking
> I might reach <u>you</u> and while I pant and struggle and
> climb the near<u>est</u> cloud, you walk out very leisurely
> in your slippers from Empyrean, and without the
> <u>slightest</u> sort of simple--I'll be a little ninny--a
> <u>little pussy</u> catty, a little Red Riding Hood, I'll
> wear a Bee in my Bonnet, and a Rose bud in my
> hair, and what remains to do you shall be told
> hereafter [L 45].

Throughout her life, others would say they did not
understand her "fine philosophy," a response Emily would
always find incredulous. She wrote Higginson some years
later, "You say 'Beyond your knowledge.' You would not
jest with me, because I believe you--but Preceptor--you
cannot mean it? All men say 'What' to me, but I thought
it a fashion--" (L 271). Unfortunately, this response to the
anomaly of an intellectual woman did not go out of style in
Emily's lifetime. [9]

As Woolf has suggested, growing up in an intellectual
miasma lowered Emily's vitality and "told profoundly upon
her work." She felt keenly an impotence to alter her status:
"Finding words of no avail, I next resorted to tears. But
woman's tears are of little avail and I am sure mine flowed
in vain. As you can imagine, Austin was victorious, and
poor, defeated I was led off in triumph" (L 23). More revealing still is this statement: "I put on my bonnet tonight,
opened the gate very desperately, and for a little while, the
suspense was terrible--I think I was held in check by some
invisible agent, for I returned to the house without having
done any harm!" (L 42). De Beauvoir has said that ". . .
anger or revolt that does not get into the muscles remains
a figment of the imagination. It is a profound frustration
not to be able to register one's feelings upon the face of the
world."[10] If she had been offered a more viable outlet for
her anger, it would not have found its way into her poetry:
"Anger as soon as fed is dead--/ 'Tis starving makes it
fat--" (P 1509). (Notice the famine images once again.)

In her poetic fantasies, Emily's frustration takes the

shape of bombs, guns, and other weapons. She executes her
domestic duties "precisely--/ As the very least/ Were in-
finite--to [her]--" only in an attempt to forget "Existence--
some way back--/ Stopped--struck--[her] ticking--through."
Ahead there are only "Miles on Miles of Nought--/ Of Ac-
tion--sicker far--." She closes the poem with the admission
that she holds her senses on not for her sake but for the
sake of others, for "'Twould start them" if they knew that
she has a bomb held in her bosom that will detonate if she
ever lets it go (P 443). In her following poem, notice her
ineffectual size, her pathetic weapon, and the giant odds she
feels she is up against:

> I took my Power in my Hand--
> And went against the World--
>
> . . .
>
> I aimed my Pebble--but Myself
> Was all the one that fell--
> Was it Goliath--was too large--
> Or was myself--too small? [P 540]

Elsewhere, she cries,

> . . .
>
> Had I a mighty gun
> I think I'd shoot the human race
> And then to glory run! [P 118]

Her best expression of impotence is the poem "My
Life had stood--a Loaded Gun." Armed with expectation and
potential, she was ready to fire but had to lie passively in
the corner until an owner "identified" her and carried her
away. "And now We roam in Sovereign Woods," and because
she now has rank, the world responds when she commands:
"And every time I speak for Him--/ The Mountain straight
reply." But she is only the agent, the instrument, of his
power. If he should abandon her or die, she will again
lapse into helplessness and oblivion:

> Though I than He--may longer live
> He longer must--than I--
> For I have but the power to kill,
> Without--the power to die-- [P 754]

She who is unable to master her life is also powerless to
terminate it. As she expresses elsewhere, life is a "Repeal-

less thing--/ A Being--impotent to end--/ When once it has
begun--" (P 565). [11]

Reality as a woman produced within Emily Dickinson
a monumental sense of loss, a factor even more important
to her art than her sense of limitation and inefficacy.    As
a person, she felt disinherited and throughout her life she
sought reinstatement of the sovereignty she felt in her "Boyhood." Her poetry is a statement of that search. As Richard
Chase has asserted,

> In Emily Dickinson's poetry, taking it by and large,
> there is but one major theme, one symbolic act,
> one incandescent center of meaning. Expressed in
> the most general terms, this theme is the achieve-
> ment of the status through crucial experiences. [12]

This is the way Emily Dickinson expresses her quest for
"Delinquent Palaces":

> A loss of something ever felt I--
> The first that I could recollect
> Bereft I was--of what I knew not
> Too young that any should suspect
>
> A Mourner walked among the children
> I notwithstanding went about
> As one bemoaning a Dominion
> Itself the only Prince cast out--
>
> Elder, Today, a session wiser
> And Fainter, too, as Wiseness is--
> I find myself softly searching
> For my Delinquent Palaces--
>
> And a Suspicion, like a Finger
> Touches my Forehead now and then
> That I am looking oppositely
> For the site of the Kingdom of Heaven--  [P 959]

This feeling of disenfranchisement was the richest
source of symbols for her poetry. As in the above poem,
they include images of position (Prince, Duke, Earl, King,
Queen); royal clothing (crowns, diadems, ermine, purple,
sceptre); and kingdom (dominion, palaces, continent, realm).

In short, maturation startled Emily Dickinson with the
awareness that being born female in a man's world is a liability for which she could never compensate--so she sought

fulfillment as a poet on her own terms.    But because she
first realized the overwhelming odds against her--because
she wanted to be a woman and a poet--she was able to produce the greatest poetry of deprivation in our language.

Paradoxically, an even larger portion of Emily Dickinson's poetry expresses the ecstasy of fulfillment.    Both her
letters and poetry give testimony that as a middle-aged person and as a mature poet, hers was a life expressed, not
a life repressed.    Her poetry of deprivation is equalled only
by her poetry of reward.    Or perhaps, as she often suggests
in her work, she could experience the heights of joy because
she had first plummeted the depths of despair.    In this spiritual adventure, she hungers for the food that will make her
grow; she plots her escape from mortal bondage; she journeys
for jewels; she seeks election as Queen, complete with throne
and crown and sceptre.    But the metaphors do not stop there,
for she succeeds ultimately on every count.    Her hunger is
surfeited; her prison becomes illusory; she is gifted with
wealth; she rediscovers her "delinquent palaces," right where
she thought she would find them.    Growth, freedom, sovereignty, wealth, and immortality--all these themes merge with
the theme of the deepening commitment of becoming and being
a poet.

In many poetic expressions, she affirms that not by
"Diminution" but by "Discipline" and "Rigor unrelieved" (P
1022) does a person acquire "a Height so high," a commitment that demands that a person know loneliness, "Alpine/
Requirements/ And Services of Snow" (P 914).    In another
poem, she reflects that the larger the life, the longer it
takes that life to round out its arc (P 1067), a statement of
consolation for the life of deprivation that she had to choose
to become a lasting poet.    Believing she was inferior in the
first place was really her greatest barrier of all:

> We never know how high we are
> Till we are asked to rise
> And then if we were true to plan
> Our statures touch the skies--
>
> The Heroism we recite
> Would be a normal thing
> Did not ourselves the Cubits warp
> For fear to be a King-- [P 1176]

The following is one of her most explicit on the subject:

> Growth of Man--like Growth of Nature--
> Gravitates within--
> Atmosphere, and Sun endorse it--
> But it stir--alone--
>
> Each--its difficult Ideal
> Must achieve--Itself--
> Through the solitary prowess
> Of a Silent Life--
>
> Effort--is the sole condition--
> Patience of Itself--
> Patience of opposing forces--
> And intact Belief--
>
> . . . [P 750]

Toward the close of her life, she wrote Mrs. Holland, a very close friend: "I think Vinnie has grown since the interview, certainly intellectually, which is the only Bone whose Expanse we woo--" (L 888). A few years earlier (1881), she asserted in a letter to Higginson, "It is solemn to remember that Vastness--is but the Shadow of the Brain which casts it--All things swept sole away/ This--is immensity--" (L 735).

Very often, she extends this theme of growth and size to include the metaphorical food and drink that nurture it. Easing her "famine" with her "Lexicon" (P 728), she learned that "The Table is not laid without/ Till it is laid within" (P 1223):

> Deprived of other Banquet,
> I entertained Myself--
> At first--a scant nutrition--
> An insufficient Loaf--
>
> But grown by slender addings
> To so esteemed a size
> 'Tis sumptuous enough for me--
>
> . . . [P 773]

Poetry also became Emily's liberator, her "escape" but in a very special sense. As a girl, she never heard the word "'escape'" without a "quicker blood." With a "flying attitude," she would "tug childish" at her bars, but would always fail (P 77). But as early as 1849, she found another way:

> I'm a 'Fenestrellan captive,' if this world be 'Fe-

nestrella,' and within my dungeon yard, up from
the silent pavement stones, has come a plant, so
frail, & yet so beautiful, I tremble lest it die.
Tis the first living thing that has beguiled my solitude, & I take strange delight in it's society.  It's
a mysterious plant, & sometimes I fancy that it
whispers pleasant things to me--of freedom--and
the future [L 27].

That "mysterious plant" held the key to prison.  Like
Emerson, she perceived that slavery is merely an attitude,[13]
that the mind itself cannot be contained.  With concentration
and discipline, the mind has the power to expand to the very
limits of Existence; only then can it explore the rim of Circumference.  So the measure of a person's freedom is really
just a measure of that person's "fall into existence."[14]  As
Emily expressed it,

> .  .  .
>
> Escape--it is the Basket
> In which the Heart is caught
> When down some awful Battlement
> The rest of Life is dropt--
>
> .  .  . [P 1347]

"Bolts of Melody" had the power to rend her prison walls:

> They shut me up in Prose--
> As when a little Girl
> They put me in the Closet--
> Because they liked me "still"--
>
> Still!  Could themself have peeped--
> And seen my Brain--go round--
> They might as wise have lodged a Bird
> For Treason--in the Pound--
>
> Himself has but to will
> And easy as a Star
> Abolish his Captivity--
> And laugh--No more have I-- [P 613]

Conversely, the "magic prison" could descend on her
whenever her concentration or poetic inspiration failed, for
whatever reasons.  When she was in Cambridge for eye treatment and ordered by her physician not to read, she felt she
was a "'Prisoner of Chillon'" and the boarding house in which
she stayed, a "'Wilderness'" and a "'Jail.'"[15]  At various

junctures in her life, she felt "The Soul has Bandaged moments" at which time she would allow "Fright" (fear of failure? of personal involvement?) to caress her.   She would suddenly flee his, Fright's, embrace, only to be "retaken" again.   As a "Felon" once again, she has "staples, in the Song":

> . . .
>
> The soul has moments of Escape--
> When bursting all the doors--
> She dances like a Bomb, abroad,
> And swings upon the Hours,
>
> As do the Bee--delirious borne--
> Long Dungeoned from his Rose--
> Touch Liberty--then know no more,
> But Noon, and Paradise--
>
> The Soul's retaken moments--
> When, Felon led along,
> With shackles on the plumed feet,
> And staples, in the Song,
>
> . . . [P 512]

Emily also compares her art and how it has changed her concept of herself in terms of material wealth.   She compares her poetry favorably to "Estate perpetual" (P 855), "reduceless Mine" (P 855), "Mint" (P 486), "Gold" (P 1351), "Pearl" (P 998), and a "Potosi .../ ... hoarded in the mind" (P 1117).   In several instances, she implies that she acquired this wealth only after a "Value struggle" (P 806):

> The Plated Life--diversified
> With Gold and Silver Pain
> To prove the presence of the Ore
>
> . . . [P 806]

In the following poem, she alludes to some crisis in her life that threatened her "Silver Shelf." The "It" in the first line is her self-regard, for she indicates in the second stanza that she only has herself to blame:

> It dropped so low--in my Regard--
> I heard it hit the Ground--
> And go to pieces on the Stones
> At Bottom of my Mind--

> Yet blamed the Fate that flung it--<u>less</u>
> Than I denounced Myself,
> For entertaining Plated Wares
> Upon my silver Shelf-- [P 747]

In many other poems, she marvels at her good fortune. It is as if she were a beggar on the street, and someone gave her a "Kingdom." (Note also her use of "Orient" and "purple.")

> As if I asked a common Alms,
> And in my wondering hand
> A Stranger pressed a Kingdom,
> And I, bewildered, stand--
> As if I asked the Orient--
> Had it for me a Morn--
> And it should lift its purple Dikes,
> And shatter me with Dawn! [P 323]

"Take all away from me, but leave me Ecstasy," she sums up in another poem, "And I am richer than than all my Fellow Men--" who, "possessing more," live in "abject poverty--" (P 1640).

Ultimately, she also realized that "Poverty of Monarchy/ Is an interior thing--" (P 803) and in countless poems, she alludes to the sovereign state of being a poet. In various poems and letters, she is an Earl, Emperor, Czar, Queen, Monarch. She uses "royal" adjectives in describing her new "title." Symbols of majesty and power grace her person. For example, in one poem she affirms that someday she will no longer be a "dull Girl." She will be an Earl with "Crests" and "Eagles" on her belt and buckles, and "Ermine" will be her "familiar Gown" (P 704).

In her letters, she more explicitly associated power with her poetry:

> What is it that instructs a hand lightly created, to impel shapes to eyes at a distance, which for them have the whole area of life or of death? Yet not a pencil in the street but has this awful power, though nobody arrests it. And earnest letter is or should be life-warrant or death-warrant, for what is each instant but a gun, harmless because 'unloaded,' but that touched 'goes off?' [L 656].

On another occasion, she reminisced: "When a little Girl I

remember hearing that remarkable passage and preferring
the 'Power,' not knowing at the time that 'Kingdom' and
'Glory' were included" (L 330).

Emily Dickinson now has that "Glory" only because
she fought to establish and sustain her integrity as a woman
artist.   Emerson was once asked if he did not think Helen
Hunt Jackson "the best woman-poet on the continent."   He
replied, "Perhaps we might as well omit the woman."[16]
In many ways, Helen Hunt was not a woman writer, for early
in her career she gave up the integrity of her vision as an
artist and became the most popular (instead of the best) woman poet of her day.   Under T. W. Higginson's approving
hand, she responded to the male criticism and was in turn
rewarded by a male culture.   Helen Hunt realized before she
died that she had compromised her art by allowing a male
criticism to define what is "writing like a woman."   And
she also realized that Emily Dickinson had not, and so, in
Helen Hunt's own words, was truly a "great poet" (L 444a).

As Virginia Woolf observed many years ago, it takes
a rare combination of genius and integrity in a woman artist
to write without compromising her perceptions, her vision,
in a patriarchal culture.   Emily Dickinson was such an artist, for never once did she seek to serve popular opinion.
When she contacted Higginson in 1862, she probably did so
because of his reputation for encouraging women artists.   In
response, she was told to read the vacuous verses of Harriet
Prescott (Mrs. Spofford).   On another occasion, Higginson
actually classed Emily Dickinson's work with that of his sister, Louisa.[17]   Likewise, Dr. Josiah Gilbert Holland, editor
of The Springfield Republican and life-long friend of the Dickinson family, said of Emily's poems, "they really are not
suitable" and "they are too ethereal."[18]   To another woman
poet who had asked about sending her work to Scribner's,
Holland answered, "I'm a bit tired of subjective poems....
Try going outside for topics, and get an interest in some
thing beside yourself and your emotions.   That is the way
to grow.   Construct more and evolve less."[19]   Clearly,
Holland's aesthetic theories were the very inverse of Emily's.

Not only was Emily Dickinson misunderstood as an
artist in her lifetime, but as a woman as well.   Her contemporaries found her "morbid and unnatural,"[20] "uncanny"
and "most odd,"[21] "partially cracked,"[22] "abnormal,"[23] and
"insane."[24]   Nursemaids told their charges that she was a
"witch" to keep them in line.[25]   In a letter to Sue, her sister-in-law, Emily once complained that she could not even

count hours, "without incurring the charge of Femina insania!"
(L 92).

Apparently, early in life, Emily Dickinson recognized
that she would have to be different to do her work.   The
deliberateness of her choice not to play the role of a "woman" of her day is everywhere mirrored in her poetry.   In
the following poem, probably written to her former best
friend and later her sister-in-law, Sue, she acknowledges
two kinds of Queenship, but also claims that the two are
separate, mutually exclusive realms:

> Ourselves were wed one summer--dear--
> Your Vision--was in June--
> And when Your little Lifetime failed,
> I wearied--too--of mine--
>
> And overtaken in the Dark--
> Where You had put me down--
> By Some one carrying a Light--
> I--too--received the Sign.
>
> 'Tis true--Our Futures different lay--
> Your Cottage--faced the sun--
> While Oceans--and the North must be--
> On every side of mine
>
> 'Tis true, Your Garden led the Bloom,
> For mine--in Frosts--was sown--
> And, yet, one Summer, we were Queens--
> But You--were crowned in June-- [P 631]

A great artist is not only born.   She must also be
made.   An artist must feel both economically and socially
free before she can feel intellectually free.   "... That five
hundred a year stands for the power to contemplate, that ...
lock on the door means the power to think for oneself...,"26
(emphasis mine) Virginia Woolf has written.   Obviously,
Emily Dickinson saw the situation in much the same terms.
Writing to Sue, she once said, "... as I sit here Susie,
alone with the winds and you, I have the old king feeling
even more than before, for I know not even the cracker man
will invade this solitude ..." (L 77).   In one poem, she
talks about what Death could offer her, but one wonders if
she is not talking about social death, withdrawal from the
world.   Note the last line:

> . . .
>
> The Things that Death will buy

> Are Room--
> Escape from Circumstances--
> And a Name.
>
> ... [P 382]

As the daughter of a well-to-do lawyer, she did not have to worry about her next meal; and, more importantly, she had a room of her own.   She knew if she relinquished either, she would die as an artist:

> I was the slightest in the House--
> I took the smallest Room--
> At night, my little Lamp, and Book--
> And one Geranium--
>
> So stationed I could catch the Mint
> That never ceased to fall--
> And just my Basket--
> Let me think--I'm sure
> That this was all--
>
> I never spoke--unless addressed--
> And then, 'twas brief and low--
> I could not bear to live--aloud--
> The Racket shamed me so--
>
> And if it had not been so far--
> And any one I knew
> Were going--I had often thought
> How noteless--I could die-- [P 486]

Virginia Woolf has also pointed out that "... it is fatal for any one who writes to think of their sex. It is fatal to be a man or woman pure and simple; one must be woman-manly or man-womanly...." She goes on to explain, "It is fatal for a woman to lay the least stress on any grievance; to plead even with justice any cause; in any way to speak consciously as a woman."[27]   An artist is doomed to mortality if her mind is distracted by "alien emotions like fear and hatred"[28] and if she allows those feelings to creep into her work.

Certainly, as much could be said of Emily Dickinson. But her art has endured for in the final analysis, "hers was the poetry of craftsmanship rather than of confession," as Robert Spiller has explained:

> Art offers two ways to those who turn to it from
> life: a blinded wandering in the deep recesses of

a sickened personality, or the depersonalized and
hard forms of disciplined and complete expression. [29]

Spiller concludes that Emily was of the latter.  For all her
exploration of the universe within, Emily Dickinson manages
to maintain an aesthetic distance.  Louise Bogan has said of
her:  "She is driven to the verge of insanity, but manages
to remain, in some fashion, the observer and recorder of
her extremity. "[30]

To charges that Emily Dickinson too often indulges in
self-pity, like a little girl whining in eternal complaint, I
think Archibald MacLeish has offered the best defense.  He
explains that Emily never wrote just for herself, for "the
voice is never a voice overheard.  It is a voice that speaks
to us almost a hundred years later with such an urgency,
such an immediacy, that most of us are half in love with
this girl we all call by her first name.... "[31]  He continues,

> ... [her voice] does not clamor at us even when
> its words are the words of passion or of agony.
> This is a New England voice--it belongs to a wo-
> man who 'sees New Englandly'--and it has that
> New England restraint which is really a self-respect
> which also respects others....  Another voice,
> might indeed have cried aloud, but in hers is quiet.
> I think it is the quietness which moves me most. [32]

MacLeish concludes, "When we drown in self-pity we throw
ourselves into ourselves and go down.  But the writer [of
this poetry] is both in it and out of it:  both suffers ... and
sees.  Which is to say she is poet. "[33]  Emily herself often
said that she could "wade Grief-- / Whole Pools of it--"
(P 252), but she could never stand the pity directed toward
her by her fellowman.  "I cried at Pity--not at Pain--" (P
588), she proclaims in one poem.

In the final analysis, Emily Dickinson wrote "like a
woman," but not self-consciously so.  Perhaps one should
say she wrote as a woman.  I contend that the observation
need not be pejorative.  Not everyone is born into privilege
and power, but everyone has experienced failure and frustration.  A gifted woman who is honest to the impulses within
her and at the same time is aware of the limitations pressed
upon her from without can produce an art that truly reflects
the human condition.  The Promethian voice of the woman
artist can speak for all, both female and male.  As an artist,

she no longer needs to apologize for the "femaleness" of her work. Woman as Artist has come of age.

## REFERENCES

1. Quotations from the letters and prose fragments are taken from The Letters of Emily Dickinson, ed. Thomas H. Johnson and Theodora Ward, 3 vols. (Cambridge, Mass.: Belknap Press of Harvard University Press, 1958). Subsequently, the letters and prose fragments will be referred to in the text only in parenthesis by the number that Johnson and Ward have assigned. With both her prose and poems, Emily Dickinson's capitalization, punctuation, and grammar, as recorded by the editors, are carefully followed.

2. "Forum: What is Female Imagery?" Ms., May 1975, p. 62.

3. S. P. Rosenbaum, ed., A Concordance to the Poems of Emily Dickinson (Ithaca, N. Y.: Cornell University Press, 1964), pp. 79-80. This count includes variations of the word "beggar," i.e., "beg," "beggared," "beggar's," "beggars," "beggary," "begged," and "begging."

4. Thomas H. Johnson, Emily Dickinson: An Interpretive Biography (Cambridge, Mass.: Belknap Press of Harvard University Press, 1955), p. 3.

5. Simone de Beauvoir, The Second Sex, trans. and ed. H. M. Parshley (New York: Alfred A. Knopf, 1953; Vintage Books, 1974), p. 376.

6. Quotations from the poems are taken from The Complete Poems of Emily Dickinson, ed. Thomas H. Johnson (Boston: Little, Brown, n. d.). Subsequently, the poems will be referred to in the text only in parenthesis by the number that Johnson has assigned.

7. de Beauvoir, The Second Sex, p. 335.

8. Virginia Woolf, A Room of One's Own (New York: Harcourt, Brace & World, 1929; Harbinger Books, 1957), pp. 55-56.

9. In fact, the noticeable paucity of women intellectuals in the nineteenth century is the subject of a Ph. D. dissertation at the University of Texas by Susan Conrad, entitled "Intellectual Women in Romantic America: Perish the Thought."

10. de Beauvoir, The Second Sex, p. 370.

11. Phyllis Chesler in Women and Madness (New York: Doubleday, 1972; Avon Books, 1972), p. 48, shows

women are more successful at attempting suicide
than actually doing it; women are as ineffectual at
taking their own lives as they are living them. As
Sylvia Plath wrote (cited by Chesler), "I have done
it again./ One year in every ten/ I manage it--."

12. Richard Chase, Emily Dickinson (New York: William
Sloane Associates, 1951; American Men of Letters
Series), p. 121.
13. Adrienne Berenson, "Emily Dickinson's Social Attitudes:
A Dissenting View," Western Humanities Review
6 (Autumn 1952): 356.
14. Roy Harvey Pearce, The Continuity of American Poetry
(Princeton, N. J.: Princeton University Press,
1961), p. 181.
15. Richard B. Sewall, The Lyman Letters: New Light on
Emily Dickinson and Her Family (Amherst: University of Massachusetts Press, 1965), p. 75.
16. Quoted in Johnson, Interpretive Biography, p. 173.
17. George Frisbie Whicher, This Was a Poet: A Critical
Biography of Emily Dickinson (New York: Charles
Scribner's Sons, 1939), p. 120.
18. Quoted ibid. , p. 121.
19. Quoted in Richard B. Sewall, The Life of Emily Dickinson, 2 vols. (New York: Farrar, Straus and
Giroux, 1974), 2:608.
20. Quoted in Sewall, The Lyman Letters, p. 65.
21. Quoted in Johnson, An Interpretive Biography, p. 159.
22. Quoted in Thomas H. Johnson and Theodora Ward, eds. ,
The Letters of Emily Dickinson, 3 vols. (Cambridge,
Mass.: Belknap Press of Harvard University Press,
1958), 2:570.
23. Quoted ibid. , 2:476.
24. Quoted ibid. , 2:519.
25. Quoted in Genevieve Taggard, The Life and Mind of
Emily Dickinson (New York and London: Alfred
A. Knopf, 1930), p. 74.
26. Woolf, A Room of One's Own, p. 110.
27. Ibid. , p. 108.
28. Ibid. , p. 61.
29. Robert Spiller, The Cycle of American Literature: An
Essay in Historical Criticism (New York: Macmil-
lan, 1955), pp. 167-168.
30. Louise Bogan, "A Mystical Poet" in Emily Dickinson:
Three Views by Archibald MacLeish, Louise Bogan,
and Richard Wilbur (Amherst, Mass.: Amherst
College Press, 1960), p. 32.
31. Archibald MacLeish, "The Private World" in Three
Views, p. 20.

32.   Ibid., p. 21.
33.   Ibid.


WORKS CITED

Berenson, Adrienne.   "Emily Dickinson's Social Attitudes:
          A Dissenting View."   Western Humanities Review
          6 (Autumn 1952):  351-362.

Chase, Richard.   Emily Dickinson.   New York: William
          Sloane Associates, 1951.   (American Men of Let-
          ters Series.)

Chesler, Phyllis.   Women and Madness.   New York:  Double-
          day, 1972;  Avon Books, 1972.

de Beauvoir, Simone.   The Second Sex.   Trans. and ed. H.
          M. Parshley.   New York:  Alfred A. Knopf, 1953;
          Vintage Books, 1974.

Dickinson, Emily.   The Complete Poems of Emily Dickinson.
          Ed. Thomas H. Johnson.   Boston:  Little, Brown,
          n. d.

_____   The Letters of Emily Dickinson.   3 vols.  Ed.
          Thomas H. Johnson and Theodora Ward.   Cam-
          bridge, Mass.:  Belknap Press of Harvard Univer-
          sity Press, 1958.

"Forum:  What Is Female Imagery?"   Ms., May 1975, pp.
          62-64; pp. 80-83.

Johnson, Thomas H.   Emily Dickinson:  An Interpretive
          Biography.   Cambridge, Mass.:  Belknap Press of
          Harvard University Press, 1955.

MacLeish, Archibald; Bogan, Louise; and Wilbur, Richard.
          Emily Dickinson:  Three Views.   Amherst, Mass.:
          Amherst College Press, 1960.

Pearce, Roy Harvey.   The Continuity of American Poetry.
          Princeton, N. J.:  Princeton University Press,
          1961.

Rosenbaum, S. P., ed.   A Concordance to the Poems of
          Emily Dickinson.   Ithaca, N. Y.:  Cornell Univer-
          sity Press, 1964.

Sewall, Richard B.   The Life of Emily Dickinson.   2 vols.
    New York:   Farrar, Straus and Giroux, 1974.

_____.   The Lyman Letters:   New Light on Emily Dickin-
    son and Her Family.   Amherst:   University of
    Massachusetts Press, 1965.

Spiller, Robert E.   The Cycle of American Literature:   An
    Essay in Historical Criticism.   New York:   Mac-
    millan, 1955.

Taggard, Genevieve.   The Life and Mind of Emily Dickinson.
    New York:   Alfred A. Knopf, 1930.

Whicher, George Frisbie.   This Was a Poet:   A Critical
    Biography of Emily Dickinson.   New York:   Charles
    Scribner's Sons, 1939.

Woolf, Virginia.   A Room of One's Own.   New York:   Har-
    court, Brace & World, 1929; Harbinger Books, 1957.

Susan Friedman

WHO BURIED H. D. ?
A POET, HER CRITICS, AND HER PLACE
IN "THE LITERARY TRADITION"*

H. D. is a major twentieth-century poet who all too
often receives the response "H. D. ?--who's he?" When
people are reminded that "H. D. " was the pen name for
Hilda Doolittle, it is generally remembered that she was
one of those imagist poets back in the beginning of the century who changed the course of modern poetry with their
development of the "image" and free verse. Her early poems,
like "Oread" or "Heat," still appear regularly in modern
poetry anthologies, but the more difficult epic poetry she
went on to write is seldom studied or taught. The canon of
her major, largely unread work is considerable: The Walls
Do Not Fall (1944), Tribute to the Angels (1945), and The
Flowering of the Rod (1946) are the three long poems of her
war Trilogy, which has recently been reissued; Helen in
Egypt (1961) is the work she called her own "Cantos"; the
newly published volume Hermetic Definition (1972) contains
three more long poems, the title poem, Winter Love, and
Sagesse; and Vale Ave is another, as-yet-unpublished epic
poem. While poetry was undoubtedly the genre giving fullest
expression to her creative energies, she also published numerous translations, acted in a movie whose script she wrote
("Borderline," with Paul Robeson, 1930), experimented with
drama (Hippolytus Temporizes, 1927), and wrote several
novels (Hedylus, 1928; Palimpsest, 1926; Bid Me to Live
(A Madrigal), 1960; and the largely unpublished The Gift),
interesting at the very least for her own style of rendering
stream of consciousness. Her memoir of Freud, Tribute to
Freud (1956), is both an impressionistic record of their sessions together and a serious reevaluation of his impact on

*Reprinted by permission of the author and publisher from
College English 36 (March 1975), 801-14.  Copyright © 1975
by the National Council of Teachers of English.

the twentieth century; it too has been recently reissued in
expanded form. Caged in a literary movement that lasted
all of six or seven years, the magnificent poet of these epics
and the writer who experimented in a wide variety of genres
is like the captured white-faced Scops owl in her poem Sagesse. While the onlookers at the zoo chatter about his com-
ical whiskers and baggy trousers, the owl who is both the
embodiment of divinity and the personification of the poet is
"a captive and in prison":

> You look at me, a hut or cage contains
> your fantasy, your frantic stare;
> . . .
>
> May those who file before you feel
> something of what you are ...
>
> . . .
>
> they will laugh and linger and some child may shudder,
>
> touched by the majesty, the lifted wings,
> the white mask and the eyes that seem to see,
>
> like God, everything and like God, see nothing. 1

As Hugh Kenner wrote in his review of Hermetic Definition,
to identify H. D. as an imagist poet is "as though five of
the shortest pieces in 'Harmonium' were to stand for the
life's work of Wallace Stevens" (New York Times Book Review, December 10, 1972). But if H. D. is not already
buried in a single moment of literary history, she is rapidly
becoming so.

Why is her poetry not read? H. D. is part of the
same literary tradition that produced the mature work of the
"established" artists--T. S. Eliot, Ezra Pound, William Carlos Williams, D. H. Lawrence. She in fact knew these artists well; she had known and almost married Pound while
the two were students in Philadelphia (H. D.'s intensely absorbing recreation of their lifetime friendship, End to Torment, is being prepared for publication); her friendship with
Williams goes back to those student days; but most important,
she was an active member of the London literary circle that
spun out the dazzling succession of artistic "isms"--imagism,
dadaism, vorticism, futurism--before the catastrophe of the
First World War smashed this coterie into the confusion of
a spiritual wasteland. Like these artists, H. D. began writing in the aestheticism and fascination for pure form characteristic of the imagists; and like them, she turned to epic

form and to myth, religious tradition, and the dream as a
way of giving meaning to the cataclysms and fragmentation
of the twentieth century.   Her epic poetry should be compared to the Cantos, Paterson, the Four Quartets, and The
Bridge, for like these poems, her work is the kind of "cosmic
poetry" the imagists swore they would never write.

The pattern of her poetic development not only paral-
leled that of more famous artists, but it was also permeated
by major intellectual currents of the century.   In 1933 and
1934 she was psychoanalyzed by Freud, an exploration deep
within her own unconscious that ultimately linked for her the
personal with the universal, the private myth with the "tribal"
myths.   At the same time that she studied with Freud, the
convinced materialist, she was a student of comparative
religion, of esoteric tradition, and, like Yeats, of the occult.
The forces perpetually at work to bring a directionless century to war were a constant preoccupation in her work.   Consciously rejecting the mechanistic, materialist conceptions
of reality that formed the faith of the empirical modern age,
H. D. affirmed a "spiritual realism" and the relevance of
a quest for intangible meanings.   Her growth into a poet exploring the psyche or soul of humanity and reaching out to
confront the questions of history, tradition, and myth places
her squarely in the mainstream of "established" modern literature.   But still, outside of a few poets like Denise Levertov, who wrote "An Appreciation" of H. D. , Robert Duncan,
and the aficionados who circulate a pirated edition of Hermetic Definition, few people read her poetry.   Once again, why?

Is her poetry just plain "bad," however serious the
philosophic and human issues she embodies in image and
epic narration?   For me, the answer is obvious--her poems
captivate, enchant, and enlighten me.   From my single,
necessarily subjective perspective, there is no doubt that
her poetry is magnificent.   But I have no intention here of
raising the thorny questions of what makes literature "great,"
who determines the standards for greatness, or even whether
the literary reputation of an author has much of anything to
do with genuine genius.   I do insist, however, that H. D.
was a serious prolific poet exploring the same questions as
her famous counterparts and thus inviting comparison with
them.   It is something of an understatement, I think, to say
that in our profession artists do not have to wear the badge
of greatness in order to have articles and books written about
them.   The simple relevance of her work to the issues and
experiments of modern poetry demands that it be studied.

And so I am still asking why H. D. 's work is buried under
a scattered knowledge of "Oread" or "Heat. "

The answer is simple enough, I think. It lies bio-
graphically and factually right in front of our critical noses--
too close perhaps to be seen easily. It lies in what makes
H. D. and her work different from a long string of more
studied poets like Eliot, Pound, Crane, Williams, and Yeats.
And it lies in the response of her critics. She was a woman,
she wrote about women, and all the ever-questioning, artistic,
intellectual heroes of her epic poetry and novels were women.
In the quest poetry and fiction of the established literary tradition (particularly the poetic tradition), women as active,
thinking, individual human beings rarely exist. They are
instead the apocalyptic Pocahontas and the demonic prostitute
of The Bridge, the goddess in the park sought by the poet
Paterson, the superficial women walking to and fro talking
of Michelangelo. They are the static, symbolic objects of
quest, not the questors; they are "feminine principles," both
threatening and life-giving, and not particularized human
beings. Women are dehumanized, while the quest of the
male poet is presented and understood as the anguished journey of the prophet-seer for the absolute on behalf of all human-
kind. For "mankind" they may be the spokesmen, but for
"womenkind" they are not. As a woman writing about women, H. D. explored the untold half of the human story,
and by that act she set herself outside of the established tradition. She became a "woman poet" in a world in which the
word "poet" actually means male poet and the word "mankind" too often includes only men. From this perspective
there are poets, and then there are the lady poets, or poet-
esses; there are people, and then there are women.

If her sex and her women subjects were not enough
to exile her from the roster of the literary establishment,
the response of many critics to her epic poetry completed
the process. Her critics have rarely forgotten that she was
a woman writing poetry. And I don't think they should have
forgotten that fundamental fact. But her appearance in criticism as "woman poet" is never positive as it should be; it
becomes instead the subtle ground on which she can be ultimately ignored. Elaborate intellectual scaffolds resting on
the fact of her sex have been constructed by some of her
critics whose net effect has been to dismiss her.

I will be concrete. In 1969 a special issue of Contemporary Literature was devoted to H. D. after years of

critical silence about her work.    It was the hope of L. S.
Dembo, Contemporary Literature's editor, who had recently
published a serious chapter introducing her late poetry, that
this special issue would spark renewed interest in her work.
It did not.    Aside from two fine reviews of her new publications (in The Hudson Review, XXVII [Summer 1974], 309-11;
Poetry, CXXIV [June 1974], 162-67), no articles or books
have followed.    Her later poetry is rarely studied in the
universities; and she is not even appearing in the wonderfully
useful bibliographies of forgotten literature written by women
and the new anthologies of rediscovered women writers (Florence Howe's No More Masks! is an exception).

    Looking at the first two articles in Contemporary
Literature's special issue--and they are both long, serious,
thoroughly researched articles by well-known scholars, Joseph
N. Riddel and Norman N. Holland--I am not surprised that
it produced more critical silence instead of new studies.
Riddel in his "H. D. and the Poetics of 'Spiritual Realism'"
and Holland in his "H. D. and the 'Blameless Physician'"
take as their starting point H. D.'s psychoanalysis with Freud
and her book about that experience.    Holland and Riddel are
absolutely correct in pointing to that experience as the key
to her poetry.    But in their hands this valuable key ends up
locking the doors to our understanding instead of opening
them as it can do.

    Although Holland and Riddel dutifully quote some of
her careful statements in Tribute to Freud--and they are as
careful as Thoreau's in Walden--about why she went to talk
with Freud, their basic analysis (particularly Riddel's) ignores
what she said about how she went to Freud as his "student,"
his "disciple," about how she saw psychoanalysis as a medium
of quest in a drifting century, about how she found with his
guidance the way to link her personal past with that of people
in all places, at all times.    Refusing to take seriously H.
D.'s own comments about the impact of Freud on her artistic
identity, Riddel and Holland dissect her with all the Freudian
terminology they can muster--as if she were a neurotic woman, a "patient" instead of the artist who warned her readers
that "in our talks together he [Freud] rarely used any of the
now rather overworked technical terms, invented by himself
and elaborated on by the growing body of doctors, psychologists and nerve specialists."    And, we might add, literary
critics.    Holland explicitly and Riddel implicitly start with
Freud's statement that a woman's "strongest motive in coming
for treatment was the hope that, after all, she might still

obtain a male organ, the lack of which was so painful to her" (Holland, p. 485). For these critics, a central issue of H. D.'s psychoanalysis is "penis envy"--in Riddel's article, it is the central issue; in Holland's essay, penis envy shares the stage with the longing to fuse with her mother, a carry-over from the oral phase. But even more destructively, in their discussion of her psyche as the generating source in her art, H. D.'s supposedly self-evident longing for a penis (don't all women want one?) becomes the focus for their discussion of her artistic identity and poetry.

Riddel, like Freud, reduces the psychology of women to a physiological level, seeing the woman's genitals as the fundamental metaphor of what he calls "feminine incomplete-ness," "inwardness," "subjectivity," and "softness" and measuring her anatomy against a male standard of power and sufficiency, the penis. [2]  Just as Freud refers in his own voice to a girl's clitoris as a "stunted penis," Riddel writes about H. D. as "phallus-less," having an "ontological depri-vation." "Suffocating" from her "feminine inwardness," Rid-del concludes, H. D. turned to the hard, male objectivity of myth, poetic form, and symbolic objects (Riddel's subjec-tive assumption that poetic form and art objects are male is not even Freudian; it contradicts what many Freudians argue: that artistic "forms" are "vessels" and represent the artists' oral wish to reunite with the mother).

While Holland is more likely than Riddel to use the careful language of H. D.'s perceptions ("again, we seem to be coming to the theme of overcompensating for what she feels is the inferior quality of her feminine body," my em-phasis), his basic thesis is still that H. D.'s creative ex-pressions are evidence for her perpetual search for the "masculinity" which was "lost" or "missing" in the first place. [3]  At the same time that she sought through therapy to "close the gap" between herself and her mother (oral stage), she transferred to Freud all the "phallic power" she had attributed to her father and her brother (phallic and oe-dipal stages). In the transference H. D. was able to absorb some of Freud's masculine power ("Fusion with a man in-sures against deficiency: thus H. D. found it easy to project into and identify with Freud"). Her poetry, with its reliance on "hard" "signs," completed the process she had begun with Freud of closing up the gaps in her body as well as her con-sciousness.

Both critics conclude that H. D.'s infantile wishes were resolved in therapy as Freud succeeded in rooting out her

penis envy, in teaching her to accept her "feminine incompleteness," in giving her "the ability to live in her wingless
self" and to discover her "woman's role." Ignoring H. D.'s
own interpretation of the "wingless Nike"--wingless in myth
so that Victory can never fly away from Athens, a positive
symbol of hope for H. D.--the critics change it into the phallus-less, powerless woman. Freud's gift to H. D. was to
resign her to the fact of her winglessness, her femininity.

Yet once having argued that Freud successfully convinced H. D. that she was a woman, both critics somewhat
inconsistently conclude that H. D.'s poetry was a product of
her unresolved penis envy. Holland writes finally that her
poems are the legacy of her continuing search for those "missing things." He generously concludes:

> I feel sadness for a woman who had to become a
> royal and mythic sign [he refers to her use of her
> initials as a pen name and her portrayal of her
> women heroes as 'hieroglyphs'] to make up for all
> those missing things. But I honor the poet. She
> did indeed close up the gap with signs and, in doing
> so, left to us a body of poems for which we can
> be grateful [Holland, p. 501].

Riddel stresses the inherent difficulty all women have in creating an artistic identity:

> The identity of the creative self as woman is threat-
> ened not only by the incompleteness of the female
> but by the insubstantiality of subjectivity.... In
> terms of the self-consciousness that forces her to
> contemplate her ambiguous role as woman poet,
> she seeks the completeness of the subject in the
> object. She must turn herself into a poem.

And since the poem is designated objective and "male" in
Riddel's scheme of things, he argues implicitly that H. D.
must abandon her identity as a woman if she is to develop
as a poet. For Riddel, not only are poems masculine, but
myths, symbols, and cult objects are linked with the "phallus ... the signifier, the giver of meaning" (Riddel, p. 462).
By what yardstick Riddel measures things like words or myths
as penis-connected or masculine, he never says. But identify
the tools of an artist's trade and the kind of images H. D.
chose with all that's masculine, Riddel definitely does do.
He comes as close as any critic to affirming that the province
of the poet is entirely masculine and the woman poet who

succeeds in writing poetry must overcome, destroy, or transcend her femininity and write like a man.

For all that the general tone of his essay appears to be detached, scholarly, and objective, Riddel's assumptions about women and women poets color and often distort his discussion of her epic poetry. Her impulse to write poetry--to handle words, to create images--originates in his perspective in her recognition of the inferiority of women and the superiority of men, in short, in penis envy. And the epic poetry of her later years which shows a turning to myth and the imagery of sacred cult objects--poetry that Riddel discusses brilliantly if his psychoanalytic framework is ignored--emerges out of her anguished search for masculine objectivity. Riddel has reduced the creative urge and poetic vision of H. D. to her desire to have what any ordinary man, poet or not, possesses from birth.

Is it any wonder that Riddel's and Holland's descriptions of H. D.'s quest for the phallus have not stimulated renewed interest in her work? Why should anyone bother reading a poet in search of "masculine hardness" when you can take your pick from among any number of "hard" male poets?

Although the work of these two critics has angered me greatly, both as a woman and as a person who sees H. D.'s poetry unjustly treated, my point is not to attack the criticism of individuals. I am far more concerned with the general issue of what impact the male-oriented criticism of modern scholarship has had on the literary reputations of women writers like H. D. I am interested in Riddel's and Holland's articles for their blatant documentation of the fact that criticism is written from a subjective male point of view; that, no matter how scholarly and well-researched such articles may be, they are not value-free.

While Riddel tends to present himself as an objective scholar, Holland himself would not disagree that all criticism is subjective. In fact, the central argument of his newest book, Poems in Persons,[4] is that all literary experiences--including the logical, careful, internally coherent work of literary critics--are necessarily subjective. But what he means by "subjectivity" (the recreation of a literary work within the terms of an individual reader's "ego identity," his or her uniquely woven pattern of childhood psychosexual fantasy) is not at all what I mean. His own "subjective" viewpoint which colors so much of what he writes about H.

D. is instead a misogynist set of psychoanalytic presuppostions about the infantile wishes of young girls which he takes to be "objective" truth. This type of political and cultural subjectivity that so pervades Holland's and Riddel's work is symptomatic of the prejudiced inadequacies of much literary criticism, non-psychoanalytic as well as that heavily influenced by Freud.

I can hear voices objecting to my generalization--you are making a mountain out of a mole hill; Riddel and Holland are only two men; dismiss them as male critics and get back to the business of criticism. It is true that by themselves they are only two men; but if they are pushed to the side as exceptions--rather than seen as examples of a hidden pattern set in bold relief--the main body of criticism can continue to put forth its mask of scholarly objectivity. In their criticism of H. D.'s works they are not simply exceptions to a generally fair rule; perhaps because of their psychoanalytic interests, their work is a more explicit version of the double standard in criticism. Vincent Quinn, for example, wrote a generally useful book on H. D., Hilda Doolittle (1967), that focuses mainly on her imagist poetry. But a subtler form of male perspective is evident in his discussion of her epic poetry. He provides a good introduction to the religious, prophetic vision of the war Trilogy--he has understood what her work is about--but he is entirely uncomfortable with it. It is too abstract, too philosophical; its theology, based on a belief in the essential oneness of divinity throughout all cultures, is confusing. As a writer of short, lyric, emotional poems about nature, love, and beauty, H. D. was at her best, in Quinn's opinion. But a double standard of judgment for men and women writers may have something to do with Quinn's evaluation of H. D.'s poetry. H. D.'s compatriots, Eliot, Williams, and Pound, left the imagist poem to write epics permeated with mythological and religious allusions and with complex philosophical abstractions; yet they are praised for the profundity of their poetic thought and not accused of abstraction. In fact, none of her late work, which always has a highly personal as well as a mythic dimension, is as abstract as a poem like the Four Quartets. But subtle enough so that even Quinn might not have been aware of his own assumptions may be the feeling that H. D.'s work was too abstract for a woman to write. The short, passionate lyric has conventionally been thought appropriate for women poets if they insist on writing, while the longer, more philosophic epic belongs to the real (male) poet. Perhaps it is this presupposition about women writers that has caused so many of H. D.'s critics (see Douglas Bush

and Thomas Swann, for example) to label her interest in
mythology "escapist." Even Linda Welshimer Wagner (women, too, can analyze from the male perspective--that has
been, after all, our training), who has some interesting comments to make on the "feminine" in Helen in Egypt, saw H.
D. 's fascination with myth as a search for "solace" and
escape.[5]  When Eliot, Pound, Williams, and Yeats show
that same rejection of materialist conceptions of reality,
they are praised for their struggle to deal with the ultimate
questions of human existence.  It is a kind of double talk
emerging out of a hidden bias that makes Eliot deeply religious, Pound profound, Crane prophetic, Williams archetypal,
and Yeats visionary while the same phenomenon in H. D. is
"escapist." If there is to be any growth in the understanding
of literature by women, or by any other group not accepted
within the recognized literary tradition, or even by the established artists, these hidden biases and the necessarily
subjective nature of all criticism (as all art) must be confronted.

H. D. 's poetry itself brings into bold relief the assumptions of her critics that have been so damaging to her reputation.  Her own explorations of women's experience and the
dilemma of women writers correct, more eloquently than I
can, the mistaken prejudices of her critics and the distorting
lens of a double standard for men and women writers.  Riddel's and Holland's Freudian conception of a woman torn with
desire to possess the penis--or at any rate something "hard"--
is nowhere demonstrated in the "woman's epic" that H. D.
writes.  Missing also are various other critical assumptions
they make:  that H. D. found her fulfillment as a woman by
resignation to "winglessness"; that the "phallic" and the
"masculine" are associated with power, myth, poetry, objectivity, and meaning in opposition to the "feminine" qualities
of weakness, softness, insubstantiality, subjectivity; and so
forth.  The more diffused, less psychoanalytic, description
of the mature poet as a fragile naiad escaping into the still
world of an imaginary Greece bears no relationship to the
H. D. who used myth to confront the most contemporary
and timeless problems in women's lives.  Even less do H.
D. 's women heroes fit the stereotypes of women in the kit-
chens of the world or in the poetry of male poets.

Winter Love (Espérance), a newly published poem of
H. D. 's (continuing in twenty-eight sections the quest of
Helen in Helen in Egypt), demonstrates forcefully how distant
the stereotypes and conventions of literature and the comple-

mentary distortions of criticism often are from the reality of
a woman's perspective.    Helen of Troy, that symbol of dangerous love and beauty in so many poems by male poets, is
in H. D.'s poem not a distant symbol, nor some soft creature
seeking to fuse with some male hero, nor a reflection of H.
D.'s willingness to accept her "ontological deprivation." Listen instead to the woman's anguish in the final section of
Winter Love as Helen gives birth to her child Espérance and
recalls the succession of lovers who have come in and gone
out of her life:

28

> I am delirious now and mean to be,
> the whole earth shudders with my ecstacy,
> take Espérance away;
>
> cruel, cruel Sage-Femme,
> to place him in my arms,
> cruel, cruel Grande Dame,
>
> to pull my tunic down,
> so Odysseus sought my breast
> with savage kiss;
>
> cruel, cruel midwife,
> so secretly to steal my phantom self,
> my invisibility, my hopelessness, my fate
>
> the guilt, the blame, the desolation,
> Paris slain to rise again
> and find Oenone and mortality,
>
> Achilles' flight to Thetis
> and the Sea (deserting Leuké),
> Menelaus with his trophies in the palace,
>
> Odysseus--take the Child away,
> cruel, cruel is Hope,
> terrible the weight of honey and of milk,
>
> Cruel, cruel, the thought of Love,
> while Helen's breasts swell, painful
> with the ambrosial sap, Amrita
>
> that must be given;
> I die in agony whether I give or do not give;
> cruel, cruel Sage-Femme,
>
> wiser than all the regents of God's throne,
> why do you torture me?
> come, come O Espérance,

Espérance, O golden bee,
take life afresh and if you must,
so slay me.

[H. D. , pp. 116-17]

In this moment of delirium, when the aging Helen sees
the lovers of her life pass before her--Paris at Troy, Achilles
in Egypt and Leuké, Menelaus back in Sparta, and finally
Odysseus, the father of Espérance--she is left with "my
phantom self/ my invisibility, my hopelessness, my fate/ the
guilt, the blame, the desolation." She is a woman used--
sought in violence by Odysseus; abandoned finally by Paris,
who returns to his first love Oenone; and Achilles, who de-
serts Helen for his mother Thetis (Menelaus is something of
a bore with his trophies and stale stories). And is the child
Espérance consolation for the emptiness of life that has left
her clinging to the only identity she has--"my phantom self,/
my invisibility"? Is he, in Freudian terms, the satisfying
sublimation for penis envy? "The whole earth shudders with
my ecstasy"; Helen cannot help but feel joy in the overwhelming experience of the birth, but mixed with this "ecstasy"
is great pain, for the Child, with the added irony of his
name, Hope, brings a special agony. Helen sees him as
linked to the older men who took from her and fled: "cruel,
cruel Grande Dame,/ to pull my tunic down,/ so Odysseus
sought my breast/ with savage kiss." For, like a lover, the
Child demands and she must give. She is not even to be
left in peace with her "phantom self," a kind of death itself
(see section 27 of Winter Love), but at least her own. To
the Child she must give milk--"while Helen's breasts swell,
painful/ and the ambrosial sap, Amrita/ that must be given";
to deny the baby is torture, to give all he demands is agony:
"I die in agony whether I give or do not give." The Child,
in taking milk and love from his mother, is bringing a kind
of death upon her: "Espérance, O golden bee,/ take life
afresh and if you must,/ so slay me." The special cruelty
is that the birth of this child should be, as his name suggests,
a woman's hope, but the Child's all-encompassing demands
mean death for Helen because once again she will have to
give and give and give, only to be left by the grown child
in the end: "take the Child away,/ cruel, cruel is Hope/
.../ cruel, cruel the thought of Love." Yet, as with her
lovers, she finally puts the Child's needs before her own;
Helen's cry in the middle of the poem to "take the Child
away,/ cruel, cruel is Hope," becomes by the end "come,
come O Espérance" as she welcomes the newborn to her
breast.

Rather than suggesting consoling escape from reality, rather than representing the acquisition of "phallic objectivity," the mythic dimension of the poem adds cruel irony to the agony of this woman, to this poetic version of postpartum depression. From the time of Homer to the twentieth century Helen has been the symbol of woman in her most perfect form. Yet this poem with Helen as the subjective voice instead of the object of some poet's glazed eyes reveals desperate unhappiness. The "Sage-Femme" (literally "midwife" in French), the "Grande Dame," who brings the child safely to term and into the world is not worshipped here by Helen as the Great Earth Mother--she is "cruel," all the more so because she and Helen are both women, sisters. And capitalization of "Child" makes explicit the parallel between Helen-Espérance and Mary-Jesus, Isis-Horus, and all the other mother figures in mythology and art. Yet instead of reveling in this mythic parallel, instead of celebrating her fulfillment as a woman, Helen cries out in agony as she once again witnesses the death of her individual self. H. D. is not writing about Helen of Troy, however; we shouldn't let the poem's ancient speaker and this whole mythic dimension interfere with the direct, contemporary, universal voice of the poem--the agony of a middle-aged woman who has given and cannot stop giving to her lovers and her children. H. D.'s poem is all about women who are driven to fulfill others' demands only to find themselves left with a "phantom self," an "invisibility," a "hopelessness."

The woman in Winter Love is lamenting "missing things," but not the missing penis of Holland's analysis. Throughout all the sections of the poem, as in many of H. D.'s epics, she searches for the missing identity, for a direction and purpose which is so often denied to women. Caught within the Freudian or even more generally male-oriented categories of her critics, this theme of missing identity or "invisibility" in the midst of love and birth could easily be twisted into evidence for the persistence of H. D.'s unresolved phallic stage, for her desire to flee "feminine inwardness," or for her attempt to acquire power by merging with a man and with the "phallic signifiers" of knowledge. But such readings would be a total distortion of what H. D. is saying--about how that "phallic power" has presented Helen with a lifetime of demands, only to desert the drained phantom in the end; about how the ecstasy of birth is mingled with the recognition of a death of the individual self. Freed from the confines of a critical cage, this poem clearly contradicts the kinds of assumptions H. D.'s critics have made as they approach her work.

Perhaps, however, my reading of one small section
of only one poem by H. D. is too limited an example upon
which to rest my case that a male-oriented bias has had
dire consequences in the understanding of H. D. 's poetry.
What about the whole sweep of her epic quests?  Do they
bear out my contention that H. D. has set herself outside
the established literary tradition by her exploration of human
experience from a woman's perspective and that conventional
male categories of literary criticism must be abandoned if
her work is to be understood?  The thematic thrust and "arguments" of her major poems do indeed reveal how mislead-
ing some of her critics have been.  In the war Trilogy, written as the German bombs created a crucible of fire out of
her home, and in Helen in Egypt, written a few years later
in quiet reflection on a war-torn century, H. D. expresses
a vision in total opposition to envy for the male world.  Both
epics are poetic arguments for a belief similar to Carolyn
Heilbrun's in Towards a Recognition of Androgyny:  the dominance of masculine values has brought destruction and suffering, like the catastrophe of the two world wars.  The
"phallus" and its weaponed manifestations are never the "signifiers" of meaning as Riddel rather self-importantly suggests;
they have been instead the destroyers of human potentiality.

In Helen in Egypt Achilles represents the "Whirlwind
of War" as the leader of the "warrior cults" of the "purely
masculine iron-ring. "  It is he who must learn from Helen
how his sword "has blighted that peace" embodied in the
Goddess and how he can become the "new Mortal" by recap-
turing the feminine values of union and creation represented
in his past by his mother Thetis and in the present by Helen
herself.  Even more explicitly in the war Trilogy, H. D.
resurrects the powerful ancient deities of the matriarchies
whom she associates with the positive values of love, peace,
regeneration, and synthesis as the poet tranforms degraded
"venery" into "veneration" for Venus, Aphrodite, Isis--the
Lady or female principle in general.  In both epics these
active, powerful forces of birth and reintegration are scarcely
similar to the placid, fecund goddesses awaiting some lance-
carrying hero for fulfillment that abound in the patriarchal
mythologies and literature.  And they bear little resemblance
to Riddel's portrayal of "soft," "weak" femininity seeking
escape into the strength of whatever he happens to label "masculine. "  In fact both epics attempt to transcend the divisions
into male and female as they reach for a vision of individual
identity, society, and religion based on an androgynous union
of the strongest and most creative aspects of the traditionally
"masculine" and "feminine. "  In so doing they reveal a writer

who believes that to rectify the understanding of women's
experience and matriarchal values leads the poet-prophet to
confront universal questions of history, time, and humanity.

    The last poem the aging, ailing poet wrote, the recent-
ly published Hermetic Definition, sharply focuses the broader
issues explored in the earlier epics to a highly personal
account of the dilemma faced by the woman poet.  As she
tries to combine the woman in love and the woman at work
into a single artistic identity, her difficulties are great, as
Holland and Riddel suggested they would be.  But totally inconsistent with her final resolution are both Holland's description of the "ego theme" by which she writes poetry to acquire
the power she associated with a whole string of male figures
since childhood, and Riddel's contention that H. D. had to
transcend her femininity to write like a man.  The poem is
first of all an implicit rejection of a Freudian tenet that infuses both Holland's and Riddel's work and our culture in
general.  Freud saw an unbridgeable chasm separating the
"masculine" woman--the active, competitive woman whose
early development was "arrested" in penis envy and its consequent sublimation into all sorts of "male" activities, and
the "feminine" woman--the passive, weak woman who had
passed beyond penis envy into an acceptance of her domestic
role. [6]  In Freud's eyes and within the perspective of the
generally acceptable attitudes which Freud's "science" did
so much to legitimize, a woman is simply not expected to be
capable of both the joys of love and motherhood and the rigors
of work beyond the home.  Yet H. D. in the poem, as in so
much of her work, portrays a woman poet simultaneously
passionate in her love for a man and in her commitment to
write poetry.

    The poet's search is not for a man to fuse with or
be like--it is precisely the opposite:  the process of the
poem's quest is how to escape from the influence of two men
in order to find her own vision and direction.  One man is
Lionel Durand, who represents for H. D. the Lover and the
Son and whom she actually met when he came to interview
her for a Newsweek review of her novel Bid Me to Live.
At age seventy H. D. fell electrically in love with Durand,
and was in fact obsessed with this love for the nine months
it took her to write the poem, as her diary of the period
reflects.  But both in her life and in the poem Durand rejected H. D., as a woman and as a poet.  His personal letters to her were polite and distant; her work, he wrote, was
"fascinating if you can stand its preciousness" (H. D., p. 7).
To deny his condemnation of her work she listens to the voice

of her guide, her Muse--once again the powerful female deity
and patron of the mysteries, not any representative of the
"phallus" or "masculine" objectivity:  Isis "draws the veil
aside,/ unbinds my eyes,/ commands/ write, write or die"
(H. D. , p. 7).  In contrast to Riddel's description of the
ambivalence of her role as a woman writer, H. D. writes
about the problem of many women writers--the ridicule they
receive from their critics and reviewers.

     Rejection by Durand leads H. D. into an intense study
of the hermetic poetry of St. John Perse.  As she is entranced
with Perse's philosophic, esoteric vision and his acceptance
of her as a poet, she gradually comes to realize that she
must pass beyond the poetry of Perse to find her own way,
one which will "recover the human equation," the human experience of her love for Durand, a dimension which is missing from Perse's more abstract, more "formal and external"
(H. D. , p. 51) poetry.  She cannot rely on any man to be
her voice.  To insure herself against "deficiency," to echo
Holland, she must speak for herself and avoid fusion with a
man, lover, or fellow poet.  Her symbolic expression of her
successful independence is this poem itself, whose writing
she images as a pregnancy and a final painful birth.  Such
a metaphor for poetic creation has been somewhat conventional in poetry by men, but coming from a woman poet it
has a special power since the woman can in fact give birth
to both human life and poetry.  Isis, the mother-goddess-
Muse, commands, directs, protects, and infuses the growing
artistic identity of the woman poet throughout the poem.  The
resolution is no easy one:  the difficulties of being a writer
are somehow part of the necessary process of writing.  But
as she closes the poem the voices of her critics must quiet
their talk of phallic power and female insubstantiality so that
they can hear the woman's voice and strength which closes
H. D. 's poetic career:

> Rain falls or snow, I don't know,
> only I must stumble along, grope along,
> find my way; but believe me,
>
> I have much to sustain me.
>
> [H. D. p. 53]

     Once again, however, the central issue at stake is
not the mistaken theories of individual critics.  What the
chasm between H. D. 's poetry and the readings of some of
her critics demonstrates is how distortions in this one case
are part of a more general pattern in criticism by which the

work of women writers is misread.   Let no one argue at
this point that as long as all reading is subjective one person's theories are as valid as another's.   It must be recognized that distortions of a literary work which result from
prejudiced political and cultural categories do have real consequences for the reputations of many writers--those of different races, nationalities, classes, and political persuasions,
as well as of sex.   These distortions play a central part in
what literature is admitted to the informal roster of the established tradition, what literature is regularly studied and
taught.   Criticism is a link of the broad cultural chain that
in this country, especially now that once excluded students
are sitting in university classrooms, does not exist for a
privileged elite alone.   Consequently, criticism does not exist
in a polite vacuum in which one person's views are as good
as another's, in a gentlemanly sort of way.   It can perpetuate
the slow burying process that is suffered by writers whose
vision and experience are somehow out of the more privileged
mainstream.   And with this burial comes the alienation of
readers who cannot find their own experience reflected in
what they study in college.

The growth of Women's Studies--like Afro-American
Studies, Puerto Rican Studies, Chicano Studies, Asian Studies,
Native American Studies--has been a necessary answer to
the closed curriculums of the established literary tradition.
There should be no doubt that poems like Hermetic Definition
and Winter Love can be studied in a course on women and
literature.   H. D. was a woman writer who faced the peculiar
difficulties imposed on women writers by the society at large
and the established literary tradition with its retinue of critics
in particular.   Although she never wrote her own A Room of
One's Own, many of her novels and poems center around the
problems of women artists and intellectuals.   In addition,
her heroes are always women; and as individuals in quest
instead of abstract symbols, the women in her work are strikingly different from those in the poetry written by her male
counterparts.   What H. D. and poets like her have to say
about women's experience and potential is as much a legitimate
focus for a course as any thematic or chronological break-
down in a college curriculum.   If literature and politics of
the thirties, or frontier literature, or the angry young men
in Britain, or the absurd in modern fiction are all valid subjects for study, then surely women and literature must also
be.

But having separate courses on women and literature

is not enough; in fact this kind of separation by itself fosters the continuation of the idea that there are poets and then women poets, artists and then black artists, literature and then radical propaganda. To say that "lost" literatures by women, blacks, and other minority groups belong in separate niches all to themselves is to claim a kind of universality for literature by white males that it does not have. The poetry of H. D. , along with that of other women and minority writers, should be as much a part of the training of a graduate student in modern poetry as the work of Eliot, Yeats, Williams, Crane, Stevens, Pound, and any other of the numerous male poets whose works are required reading in the universities. H. D. is a part of modern poetry--that she was a woman writing about women should not exclude her from "The Literary Tradition." What she has to say about women and men in her poetry should be as much a part of any class as what Pound or Eliot have to say about men and women. If the elite of acceptable literature will have explored the experience of only half the human race (at best), with this incompleteness, this subjectivity, it will have lost a profound understanding of its own humanity. For when men see women in terms of stereotypes, they also understand themselves inadequately.

## REFERENCES

1.  Sagesse, in Hermetic Definition (New York: New Directions, 1972), p. 59. This volume will hereafter be referred to in the text as H. D. I am grateful to Norman Pearson, H. D. 's literary executor, for the suggestion that the caged owl of the poem is the aging poet herself.
2.  For Riddel's references to the inferior anatomy of women and the spiritual or psychological consequences, see his "H. D. and the Poetics of 'Spiritual Realism,'" Contemporary Literature, X (Autumn 1969), 448, 453-54, 455, 456, 459.
3.  For Holland's references to genitals as representations of physical and psychical inadequacies, see his "H. D. and the 'Blameless Physician,'" Contemporary Literature, X (Autumn 1969), 476, 482, 483, 485, 486, 490-91, 493, 497, 499-500, 501, 502.
4.  Norman Holland, Poems in Persons: An Introduction to Psychoanalysis and Literature (New York: Norton, 1973). Two thirds of this book uses H. D. as a case study for his broader argument concerning

psychoanalytic criticism as a general method.  His
Contemporary Literature article appears with few
changes as Chapter One where his argument is more
clearly seen as a method of tackling any writer,
male or female.  Many of the stylistic changes
are eliminations of Freudian terminology ("anal,"
"phallic," "oral," etc.); some of the "penis envy"
language has been softened or diffused.  But his
argument that H. D.'s childhood "phallic stage"
left within the adult poet a sense of longing for
the penis her mother and father never gave her is
as much present as ever in spite of the "gentler"
language.

5.   Wagner's article, "Helen in Egypt: A Culmination," is
in Contemporary Literature, X (Autumn 1969), 523-
36.  See also Thomas Swann's The Classical World
of H. D. (Lincoln: University of Nebraska Press,
1962) and Douglas Bush's Mythology and the Romantic Tradition in English Poetry (Cambridge, Mass.:
Harvard University Press, 1937), pp. 497 ff.

6.   See Sigmund Freud, "Femininity," in New Introductory
Lectures, trans. James Strachey (New York: Norton, 1964), pp. 112-35; Freud, An Outline of Psychoanalysis, trans. James Strachey (New York:
Norton, 1949), pp. 80-99.

Suzanne Juhasz

"THE BLOOD JET":
THE POETRY OF SYLVIA PLATH*

Sylvia Plath is the woman poet of our century who sees
the double bind inherent in trying to be both woman and poet
with the coldest, most unredeeming clarity: her life and her
art embody her attempts to find a solution. She never finds
one. The conflict as she experiences it is between her woman's body (object, all surfaces, illusion; or else inner space,
fertility, but also, in the end, illusion) and her poet's mind
(vision, reality, and death). As a person who sees division,
separation within her very self, who is conscious of surfaces
and interiors everywhere and of the gap between them, she
sees the pulse of life as the movement towards disintegration; the stasis of death as the only integration. Her later
poetry enacts symbolically the struggle between life and death
which is occurring in her consciousness, in her life. Over
a period of ten years her art develops from a glittery poetry
of surfaces, in which the poet, observing the external world,
orders and controls it through the power of her language to
dissect and reassemble, to a poetry of engagement and integration, in which the sole source of reality is her own consciousness, in which objects from the external world are
meaningful only as they define that consciousness, in which
the outside world has been pulled inside the mind.

Plath killed herself at the age of thirty-one. The fact
of her death is what is to many the most important thing about
her, what has allowed her to be appreciated and even vener-
ated as a wonderfully sensitive soul who transcended life by
death and art; a myth; a prophetess. Certainly not a woman;
"hardly a person at all."[1] The particular, real issues and

_____

*Reprinted by permission of the author and publisher from
Juhasz's Naked and Fiery Forms: Modern American Poetry
by Women; A New Tradition (New York: Harper & Row,
1976), pp. 85-116. Copyright © 1976 by Suzanne Juhasz.

experiences with which her last poems deal, those which
shaped her life and occasioned her death, the forms and tech-
niques that she found for expressing them, these need not
concern or threaten anyone.    Yet in my own reaction to and
analysis of Plath's poetry, I would in no way discount her
death.    It is of supreme importance, because it is to that
death that both her life and art led her.    A life and art that
both resulted from the fact that she was a woman poet.

1.    "When on tiptoe the schoolgirls danced"

Sylvia Plath suffered in an extreme form from the woman artist's need to reconcile her two roles, woman and
poet; from the necessity of living with what may seem her
two selves.    The exaggerated nature of her situation and her
suffering seems to have resulted from the peculiar temporal
and social context in which Plath's life and art grew:    the
fifties, New England, the middle class.    Sylvia Plath as
high school and college superachiever, the prettiest, the
most popular and the smartest, with her dark red lipsticked
smile, her carefully waved hair, a perfection of surfaces,
was in discord with another "self":    the poet whose words
could destroy surfaces and open inner places, inner wounds,
inner emptiness.

Roles are not really selves, although they may seem
so to the person enacting them.    To talk about the conflict
Plath experienced as woman and poet, as body and mind, is
not to talk in the jargon of psychiatry about split personalities
and pathological mental states.    Role conflicts occur in everyone; but if they are too extreme and too prolonged they can
surely have unpleasant consequences, especially if the conflict occurs between roles so primary to the personality that
neither can be readily eliminated.    I think that Plath's suffering was caused by such a role conflict and by the measures
she took at various stages of her life to try to ease the strain.

In high school Plath seems to have swallowed whole
the myth of the all-round student and projected it back to
the world as only one so capable and thorough as she could
do, achieving a perfection of the role:    editor, actress, sorority girl, and tennis and basketball player.    She was also
writing, taking that as seriously as she took everything else
about herself:    she had sent forty-five pieces to Seventeen
before the acceptance in March, 1950, of a short story.    The
tale continued at Smith College:    scholarships, awards and

prizes of all kinds came to her, seemingly for the asking.

For the bright young woman in American high schools of the fifties, there was one way only to validate the possession of an intellect: by proving that she was as pretty, as popular, as "normal" as anyone else. Plath seems to have pulled it off "exceptionally well." (The quote is from "Lady Lazarus" and refers to her skill at dying. But that came later.) Having proved her normalcy (femininity), she could also pursue scholarly activities.

Yet college was interrupted by the depression and suicide attempt that she made famous in her novel (written a good many years afterwards) The Bell Jar.

> ... I felt dreadfully inadequate. The trouble was, I had been inadequate all along, I simply hadn't thought about it.
>
> The one thing I was good at was winning scholarships and prizes, and that era was coming to an end. 2
>
> I hadn't washed my hair for three weeks, either.
>
> I hadn't slept for seven nights....
>
> I saw the days of the year stretching ahead like a series of bright, white boxes, and separating one box from another was sleep, like a black shade. Only for me, the long perspective of shades that set off one box from the next had suddenly snapped up, and I could see day after day glaring ahead of me like a white, broad, infinitely desolate avenue.
>
> It seemed silly to wash one day when I would only have to wash again the next.
>
> It made me tired just to think of it.
>
> I wanted to do everything once and for all and be through with it [pp. 104-05].

The Bell Jar is a writer's attempt to understand and to analyze her own mental condition: it is interpretive, but it does nevertheless point to elements of the situation that help explain why at precisely this moment the gears that were working at such top speed came to a grinding halt. A feeling of insecurity, puzzling to many who knew only the surface Sylvia Plath, is documented also in her letters and

confidences of the period: "for the few little outward successes I may seem to have, there are acres of misgivings
and self-doubt. "3   There are overtones of both false modesty
and adolescent exaggeration here, but the feeling that prompts
the statement seems genuine.   And understandable, given the
conflict she must have experienced between her long devotion
to maintaining that surface perfection and her doubts about
its validity--and even its reality.

        The overt "symptoms" of her depression, not washing
her clothing or her hair, not keeping up her feminine appearance, not keeping up appearances, send a clear message to
the world: I have stopped playing my role.   Why?   Because,
as the quoted passage reveals, another vision has interfered
with, has short-circuited the dictates of society: a vision
of life as a prison of bright meaninglessness; of her own
life as she had been busy creating it.   A life which from
her changed perspective hardly seems worth the trouble.
The vision was not sent to her; it came from within herself,
from a part of herself she had been carefully ignoring because
such a penetrating kind of insight could destroy her all-im-
portant surfaces.   It has already begun to do so by forcing
her to question those ritual acts of hairwashing, dressing
well--of looking pretty.   The vision leads to an attempt at
death, at "being through with it. "

        Yet when the suicide attempt proves abortive, and
after the care of the psychiatrists, Plath seems to get back
on the track.   She finishes Smith with glory, goes off for
two postgraduate years at Cambridge, marries a rising young
British poet, and returns to America to teach at Smith, carrying out her program for success with her old skill and
determination.   It is from this period (1955-1959) that the
poems of her first book, The Colossus, come.

2.   "And heart's frosty discipline/
        Exact as a snowflake"

        "She wrote her early poems very slowly," writes her
husband, Ted Hughes.   "Thesaurus open on her knee, in her
large, strange handwriting, like a mosaic, where every letter stands separate within the work, a hieroglyph to itself. "4
This is a glittery, brilliant, self-conscious poetry of surfaces, a cold poetry: Sylvia Plath's diamond gift to the
world.   Commentators on the verse of The Colossus are
always picking out influences, naming Roethke, Stevens, Law-

rence, Thomas.  Certainly they are there, for this is the
poetry of a woman who has studied hard in the school of
modern poetry and, as always, learned her lessons well.
She observes the world around her and claims it as her own
by imposing order, the order of language, upon it.  She has
an eye, an ear:

> "The pears fatten like little buddhas"
> ("The Manor Garden")

> In their jars the snail-nosed babies moon and glow.
> He hands her the cut-out heart like a cracked heirloom.
> ("Two Views of a Cadaver Room")

She has, as well, a vision:  the perception of the worm in
every apple core that breeds in her a bitter humor, a delight in the knowledge of disintegration and death.  These
elements give a focus to her observations:

> ... the gross eating game
> We'd wink at if we didn't hear
> Stars grinding, crumb by crumb,
> Our own grist down to its bony face.
> ("All the Dead Dears")

Yet the vision seems often precocious.  Precocious because
it expresses knowledge without experience.

"Man in Black," for example, a poem which contains
the death motif central to all of Plath's poetry, is essentially
a landscape.  The poet as watcher creates a scene.  She
first dissects it into its components, then reassembles it,
having found its fulcrum, its significance as a unit of related
elements.  The components of this scene are rocks ("three
magenta/ Breakwaters" which "take the shove/ And suck of
the grey sea/ To the left"), the sea ("the wave/ Unfists
against the dun/ Barbwired headland"), an island prison, ice,
rockpools, and cliffs:

> ... and March ice
> Glazes the rock pools yet,
> Snuff-colored sand cliffs rise

> Over a great stone spit
> Bared by each falling tide.

Finally, a man, who strides out in a "dead/ Black coat,
black shoes," with black hair, "till there you stood."  We

might assume that the man is the human element in the scene,
but the language describing him divests him of his humanity.
He is further dissected into components--coat, shoes, hair,
not a whole man; and he is black, dead.   The natural world,
on the other hand, is vital and active:   the sea shoves and
sucks, the wave is a fist, the ice acts upon the rock pools,
glazing them, the cliffs rise, each falling tide bares the
stone spit.   Yet the man is nevertheless the focus of the
scene, its "fixed vortex," so that the word around which the
poem turns is the "till" in the final line just quoted:  "till
there you stood,"

> Fixed vortex on the far
> Tip, riveting stones, air,
> All of it, together.

The man walks out on the stone and then stops.   Then his
negativity, his absence of life, makes sense of the March
landscape, stills its frenetic energy, rivets, fixes it into
stasis:  the stasis already implicit in its iciness, its bare-
ness--the stasis of death.   This is a poem about death in
life.   It is of course Plath's perception of the death-elements
in man and in nature that allows her to compose the scene
as she does, so to say that she is absent from the poem is
wrong.   But her participation is external, as it is in most
of her poems about scenes from nature or society, the majority of the poems in The Colossus.   What is most important about poems such as "Man in Black" is the element of
control which they manifest:  a firm and skillful control over
language which results in control over the external world.
Having divided it into its component parts and then reassem-
bled those elements according to her own concept of order,
they belong to her and therefore (hopefully) do not threaten.
It is understandable that a person who sees division, separation in her very self, who is morbidly conscious of surfaces and interiors and of the gap between the two, will be
aware of corresponding states in the external world.   At
this stage in her poetic development, she seems to believe
in the power of her own will to control the world, even as
she kept herself in control through the same kind of effort.

Not all of the poems of The Colossus are about nature; at times the poet herself is a major actor in the narrative.   But always the principles of objectivity and distance
are fundamental.   For example, in "Two Views of a Cadaver
Room," the personal experience, that of visiting a dissecting
room, is neatly balanced against a description of a Brueghel

canvas.  The title makes the connection:  both are versions
of the human condition--the world is one big cadaver room!

Even in Part I, the "personal" experience, Plath acts
as detached observer, describing with imagistic if not clinical
detail the four bodies, "black as burnt turkey,/ Already
half unstrung"; the medical students, "the white-smocked
boys"; one cadaver in particular, held together by "a sallow
piece of string," a "rubble of skull plates and old leather";
and the fetuses in jars, "the snail-nosed babies" that "moon
and glow. "  When she is forced into physical contact with
the "cut-out heart," she describes it as being presented to
her like "a cracked heirloom," thereby commenting upon the
student's pride in his work, work which she, however, considers both ominous and ludicrous.  Such is the effect of
the images she creates, which are oblique reports of her
reactions, opinions.

When she turns to "Brueghel's panorama of smoke
and slaughter," she concentrates upon the only two people in
the canvas who are "blind to the carrion army": two lovers,
lost in blue satin skirts, music, and one another: "deaf to
the fiddle in the hands/ Of the death's head shadowing their
song. "  Again, the sense of the ludicrousness of human life,
now attempting love (as before, in the cadaver room, attempting knowledge or salvation) in the face of prevailing death,
is omnipresent, and is driven home with a flourish of irony
in the concluding couplet:  "Yet desolation, stalled in paint,
spares the little country/ Foolish, delicate, in the lower
right-hand corner. "  Only art, which is not, the poet points
out, reality ("stalled in paint") can keep alive such a moment,
a moment delicate but ultimately foolish.

One poem in the volume, however, "The Disquieting
Muses," is to some degree different from those I have been
discussing.  Like the others it transposes personal drama
onto a more "objective" level:  in this case, to the realm
of fairy tales.  It externalizes elements from Plath's psyche,
her poetic impulses or vision, into three ladies, three evil
fairies, three disquieting muses.  But this poem nevertheless
resolutely attempts to describe, to reveal that aspect of
self:--the very one which is being suppressed or certainly
harnessed in poems like "Man in Black," or "Two Views of
a Cadaver Room"--the one which led her at nineteen to attempted
suicide.  Perhaps because of its difference in approach, the
poem's language is different, too:  both more narrative and
less image-laden, less baroque.

> Mother, mother, what illbred aunt
> Or what disfigured and unsightly
> Cousin did you so unwisely keep
> Unasked to my christening, that she
> Sent these ladies in her stead
> With heads like darning-eggs to nod
> And nod and nod at foot and head
> And at the left side of my crib?

In the first stanza explicit analogy sets up what will be the underlying allegory for the poem: Plath is a Sleeping Beauty, and contesting for her soul are her real mother (to whom the poem is addressed) and three evil fairies.

Throughout the poem's narrative, mother and god-mother vie to teach the poet-princess her lessons. In each stanza the dark and passive power of the three "mouthless, eyeless" ladies sabotages the energetic, optimistic work of the mother, whether it be at dancing, music, or life: "I learned, I learned, I learned elsewhere. / From muses un-hired by you, dear mother."

The poem concludes with a vision of the mother's final defeat:

> I woke one day to see you, mother,
> Floating above me in bluest air
> On a green balloon bright with a million
> Flowers and bluebirds that never were
> Never, never, found anywhere.
> But the little planet bobbed away
> Like a soap-bubble as you called: Come here!
> And I faced my travelling companions.

The reality principle has been invoked with finality. Your vision of life was a dream, mother, says the poet: a soap-bubble, a never-never land that is not real. And you are part of it, mother; you aren't real, either. What are real, the final line indicates, are my "travelling companions." I go with them because they have become me and I them, they are inside of me, they are me.

> Day now, night now, at head, side, feet,
> They stand their vigil in gowns of stone,
> Faces blank as the day I was born,
> Their shadows long in the setting sun
> That never brightens or goes down.

And this is the kingdom you bore me to,
Mother, mother. But no frown of mine
Will betray the company I keep.

Here is yet another vision of death, a spiritual death which
the poem transforms into a physical one. The godmothers
who stood by the cradle with their christening wish have
achieved their prophecy as they stand, carved angels, by
the tomb. Theirs is the kingdom of death. But of course
the speaker is not really dead, she is speaking the poem.
Then what is this death that she is living, a state characterized by shadow and blankness on the part of both muses
and poet (for her face, like theirs, has become totally ex-
pressionless, hiding their existence inside her, their presence
from the outside world)? It is the state in which she can
make poetry: for these evil fairies are her muses, and the
gift they have given her is the power to see the real. The
real is disquieting--frightening, because it contains within
itself at all times the existence of death; but the ability carefully hidden inside herself ("no frown of mine" betraying its
existence) for many years: that force which will produce
the exceptional poetry of her last years.


3.   "I may be ugly and hairy"

In the final three years of her life (1960-1963) Sylvia
Plath gave up her plans to be a professor of literature and
turned completely to writing poetry, settled in England, gave
birth to two children, separated from her husband, and twice
attempted suicide. During this period she wrote a poetry
that at last manifested the reality of her experience as a
woman and poet.

"She is a very different woman in the last long year
of her life," writes her critic and admirer, Charles Newman.
"Photographs at the time indicate that she had lost all resemblance to the Smith girl who won the Mademoiselle fiction
contest. She is deliberately dowdy, hyper-English, very
much the mother and established poetess."[5] The change in
appearance seems linked to the change in the poetry itself.
Esther Greenwood of The Bell Jar, in refusing to wash her
hair or change her clothes, is rejecting a complete and
carefully cultivated image of herself, her role as American
Girl, the Great Virgin Sex Queen. But to appear drab and
dowdy is not, I do not think, to take on another surface,
another role, that of the British "Mum." It is rather a

negation of surfaces: it is to not do the work, to reject the
feminine body by refusing to anoint and decorate and worship
it.  It is, in consequence, to reject the body-as-object as
she herself had created it.

In a thinly veiled allegory about her perception of
her "two selves," "In Plaster" (March, 1961), a poem describing a woman wearing a cast, Plath comments upon the
relation between the surface woman and the one "inside."

... There are two of me now:
This new absolutely white person and the old yellow one.
                              [Crossing the Water6]

The surface woman, the plaster woman, is cold, white, beautiful, tidy, calm, patient, and thinks she is "immortal."  At
first the woman inside is kind to the plaster woman: "I
realized what she wanted was for me to love her"; "Without
me, she wouldn't exist, so of course she was grateful. / I
gave her a soul."  Then she realizes that a death struggle
is occurring between them:

And secretly she began to hope I'd die.
Then she could cover my mouth and eyes, cover me
          entirely,
And wear my painted face the way a mummy-case
Wears the face of a pharaoh, though it's made of mud
          and water.

The inner woman's problem is that she has grown dependent
upon the surface woman: "She's supported me for so long I
was quite limp."  But in the final stage the inner woman is
plotting her revolution:

I used to think we might make a go of it together--
After all, it was a kind of marriage, being so close.
Now I see it must be one or the other of us.
She may be a saint, and I may be ugly and hairy,
But she'll soon find out that that doesn't matter a
          bit.
I'm collecting my strength; one day I shall manage
          without her,
And she'll perish with emptiness then, and begin
          to miss me.

As a poem this narrative remains grounded in its
allegorical mechanics, but as a piece of self-analysis its

perceptions point to the nature of her conflict and to her decision during this period to resolve it.   She had decided to
place her faith in the inner woman because she had seen with
clarity that the cold and perfect surface woman was an illusion.   Certainly the struggle between them had been destructive, but now she would annihilate once and for all that cold,
sterile, woman/body/object self and free her creative impulses and vision, the "inner" self.

Her change in appearance follows Plath's rejection of
America and of the profession for which she had been training most of her life:  that of teacher/scholar.   She chooses,
instead, England, poetry, and motherhood.   She chooses
another body image which seems to be a more suitable ves-
sel for her mind and soul.   Another form for woman:  no
longer sex-object but mother; no longer the narcissistic ste-
rility of surfaces, but the nurturant fertility of inner spaces,
of the womb.   Her woman's creativity (children) and her
poet's creativity (poems) will coincide and correspond, and
she will no longer be two warring selves but one whole person:  the woman poet.   In the process she rejects as unreal
all surfaces, all externals, even as she affirms the inside
rather than the outside of her body.   The poetry of this period reflects her attitude:  in it objects from the external
world are meaningful only as they define her own consciousness.   She pulls the outer world inside her mind, inside her
poetry.

Her decision to commit herself to poetry results in
an engagement that had been missing from her earlier work.
For Plath poetry had always been symbolic action.   In The
Colossus she had used language to impose an order upon experience, but the order in her poems contradicted her vision
of reality as fragmented and perpetually disintegrating.   Only
in a poem could the world be composed and controlled, and
so poetry was artificial; it lied.   In the later poetry she
begins to tell the truth.   When she comes to see that reality
resides in her own mind, words and poems become as real
as anything else.   The expression of her vision in words
unleashes reality, for her poems describe what is real:  her
own consciousness.   The action that is poetry is recognized
as symbolic action, but the symbols now reflect rather than
counteract her own life.

The poems of these final years render in symbolic
action her personal battle between life and death.   It appears
that in committing herself to her artistic and bodily creativity
she had not alleviated the struggle but rather had heightened

it.    First, because the positive values of motherhood were outweighed in her life by its negative ones.

There may have been, for a short while at least (during pregnancy, right after birth) a respite from the long conflict between body and mind, woman and poet, that had plagued her for so many years.

> When I walk out, I am a great event.
> I do not have to think, or even rehearse.
> What happens in me will happen without attention.
> The pheasant stands on the hill;
> He is arranging his brown feathers.
> I cannot help smiling at what I know.
> Leaves and petals attend me.    I am ready.

So the voice of the mother in Plath's lengthy exploration of maternity, Three Women (Crossing the Water), describes the condition of unity between one's own body and the body of the world that the woman entering into childbirth feels.

But when pregnancy and childbirth are over, what is left is the child, who presents two major problems.    First, one spends more time cleaning and feeding and cleaning than simply loving: "Meanwhile there's a stink of fat and baby crap" ("Lesbos").    The late poems were all written before eight a. m. , during the early morning hours before the children woke and her life as a mother (rather than poet) began.    The conflict had surely returned in another form. The second problem is that one cannot keep a child: slowly, from birth, the mother watches her perfect creation corrupted from her by the world which has already corrupted herself.

> How long can I be a wall, keeping the wind off?
> How long can I be
> Gentling the sun with the shade of my hand,
> Intercepting the blue bolts of a cold moon?
>                                     [Three Women]

The two kinds of creativity are not the same; there remains a gap between woman and poet.

As poet, Plath sees with increasing clarity this gap. She sees as well the existence of life and its inevitable corruption into death.    The forces in her that gave rise to her awareness of and fascination with death are surely complex; but surely the fact that she existed for so long with a sense of her own self as disparate, bifurcated contributed to a desire for wholeness which she could equate only with death. The pulse of life was the movement towards disintegration: the stasis of death brought integration. And perfection. For Plath had viewed perfection as a solution to her problem, a perfection that she had been led to believe was achievable through talent and sheer will power. She needed to be good at everything because in that way she could be everything: woman and poet. Although this program proved impossible, she was left with her belief in perfection. There was perfection in death.

The nature of her struggle between the forces of life and death is revealed in the vocabulary as well as the themes of her poetry. Plath's poetic vocabulary is always value laden: words like "white" or "red," "moon" or "heart" carry with them a set of symbolic associations whenever they appear, creating both emotional and conceptual resonances and meanings. Blood, flowers, babies, pain, cries, breath form image clusters (units of experience) that compete for Plath's favors with emptiness, purity, colorlessness, perfection, stars, moon, snow; with "the cold dead center/ Where spilt lives congeal and stiffen to history" ("A Birthday Present"). Poetry, "the blood jet," starts in life but moves towards death: "there is no stopping it" ("Kindness").

### 4. "The woman is perfected"

A selection of poems from the last nine months of Plath's life was published posthumously in 1965 by her husband in Ariel. In 1971 appeared Winter Trees, containing more of the final poems; then Crossing the Water, transitional poems from the period between The Colossus and the Ariel poems. Ariel caused Plath's fame, her myth: its poems fully realized, powerful, and vital.

The themes of these last poems all intertwine. There are poems concerned with various aspects of womanhood, the particular experiences of motherhood, emotional life and fantasies, nature (as much emotional life and fantasy as anything else), the life-death battle, a primary element in the emotional and fantasy life, and a myth for the life-death battle, the bee poems. The themes are so intertwined because all are manifestations of the consciousness of Sylvia Plath. The struggle between life and death may not always be the ostensible or overt subject of a poem, but the perceptions and ideas of a consciousness that is struggling between life and death not only color but indeed control the vision of every poem produced.

Yet the war between death and life is an ongoing process, and the poems as they evolve arrange and rearrange the symbols for elements of the poet's experience. These arrangements indicate the progress, the direction of the struggle itself.

In "Tulips" (1961), Plath describes herself as hospital patient, recovering from an appendectomy. In this poem the desire for death is overcome by the force of life. In long lines of narrative the poem sets up a series of external correspondences to the poet's psychological state. Through her very perception of these "correspondences" as they actively exist and interact, the poet undergoes a gradual change in her condition.

She is "nobody": she has "let things slip, a thirty-year-old cargo boat"; she is "swabbed clear of her loving associations," "a nun," who has "never been so pure." She perceives the hospital and all associated with it as agents that assist in her quest for non-being: "I have given my name and my day-clothes up to the nurses/ And my history to the anaesthetist and my body to the surgeons."

... it is winter here.
I am learning peacefulness, lying by myself quietly
As the light on these white walls, this bed, these hands.

If the season of hospitals is winter, its element is water. The nurses are gulls: they "pass and pass, they are no trouble,/ They pass the way gulls pass inland with their white caps." Her body is a pebble to them: "they tend it as water/ Tends to the pebbles it must run over, smoothing them gently." Their bright needles bring her numbness, sleep. She wants the freedom, the peace that she identifies with the gift of death.

How free it is, you have no idea how free--
The peacefulness is so big it dazes you,
And it asks nothing, a name tag, a few trinkets.
It is what the dead close on, finally: I imagine them
Shutting their mouths on it, like a Communion tablet.

But there is an alien presence in this wintry mindscape. The poem opens with it: "the tulips are too excitable."

While the first five stanzas commemorate the force and fascination of death, culminating in the vision of the dead shutting their mouths on its great freedom and peacefulness, the
irritant, the presence of the tulips, continues to bother and
is perhaps the cause of such an extended paean to non-being.
In the first stanza the poet argues: "I am nobody; I have
nothing to do with explosions." Again, she begins the fifth
stanza, which ends with the reference to the Communion
tablet, arguing: "I didn't want any flowers, I only wanted/
To lie with my hands turned up and be utterly empty."

But the tulips cannot be ignored. They are "too red";
they watch, they breathe, they move. Their redness hurts:
it "talks to my wound, it corresponds." They breathe "like
an awful baby." They weigh her down although they seem
to float: "Upsetting me with their sudden tongues and their
colour." And they watch; they turn to her, make her see
herself:

> ... flat, ridiculous, a cut-paper shadow
> Between the eye of the sun and the eyes of the tulips,
> And I have no face, I have wanted to efface myself.
> The vivid tulips eat my oxygen.

The two stanzas of describing the tulips, of analyzing why
she resents their presence, are already enough to cause her
to notice a sun outside, to see herself in a new light, to
begin to want to breathe the oxygen that the tulips are "eating." The tulips "correspond" to her wound, because like
them she is alive, and their living presence forces her living
response.

The concluding two stanzas are vivid with color and
noise, as life, once acknowledged, seems to explode around
the poet: "Now the air snags and eddies round them the
way a river/ Snags and eddies round a sunken rust-red engine." The icy sea has become a turbulent river; she is
caught up in it. For the season is changing: "the walls,
also, seem to be warming themselves." The final correspon-
dence is at last made: there is no escaping it. Even as
the tulips open "like the mouth of some great African cat,"
so she becomes aware of her heart:

> ... it opens and closes
> Its bowl of red blooms out of sheer love of me.
> The water I taste is warm and salt, like the sea,
> And comes from a country far away as health.

As the tulips become a fierce, warm-blooded African cat,
so her own heart becomes a bowl of flowers, the tulips themselves.  Her heart equals flowers and flowers equal animals
because all are alive, full of color, full of motion.  So, too,
is the sea, once the ice has melted from its surface (from
all the heat, the warmth of breath and blood) and it too can
flow freely.

It is Plath's method to express her ideas in terms of
such "correspondences": the quality of her vision (here,
one that sees gulls and pebbles, babies and African cats) has
always set in motion the symbolic action of her poems.  What
is different now is that the person having that vision is a
part of it and affected by it:  what and how the poet "sees"
affects what happens to her in the poem, even as what happens to her as the main character in the poem affects what
and how she sees.  In this instance the positive power of
life (flowers, babies, redness, breath) overwhelms the negative pull of death (whiteness, winter, ice, snow, passivity,
purity, emptiness, peacefulness, freedom); and the action of
the poem is the battle that is waged.  The detached and
distant observer is no more.

In the last poems the love between mother and child
is described again and again.  It appears as the strongest
agent for life, having the most powerful hold upon the poet.
In Three Women, women in a maternity ward speak of their
experience of motherhood.  The first woman, committed to
maternity and nothing else, is linked to the physical world:
"I am slow as the world"; "I am breaking apart like the
world"; "I am a river of milk. / I am a warm hill."  The
second woman has had a series of miscarriages:  she cannot
carry a child to term.  She equates her condition with death
and masculinity.

> When I first saw it, the small red seep, I did not
>     believe it.
> I watched the men walk about me in the office.  They
>     were so flat!
> There was something about them like cardboard, and
>     now I had caught it,
> That flat, flat, flatness from which ideas, destructions,
> Bulldozers, guillotines, white chambers of shrieks
>     proceed,
> Endlessly proceed--and the cold angels, the
>     abstractions.

The third woman is a college student having an illegitimate

child that she does not keep. She equates the child with danger for her freedom, for her seriousness. She speaks of
her "red, terrible girl" whose cries are "hooks that catch
and grate like cats." Near the end, when she has returned
to the university, she tries to praise her lack of attachments,
her aloneness.

> It is so beautiful to have no attachments!
> I am solitary as grass. What is it that I miss?
> Shall I ever find it, whatever it is?

But she has underestimated the power of maternity, of the
love that she has given up. Some feminists have attacked
Three Women because it is virtually a hymn to motherhood,
to the woman's body as a physical instrument. Yet surely
the poem must be viewed in the context of Plath's art, and
life, as the expression of a yearning for a simple commitment
that it is impossible for her to make, no matter how fiercely
she feels its call and gifts. In maternity and in maternal
love the elements that Plath has always associated with life--
pain, cries, breath, redness, blood, love, and babies--come
together. Yet as symbols for life the mother and child are
as impermanent, as fluid as the elements of which they are
composed. Love is not enough to fix them; the perfect child
will leave the mother, will enter the world, will know death:
"O golden child the world will kill and eat" ("Mary's Song").

One cannot find one's own perfection through another
human being, even one's own child. This is the lesson that
Plath learns from trying to do it. Forever seeking perfection, first in herself (but finding it to be a lie, a farce, an
illusion), she then seeks it in her children: "Your clear
eye is the one absolutely beautiful thing," she writes in
"Child." She wants to fill the child's eye, as a poem, with
the beauty and good of the world as she sees it: she wants
it to be a mirror, reflecting back the images of perfection
that she cannot make in herself: "Pool in which images/
Should be grand and classical." But there is no help for it:
the child's eye reflects herself, reflects the world: "this
troublous/ Wringing of hands, this dark/ Ceiling without a
star." If one seeks perfection, as Plath did, there is finally
only one source left: death.

"Edge" (Ariel) was written during the last week of
Plath's life. It is as spare and terse as "Tulips" was narrative and conversational. It is nothing but vision: a vision
of herself, now, no longer operating in any external world.

Elements from the physical world are useful, valid, real
only as they help her to define with words her own consciousness.   She has come to see with an awful clarity that the
only reality is what she makes.   She did not make herself.
She made her children and her poems; and she can make her
death.   In her poem she makes that death with words.

> The woman is perfected.
> Her dead
>
> Body wears the smile of accomplishment,
> The illusion of a Greek necessity
>
> Flows in the scrolls of her toga,
> Her bare
>
> Feet seem to be saying:
> We have come so far, it is over.

Perfection, accomplishment, death--these ideas are embodied
in the corpse of a woman.   The very folds of her clothing
are in exactly the right position, as if fated to be there;
everything about her form is correct, exact, the fulfillment
of her destiny.   So I paraphrase Plath's figure of speech,
but the form in which she expressed this thought is itself
significant:   the way in which the concepts "illusion" and
"necessity" take action (flow) and physical shape in the scrolls
of a toga represents the merging of concept and object which
is the subject of the poem.

     This woman is a mother; but here the problem of
losing the child to the world has been solved, for the children, too, are dead:

> Each dead child coiled, a white serpent
> One at each little
>
> Pitcher of milk, now empty.

In this poem the opposition between images and symbols--red
vs. white, blood vs. ice--that occurs in so many of her works
has been reconciled, or surmounted.   Dead, a child is white.

> She has folded
>
> Them back into her body as petals
> Of a rose close when the garden
>
> Stiffens and odours bleed
> From the sweet, deep throats of the night flower.

Children, flowers, and blood still go together, but it has
been understood here that flowers also die, that the blood
which pulses through the veins and symbolizes life is the
same blood that flows out to create death.  Returned to their
original unity with the mother, the children have therefore
recaptured their prelapsarian perfection.

> The moon has nothing to be sad about,
> Staring from her hood of bone.
>
> She is used to this sort of thing.
> Her blacks crackle and drag.

The moon, as in many Plath poems, remains the proper
light, and audience, for a death-scene:  her cold and carved
whiteness reflects and illuminates the cold corpse with its
sculptured form.   The woman has become her own tombstone,
her own monument.

In his study of suicide, The Savage God (New York,
1972), Alvarez argues quite convincingly that in her last
suicide attempt, as in all of her former attempts, Plath did
not really mean to die and tried to make it possible for
someone to save her; but that a series of unfortunate coin-
cidences prevented that salvation from occurring.  He may
well be correct:  many people attempt suicide as an ultimate
gesture, the most extreme and the strongest that they know,
that says in effect:  help me! pay attention to me!  I cannot
manage things alone!  I need help!  Surely the social and
physical conditions that Plath was experiencing in her last
months--a bitter winter, frozen pipes, no telephone, unpre-
dictable heat and electricity, no help with the children,
separation from her husband, her own illness--were the
mitigating circumstances that caused intense depression, a
feeling that she could no longer go it alone and needed help.
She did not have to die in the winter of 1963.   But it seems
inevitable that at some point she would have caused her own
death.   Its attractions were so very great for her, because
there was, finally, no solution to her life.   She is the woman
poet of our century who sees the problem, the situation of
trying to be a woman poet with the coldest and most unredeeming clarity, and who, try as she might, finds no solution.
Being the best poet, being the best mother will not solve the
problem, because there remains the yawning gap between
poet and mother, her sense of herself as not one but two.

Her death, because it is no solution, proves the impossibility of what she set out to do, which may be why she has been such a satisfying idol for both those who do not believe that women have a right to be both women and poets and those who believe in the right, but as an ideal that can never be achieved in the practical world.   Surely she was a victim of her situation, yet others before and since in a similar situation have not responded exactly as she did, either because they did not perceive it as she did or because they found other ways out of it.   Ultimately, we cannot distinguish between her situation, herself, and her art.   She would not have killed herself if she had not been in that particular situation and had not perceived it as she did, but neither would she have been the woman she was, the poet she was, if she had not lived and written under those conditions.

Yet her death was in every sense tragic because it was not necessary; because the social and psychological pressures that led her to it need not have existed--need not exist. When I read Plath's poetry, I am frightened by it, but I am not led, as she was, through it towards death.   It makes me want more than ever to be allowed to live; to fight to be able to live as both woman and poet; to make it possible for these to be harmonious facets of one person.   Because Plath lived, and died, and wrote as she did, this goal has become more possible.   Her courage to work from the reality that she knew can be emulated; her defeat in the face of that reality can be a lesson to avoid.

REFERENCES

1.   Robert Lowell, Introduction to Ariel (New York:   Harper
        & Row, 1966), p. vii.
2.   The Bell Jar (New York:   Harper & Row, 1971), p. 62.
3.   Lois Ames, "Notes Towards a Biography," in Charles
        Newman, ed. , The Art of Sylvia Plath:   A Sympo-
        sium (Bloomington:   Indiana University Press,
        1971), p. 160.
4.   "Notes on the Chronological Order of Sylvia Plath's
        Poems," in Newman, p. 188.
5.   "Candor Is the Only Wile:   The Art of Sylvia Plath," in
        Newman, p. 46.
6.   New York:   Harper & Row, 1971.

Rise B. Axelrod

## "I DARE TO LIVE": THE TRANSFORMING ART OF ANNE SEXTON*

No longer in a merely physical universe, man
lives in a symbolic universe.... Instead of dealing with the things themselves man is in a sense
constantly conversing with himself [Ernest Cas-
sirer, An Essay on Man].

Where there is no vision, the people perish [Pro-
verbs, 29:18].

As animal symbolicum, or symbol-maker, each person lives in a world of abstraction, or other-reality distinct from the world of multiplicity and sense experience.
Civilization, that accumulation of symbolic constructs, forms
a buffer between the individual, the internal self, and nature,
the world without. "This capacity for living easily and fa-
miliarly at an extraordinary level of abstraction," is, as
William Barrett explains in Irrational Man, both the source
of our immense technological power and the source of that
"desolating sense of rootlessness, vacuity and the lack of
concrete feeling that assails modern man in his moments of
real anxiety."[1] The inevitable dead end of our epistemology
is Nothingness: the tragedy of modern existence is that we
are irrevocably alienated, cut off from our roots, imprisoned
in the narrow cell of our own self-consciousness. Yet the
poet in our time seeks to free the self from the deadly effect
of symbolic entrapment. This quest for unification of self
with other is the ultimate aim of Eros, the liberating and
creative life force. In her poetry, Anne Sexton plunges into
the abyss of the isolated self and touches sources of regeneration. In her early books, To Bedlam and Part Way Back,

*Reprinted by permission of the author and publisher from
Concerning Poetry 7, 1 (Spring 1974), 6-13. Copyright ©
1974 by Concerning Poetry.

All My Pretty Ones, and Live or Die, she explores the dark
depths of her own consciousness. In the later three books,
Love Poems, Transformations, and The Book of Folly, she
experiments with mythopoeia providing possibilities of re-
connection, and hence of rebirth. [2] Thus the movement of
Sexton's poetic is dual: centripetal as well as centrifugal.
The inturning therapeutic mode analyzes the "cracked mirror"
of the self in search of the origins of dissolution.  The second, more visionary mode allows the resurrection of the
true self and its reunification with others.

     Anne Sexton's early poetry takes place in Bedlam,
the realm of extremity and madness.  She explained, in a
Paris Review interview: "I was a victim of the American
Dream....  The surface cracked when I was about twenty-
eight.  I had a psychotic break and tried to kill myself."[3]
In the seminal poem, "For John, Who Begs Me Not to Enquire Further," that cracked surface of her brittle system
of symbolic constructs is transformed into an image of "the
cracked mirror," an image of her own and the world's insanity:

> Not that it was beautiful,
> but that, in the end, there was
> a certain sense of order there;
> a something worth learning
> in that narrow diary of my mind,
> in the commonplaces of the asylum
> where the cracked mirror
> or my own selfish death outstared me.

In this mirror, the poet comes face to face with her own
disintegration, and with her ambivalent movement toward
death.  Evidences of the fragmentation of her psyche are
scattered throughout the poetry in synecdochic images.  Her
very life is a burden: "lugging myself as if/ I were a sawed-
off body/ in the trunk" (LD 87).  Not only is her body irrevocably severed from her mind by a strictly enforced Cartesian dualism, but it is in revolt.  In the mad-house, the
poet tries to do therapy:

>              I make
> moccasins all morning.  At first my hands
> kept empty, unraveled for the lives
> they used to work.  Now I learn to take
> them back, each angry finger that demands
> I mend what another will break
> tomorrow [B 3].

Those empty, death-embracing hands and those self-motivated, self-destructive fingers resist making a "mock of sin." They resist overturning the abstract system of guilt and repression, and so resist being cured, resist wholeness.

The "cracked mirror" also reflects the narcissistic self unable to perceive a world outside itself. According to Martin Heidegger, after Plato's Cave of Shadows each individual was trapped in solipsism.[4] In "The Double Image," Sexton has a corresponding "cave of the mirror," where two portraits, the dying mother and the suicidal daughter, face each other, mirroring each other's death and identity:

> my mocking mirror, my overthrown
> love, my first image.  She eyes me from that face,
> that stony head of death
> I had outgrown.
> . . .
>
> And this was the cave of the mirror,
> that double woman who stares
> at herself, as if she were petrified
> in time....

The portrait of the mother is a death mask, "petrified" in as well as by time and inevitably frightening to any witness. But to confront death in a double image of oneself forces one to view the abyss from a fragile precipice.  For in the mother's death, the poet cannot escape the vision of "my mocking mirror"--her own failed suicides.  Add guilt to that death and imagine the innumerable horrors the poet must suffer. The mother could not forgive her daughter's suicide attempts and held them responsible for her own death: "As if death were catching/ ... as if my dying had eaten inside of her/ ... [she] said I gave her cancer."

Traditionally, Western society offers two means of dealing with death:  the economic institution of hereditary property and the religious promise of immortality.  Sexton experiments with both of these systems, only to discover their ultimate inadequacy.  In "The Division of Parts" and "All My Pretty Ones" she "shuffles" through "the love and legal verbiage" of both parents' wills.  This ritual sorting and cataloguing of her inheritance is likened by Sexton to "piling stones one on top of the other."[5]  These "gifts" are deadweight which "settle on [her] like a debt"; but through the verbal piling process she is able to bury her parents, their deaths, and her guilt under an avalanche of physical material. Yet this escape from feeling into factuality ("Time, that rearranger/ of estates, equips/ me with your garments, but not with grief") proves unsuccessful, for even in her numbed sleep, nightmare visions violate her bed. The demon cannot be exorcized because the "brave ghost" is the mother, the double image, the self. Avoidance of death through materialism is really equivalent to a flight into schizophrenia and death itself.

The alternative religious solution is desperately sought by Sexton, but it too proves impossible, at least at this stage in her writing. Yearning to believe in the Resurrection and the mythology of eternal life, she is unbearably constrained by the physical reality of the Crucifixion. Christ's passion is too real, his human suffering too recognizable. Sexton's Protestantism prevents her from acceptance of the miracle: Christ is too much man to be God. She sadly states, "Need is not quite belief" (A 22). Worse still is her horrorific conclusion, for without a Heaven, without a God to rescue us from death, the fiction of Christ's resurrection becomes a cruel joke. His death, like our own, is a grotesquery. There is no escape from total annihilation: "Unto the bellies and jaws/ of rats I commit my prophecy and fear./ Far below The Cross, I correct its flaws./ We have kept the miracle. I will not be here" (A 26). Thus, these imperfect systems rather than providing succor only aggravate the pain, forcing the poet to acknowledge the very truth she wishes to avoid.

"The only way to escape the abyss," Cesare Pavese claims, "is to look at it, measure it, sound its depths and go down into it."[6]   Through a suicidal leap into the void at the core of being, Anne Sexton finds the means of liberation. By taking death into oneself, she says, you "have possessed the enemy, eaten the enemy,/ have taken on his craft, his magic" (LD 58). Suicide then is an attempt to conquer death, to master the existential dread, the fear that "in the end ... drowns you" (LD 17). Besides this will to power over one's daily dying, the "suicide impulse" can be, as James Hillman explains in Suicide and the Soul, "a transformation drive."[7] Oftentimes, the suicide finds it necessary to wrench herself violently out of one inadequate order of reality into another reality. In "Kind Sir: These Woods," Sexton describes this process in terms of a childhood game: "It was a trick/ to turn around once and know you were lost;/ ... O Mademoiselle,/ the rowboat rocked over. Then you were dead./ Turn around once, eyes tight, the thought in your head." This playing with dislocation, madness, and death becomes

for the adult a terrifying but necessary experience. As the
poem's epigraph from Walden advises: "Not till we are
lost ... do we begin to find ourselves." Like Thoreau, the
poet in search of an authentic self realizes the therapeutic
necessity of throwing off all the unnecessary surplusage of
civilization and going naked into the woods of the psyche:

> And opening my eyes, I am afraid of course
> to look--this inward look that society scorns--
> Still, I search in these woods and find nothing worse
> than myself, caught between the grapes and the thorns.

This initial, self-analytical "inward look" into the
"Heart of Darkness" leads Sexton to the wisdom of accepting
her genuine self ("love your self's self where it lives" [B
54]). Only then is she enabled to escape solipsism and death
through the emergent, coalescent poetic vision: "In a dark
time, the eye begins to see."[8] Imagery of the eye and seeing
is, therefore, pervasive in Sexton's poetry. Blindness suggests death: it is a playful confrontation with the void ("eyes
tight" shut in a childhood game [B 5]), or a desperate recognition of helplessness ("I come like the blind feeling for
shelves" [LD 18]). This sense of extremity, of consciousness
turned upon itself, adrift in Nothingness, is characteristic
of existential anxiety: "They turned the light out/ and the
dark is moving in the corner" (B 8). In suicide, like schizophrenia, one "will enter death/ like someone's lost optical
lens" (LD 75); consciousness is divorced from being, the
"eye" is estranged from the "I." But even at this radical
moment of denial of life and vision ("my head in a death
bowl/ and my eyes shut up like clams" [F 36]) a vital coun-
terforce is at work: "I have one glass eye. / My nerves
push against its painted surface/ but the other one/ waiting
for judgment/ continues to see" (LD 22). Self-analysis is
a re-education, a revision, a sharpening of one's latent vision
("eyes circling into my childhood,/ eyes newly cut" [LD 7]).
The process of freeing vision is regenerative: "I was the
one/ who opened the warm eyelid/ like a surgeon" (LD 9).
Not only is the self reborn, but others are "brought forth"
also by means of this mystical caesarean section. For Sexton, poetic vision is true vision. Poetry liberates one from
the "labyrinth" of inward existence, by soaring Icarus-like
"into that hot eye," the sun, visionary source of life, seer
and seen (A 8).

The only way to defeat death and abstraction, then,
is through the liberation of vision, or true seeing. "Poetic

creation," Carlyle observed, "What is this but seeing the
thing sufficiently?" Poetry of this order reconnects the self
with the roots of being. It "milks the unconscious," as
Sexton explained to the Paris Review (p. 162), signifying a
return to primal unity through the primordial model of wholeness and psychic comfort. A visionary poet like William
Blake, Anne Sexton seeks to break through the "walls" of
abstraction which enclose and pervert the creative life force,
Eros, or the Blakean equivalent, Los. Mythology and ritual,
which should ideally protect Eros, serving as a second womb
for the emergent self, have now become repressive systems
of moral, religious, and philosophical dogma. Therefore,
instead of fulfilling the traditional role of witness and midwife
of ritual rebirth, the modern seer must create new and viable
myths of the self. The Confessional poetic is an attempt to
extend the role of the visionary poet. By regarding the self
as an archetype, the poet becomes a participant in, as well
as herald of, rebirth. Sexton's early poetry creates a "mythology of the lost self";[9] her more recent volumes explore
other archetypal realms of human experience: the myth of
the body (Love Poems), the mythology of sexual maturation
(Transformations), and the myth of the other (The Book of
Folly). Her theme in these later books is not disunion but
reunion, not loss but discovery.

   In Love Poems, the Cartesian separation of mind and
body is tentatively bridged by liberation of Eros, the uniting
force of love. Sexton acknowledges the internal conflict between the death and love impulse, between Thanatos and Eros:
"When I lie down to love, / old dwarf heart shakes her head"
(A 10). "Old dwarf heart" signifies instinctual repression,
the internalization of original sin and human mortality. Nevertheless, Sexton is affirmative in the midst of contradiction,
advising acceptance of the self in all its multiplicity; she
would assert with Blake, "Without Contraries is no progres-
sion. Attraction and Repulsion, Reason and Energy, Love
and Hate, are necessary to Human existence." Countering
"old dwarf heart," these love poems are a celebration of
the body, so long disconnected and lifeless, like the synedochic
hand in the poem "The Touch." Through touch, connection
with a lover, the hand is revitalized and the body is resur-
rected:

> Your hand found mine.
> Life rushed to my fingers like a blood clot.
> Oh, my carpenter,
> the fingers are rebuilt....

Nothing will stop it, for this is the kingdom
and the kingdom come.

The lover is a "composer" (LP 3), a musician who performs
his art upon the body, "the valley of my bones,/ ... / A
xylophone maybe with skin/ stretched over it awkwardly./
Only later did it become something real" (LP 4). Once awak-
ened, the poet accepts her womanhood with ecstatic, Whitmanesque expansiveness:

> Sweet weight,
> in celebration of the woman I am
> and of the soul of the woman I am
> and of the central creature and its delight
> I sing for you. I dare to live [LP 12].

Through this joyful reintegration of the self, Sexton transcends
the boundaries of time and space and individual separateness.

In love, wholeness has finally become realizable for
Sexton. Yet she remains intensely aware of the difficulties
inherent in sustaining love relationships. Many of the Love
Poems are really "ironic love poems," as Robert Phillips
claims, "speaking more of alienation than of conciliation."[10]
Sexton emphasizes at times the predatory character of love
affairs, each participant involved in a big game hunt for self-
fulfillment; lovers "are a pair of scissors/ who come together to cut," not complementary parts of John Donne's
marriage compass (LP 57). But even if these poems present
failures, they are consistently positive in their renunciation
of destructive societal taboos. "The Ballad of the Lonely
Masturbator," for example, breaks conventional silence upon
a forbidden subject. But it is even more revolutionary in
its assumption that sexual satisfaction can be achieved by a
lone woman. Love affairs, as well as masturbation and its
metaphorical equivalent, poetry writing, are all basically
positive and creative experiences. These poems "come
about," as Sexton explained, "as a result of new attitudes,
an awareness of the possibly good as well as the possibly
rotten. Inherent in the process is a rebirth of a sense of
the self, each time stripping away a dead self."[11]

The cultural mechanism responsible for directing and
easing the difficult rebirth into sexual selfhood is the rite
of passage. In her book of adaptations of Grimm fairy tales,
Transformations, Sexton makes explicit the mythology of
maturation and satirically criticizes societal repressiveness.

"Old dwarf heart" appears here in the guise of Rumpelstilt-
skin. In him Thanatos is victorious over Eros; he is the
symbol of impotence, "a monster of despair. / ... all decay"
(T 17). The process of seduction is seen as an unnatural
persecution and crucifixion of instinctual need by inhibitory
institutions. In the Blakean tale "The Wonderful Musician,"
the symbols of sexuality are perversely transformed into
mercantile and measuring systems. The female bird "lay
as still/ as a dollar bill" and the male "drowse-belly" snake
"lay as still as a ruler." Not only is Eros murdered, but
the wronged animals are prevented by legal restraint, in the
person of the Woodcutter, from avenging themselves; revolution and rebirth are made impossible. Institutional repression exercised by the executioner, the Eichmann or repressive mother, is responsible for the degraded, balked state
of our culture.

In Sexton's vision, neither the ending of the fairy tale
nor the American Dream which the ending represents culminates in happiness. Rather, the maturation signalled in the
completion of courtship--the institution of marriage--is really
a deathly stasis:

> His tongue lay in her mouth
> as delicately as the white snake.
> They played house, little charmers,
> exceptionally well.
> So, of course,
> they were placed in a box
> and painted identically blue
> and thus passed their days
> living happily ever after--
> a kind of coffin,
> a kind of blue funk [T 14-15].

Marriage is an unconsummated image of consummation: when
the man first ate the white snake he became magically attuned
to nature and put into communication with universal truth
("he heard the animals/ in all their voices speak"), but when
he transfers this power to the woman, nothing happens, nothing at all.

Finally, Anne Sexton explodes the myth of the other-
as-alien and successfully breaks free of the narrow prison
of self-consciousness. Through the visionary medium of
personae, the poet actually embodies another individual and
in dramatic narrative re-enacts that person's life experience,

which, though evocative of Sexton's own, remains unique.
Similar to William Butler Yeats's use of mask, Sexton's
assumption of personae is an expression of Eros, creative
life that "is a re-birth as something not oneself, something
which has no memory and is created in a moment and perpetually renewed."[12] This demonstration of poetic reincar-
nation in effect conquers human alienation and even death.

The protagonists of Sexton's dramatic poems fall into
three categories: strangers whose suffering parallels the
poet's (lonely women, soldiers facing death, mothers renounc-
ing children); dead relatives, particularly a great-grandfather
who symbolizes her New England Gothic origins and a great-
aunt whose madness duplicates her own; and Jesus Christ,
whom the poet is finally able to accept as a model. The
most significant poems of this last-named kind are "The
Jesus Papers" which appear in The Book of Folly, the title
of which is adapted from Erasmus' The Praise of Folly. In
his treatise, Erasmus called for the imitation of the life of
Christ, a reunion of religion with the body, and the overthrow of institutional piety and dogma. In poems which celebrate the human experience of Christ, Sexton is able to
balance her earlier despairing vision of the crucified Christ's
grotesque suffering. She has learned to identify herself with
Christ in his essential humanity. The Resurrection has finally become a realistic and viable concept for her, when
seen through the visionary eye of poetry, that divine folly.

Beginning with the courage to seek the self's dark
truth, however hidden away and horrible, Anne Sexton discovered a deep wellspring of poetic power. Her insight has
made outsight possible; her poetry has become both an interior
and exterior quest for meaning. Like a Phoenix, she rises
out of the ashes of her own selves, in each successive book
creating herself and her world anew. In this act of creative
imagination--which ultimately aims to mend the "cracked
mirror," to reunify the poet with her real inward and outward
universes--Anne Sexton profoundly fulfills E. M. Forster's
prescription for our modern Cartesian dilemma: "Only Connect."


AFTERWORD (1977)

When I heard of Anne Sexton's untimely death in fall
of 1974, I felt a tinge of glad relief amid the sense of loss
and sorrow. It seemed to me that in finally yielding to that

necessity, Sexton had at last reached the end of her "hegira," her trip "undertaken as a means of escaping from an undesirable environment, or as a means of arriving at a highly desirable destination."[13]  Sexton's ouevre is her last will, her testament to the awful beauty of the world which offered her so much pain and joy.

In the three books published since my essay was originally written--The Death Notebooks (1974), The Awful Rowing Toward God (1975), and 45 Mercy Street (1976)--Anne Sexton continues her long and torturous journey from alienation to reconciliation.  In the celebratory Death Notebooks, she rejoices in the possibility of rebirth through the power of art to transform "the abyss" into a "God Spot."  The first posthumous volume, The Awful Rowing Toward God, shows even more clearly her deepening religious sensibility, her growing conviction of the interconnectedness and perhaps even the unity of imagination and God.  Her voyage is, as it should be, both an inward journey and an arrival at a distant shore. Although she must exorcise the horror of herself by cutting out "the gnawing pestilential rat" within, Sexton will not deny the sanctity of her being.  For this ugliness too is part of God's domain, and she knows that he is certain to "embrace it."  In 45 Mercy Street, edited with grace by her daughter Linda Gray Sexton, Anne Sexton embarks upon her final journey, an "hegira" simultaneously into past and future, seeking both self and communion with the other.  Wanting desperately to "own the past," both to claim it and to confess it, Sexton imaginatively returns to the critical age ("twenty-eight, or is it forty-five?"), the time at which her poetic journey began. From this starting point, this reclaimed origin, she begins again for the last time the long journey home.  In the volume's last poem, "The Consecrating Mother," she stands Whitman-like before the sea, committing herself to "its destiny":

> I am that clumsy human
> on the shore
> loving you, coming, coming,
> going. . . .

## REFERENCES

1.  Irrational Man (Garden City, N. Y.:  Doubleday Anchor, 1962), p. 31.
2.  Quotations from Anne Sexton's poetry will be indicated

parenthetically in the text by volume symbol and
page reference.  All volumes bear the same pub-
lisher imprint.  To Bedlam and Part Way Back
(Boston:  Houghton Mifflin, 1960) (B); All My Pretty
Ones (1962) (A); Live or Die (1966) (LD); Love
Poems (1969) (LP); Transformations (1971) (T);
The Book of Folly (1973) (F).

3.  Barbara Kevles, "Anne Sexton:  The Art of Poetry,"
    Paris Review, 13 (August 1968), p. 160.
4.  Barrett, pp. 225-26.
5.  Charles F. Madden, ed., Talking with Authors, inter-
    view April 13, 1964 (Carbondale:  Southern Illinois
    University Press, 1965), p. 161.
6.  Quoted in A. Alvarez, The Savage God (New York:  Ban-
    tam, 1972), p. 136.
7.  Suicide and the Soul (New York:  Harper-Colophon,
    1964), Chapter 4.
8.  Theodore Roethke, "In a Dark Time," Collected Poems
    (Garden City, N. Y.:  Doubleday, 1966), p. 239.
9.  Robert Phillips, Confessional Poets (Carbondale:  South-
    ern Illinois University Press, 1973), p. 8.
10. Phillips, p. 82.
11. Paris Review (note 3), p. 163.
12. Quoted in Richard Ellmann, Yeats--The Man and the
    Masks (New York:  Dutton, 1948), p. 174.
13. 45 Mercy Street (Boston:  Houghton Mifflin, 1976), p.
    1.  The other two volumes discussed in this After-
    word bear the same publisher imprint.

Dianne F. Sadoff

MYTHOPOEIA, THE MOON,
AND CONTEMPORARY WOMEN'S POETRY*

Mythology and archetype, male-imagined fables of identity, mythopoeic approaches to literature, all force feminist
critics to confront, accommodate, or transform an exaggerated gender-based description of culture.   Jung's apparently
innocent definition of archetypes as "formal factors responsible for the organization of unconscious psychic processes,"[1]
however, leads directly to exaggerated notions of masculine
and feminine; to that problematic archetype, the anima, and
its more problematic counterpart, the animus; and to passionate academic arguments about androgyny.   In his article,
"Androgyny: The Sexist Myth in Disguise," Daniel A. Harris
concludes that the entire concept of androgyny, which is based
on anima-animus readjustments, has "no positive value" in
liberating the study of literature from stereotypes, since the
anima is itself a gender-based stereotype.[2]  Harris quotes
many of Jung's objectionable passages about the anima from
The Archetypes and the Collective Unconscious, including the
famous ones in which Jung implies the anima is man's bitch
and burden: "She is the serpent.... She intensifies, exag-
gerates, falsifies, and mythologizes all emotional relations
with [a man's] work and with other people of both sexes....
She is full of snares and traps, in order that man should
fall, should reach the earth, entangle himself there, and stay
caught, so that life should be lived."[3]  Harris then quotes
passages from "Woman in Europe" which delineate the crux
of the anima-animus problem:  the anima affects the male
positively by making him intuitional, integrative, less aggressive, and negatively--if the conscious life is unbalanced--by
making him "touchy, irritable, ... jealous, vain, and un-
adjusted";[4] the animus apparently affects the female solely
by "stop[ping] up the approaches to her own feeling.   She may

*Reprinted by permission of the author and publisher from The
Massachusetts Review 19, 1 (1977).   Copyright © 1977 by the
Massachusetts Review, Inc.

even become frigid. "[5]   The masculine intellectual, rational,
and judgmental animus, then, resides in the female unconscious; but since these are the very aspects of the intellect
our society values, Jung immediately implies that women
are all soft-headed by nature, that intellectual women are
animus dominated and overly-masculine, and that non-aggres-
sive men are somehow unpleasantly effeminate.

Although I am tempted to agree in part with Harris'
responses to the concept of androgyny and to his analysis of
the animus problem, we cannot ignore the fact that men and
women are to each other "the opposite sex." Harris also
fails to recognize that Jung and his followers try valiantly
to deal with the thorny anima-animus problem.   In his last
published volume, Jung becomes aware he has slighted women's consciousness in the bulk of his writings; he attempts
to soften the implication that all intellectual women are "masculine" by referring to a feminine archetype, the moon:
"Luna is primarily a reflection of a man's unconscious femininity, but she is also the principle of the feminine psyche,
in the sense that Sol is the principle of a man's.... If,
then, Luna characterizes the feminine psyche and Sol the
masculine, consciousness would be an exclusively masculine
affair, which is obviously not the case since woman possesses
consciousness too." Jung solves this problem by deciding
that woman's "consciousness has a lunar rather than a solar
character.   Its light is the 'mild' light of the moon, which
merges things together rather than separates them.   It does
not show up objects in all their pitiless discreteness and
separateness, but ... blends in a deceptive shimmer the
near and the far ... into an unsuspected unity. "[6]   Jung now
allows women intelligence, but the equivocal rhetoric of this
passage demonstrates Jung's deep belief that female consciousness is somehow more mysterious and less verifiable than
is male, and must, therefore, fail to make adequate judgments
and distinctions.

Other Jungians have made perhaps more satisfying
accommodations with the animus problem; Emma Jung, for
example, both apologizes for and clarifies her father's thinking.   "Confronted with ... the animus," she writes, "the
woman's task is to create a place for it in her life and personality, and to initiate some undertaking with the energy
belonging to it....   Only when this masculine entity becomes
an integrated part of the soul and carries on its proper function there is it possible for a woman to be truly a woman in
the higher sense, and, at the same time, also being herself,

to fulfill her individual human destiny."[7]  Unfortunately, however, Emma Jung, like her father, asserts that women's intellect and creativity are basically different from those of men: feminine mentality has an "undeveloped, childlike, or primitive character; instead of the thirst for knowledge, curiosity; instead of judgment, prejudice; instead of thinking, imagination or dreaming; instead of will, wishing."  And on creativity, Emma Jung's ideas deny women genius: "There are many women who have developed their powers of thinking, discrimination, and criticism to a high degree, but there are very few who are mentally creative in the way a man is.... The creativity of woman finds its expression in the sphere of living, not only in her biological functions as mother but in the shaping of life generally....  The development of relationships is of primary importance in the shaping of life, and this is the real field of feminine creative power."[8]  Despite Barbara Charlesworth Gelpi's response to Emma Jung, "The Androgyne," in which she argues that Jung attempts to "overcome the universal denigration of the feminine,"[9] Jung's article appears saturated with a now-familiar female fear of the intellect, of ambition, of discipline, and of rigor.

The female Jungian, Irene Claremont de Castillejo, deals most successfully with the animus problem.  Although she believes women experience stronger ties to "undifferentiated thinking" than do rationalistic men, de Castillejo refuses to accept Jung's anima-animus equation, and admits the "notion that [women] were only intelligent people by virtue of an animus had grated uneasily" on her.  De Castillejo solves the problem ingeniously; by following Erich Neumann and refusing to use the term "soul" interchangeably with "anima," as Jung does, she decides that the "ego is masculine in women as well as in men, [and] that the soul appears as a feminine figure not only in men but also in women."[10] Although she seems only to have inverted the troublesome categories of masculine and feminine, de Castillejo's theories finally allow women to be intelligent rather than either unconscious or animus-ridden.

Like female psychologists, female literary critics must also confront masculine definitions of femininity.  The landscape of our mythology reflects masculine activity and female passivity: the land, with its hills, rills, chasms, and wooded caverns is female; the sea, source of all life, the symbol of womb toward which we journey in regression, the fluid of undifferentiated being, unconsciousness, and pre-separation bliss is female.  The impregnating sky is masculine, and the male hero moves over the landscape, questing after his identity and immersing himself in the unconscious sea. Woman becomes passive nature, man its active and heroic inhabitant. Ellen Moers helps us deal with the ways women writers inhabit this mythological landscape; rather than reject female landscape because of its masculine tradition, Moers discovers that women writers adopt the landscape for their own works, and explore female identity by transforming the perspective from which we view female landscape. [11] In this way, women writers appropriate a male tradition, yet make it reflect feminine issues and concerns.

In addition, women writers will now remind the literary community of the ways mythology stereotypes women. Adrienne Rich, in response to Galway Kinnell's plea for a return to mythopoeic perceptions, believes that masculine imaginations of woman as "eternal mystery" reveal male fear of the female, and result in patterns of extreme idealization as well as "objectification and domination" of women by men. Rich asks the male poet to reject his "handed-down myths," and calls for a "new bisexuality in poetry written by men"; her example of the bisexual poet is Walt Whitman, whose acceptance of both masculine and feminine imaginations allowed him to experience the being in himself capable of "tenderness, vulnerability, [and] mutuality."[12] Rich's article demands just what women writers and feminist critics now exhort from the culture: a wholesale revaluation, a transformation, even a rejection of traditionally masculine archetype and mythopoeia.

II

As Jung knew when he attempted to modify his thinking about female consciousness, man has for centuries associated the moon with all aspects of woman and her sexuality. In patriarchal cultures, the incestuous moon goddess, wife of the sun, gives birth to a son who dies and is born again and who then becomes her lover; she is the archetypal Great Mother. In matriarchal cultures, the Great Mother can also be a Virgin, an unmarried goddess who is not related to a god as wife or counterpart, but is singularly herself, and her own mistress. This moon goddess, however, can also be a prostitute, and can demand ritual prostitution of her female virgin attendants in order to liberate them from individual, egoistic sexuality. [13] Whether wife, Great Mother, sacred prostitute, or virgin, then, sexuality is central to the moon goddess's identity and to the worship of her.

The moon's most important earthly influence, fertility, relates directly to her sexual function.  She presides
over agricultural planting, growth, and harvesting; in some
cultures she presides over pregnancy and childbirth--in the
mythology of the Maori, the male opens the vaginal canal,
but the moonbeam fertilizes the ovum (Harding, pp. 21-24).
But the fertility-bringing moon, because of her phases, becomes dualistic, or sometimes triune:  she brings life during
her crescent, but death and destruction during her waning
phase.  In Greek mythology, the goddess of love, Aphrodite,
represents the bright moon, while Hecate, goddess of sorcery
and witchcraft, represents the dark moon.

The moon's phases also account for man's association
of the moon with femininity.  Like the moon, women have
monthly cycles, and in all branches of the Indogermanic family of languages we find cognates for "month" and "moon. "
Male fear of and bafflement about female menstrual cycles
undoubtedly caused this association in primitive times; the
Maori called menstruation "mata marama," or moon sickness.
The Babylonians associated the full moon with Ishtar's menstrual period; this time was "sabattu," or evil day of Ishtar,
hence our "sabbath," which is now observed at each of the
moon's phases rather than only during her full moon (Harding,
pp. 56-62).  By extension from phases and their relation to
the menstrual cycle, man associates the moon with fickleness,
lunacy, and inspiration:  "In these unaccountable qualities of
the moon['s phases], man has seen a symbol of woman's nature which to him appears erratic, changeable, fickle, not
to be relied on" (Harding, p. 65).  Because the waning moon
presides over storms and other natural disturbances, she
brings lunacy, insanity, but also vision; unlike the sun, which
reliably rules the day, the changeable moon rules the night,
and becomes associated with the unconscious, with genius
and abnormality, with inspiration and religious ecstacy, with
madness and lunacy (Harding, p. 114).  In Greek mythology,
for example, Cybele blasted her son Attis with ecstacy which
drove him mad.

What, we might then ask, does all this moon mythology
mean?  What cultural fantasies about the female does it reveal, or what needs does it fulfill?  If, like Jung and Harding,
we assume all primitive myth is projection of the unconscious
onto the natural world, we must interpret moon mythologies
as man's protection from his fear of woman, the other; menstruation, pregnancy, motherhood, and the complexity of human sexuality all separate women's experience from men's

and often complicate relations between the sexes.    Each aspect of the moon goddess's qualities also protects man from the feminine within himself and allows him to project that quality onto woman and her goddess, the moon.    Most moon legends also reflect the culturally dualistic portrayal of woman:  the virgin and the whore, the source of inspiration and madness, the life-giver and life-destroyer.[14]   When a woman writer encounters these mythologies, she must reinvent, revise, and transform them to fit her own female body, her female identity, her unique female experience.    Contemporary women poets correct dualistic moon myths by re-examining both aspects of the moon goddess, the virgin and the prostitute; but now the virgin goddess embodies female self-doubt and fear of sexual involvement rather than the male-imagined chaste, cold, fickle moon, and the prostitute goddess embodies the transforming power of female sexual desire rather than the male-imagined Great Mother.    Myth and archetype are reimagined female.

III

Denise Levertov, for example, uses the moon's cycles and phases as emblem of natural growth and change in O Taste and See and in Relearning the Alphabet.[15]   Levertov's poetry celebrates process:  the recurring cycles of nature, the natural unity of birth and death, the reciprocities of imagination.    In "Another Spring," for example, Levertov deals with the natural dialectic which unites opposition and repetition through process; she imagines "in the gold mouth of a flower/ the black smell of spring earth" ($\ell\ell$. 1-2):  mouths golden, full of opening and desire, speaking of birth and renewal, bite through and into an earth made from death.    Human beings, existing in this repeating cycle of death and rebirth, recapitulate Adam and so "Death in us goes on/ testing the wild/ chance of living" just as "Adam chanced it" ($\ell\ell$. 9-12).    The moon and the sky mirror the earth's cycles and repeat its paradoxical golden and black colors, as Calavera unites gold ore in a black earth with seasonal renewal:  "Golden-mouthed, the tilted smile/ of the moon westering/ is at the black window,/ Calavera of Spring" ($\ell\ell$. 13-16).    The poem, then, creates dualism--birth and death, winter and spring, new moon and old moon, Adam and we moderns-- then gathers duality into ever expanding cycles, moon phases, and unifying patterns.    The poem closes with a celebration of process-as-unifier of human and natural time:  "I am speaking of living,/ of moving from one moment into/ the

next, and into the one after" (ℓℓ. 18-21); death is "in the
spring air" and air "means/ music to sing to" (ℓℓ. 22-24).
The Westering moon, its cycles as unifier of oppositions,
becomes an emblem of natural wholeness.

The moon also participates in Levertov's poems about
the process of the imagination, which resembles the process
of nature: it appears in opposite guises which can be seen
dialectically as one; it creates continuity amidst discontinuity;
it unifies the subjective poet with the objective world.   But
the imagination is also wholly different from nature; it is
inspired, it is lunatic, it is the dark side of the moon.   The
poem "In Mind" juxtaposes apparently opposite women; one
an innocent, natural woman, "smelling of/ apples or grass"
who is "kind," "very clean," and "without ostentation" yet
has "no imagination" (ℓℓ. 3-10); the other a "turbulent moon-
ridden girl" who is either girl, "old woman," or "both," who
dresses in paradoxical "opals and rags, feathers/ and torn
taffeta," and who "knows strange songs" and is "not kind"
(ℓℓ. 12-17).   One woman is nature, the other the imagination; the poem structures a paradox within a dualism.   Yet
the wholesome woman and the moon-ridden lunatic both live
"in mind"; old and young, riches and rags, the imagination
and nature, couplets as well as solitary, fractured lines,
all are contained in the complex, paradoxical imagination of
the woman poet who creates herself.

In the opening poem of O Taste and See, "Song for
Ishtar," Levertov invokes the Babylonian moon goddess as
emblem for the female imagination; the poet is a "pig," the
moon goddess a "sow," and the poet becomes one with the
world by having sexual intercourse with the moon.   But this
intercourse is not simple; the masculine "pig" poet lives in
an implicitly female landscape, a "hollow" filled with mud--
and later in the book, in "Hypocrite Woman," Levertov calls
the female genitals, "caves of the Moon."   And the moon's
shining penetrates the poet's hollow, as the moon assumes a
masculine sexual identity regardless of her femininity.   Ishtar,
oldest of moon goddesses is, however, androgynous; her
worshippers invoke her as "Oh my God and my Goddess"
(Harding, p. 94).   This sacred sexual act mirrors the union
of opposites throughout the poem:  the muddy hollow "gleams/
and breaks in silver bubbles"; desire is "black" with the
moon's "great shining."   And the moon's duality--her aspects
of life-giver and life-destroyer--become one through desire:
"When she opens her white/ lips to devour me I bite back/
and laughter rocks the moon" (ℓℓ. 8-10); at the end of the

poem, both participants lose their separate characteristics
as pigs and moonbeams get all mixed up and the lovers "rock
and grunt, grunt and/ shine" (ℓℓ. 12-13). The final, one
word line, "shine," reaffirms the joy of becoming one with
Ishtar, as well as the peace and tranquility of closure and
of orgasm. The process of the imagination is sexual, as
the poet interacts with nature and the imagination makes him
one with it; and this imaginative process, like Ishtar, is
androgynous, and affirms the multiple sexuality of the poet,
who, both male and female, sexualizes experience and makes
it joyful.

Levertov's Relearning the Alphabet emphasizes duality
and the struggle to change, rather than the achieved unity of
the earlier O Taste and See; the book moves from "Elegies"
to "Relearning the Alphabet," with "Wanting the Moon" as
middle transformational section. Death and dualism imply
frustration and loss, and the section named for the moon
longs for--hungers after--eventual unification of opposites:
moon and not-moon, man and woman, vision and barrenness.
Again, imagination is desire; sexual intercourse creates unity.
An implicit Leda poem imagines Zeus's rape of the swan as
poetic transformation; the poet "rise[s] up/ with changed
vision,/ a singing in [her] ears" ("Wings of a God," ℓℓ. 22-
24). The woman poet longs for the moon, and "not the moon";
for a "flower on the other side of the water," and "not a
flower"; for a "young man," a "jester" whose face, like lan-
terns and the moon, "is awake with its own light," and whose
loving joy when united with the woman poet's imagination
would create wholeness ("Wanting the Moon, I"). But rape
is not love, and longing is not cured; the poet goes on "Waiting," "Wanting the Moon, II," "Craving" with "A Hunger,"
wanting to "seize/ the gaiety of change from within" by becoming a cloud, wanting to cure change by lying down "in
the dreams/ of a young man." The woman poet craves man;
the swan craves immortality through sexual intercourse with
the god.

Toward the end of this moon section, a final moon-
poem completes our equation: moon equals desire. In
"Adam's Complaint," we moderns once more recapitulate the
first man because desire never fulfills itself, either in individual lives or throughout human history. "Some people,/ no
matter what you give them,/ still want the moon"; give them
bread, salt, and meat, they are "still hungry"; give them the
marriage bed and a cradle, "still empty arms"; give them
land, "still they take to the roads"; "dig them the deepest

well,/ still it's not deep enough/ to drink the moon from"
(ℓℓ. 1-16).  The paradox of human desire demands continual
and escalating fulfillment; the poet relates this lesson cyni-
cally, yet with a certain sad humility, since the poet too
wants the moon, can never get enough fulfillment, can never
drink deeply enough of the moon's desire.

Yet this very hungry, devouring desire transforms
"Elegies" into "The Singer," then into "A Tree Telling of
Orpheus," and, finally, into "Relearning the Alphabet."  In
"The Singer," three adjacent moon poems sum up the emerging transformational model:  in "Equilibrium," a woman hungers for sexual fulfillment, hating "the single ocean,/ the
one moon" (ℓℓ. 27-28).  In "Secret Festival; September
Moon," the moon presides over the beginnings of fulfillment
and harmony:  a "pandemonium of owls" sings an "antiphonal"
song with fox "obbligato"; the owls "raise/ the roof of the
dark," and "ferocious [is]/ their joy in the extreme silver/
the moon has floated out from itself" (ℓℓ. 1-17).  In "Moon
Tiger," the personified animal moon prowls around a dark
bedroom with twin beds; the passive, frightened speaker whispers to her companion, "I'm coming in with you" (ℓℓ. 18),
and sexual unity appears possible.  This section of the book
emphasizes singing and art, and works toward the section
which is the sole poem, "A Tree Telling of Orpheus"; the
transformational tree is often home for the changeable moon
in mythology, and both here work toward the liberation of
imagination through desire as well as toward the making of
art.

In the final "Relearning the Alphabet," the poet creates
a microcosm of the book's entire transformational structure.
The search for joyful, spontaneous imaginative expression,
for desire fulfilled, culminates in the acceptance of process
and "the grace of transformed/ continuance" (G).  Searching
for "'Imagination's holy forest,'" the woman-poet once more
envisions the jester, "someone dreamed/ on the far bank,"
or "seen/ in epiphany" (I, J).  And the moon, desire, is
again the transformational agent, its chaste fire the burning
away to vision:  the woman poet "wanted/ the moon and went/
out to sea to touch/ the moon" (M), hoping to be "burned
by the cold moon to cinder" (N).  The moon's cold burn
transforms absence and the desire for permanence into acceptance of process, of "transformation, continuance," faith,
and "acts of magic" (R).  The poem, built on a transformational model, discovers transformation as the center of human
experience; continual change, like the moon's phases, becomes

the goal of both life and art.  In microcosm, then, and in
macrocosm, <u>Relearning the Alphabet</u> finds joy through acceptance of human process and imagination; the woman poet
touches the moon, is changed by it, and experiences the joy
of both time and sexuality by doing so.

Nancy Willard's poetry, like Levertov's, celebrates
the life of the imagination.  <u>Nineteen Masks for the Naked
Poet</u>[16] creates a cosmology in which sun and moon, poet and
wife dance a neo-surrealist series of attitudes toward creation
and transformation, toward "naming" and the imagination.
In "The Poet Loses His Name in a Well," the poet's name
rescues and re-creates himself and his material existence:
"The poet whistled.  He called himself/ to come out of the
twilight. /  His name swam up like a dog. /  Clean as a
pebble," the "peddler sang in its jaws" (ℓℓ. 12-17).  When
the poet "Plants a Forest in His Wife's Marimba," the act
of naming or imagining creates real yet visionary products;
the poet "plays and remembers their names,/ ROSA, ROSA-
LINE, ROSEANNA, ROSEMARY,/ and out of the wood they
come,/ rose trees with flowers like eyes" (ℓℓ. 10-13).  The
creations of his imagination then absurdly and obediently become part of his daily life; the roses "are bringing him cof-
fee, laying the table/ and singing his wife to sleep" (ℓℓ. 17-
18).

The act of naming also creates song, the poem; the
poet is singer and maker, and the song is the body remade
through its singing: "Every spring his own body astounds
him. /  His old skin unravels,/ he knits it into a new song"
("Two Hundred Cats Apply Their Tongues for His Bath,"
ℓℓ. 16-18).  In these poems, language is of the body and is
the body; the name must be the thing and become the thing.
When "The Poet Enters the Sleep of the Bees," he discovers
the bees "making a lexicon/ of the six-sided names of God,/
<u>Clover's breath, dewflesh,</u>/ ritual of the thorn, a definitive
<u>work</u>/ to graft the names to their roots" (ℓℓ. 4-8).  Just as
bees create honey, so the poet creates language, and the
poet hears "ten thousand tongues flowing along like gold" (ℓ.
22).  Language sweetly embodies and creates enjoyment.

The moon's role in this poetics becomes, paradoxically,
inspiration and destiny.  In "The Poet Tracks Down the Moon,"
the female moon-as-inspiration is active, "barking/ and humming and turning around on her nest" (ℓℓ. 1-2); she radiates
the bodily light of inspiration, "this quartz quail,/ this silver
truffle slivering into the dark" (ℓℓ. 4-5).  But when the poet

sets out to catch the tricky moon, she decides to catch the
poet; she "turns out her light,/ leaves her skin under a bush
like patience,/ and covers her tracks with a sigh" (ℓℓ. 6-
8); into the river, "she throws the first letter/ of her language, the crescent, the open trap./ It stands for <u>canny</u>
and <u>clever</u>" (ℓℓ. 9-11). The poem parables the creative process: as the poet enters his transformational imaginative
world, language and inspiration entrap him. The moon "bangs
her thin wire around his ankle,/ hangs her tiny hook in the
gills of his heart" (ℓℓ. 14-15); he is fish for her net.

But the moon's phases also create unchanging, static
"destinies," and her power can become tyrannical. When
"The Poet invites the Moon for Supper," he refuses to become
the moon's heir, to marry the moon-offered snow, to become
immortal like the moon. The poet here denies the patriarchal
notion of reputation, and affirms instead the kinship of human
process and the act of creation. When he dies, the poet will
be devoured by the "mouth of the earth"; he will be part of
its natural mortality: "I am a song./ Someone is writing me
down / I am disappearing into the ear of a rose" (ℓℓ. 12-16).
Despite the moon's immortal power, however, in her "Tenth
Street kitchen," the baker's wife creates her own version of
the universe, and replaces the moon as female-inspiration:
a bride and groom "stand up/ on the great imagination; he
gathers the "dark strands/ of the poem like a tide," and
turns "his face toward the sun" (ℓℓ. 7, 9-10, 15). But he
uses his wife's homemade domestic implements in his ascen-
sion: her buttercup-colored dustpan "fan[s] out" behind him
"like a saffron cape"; her glasses on his nose "polished/
themselves to crystals"; her "simple sink" rides him "into
heaven" (ℓℓ. 11-16). The poetic act parodies the domestic
act, and vice versa. In addition, the poet's wife creates
his visions. Her handmade doors are thresholds of perception and creation: "If she made a revolving door,/ summer
and winter would run like mice in a wheel./ If she made a
door for the moon,/ the dead would cross over" ("The Poet's
Wife Makes Him a Door so He Can Find the Way Home," ℓℓ.
2-5). Her doors become mirrors of self-discovery, yet can
be mirages, making "palm trees and parrots" to call the
poet's name (ℓ. 12). While the poet drags himself over the
desert in "search of his Heart" (ℓ. 8), his wife builds and
rebuilds, creates and recreates, and controls the visionary
doors of the imagination. Although the title, "poet," belongs
to the male, the female is fully as creative as he is; these
poems satirize the roles of "poet" and "wife," yet make the
two partners in the creative process, as imagination becomes
a truly androgynous business.

Diane Wakoski's moon poems, unlike Levertov's and
Willard's, deal not with the imagination but with persona.
In <u>The Motorcycle Betrayal Poems</u>, Wakoski creates an entirely consistent personal moon mythology: "I am/ the moon./
My name,/ Diane."[17]  But here, Diana, the chaste huntress,
becomes sexually devouring Diane, the female bank dick who
is both victim and "hit woman."  Every man she loves be-
trays this Diane; she has lost her children, lost her husband,
lost "everything a woman needs, wants" (p. 14).  She tires
"with the burden of being alone," of living a "self-sufficient/
lonely/ life," of being "isolated and empty" (pp. 44, 46).
This selfless woman turns to men to give her life meaning;
like the moon she is, she continually "lives/ in" a man's
"reflected light" (p. 55).  Yet ironically, the very men she
loves will inevitably betray, abandon, and victimize her;
these motorcyclists who tinker with machines, wear mus-
taches, and shoot from the hip become Diane's heroes, despite their disregard for women.

This female victim also has a long history of suffering; her first betrayer was her own father: "the man who
rejected me and left me/ when I was 2" (p. 59).  And the
child is mother to the woman; the father-loving and father-
hating little girl creates as an adult that same fatherly betrayal with a sexual twist which combines abandonment with
symbolic rape.  The "hefty" woodsman who "chop[s] down
[her] trees," and "stomps into the heart of this/ forest,"
her body, who "unlike George Washington" tells "many lies,"
merely adds a sexual objectification, violation, and use to
the sins of the father (p. 144).  Diane re-enacts her little
girl abandonment by masochistically choosing the strong,
heroic, George Washington types she knows are really brutes.
"Every woman adores a fascist," Plath says with cynical
irony, and Diane's self-pitying lament admits--and revels
in--such victimage.  From this perspective, the real betrayer
of this continually betrayed persona is herself: "My face
has betrayed me again," she says, "my face shimmering
and flat as the moon/ with no features."  The "great betrayer" is the one she "sleep[s]/ with at night"--her "own face"
(pp. 11, 14, 15).  Unable to admit the depth of her self-
betrayal, this persona blames her misfortunes on "ugliness."
Diane sums up this aspect of her experience as victim and
self-victim: "Woman is a wound" (p. 156).

In order to combat such victimage, the woman persona
must cultivate toughness.  She advertises for a husband in
an ironic, self-congratulatory tone: "You might as well not

apply for the job/ if you don't have/ a mustache," but "if
you think you qualify,/ write in for the application forms";
"I am known," she says, "for my discrimination" (pp. 36-
39).    Diane imagines herself motorcyclist, or motorcycle,
a "tuned-up engine" for "turn[ing] on" (p. 19).   Male disregard for the charged-up "beautiful little engine" makes Diane
a murderer, an ironic inversion of Diana's response to Ac-
taeon's sexual approach.  "Love Letter Postmarked Van
Beethoven" details the bullets from a .38 caliber Thompson
Contender this Diane discharges into the backs of her unre-
sponsive lovers:  "One for my father who deserted me and
whom you masquerade as,/ every night, when you don't come
home" (p. 16); one for the first lover, who refused to marry
her; one for the men who loved other women, making her
feel "ugly, undesirable" (p. 17).   The poem's violent rhetoric
climaxes with five final reasons for murder, and with five
lines beginning with the phrase, "a bullet ... "; structure and
rhetoric substitute aggressive masculine sexual "shooting"
for the experience of tender loving the woman really desires;
as in yet another version of self-betrayal, Diane refuses to
accept her female sexuality.

But the role of male manqué finally does not suit
Diane; this tough, sexually aggressive bitch concludes her
outrage quite penitently, feeling, she says, "ashamed of my
anger/ at you/ whom I love/ whom I ask for so much more
than you want to give" (p. 18).   The outraged murderess
merely fronts for the hurt, empty child-victim; the tough hit
woman is a role developed to hide the vulnerability Diane
fears revealing to the brute men she inevitably falls for.   The
final poem in the book admits this dualism:  "I could not wear
that pink dress tonight./   It betrayed all that was strong in
me./   The leather boots I wear to stomp through the world
...."   The woman fears her "own vulnerability," fears "everything that hurts" (pp. 157-59).

The perfect parable of Diane's dualistic moon-goddess
role in the book is "The Lament of the Lady Bank Dick," in
which Diane becomes a fantastical version of James Bond,
chasing gangsters around Europe in her Maserati, wearing a
trench coat--but with "Belgian lace, thin silk, and French
perfume" underneath.   She says of Tony Tansanite, the hero-
criminal she chases, "You like/ the idea of the woman/ who's
the dick,/ the one with all the strength behind her eyelashes. "
In this fantasy, the sexually aggressive woman again becomes
the male manqué, and a gun substitutes for the missing penis:
"I, the lady bank dick/ threatening your masculine role/ with

the . 22 pistol/ I always carry hidden/ in a place only you'd/
think to look. " But the role of lady bank dick, demeaning
as it is to all that is female, paradoxically builds sexual
humiliation and defeat into the chased and chasing relationship: "You must kill me--for I'm the cop/ and you're the
robber.... I must be destroyed because my role serves me/
as the woman who chases you. " And the fantasy of lady cop
only disguises the fantasy of being murdered, or, since sex
and killing become motivationally interchangeable, being raped.
To prove she is really a woman and "still, so very soft"
under the paraphernalia of copdom, the female will "contra-
'dick'-t" her title, will "die/ any time,/ a hundred machine-
gun holes lacing [her],/ proving [her] womanly parts. " Her
"final act," she says, "would be to throw/ all my guns/ in
your lap"--to give up her role as masculine shooter-from-
the-hip, and become the little-girl female again (pp. 93-97).

Despite all her sexual aggression and its resultant
humiliation, then, this Diane really wants to be the chaste
huntress Diana, her namesake; since she fears the female so
thoroughly, her only choice if she gives up her facade of
masculinity is to become virgin.  The most positive poem
in the book, for example, presents "My Hell's Angel," as
Diane meets yet another motorcyclist, this time on a beach,
and they discuss aggression.  She admires him precisely
because he "wants to challenge every man/ to fight him.  He
wants to prove his body against every man" (p. 28).  Despite
the sexual paraphernalia of beach, bikini, and motorcycle,
however, he makes no sexual advances, and she makes none.
The poem concludes with exhiliration, with sharing: the
chasing Diane is the chaste Diana, who longs only to talk to
a man, and to admire his masculine self-esteem.  This persona Diane represents all aspects of what Harding calls, "the
Virgin Goddess": she is cold, and experiences no love, but
only a hard desire; she chases men, but remains uninvolved
with them, seeking only power and conquest, regarding love
only as a game and a technique of seduction, yet convinced
she "falls in love with the various men whom she meets and
subdues" (Harding, pp. 118-20).  This woman, whom women
hate and men eventually abandon, is represented by the dark
moon and by the chaste Diana, who kills men if they dare
approach her sexually.  This woman fears her own femaleness,
and especially her sexuality, and appears tough in order to
create and maintain her power over men.

Other poems in the book admit the struggle to maintain
the dualism of powerful seductress and fearful virgin, and

demonstrate that playing the role of lady bank dick, of "hard
rock" (p. 66), creates inner deadness.  The modern, demy-
thologized moon becomes this basically sterile version of
Diane, with a "complicated geography" (p. 54).  The astronauts' first moon landing makes Diane feel "a strange kind
of dubiousness" about the moon, "an image which, as a poet
and as a person named after the moon, I had begun to think
of as my own property" (p. 98).  This no longer romantic
moon becomes dead and dry, a "heavy," "dead crust" which
Diane, being the moon goddess, must learn "to lift in each
foot" (p. 49).  Love is moist, but this sterile moon exudes
"a hot breath of air" (p. 56).  The poem "I Lay Next to
You All Night, Trying to Understand the Watering Places of
the Moon" explores this moist-dry dualism; the "dry and
restless," "dead Moon" needs water, but cannot escape the
"hot and thirsty" sun or its "gravity" (pp. 62, 64).  Part of
the dryness, then, results from Diane's dependence on men
and her lunatic frustration: "The moon is murdered by/ the
movement/ of the earth on its axis.... Same. / When I
am with you/ I'm a different person/ than alone"; the moon
"lives/ in reflected light/ and of course/ that it causes the
tides/ and madness" (pp. 53-55).  This persona longs to
partake of the moon's other functions, of its fertility, of the
periods when "flowers and beans grow fatter/ under its full-
ness" (p. 55).  Loving sex would create this fertile moisture,
and lunacy would cease: "The night you come home to me/
the moon will be full/ and someone else's madness/ will
start" (p. 57).  But this fulfillment appears impossible, so
lunacy continues; we are left with the inevitable feeling that
the moist-dry dualism fills Diane's life "with paradox":
"Those who most need love/ are the unloveable" (p. 56).

But the Virgin Goddess can also long to change her
dualistic dependence on and rejection of men.  The modern,
sterile Diana is possessed, colonized, made into "American
territory," as she is sexually dominated and objectified by
men like the astronauts (p. 102).  The chaste Diane says,
"I am something/ no one has ever touched,/ ...  / Something
dreamt of,/ a place to put a flag,/ something to conquer"
(p. 99).  "Everyone wants," she says, "to use me,/ to put
a missile base on me,/ to extract my ore,/ to bounce radio
waves off me."  In this particular poem, Diane-moon refuses
to be owned, and attempts to give up her extreme dependence
on men.  She becomes confused; she is "old moon,/ Young
moon," and doesn't "even know what [she is] any more"; but
she also senses she must give up her victimization for self-
esteem: "I'd invoke myself,/ Diane,/ the moon,/ make love

to myself" (p. 101). Diane hopes for transformation because
she is moon goddess; her own phases and cycles presage
change, renewal, and rebirth from virgin bitch into true
virgin, the woman in control of her life but not afraid of
intimacy and female sexuality. But Diane cannot give up the
sun's light, the glory of male acceptance, and later in the
book she admits she "needs, wants" yet cannot "be possessed"
(p. 155). The entire dualistic moon-myth comes together in
this final admission of female failure: Diane cannot be but
longs to be the property of men; as sexual huntress she becomes victim, so must hid her vulnerability and play "tough
broad." Inevitably all men betray her, and she is left alone,
and empty.


                                IV


        These three contemporary women poets, then, recreate
moon as image and mythology from a female perspective, and
reimagine all aspects of the goddess's character: her inspiration, her lunacy, her duality, and most important, her sexuality and her cyclic nature. Precisely because the moon
presages change, because her phases imitate the rhythms of
feminine time, Levertov, Willard, and Wakoski create an
aesthetics of change in which the moon becomes transformational agent; whether the moon is image, as in Willard and
Levertov, or mythological goddess, as in Wakoski, she participates in a poetics which desires female change, growth,
and rebirth. Female poets, then, reappropriate older patterns of transformation, which, according to Erich Neumann,
were in primitive cultures the domain of the female: "In
this matriarchal world, the spirit world of the moon, corresponding to the basic symbolism of the Archetypal Feminine, appears as a birth--and indeed as rebirth. Wherever
we encounter the symbol of rebirth, we have to do with a
matriarchal transformation mystery, and this is true even
when its symbolism or interpretation bears a patriarchal
disguise."[18] Moon goddess and female create spiritual transformation.

        Levertov's poetry celebrates this alteration in the fe-
male experience; her poems imagine the moon's transforming
fire creating joyful change, acceptance of natural process,
and the partnership of men and women who love one another.
The power of female sexuality, which is imaginative energy,
recreates woman and joins her with a man and with the world.
Like Levertov, Willard celebrates the powers of the imagination, but unlike Levertov, she emphasizes the contrasexual

aspect of the creative process in which the marriage of masculine and feminine produces wholeness, or spiritual union. The poet and his wife both participate in poetry-making, and their marriage, in effect, recreates the universe: together they harness the powers of the imagination and re-name the cosmos; they imitate, re-imagine, and assume the moon's inspiration, transforming her inflexible phases into the shining material of the imaginative process.

Unlike both Willard and Levertov, Wakoski writes a document of female failure to change; her persona, Diane, attempts to imitate the fertile, moist aspect of the dual moon goddess, but fearing her own femininity, ends up the bitch goddess or negative female, the chaste Diana, fearing the male she inevitably loves, punishing him for his sexual approach, and eventually finding herself abandoned by him. The failure of the female persona informs us as fully about women's experience as does the success of Levertov's and Willard's transformational poetics; the moon's cycles, the goddess's duality, allow sexual and imaginative failure as well as transformation and rebirth. While Levertov and Willard solve the anima-animus problem by uniting the female with the male in sexual or contrasexual union, Wakoski falls into the animus trap; her persona, afraid of her sexuality, represses the feminine and causes energy to flow destructively into the masculine aspects of her psyche. Diane's self-doubt makes her hate men without fully realizing it is herself she truly hates.

Regardless, then, of female success or failure in a poetics of transformation, moon mythology and imagery no longer portray women from a masculine perspective. Levertov, Willard, and Wakoski transform the female experience into poetry; they imagine sexuality and change from a female point of view, and with the fully feminine voice.

## REFERENCES

1.  C. G. Jung, "Synchronicity: An Acausal Connecting Principle," in The Structure and Dynamics of the Psyche, from The Collected Works of C. G. Jung, VIII (New York: Pantheon Books, 1960; Bollingen Series XX), p. 436. See also C. G. Jung, "Archetypes of the Collective Unconscious," in The Archetypes and the Collective Unconscious, from The Collected Works of C. G. Jung, IX, I (New York:

Pantheon Books, 1969; Bollingen Series XX), pp. 5-6.

2. Women's Studies, 2 (1974), 171. This entire issue debates the concept of androgyny from feminist perspectives.

3. Jung, The Archetypes, pp. 28, 70, 26; Harris, p. 179.

4. Jung, The Archetypes, p. 70.

5. C. G. Jung, "Woman in Europe," in Civilization in Transition, from The Collected Works of C. G. Jung, X (New York: Pantheon Books, 1964; Bollingen Series XX), p. 119; Harris, p. 180.

6. C. G. Jung, "The Personification of the Opposites," in Mysterium Coniunctionis, from The Collected Works of C. G. Jung, XX (New York: Pantheon Books, 1963; Bollingen Series XX), p. 179.

7. Emma Jung, "On the Nature of the Animus," in Women and Analysis, ed. Jean Strouse (New York: Grossman, 1974), pp. 257, 260.

8. Emma Jung, pp. 241-42.

9. In Women and Analysis, p. 262.

10. Knowing Woman: A Feminine Psychology (New York: Putnam, 1973), p. 170. See also Ann Belford Ulanov, The Feminine in Jungian Psychology and Christian Theology (Evanston, Ill. : Northwestern University Press, 1971), p. 269: "The highest phase of confrontation and individuation in both sexes is initiated by the feminine: for the man, through the anima, which leads to the self; for the woman through the feminine self, not through any contrasexual elements.... It is the feminine which completes the individuation of each sex."

11. Literary Women: The Great Writers (Garden City, N. Y. : Doubleday, 1976), ch. 11, "Metaphors: A Postlude."

12. "Poetry, Personality, and Wholeness: A Response to Galway Kinnell," Field, No. 7 (Fall 1972), pp. 13, 17-18.

13. M. Esther Harding, Woman's Mysteries, Ancient and Modern (New York: Putnam, 1955), pp. 88-97, 103-04, 144-53. I am much indebted to Harding's survey of moon mythologies; further references to specific passages in her book will appear parenthetically in my text.

14. Wendy Martin, "Seduced and Abandoned in the New World: The Image of Woman in American Fiction," in Woman in Sexist Society: Studies in Power and Powerlessness, ed. Vivian Gornick and Barbara K.

Moran (New York: Basic Books, 1971), pp. 329-
46, bases her well-known article on man's need to
define woman as dualistic.

15. (New York: New Directions, 1934), and (New York:
New Directions, 1970). All references in my text
are to these editions.

16. (Santa Cruz, Calif.: Kayak Books, 1971). All references in my text are to this edition. Some of
these poems also appear in the Norton edition of
Willard's Carpenter of the Sun (New York, 1974).

17. (New York: Simon and Schuster, 1971), p. 99. All
page references in my text are to this edition.

18. The Great Mother: An Analysis of the Archetype (New
York, 1955), pp. 58-59. See also ch. 15, "Spiri-
tual Transformation," and Ulanov, Pt. III, "The
Psychology of the Feminine."

Suzanne Juhasz

## THE FEMINIST POET:
## ALTA AND ADRIENNE RICH*

The feminist poet finds "woman" and "poet" to be political words. Through art that reflects, expresses, creates
her life, she both validates herself as she is and works towards the revolution, the transformations that she desires:
"breaking down the artificial barriers between private and
public, between Vietnam and the lovers' bed" (Adrienne Rich). 1

Writing poems from personal experience, feminine
experience is an act both necessary and vital to the revolution that is occurring. This revolution must begin in the
mind, for consciousness needs to be raised before public
change can take place. Consciousness of oppression; consciousness of identity. As long as women believe in the
definition of themselves created by a male culture, they can
not know themselves to be oppressed. People born to be
slaves, who need and want other people to "take care of"
them, who see themselves as inferior, are by definition not
oppressed when others allow them to play out this role. Step
1 has been to realize that women are not what we have been
told about ourselves. Step 2 is to find out who we are.
Starting all over again. We need before us the evidence in
many forms of women and their lives. Feminist poets are
giving us these lives.

The life that she will offer needs not only to be validated; it needs to be changed. As feminists, we work for
affirmative action and child care centers, but we work as
well at individual lives. The poems that feminists write are
acts that change their lives; change, also, the lives of those

*Reprinted by permission of the author and publisher from
Juhasz's Naked and Fiery Forms: Modern American Poetry
by Women; A New Tradition (New York: Harper & Row,
1976), pp. 177-204. Copyright © 1976 by Suzanne Juhasz.

who read and hear.    Through seeing who we are, we change;
through saying who we are, we change; through seeing and
saying who we might become, we start to change into her.

Yet although women share much because of the fact of
their sex, each woman encounters feminine experience with
her own individuality.    Consequently, the forms that women
seek in art for expressing that experience must of necessity
be varied.    Finding oneself means finding one's own voice;
and this voice, to turn into a poem, must, in Adrienne Rich's
words, be that "of someone who knows the rhythm of his or
her own energy and blood."[2]    There is no one rule for feminine form, precisely because it needs to be an articulation
of the person, an extension of the person.    Yet this very
commitment to the self in poetry is feminine and feminist.
The need to validate the personal and the private as legitimate
topics for public speech is particularly feminine; the need to
integrate the private and the public is particularly feminist;
"But I don't see a radical feminism as preceding from anything but a connection between inner and outer.    We are attempting, in fact, to break down that fragmentation of inner
and outer in every possible realm.    The psyche and the world
out there are being acted on and interacting intensely all the
time" (Adrienne Rich).[3]    The rules for the private sphere
(woman's place) have heretofore not applied to the public
sphere (man's world).    Now feminist poets are working to
integrate their own lives and that of the world.

In the late sixties and early seventies, an explosion
of poetry by women occurred:  existing writers have been
discovered, new writers have been published.    Certainly,
this interest in women poets has been related to the existence
of the women's movement at large.    Certainly, women writers
are being published today who would not have been ten years
ago.    Yet this fact does not itself prove faddishness or lack
of quality in such work.    It points rather to changes in the
very way in which poetry is being evaluated.    The recognition
that women can be poets acknowledges as legitimate poetry
with themes hitherto omitted from the canon, or familiar
themes treated from a different perspective.    It acknowledges
as well changes in poetic form:  "but is it poetry?"

Recently, I received a rejection slip from a well-mean-
ing editor who, while admitting the "necessary" nature of my
poems, took issue with the fact that my poems "said it all."
"Try more denotation ... .synecdoche, metonymy, suggestion,"
he said.    Yet I and many feminist poets do not want to treat

poetry as a metalanguage that needs to be decoded to reveal meaning. Poetic language must always be language, not the "thing," so that what we call poetry is made from the inevitable yet always wonderful tension that exists between body acts and language acts. Among many feminist poets, however, there is a need to reveal rather than to conceal, to use a language bare not only of adornment but of obliqueness.

Mary Mackey, in "Women's Poetry: Almost Subversive," describes recent poetry by women this way:

> ... right off the bat they tend to commit the unpardonable sin of speaking clearly. Poems by women often make statements that can be understood by everyone, statements like:
>
>> I have no color belt in karate.
>> I only know how to kill.
>
> Why a poem as blunt as that is positively unprofessional. A six year old could read it. If everyone went around writing poetry like that, they'd have to give up teaching it in the universities. Obviously the woman who produced it must be a bit simpleminded. Apparently she had blithely assumed the relation between poet and reader must be one of equality rather than between priest and worshipper.
>
> Speak clearly? Right out of your own life? It's naked, indecent, obviously unpublishable. Besides, sometimes a poem that doesn't hide behind symbols, tropes, and obscure allusions sounds a little clumsy, a little plain.
>
> Clumsy like a scream.[4]

Mackey is pointing to another way in which feminist poetry is a political act. In speaking as it does, it alters the communication between poet and reader/ listener itself in accordance with feminist values, promoting nonhierarchical interchange rather than a power trip. Mackey observes that poetry by men has always been part and agent of the patriarchy:

> Because to be published a poem must be obscure, symbolic, magical, abstract, inaccessible. If it contains a few words in Sanskrit or an indirect reference to a 16th century Moldavian archivist, so much the better. A poem, to be published, must make the reader feel overawed, inadequate, a little

> thick-headed; it must, in turn, make the poet seem
> superior, in control, a high priest whose talent,
> art, and knowledge are beyond those of the ordinary
> person. [5]

Now, however, women poets are beginning to be published, and one reason is that there is a visibly expanding
audience for their work:  so many women who always thought
that "poetry had nothing to say to me" are hungrily reading
and asking for more names.   More importantly, perhaps,
women are publishing themselves.   Women's presses and
periodicals now exist throughout the country so that women's
voices can be heard.   Some of the most radical of these
voices are not yet listened to at the New York publishing
houses (and some, like Judy Grahn or Susan Griffin, do not
want to be published by the very establishment against which
they are in revolt), but the readers care little about where
the book comes from; they are concerned with what it says.

Women's voices in poetry are high and low, elegant
and harsh.   Sometimes they talk, sometimes they sing, but
they tend to share two characteristics:  they are strong and
real.   Alta and Adrienne Rich can represent two extremes
of feminist poetry:  the distilled colloquial of Alta, whose
emotions are on the surface of her skin and her poems; the
surrealism of Rich, whose words are pared and chiseled to
the cold bone of vision.   I chose them from among many:
Erica Jong, Diane Wakoski, Susan Griffin, Judy Grahn, Kathleen Fraser, Marge Piercy, Robin Morgan, Margaret Atwood,
Lynn Strongin, Lynn Sukenick, Lynn Lifshin, and others whose
work continues to surface.

Alta:  "i stand in my own pain / & sing my own song"

Alta was a feminist poet way back when (in the sixties!) there was not so much company.   In 1969 she founded
and still operates one of the country's first feminist presses,
Shameless Hussy Press.

> Euridice
>
> all the male poets write of orpheus
> as if they look back & expect
> to find me walking patiently
> behind them.   they claim i fell into hell.
> damn them, i say.
> i stand in my own pain
> & sing my own song. [6]

It is only recently that she has been represented in any national anthologies, a recognition that has come from women. [7] An important fact, because the most common negative response to her poetry is: "It isn't poetry." Who says? People who don't like what she writes--a vicious kind of circle. Don't like it (we are now at an emotional, not an intellectual or theoretical, level) because it is shocking. Why shocking? In its anger (and joy) it does not lie. It isn't true life, it is poetry, but the electric connection between the two kinds of truth is not severed. For some, the poems are too honest: "how can i do this?/ how can i write this need?/ have i no shame?" she herself asks. [8] But it is necessary that the need be written: "because my song is my life/ & you cant have just my poems. / we're a package deal." (The title of the poem quoted makes a telling comment: "--we want yr words, alta, we just dont want you. --woman on the staff of it aint me, babe.")

Honest, these poems lack "decorum," that heretofore primary criterion for women's language. The shock when they speak to men (in this case, her husband): "take me to the woods sometime instead of/ your girlfriend/ see how you like it." They shock more profoundly when they speak to women--not through men, because of men, about men, or for men--but to women directly.

> can we speak true & trust?
> what is this need i have
> to know a woman as friend?
> to know you, andrea, as well as
> i know the pain in yr poems.
>
> where are you turning we're
> opening we're opening hold
> my hand my body's opening[9]

They shock not only because they overturn stereotypical male/female relationships, but because they break down all protective barriers of politeness that isolate one human from another:

> i havent written about this
> because its going to hurt.
> it's going to hurt her & it's
> going to hurt me.
> she's never said
> "stop being racist"
> & i've never said

"do i act like i been raised
english?"
i call her when i'm in trouble,
but it was 2 years
before i went to see her in her home.
    ["Alchemy," I, I am Not a Practicing Angel]

A Confusion of Musk

when we knelt side by side
the smell of us rose between our legs
& i couldnt tell, after the first shock
(that means i want her!)
i couldnt tell if it were yrs or mine.
    [I Am Not a Practicing Angel]

        Alta writes of the moments we try to ignore or forget
about ourselves and others ("ever since i suggested/ we make
love/ she hasnt let me/ touch her/ am i so vile"), because
she is fighting a revolution that is not only for women but
for love itself: "so that we are both fully exposed, & vul-
nerable to each others love."[10]

        Alta is shocking for another reason:   she is funny.

euch, are you having yr period?
why didn't you tell me?
i shoulda fucked him ina dark.
he coulda-thot bloody sheets
look ma a virgin
    [No Visible Means of Support]

if yr not good to me,
you'll have to watch your step.
i have friends in low places.
    [I Am Not a Practicing Angel]

i beat off after every meal.
havent had a cavity for years!
    [I Am Not a Practicing Angel]

There is always a gasp of pain in our laughter for these poems,
as there is in Alta's wry wit when she writes them.   It is
allowable for people in pain to laugh at themselves (it eases
the hurt and keeps them from resisting), but they are not
supposed to use their humor as a way of fighting back.   Alta's
wit threatens, because it helps bring pain into full consciousness, which is the first step.

Elaine Gill calls Alta's lyrics "terse" and "pure."[11] It is the distillation of experience that her words achieve that accounts for this purity; it is their engagement with experience at a level of direct feeling that accounts for the terseness.

> first pregnancy:
> lonely & big
> a couple of time i cried
> hearing you
> beating off under covers.
> [Song of the Wife/Song of the Mistress]

> you think weeping sounds bad,
> you should hear me laugh
> [No Visible Means of Support]

> To My Children on a Trip
>
> they don't need my fear
> riding along with them
> like an unwanted ghost.
> [No Visible Means of Support]

The compression in such poems results in an accompanying expansion, which however takes place in the mind of the reader/listener. I am talking about the impact from these poems, an afterimage or aftertaste, a reverberation that occurs when the poem connects to a place of feeling within me.

But is it poetry?

> this ain't a poem, it's just something i have to say:
> if yr planning an abortion, because yr afraid
> of social censure, or afraid you wont be able
> to support yr child, don't do it.
> society is what has to give,
> not our children.
> [I Am Not a Practicing Angel]

In a prose article on women's poetry, "TELL IT LIKE IT IS," she also discusses this question:

> IT'S DIFFICULT TO BE CLEAR & NOT ONE DIMEN-
> SIONAL. ONLY A GREAT WRITER CAN DO IT.
> SO MANY POEMS ARE JUST STATEMENTS: WITH
> POLITICS BEHIND THEM, IT DOESNT REALLY MAT-

TER IF THEYRE TIMELESS ART.  BUT THESE
POEMS ARE VALID NOW, & THEY SHOULD BE
HEARD NOW.  THE POEMS PEOPLE NEED IN
2072, THEY'LL READ (I HOPE) IN 2072.  & I
HOPE A LOT OF THE BATTLES WE'RE FIGHTING
NOW WILL BE WON, EVEN IF IT MEANS 1/2
OUR WORK WILL BE IRRELEVANT.  WE MUST
WORK TOWARDS OUR OWN OBSOLESCENCE. [12]

With a strong political imperative behind her work,
Alta is making a distinction, not between poems and non-
poems, but between time-bound and timeless art.  She is
writing, not for eternity, but for now.  Yet when Alta is
very good, and often she is, her poems express the human
spirit on a level that might very well be timeless--who can
know?  What her comment and the poem quoted above under-
line is the reason why, for any superior poem on a page,
there are others less successful, because they don't work
(at the level of distilling and integrating language and experience) so well.  They are there on the page anyway, because
they continue to be "something i have to say."  For Alta,
that is sufficient reason for their presence.

Alta's poems come out of private and politicized woman's experience.  She writes to and about her lovers (female and male), children, friends, and enemies; she writes
out of longing, anger, pain, desire, frustration, joy, loneliness, bitterness, pride.  These intensely personal emotions
are political, because Alta is conscious of the fact that her
own suffering can speak to others, too; that ultimately it
must speak to others if ever it is to be overcome.

the wound of crying alone.
of being the voice that fits no ear.
no shelled ear catching the screech
of this wound, the wound of hearing our own
screams uninterrupted,
bouncing back from concrete & glass
& our ears ache & our throats crack dry &
only the other screams that sometimes bounce
back from other concrete walls interrupt
our pain / & the double pain easier because
another spirit wants out, another
person in pain wants to care &
the wounded recognize each other.
our wounds will heal us.
["The Wound Will Heal Us"][13]

Poetry is a way of speaking: "your tiny body warms my breast"; "i promised i would but i can't. So what else is new?"; "if you won't make love to me, at least/ get out of my dreams!" It is the poem itself that serves as the agent of connection between people. For the poem to work, the reader/listener has to take part (as herself/himself, as the person to whom the poem is addressed, as the speaker of the poem). To cause such response, this kind of poem usually does not use the imaginative transformations of fig- urative language. Rather, it calls on the impact of the literal detail to fly directly like an arrow, to touch feeling to feel- ing. There is in such poetry an inherent distrust of a lan- guage (a sexist language) that has always before been used to deceive, to distance, to separate: "my history books lied to me. they said i didn't exist"; "--dont tell anyone about our affair. i intend to run for city council. --/--bob."

> how can i reach out with poetry
> when words are such faulty fingers?

To work, poetry must be removed from the realm of "fantasy": "come honest to the bone./ peel away the lies/ (i'm afraid)," she writes in a poem called "ITS THE REAL THING IN THE BACK OF YOUR MIND." A difficult thing to do: "its not that i lie, its just/ sometimes i like to hide a little bit./ that's a lie, i dont like/ to have to hide at all." But this poem itself persists in revealing, baring its speaker as it, and she, look at her hands, with nails that aren't pret- ty, hands that "are strong & can make music/ & fix a press"; at her titties that are "funny" because "those children loved my milk"; at her scarred skin and high cheekbones:

> ... i dont
> look like what youve been taught to want.
> my body looks like me, like a strong woman
> who has survived a lot & come out
> dancing.
> here i am.
> (i'm afraid)
> here i am ...
>
> it's my face & i stand behind it.
> here i am.

It is the poem that brings Alta to make the final declaration without, finally, the refrain of fear. The poem works to make language (and people) honest. It works to evoke "rec- ognition"--in this way, to heal.

"Could a poem be a cup/ to pour our joy into?" she
writes in a poem whose title itself supplies the answer: "ANY-
BODY COULD WRITE THIS POEM. ALL YOU HAVE TO SAY
IS YES. "

## Adrienne Rich: "the field of the poem wired with danger"

Adrienne Rich is a feminist poet who has struggled
over a period of many years to become one. She is today
one of the strongest and clearest advocates of a feminist
philosophy that has changed her poetry, changed her life, by
bringing about a closer integration of the one with the other.
In 1973 she concludes her poem "Re-forming the Crystal"
with this description of the poem--the woman's poem, one
element of an interrelated web of act and dream.

> Tonight if the battery charges I want to take the
> car out on sheet-ice; I want to understand my fear
> both of the machine and of the accidents of nature.
> My desire for you is not trivial; I can compare it
> with the greatest of those accidents. But the energy
> it draws on might lead to racing a cold engine,
> cracking the frozen spiderweb, parachuting into the
> field of the poem wired with danger, or to a trip
> through gorges and canyons, into the cratered
> night of female memory, where delicately and with
> intense care the chieftainess inscribes upon the ribs
> of the volcano the name of the one she has chosen. 14

Rich's recent poetry conjoins long open prose lines
with tense sharp blunt verse units: Whatever forms that
will, as she says in "Planetarium," 1968, "translate pulsa-
tions/ into images. "15 She seeks words that do not lie by
standing separate from experience but speak truth through
connection to the speaker's own energy and blood. Her poetry
offers visions of a patriarchal culture that oppresses, destroys, gives birth only to death; of women being reborn into
selfhood, power, and hopefully salvation; of things as they
are and as they might be. The poetry that she writes today,
its language as well as its themes, is the result of a long
process of learning to look "nakedly/ at the light" (as she
says in "From the Prison House," 1971)16 and to find the
words for what she sees.

Looking back at her early poetry, Rich has written:

I know that my style was formed first by male

poets: by the men I was reading as an undergrad-
uate--Frost, Dylan Thomas, Donne, Auden, Mac-
Niece, Stevens, Yeats.  What I chiefly learned
from them was craft.  But poems are like dreams:
in them you put what you don't know you know.
Looking back at poems I wrote before I was 21,
I'm startled because beneath the conscious craft
are glimpses of the split I even then experienced
between the girl who wrote poems, who defined
herself in writing poems, and the girl who was to
define herself by her relationship with men. [17]

W. H. Auden concludes his introduction to her first
volume of poems, A Change of World, with this praise: "The
poems a reader will encounter in this book are neatly and
modestly dressed, speak quietly but do not mumble, respect
their elders but are not cowed by them, and do not tell fibs;
that, for a first volume, is a good deal."[18]  Patronizing
words, but also truthful; for as a young poet Rich (As well
as Auden) accepted the models provided by her patriarchal
world and literary tradition.  This is poetry with wraps on,
carefully, tightly constructed so that the play of words is
foregrounded, so that emotion is generalized.

Boundary

What has happened here will do
To bite the living world in two,
Half for me and half for you.
Here at last I fix a line
Severing the world's design
Too small to hold both yours and mine.
There's enormity in a hair
Enough to lead men not to share
Narrow confines of a sphere
But put an ocean or a fence
Between two opposite intents.
A hair would span the difference.

Regular meter and rhyme, distance and generalization, combine to create the discrete decorum of her language.  This
poem refers to profound interpersonal conflict, but who is
feeling, what is felt, are never identified, alluded to only as
"what has happened here."  The nature of the struggle becomes
"two opposite intents."  While the first six lines refer specifically if obliquely to a "me" and a "you," the issue that
the poem is considering, the importance of seemingly small
differences, has been generalized by the last six lines:

"Enough to lead men not to share." The precision and ele-
gance of the poem with its strongly conceptual vocabulary
(of "world," "line," "design," "enormity," "confines," "intents," "difference") helps create the strong but subtle distinctions and boundaries that are described: "Here at last
I fix a line/ Severing the world's design." Although the poet
considers her subject from on high, at all times distant,
distinct, objective, that subject is, nevertheless, relationship:
specifically, the intimate relationship between woman and man,
Rich's abiding concern throughout her career. If into the
early work she has put "what you don't know you know," the
process of her development as a poet has been to come to
consciousness--to know what she knows. The forms and
the very language of her poetry have aided in that process
as much as they have expressed it:

> Perhaps a simple way of putting it would be to
> say that instead of poems about experiences I am
> getting poems that are experiences, that contribute
> to my knowledge and my emotional life even while
> they reflect and assimilate it. In my earlier
> poems I told you, as precisely and eloquently as
> I knew how, about something; in the more recent
> poems something is happening, something has
> happened to me and, if I have been a good parent
> to the poem, something will happen to you who
> read it. [19]

By Snapshots of a Daughter-in-Law,[20] a crisp and
matter-of-fact statement of ordinary detail ("These old
tears in the chopping bowl" ["Peeling Onions"]) balances
against the old elaboration of figure. Both are turned more
and more to the elucidation of the intimate moment itself,
as in these lines from "A Marriage in the Sixties":

> Today we stalk
> in the raging desert of our thought
> whose single drop of mercy is
> each knows the other there.
> Two strangers, thrust for life upon a rock,
> may have at last the perfect hour of talk
> that language aches for; still--
> two minds, two messages.

Talking about the title poem in that volume, Rich calls it
still "too literary, too dependent on allusion; I hadn't found
the courage yet to do without authorities, or even to use the
pronoun 'I.'"[21] The transfers of figurative language can

either move away from the particular (as in "Boundary") or
into it; in the late fifties and early sixties, Rich's poems
are capable of both movements.  In "A Marriage in the Sixties" the moment of felt separateness between husband and
wife is seen as a kind of intimacy; the quoted lines describe
an internal landscape that is bare and full of pain:  the mind
is a "desert" that is "raging."  The single source of life in
this barrenness is the fact that each is aware that the other
also inhabits the same separate place.  Then the focus nar-
rows; the couple are two strangers, thrust for life upon a
single rock.  The possibility of union ("the perfect hour of
talk/ that language aches for") is denied by the poem's bleak
images of loneliness--"two minds, two messages."  Although
concentrating upon the moment, Rich's language, with its
vocabulary of "thought," "mercy," "life," "talk," "language,"
"mind," and "messages," is still constantly conceptualizing.
In her poetry as in her life, Rich struggles with that primary
separation between physical experience and intellectual interpretation.

"Novella," 1962, is a spare poem of literal detail, of
quarrel between man and woman, in which separation is revealed and enforced by the verse sentences themselves:  each
character is confined to her/his own.

> One gets up, goes out to walk.
> (That is the man.)
> The other goes into the next room
> and washes the dishes, cracking one.
> (That is the woman.)

The poem continues accordingly:  "She has no blood left in
her heart"; "He has forgotten the key."  The man leaves and
comes back:  "The door closes behind him"; he "hears sob-
bing on the stairs."  Suddenly, in the closing two lines, the
focus of the poem expands to include the world of which this
house and this couple are one small part:  "Outside, separate
as minds/ the stars too come alight."  The poem has expanded,
as well, into figurative language that aligns internal and external worlds to comment on the universal condition of separation and pain that this woman and this man embody.

Yet Rich has written in a notebook at about this time:

> Paralyzed by the sense that there exists a mesh of
> relationships--e. g. between my anger at the chil-
> dren, my sensual life, pacifism, sex, (I mean sex

in its broadest significance, not merely sexual
desire)--an interconnectedness which, if I could
see it, make it valid, would give me back myself,
make it possible to function lucidly and passionately.
Yet I grope in and out among these dark webs. [22]

The existence of such interconnectedness is sensed only during these years; for the world of people and events as she
experiences it, as her poems analyze it, gives back nothing
but disconnection, separation, loneliness.   The "mesh of
relationships" is sensed deep within herself but is refused
entry into the world.

    It might be that language could be the midwife for such
a birth.   The first stanza of "The Well" (Snapshots of a
Daughter-in-Law) lists discrete objects that have fallen into
a well ("an old trash barrel") in November:  leaves, cores
of eaten apples, scraps of paper.   The second stanza includes
the presence of the poet and her attempt to bring about wholeness with her language, "that word."

>           But I come, trying
>           to breathe that word
>           into the well's ear
>           which could make the leaves fly up
>           like a green jet
>           to clothe the naked tree,
>           the whole fruit leap to the bough,
>           the scraps like fleets of letters
>           sail up into my hands.

In this vision of possibility, figurative language again makes
its entrance into the poem.   The well is personified (it has
an ear) and is thus related to the human world.   The leaves
would return like birds, like water to clothe a body-tree, so
that many elements in nature unite in the act; language itself
(the scraps of paper) would become boats, bearing messages
into her hands.   In other words, the vision of wholeness and
connection between seasons and persons and things is achieved
in the poem through figures of speech that connect what have
hitherto been discrete units of experience.   Yet even in this
poem, which remains language and not physical act, the wholeness is viewed as possibility only.   That is because language
itself is suspect.

    In "Two Songs," 1964, from Necessities of Life,[23]
Rich discovers in trying to write about her own experience

of sexuality a difficulty in using the language ordinarily assigned to it: "sex, as they harshly call it"; "that old 'last
act.'"   Each of the two short poems is a movement between
an existing vocabulary, which must instruct sensation as
much as it describes it ("and longing for that young man/
pierced me to the roots/ bathing every vein, etc.") and her
own unnamed truth of feeling.

> Sex, as they harshly call it,
> I fell into it this morning
> at ten o'clock, a drizzling hour
> of traffic and wet newspapers.
> I thought of him who yesterday
> clearly didn't
> turn me to a hot field
> ready for ploughing,
> and longing for that young man
> piercéd me to the roots
> bathing every vein, etc.

She lodges this experience in her own actuality, enumerating
hour and weather.   Naming it "sex," she tries to use the
literary language for it.   Except that he "clearly didn't"--and
in her poem that phrase is one line juxtaposed against the
language of literary cliché--"turn me to a hot field."

> All day he appears to me
> touchingly desirable,
> a prize one could wreck one's peace for.
> I'd call it love if love
> didn't take so many years
> but lust too is a jewel
> a sweet flower and what
> pure happiness to know
> all our high-toned questions
> breed in a lively animal.

She identifies the man as "desirable" and "a prize"; can't
call what she feels "love" because the definition she knows
for love won't work here; ends by calling it lust and rede-
fining that term to fit with metaphors that could do as well
for love: jewel, sweet flower.   The ending of the poem is
ambivalent, skirting the language issue and opting for the
validity of lust, now that she's named it that, for the animal-
ity of thoughtful humans.   But the second song centers once
more on language.

This poem's beginning parallels the start of the first,

offering a cliché definition of sex, "that old 'last act,'" followed immediately in the next line by a demurral, "And yet
sometimes." Trying to talk about her feeling of being outside
herself ("all seems post coitum triste/ and I a mere by-
stander"), she takes literally and develops dramatically yet
another sexual cliché: "Somebody else is going off,/ getting
shot to the moon." A moon race! The couple lie at a crater
edge, she arriving split seconds after he does. The he
speaks:

> in a different language
> yet one I've picked up
> through cultural exchanges ...
> we murmur the first moonwords:
> Spasibo.  Thanks.  O. K.

Now Rich specifically equates that other language, the
one that is foreign to her but which she has "picked up" and
learned to use, as that of men. In later books, she will
focus all of her energies on forging a new language, because
the language of a patriarchy is both false and destructive.
But here she is still at the point of identifying its essential
alienness to her; with wit she is playing with the images that
such an observation has offered her.

By 1968, in "Implosions" (Leaflets), she can clearly
identify her purpose as an artist working with language: "I
wanted to choose words that even you/ would have changed
by"; "Take the word/ of my pulse, loving and ordinary."[24]
(In 1972 she will say "that people turn to what they at least
call poetry when they're trying to break out of an extreme
situation. Because poetry's got that incredible connection
with speech. It seems like almost the most human thing
you can do." When the interviewer asks her when these
urgent voices turn into poems, she answers: "When it's the
voice of someone who knows the rhythm of her own energy
and blood.")[25] In "Implosions" she shows herself as aware
of the extremity of her situation--"All wars are useless to
the dead"--and of the difficulty of bringing about the peace
through change that she desires:

> My hands are knotted in the rope
> and I cannot sound the bell
>
> My hands are frozen to the switch
> and I cannot throw it
>
> The foot is in the wheel

Difficult because she is caught in the very situation that she
needs to change, as her images show.   The primary situation
is still the sexual one, so that the need is somehow to unite
with the enemy:

> Send out your signals, hoist
> your dark scribbled flags
> but take
> my hand

The poem makes language the metaphor, the means ("sig-
nals," "dark scribbled flags") for connecting.   The poet now
knows she must do more than describe that loneliness and
separation, as she used to do, for its implications are more
deadly than she had understood.   "But revolutionary force has
got to have behind it so much more understanding of what
we're all about, of whether a whole new set of relationships
is possible.   It has to begin at the sexual level."[26]   She has
to try to help:

> When it's finished and we're lying
> in a stubble of blistered flowers
> eyes gaping, mouths staring
> dusted with crushed arterial blues
>
> I'll have done nothing
> even for you?

The change in Rich's thinking about language and its
relation to society must necessarily lead to changes in her
own poetry.   In her earlier work, she generalized and uni-
versalized her concern with the personal to make it acceptable
as poetry.   Abstractions combined with the extensions of
figure helped accomplish this for her.   But now she sees
the essential rather than arbitrary or superficial connection
between private and public.   She begins to place thematic
focus directly upon "the lovers' bed" but still has the problem of having to make the connections with language.   In
their very form, many of the poems in Leaflets show her
struggle:

> Something broken    Something
> I need    By someone
> I love    Next year
> will I remember what
> This anger    unreal
>                         yet
> has to be gone through

              The sun to set
              on this anger
                        I go on
              head down      into it
              The mountain pulsing
              Into the oildrum      drops
              the ball of fire.
                   ["Nightbreak"]

Rich is breaking down poetic language itself in order to be
able to recompose it.

    In The Will to Change and Diving into the Wreck, a
new quality of language irradiates Rich's poetry.  Many of
the poems themselves are manifestos of her new aesthetic:

              I have been standing all my life in the
              direct path of a battery of signals
              the most accurately transmitted most
              untranslatable language in the universe
              I am a galactic cloud so deep    so invo-
              luted that a light wave could take 15
              years to travel through me      And has
              taken      I am an instrument in the shape
              of a woman trying to translate pulsations
              into images       for the relief of the body
              and the reconstruction of the mind.
                   ["Planetarium," 1968]

The rhythms of this inner focusing are steadier, longer;
pauses occur as breaths within the line as well as after it;
statement is permissible--any language form that will translate "pulsations into images," as she now identifies the work
that must be done.

    Complementary to "Planetarium" is another manifesto,
written three years later in 1971, "From the Prison House,"
describing "another eye" that has opened underneath her lids.
This eye "looks nakedly/ at the light."  It observes the external world and sees "detail not on TV," such as "the fingers of the policewoman/ searching the cunt of the young
prostitute."

              This eye
              is not for weeping
              its vision
              must be unblurred

though tears are on my face

its intent is clarity
it must forget
nothing

Here the form is sharp, short, blunt, literal.  This eye
looks out, not in, so that the two poems taken together are
mirror images of the same process.  There is urgency in
the looking "From the Prison House," which its staccato
lines communicate.  "What we see, we see/ and seeing is
changing," she writes in "The Blue Ghazals" (The Will to
Change).  In order to succeed, the sight must be unblurred,
excruciatingly clear.  One way to translate seen images into
words is to pare language, likewise, to its essence, to reduce words to clear unshadowed counters, bone black on the
white page.  For "this is the oppressor's language," as she
observes in a long poem on the subject, "The Burning of
Paper instead of Children" (The Will to Change); "Yet I need
to talk to you."  This talking must be done with scrupulous
care, being aware at all times of that language.

Our Whole Life

Our whole life a translation
the permissible fibs

and now a knot of lies
eating at itself to get undone

Words bitten thru words

meaning burnt-off like paint
under the blowtorch

All those dead letters
rendered into the oppressor's language

Trying to tell the doctor where it hurts
like the Algerian
who walked from his village, burning

his whole body a cloud of pain
and there are no words for this

except himself
    [1969, from The Will to Change]

This poem identifies language as absolutely central to the act
of living as well as to the art of poetry; central to the identification of the self, to the relation between selves.  Its primary metaphor begins the poem: Life = a translation; it

equates language and lives.  With a series of such metaphors,
the poem urges that the most important action of our lives
be to live the truth.  The poem's own words become agents
of the truth that lies beneath the knot of lies; each new metaphor functions like "the blowtorch" to burn to the meanings
underneath.  The final image insists upon the truth of metaphor itself.  Lives are language, and the words we use to
show this must come from the same place as the breath itself:  "there are no words for this/ except himself. "

Thus work on language does not exist in a separate
compartment from other political enterprises as Rich understands it in the late sixties and early seventies.  To resee
and reexpress:  see the existing damages and dangers, express the realities that have been hidden or lied about or
have not yet been born:  this is her purpose as a feminist
desirous of saving the culture, and poetry can be one medium
in which this action occurs.

> We need a poetry which will dare to explore, and
> to begin exploding, the phallic delusions which
> are now endangering consciousness itself. [27]

> I don't know how or whether poetry changes any-
> thing.  But neither do I know how or whether
> bombing or even community organizing changes
> anything when we are pitted against a massive
> patriarchal system armed with supertechnology.
> I believe in subjectivity--that a lot of male Left
> leaders have turned into Omnipotent Administrators,
> because their 'masculinity' forced them to deny
> their subjectivity.  I believe in dreams and visions
> and 'the madness of art. '  And at moments I can
> conceive of a woman's movement that will show
> the way to humanizing technology and fusing dreams
> and skills and visions and reason to begin the
> healing of the human race. [28]

> One thing I am sure of:  just as woman is be-
> coming her own midwife, creating herself anew,
> so man will have to learn to gestate and give
> birth to his own subjectivity--something he has
> frequently wanted women to do for him.  We can
> go on trying to talk to each other, we can some-
> times help each other, poetry and fiction can show
> us what the other is going through; but women can
> no longer be primarily mothers and muses for
> men:  we have our own work cut out for us. [29]

"Subjectivity" becomes a key word in Rich's recent discussion of politics and art, because it is that force that must be recognized, validated, and included in any endeavor if the real interrelation between private and public, inner and outer, is to occur.   For herself as poet, subjectivity means finding words and images that can establish those connections.   Yet Rich is always a thinking and thoughful woman; she does not, as T. S. Eliot wrote (albeit questionably) about the English metaphysical poets, "feel [her] thought as immediately as the odour of a rose."[30]   She is no Alta--nor need she be!   In her recent poetry, she includes the subjective by offering clear, careful depictions of an ordinary world that is always symbolic because its terrain is both inner and outer:   the world of dream and of waking.

> The tragedy of sex
> lies around us, a woodlot
> the axes are sharpened for.
> The old shelters and huts
> stare through the clearing with a certain resolution
> --the hermit's cabin, the hunters' shack--
> scenes of masturbation
> and dirty jokes.
> A man's world.   But finished.
> They themselves have sold it to the machines. . . .
>
> Nothing will save this.   I am alone,
> kicking the last rotting logs
> with their strange smell of life, not death,
> wondering what on earth it all might have become.
> ["Waking in the Dark," from Diving into the Wreck]

> even you, fellow-creature, sister,
> sitting across from me, dark with love,
> working like me to pick apart
> working with me to remake
> this trailing knitted thing, this cloth of darkness,
> this woman's garment, trying to save the skein.
> ["When We Dead Awaken," from Diving into the Wreck]

"The tragedy of sex" = "a woodlot/ the axes are sharpened for"; "this trailing knitted thing, this cloth of darkness,/ this woman's garment" is at the same time a literal piece of knitting and a symbolic form for the lives of women. This is the kind of image that Rich creates out of the pulsations she experiences; with the stark lucidity that has become the primary characteristic of her poetic language, she envisions the world of masculine destructiveness, the world of women attempting rebirth in (and on) their own terms.

More and more she sees beyond the present moment
into the process that will create a new world. Everywhere
in her poetry a fire of creativity rises up against man's ice
of impotence.

> raking his body down to the thread
> of existence
> burning away his lie
> leaving him in a new
> world; a changed
> man
> ["The Phenomenology of Anger," 1972]

> ... the mirror of the fire
> of my mind, burning as if it could go on
> burning itself, burning down
> feeding on everything
> till there is nothing in life
> that has not fed that fire
> ["Burning Oneself Out," 1972]

we talk of destruction and creation
ice fists itself around each twig of the lilac
like a fist of law and order
your imagination burns like a bulb in the frozen soil
the fierce shoots knock
at the roof of waiting

when summer comes the ocean may be closed for good
we will turn
to the desert
where survival
takes naked and fiery forms
["Blood-Sister," 1973]

... Dawn is the test, the agony
but we were meant to see it:
After this, we may sleep, my sister,
while the flames rise higher and higher, we can sleep.
["White Night," 1974]

In articulating these images of the mind, bringing
them into consciousness and into focus in black words on
white paper in the waking world, she is helping to bring about
the new world. Her focus is on the process for change, and
all of these visions of possibility begin in the carefully ob-

served domestic world. "White Night," the ending of which
I have just quoted, begins: "Light at a window. Someone
up/ at this snail-still hour. " An everyday (or everynight)
event, yet pulsing with political significance, as the following
lines that complete the image indicate: ". . . I've had to
guess at her/ sewing her skin together as I sew mine/ though/
with a different/ stitch. " This form, validating the personal,
fusing the private and the public, is feminine and feminist.

The change in Rich's poetry has represented her attempt to "function lucidly and passionately" in the world by
bringing her sense of interconnectedness into it by means of
the poem. Her early work articulated the separation she saw
between people in the world, between herself and the world,
between aspects of her self, between her self and the poem.
Her poetic language created those separations in art by forms
that distanced, generalized, impersonalized experience. Her
work on language has been to use it as a force for integration, for permitting the subjective entry into the world.
Rich's language, broken down and reformed, is now a living
extension of her mind. Her poetic images integrate dream
acts and waking acts in a conceptual but physically precise
way--what I have earlier called surrealism.

Consequently, when she describes the poem itself in
1974, it is solid, active, ordinary, and full of power; it is
a part of the world and an act towards the new one; it contains within itself the fire of birth. These words conclude
a poem called "The Fact of a Doorframe":

Now, again, poetry
violent, arcane, common,
hewn of the commonest living substance
into archway, portal, frame
I grasp for you, your bloodstained splinters, your
ancient and stubborn poise
--as the earth trembles--
burning out from the grain

## Feminist Poetry: "violent, arcane, common"

Adrienne Rich and Alta are very different kinds of
poets, even as they are very different kinds of women. Yet
each speaks as a woman, and each seeks a language that
will honestly express that self. In her own way, each poet
has used her art to validate the personal and the private as

legitimate topics for public speech; each has used her words
to integrate the private and the public.    Each has seen poetry
to be an aspect of political feminism, and as a poet each
has based the revolution in the language act, reshaping words
into forms that can give us lives, and life:   re-forming the
crystal.

There is also an important difference between the
poetry of Rich and Alta.    Rich has worked hard and well to
create a form that will articulate her radical politics, but
that form itself is not radical.    First, because Rich's new
forms are still a development from her old.    Her feminism
has brought her to a place where poetry and self are not at
odds but at one, but that self did learn its craft in the fifties, and that self is primarily controlled by the mind.    Rich
is an intellectual, and her poetry, which is mind-poetry,
works by blowing our minds.    Her forms are neither shocking
nor threatening, although her ideas may be.    Alta's poetry,
on the other hand, confronts the reader in the pit of her
stomach, in the genitals, in places that are not traditionally
associated with the high art of poetry.    Which is the point.
Alta's art is not high but low, not elitist but popular, not
timeless but time-bound, not universal but particular.    Her
feminist aesthetics, hand in hand with her personal inclina-
tions, demand this.    Alta's very forms--her vocabulary, her
literalness, her brevity (the epigram is inferior to the epic,
says tradition)--are radical and shocking and threatening.
How does one evaluate such poetry?    But is it good?

My own answer to these questions is that a poem works
if it lives up to itself; if it fulfills the requirements that it
has set up for itself.    The philosopher Kenneth Burke defined
form as the arousing and fulfilling of desires,[31] a definition
that includes the reader in a similar process.    Such a definition contains no built-in ranking system:  it does not call
one form better than another.    Yet a poem can work and not
be good.    It can be dull or ordinary or superficial in its
solutions and statements.    A good poem works powerfully and
accurately to communicate between poet and reader or listener.
When the power and accuracy of the words in their created
form link poet and poem and reader in an instant of light,
that, to me, is a good poem.    When Alta achieves the distill-
lation and subsequent expansion that I have described, when
her poems are tight as a fist, when every word works not
only better than any other word in its place could work but
also with excitement and power, then Alta is very good.    Yet
Alta will print poems that do not work this well simply be-

cause of their message, their theme or statement.  At this
point, I think, politics and art part company.  And I can
continue to respect the political philosophy that tells Alta to
print the lines, even if I do not want to call the lines poetry.

Rich's early poetry usually works, and for many years
it has been considered good.  But its success seems to be a
technical one, and those granting the mantle did not seem to
be concerned about the excitement of language that is part
of a communication process created only when the poet is
connected to her poem.  Here my criteria differ from that
of some other critics, for while I can appreciate a cold pure
form, I do not, anymore, usually like it.  Today Rich writes
as herself, using all her skill with language to that end and
purpose.  I think she is very good.

But is it poetry?  Not only Rich and Alta, but all women who write as women, each woman who writes as herself, continue to face this ultimate of questions.  The question comes from the heart of sexism, from the heart of a
culture that has made rules for everything, including art,
that uphold its values.  Women's poetry is so threatening
because it does provoke the ultimate questions.  It is not
that everything women do as poets is different from what men
do, or that women use words in ways that men don't, or
can't, but that many of their ways are different, and that
their ways are for the purpose of expressing in art their
real selves, not the selves that have been created for them.
To do this in a patriarchy is revolutionary.

Establishment poets and critics are forever talking
about timelessness and transcendence and universality in art,
condemning many women and minority artists, in accordance
with these criteria, as being "limited," or as nonartists.
By not universal they mean, however, not including me, the
man.  The traditional criteria for poetry have described the
poetry that men have made; it has been "universal" because
it has described the experience of MANkind.

Webster defines a poem as "an arrangement of words
in verse; especially a rhythmical composition, sometimes
rhymed, expressing facts, ideas, or emotions in a style more
concentrated, imaginative, and powerful than that of ordinary
speech."  A poet is "a person who writes poems."  Poetry
is "poems, poetical works, the writing of poetry."  These
broad definitions do not exclude Alta; it is applied and culture-
bound criteria that exclude her.  Yet the very concentration,

imagination, and, above all, power of feminist poetry today threaten the patriarchy because it is poetry, and because, whether or not they acknowledge its right to existence, whether or not they stamp it with the seal of approval, POEM, it goes on working as poetry ought, to affect minds, lives, and culture itself.

## REFERENCES

1. Diving into the Wreck (New York: W. W. Norton, 1973), back cover.
2. David Kalstone, "Talking with Adrienne Rich," Saturday Review: The Arts 4, no. 17 (April 22, 1972): 57.
3. "Three Conversations," in Barbara Gelpi and Albert Gelpi, eds., Adrienne Rich's Poetry (New York: W. W. Norton, 1975), p. 114.
4. Mary Mackey, "Women's Poetry: Almost Subversive," Small Press Review 11, vol. 3, no. 3: 17.
5. Ibid., p. 17.
6. I Am Not a Practicing Angel (Trumansburg, N. Y.: The Crossing Press, 1975), p. 8.
7. Her work has been published in such anthologies as Florence Howe and Ellen Bass, eds., No More Masks: An Anthology of Poems by Women (New York: Anchor Books, 1973); Elaine Gill, ed., Mountain Moving Day: Poems by Women (Trumansburg, N. Y.: The Crossing Press, 1973); Jean Malley and Halé Tokay, eds., Contemporaries (New York: Viking Press, 1972).
8. No Visible Means of Support (San Lorenzo, Calif.: Shameless Hussy Press, 1971), p. 30.
9. Letters to Women (San Lorenzo, Calif.: Shameless Hussy Press, n. d.).
10. I Am Not a Practicing Angel, pp. 51, 80.
11. Elaine Gill, Introduction to Mountain Moving Day, p. 8.
12. "Tell It Like It Is," Small Press Review 11, vol. 3, no. 3: 3.
13. No Visible Means of Support, p. 41. The remaining poems quoted are from this collection.
14. Poems: Selected and New, 1950-1974 (New York: W. W. Norton, 1975), p. 228.
15. The Will to Change (New York: W. W. Norton, 1971), p. 13.
16. Diving into the Wreck, p. 17.
17. "When We Dead Awaken: Writing as Re-Vision," College English 34 (October 1972): 21-22.

18.  W. H. Auden, Introduction to A Change of World (New
     Haven, Conn. :  Yale University Press, 1951), p. ii.
19.  "Poetry and Experience:  Statement at a Poetry Reading,
     1964," in Gelpi and Gelpi, eds. , Adrienne Rich's
     Poetry, p. 89.
20.  Snapshots of a Daughter-in-Law (New York:  W. W.
     Norton, 1967).
21.  "When We Dead Awaken:  Poetry as Re-Vision," p. 24.
22.  Ibid.
23.  Necessities of Life (New York:  W. W. Norton, 1966),
     p. 22.
24.  Leaflets (New York:  W. W. Norton, 1969), p. 42.
25.  Kalstone, "Talking with Adrienne Rich," p. 58.
26.  Ibid.
27.  "Caryatid," American Poetry Review 2, no. 3 (May/
     June, 1973):  11.
28.  Kalstone, "Talking with Adrienne Rich," p. 59.
29.  "When We Dead Awaken:  Writing as Re-Vision," p. 25.
30.  T. S. Eliot, Selected Essays (New York:  Harcourt,
     Brace & Co. , 1950), p. 247.
31.  Kenneth Burke, "Lexicon Rhetoricae" in Counter-State-
     ment (Los Altos, Calif. :  Hermes, 1953), p. 124.

R L Widmann

# THE POETRY OF CYNTHIA MACDONALD*

Cynthia MacDonald's Amputations[1] is a collection of
stark visions, of the "grotesque," of the minutiae of living,
of the archetypal "American experience," an articulation of
victimization.  Her poems in this volume range widely in
subject matter, but underlying all of them are her witty perceptions of the kinds of realities shown in Diane Arbus' relentless camera.  But MacDonald goes beyond Arbus in stark-
ness of presentation.  Where Arbus is content to show us
the shell of people, MacDonald goes inside the skull of the
shell.  What we see is not especially pleasant, but MacDonald's elan in presenting it mitigates the horror (if only slightly), so as to make bearable and tolerable that which, from
our mythic or collective unconscious, is essentially unbearable
and intolerable.

Despite a tendency toward images of nightmare, madness, and fantasy, MacDonald does not write from a position
of woman-as-poet-and-incipiently-mad, as do the confessional
poets, Plath and Sexton.  Rather, MacDonald chooses as terrain the emotional minefields of the "American experience"
and deals with maturing women, passing through adolescence
into motherhood, in novel and provocative ways.

The themes in Amputations are powerful ones.  Mac-
Donald confesses to the arbitrary strangeness of the experience of being a poet in "Breaking Seals" where the persona
is Esmerelda, the Seal Lady Wizard, who tames seals just
as MacDonald tames the words that she stuffs into her own
poems.  Or, she examines the nuclear family and finds it
not only wanting and destructive, but especially silly, as in
the poem, "A Family of Dolls' House Dolls," narrated by a
persona who is both girl child and adult woman; here the

*Reprinted by permission of the author and publisher from
Concerning Poetry 7, 1 (Spring 1974), 19-26.  Copyright ©
1974 by Concerning Poetry.

doll family either fights or denigrates each other.   Or, the
anxieties of motherhood are depicted in "Twice Too Long,"
where a mother bears a dwarf who will then not stop growing.
This mother's journey to an endocrinologist only results in
the application of female hormones, which encourage the mon-
ster-child to keep growing to the enormous height of eleven
feet.   The mother, having attempted to "compress or ampu-
tate," is carted off to Bellevue and the child lives in the
living room, chewing up any observers who declare it is
"too long," and depositing them "in the plant-filled Minton
jardiniere (where/ They make excellent fertilizer)," for, as
MacDonald concludes, "It believes in growing things." The
hideous irony and puns of this poem inform most others in
the collection.   Motherhood and the position of woman-as-
creator-and-nurturer are depicted savagely and clearly.

MacDonald certainly depicts the Woman as Outsider.
MacDonald's searing and caustic vision, though, is reserved
for the readers who are able to confront the pain of amputation from old castes of thought, old molds, old categories.
American women, far too accustomed to Us-As-Castrating-
Bitch, will revel in the poem, "Objets d'Art," where the
persona, obviously female and seventeen, enters a men's
room in the Dakar Station, where a man tells her, "You're
a real ball cutter" ($\ell$. 3).   Rather than cringe in shame at
having been detected and thereby "named," the persona turns
this social gaffe from infelicity into imagistic truth, for she
goes on, "I thought about that/ For months and finally de-
cided/ He was right" ($\ell\ell$. 3-5).   The poem then sweeps on
through a recounting of her collection and perfecting of methods.   She admits, "Until then/ I had never thought of trophies" ($\ell\ell$. 7-8).   As a dutiful American, given to collecting
trash and impedimentia of all kinds, the persona approaches
the problem of preservation seriously and thoughtfully.   After
she finds that "pickling worked/ But was a lot of trouble,"
she discovers that American technology has the answer:   "Freez-
ing" ($\ell\ell$. 9-10).   And shortly the first freezer "is filled
with rows and rows of/ Pink and purple lumps encased in
Saran Wrap" ($\ell\ell$. 13-14).   The reader is, of course, shocked.
But the shock comes not from any precious morality, lingering in our Puritan consciousness.   Rather, MacDonald's tech-
niques shock the reader, who sees that the poet is attempting
to articulate and be arbiter between the woman's unspoken
fantasy and its actualization in time and space.   American
women are too often cast as objects of shame and denigration
as either a whore/scarlet woman or as Virgin Mother; both
images in American literature are stultifying and limiting.

MacDonald's persona in "Objets d'Art" represents a great
leap upward and forward.  She is no longer frozen in traditions clearly outmoded, is not domesticated to psychoanalytic
Freudianism or unsatisfactory roles; this persona looks at
us and says, "I'm willing to cut you up, baby, should you
wish to be cut."  Here is a woman acting out her psychic
experience of confrontation and its accompanying oppressive-
ness, both of which cause distressing conforming to traditional roles in male-female sexual experiences.  This persona, adopting the role of the gutsy seventeen-year old who
is shoved smack-dab up against the reality of male fantasy
that all women are castrators at heart, turns the male fantasy against itself, as she becomes the model of wife-mother-
of-the-plains/frontier, who is a Preserver.  But instead of
canning beans, tomatoes, dill pickles, this persona preserves
testicles.

        The second stanza of the poem moves into new ter-
ritory.  We learn that she has "more subjects than I can
handle,/ But only volunteers" (ℓℓ. 15-16).  American males,
domesticated to violence of the spirit and the person, willingly accede to this persona.  She turns the down-home, folksy
craft of making preserves into the fantastic and grotesque
mode of the "art like hypnosis" (ℓ. 16) where the victim
must be willing.  In MacDonald's harsh judgment, the American male, fraught with anxieties about his sexual potencies,
willingly seeks the bitch or whore who will castrate him,
commercialize him.  The poem bitterly concludes:

If you desire further information about the process and
The benefits, please drop in any night from nine to twelve.
My place is east of Third on Fifty-sixth.
You'll know it by the three gold ones over the door
                                              [ℓℓ. 17-20].

As we are jerked from the homespun American Frontier spirit of the first stanza, into the crass commercialization of
the second, we recognize the mythic quality of MacDonald's
art.  She, in celebration of archetypes, here says that we
are all victims and castrators.  Although women have been
chiefly defined as castrators, the complicity of the males in
allowing and encouraging detesticularization has been an impetus in maintaining this degrading and dehumanizing experience.  As MacDonald shows us in the second stanza, we
can only draw the conclusion that victims (males) are in
control of the fantasies of the victimizers (females).  The
victimizers or castrators, as good American consumers,

buy sufficient Saran Wrap and Amana freezers to preserve
the ill-gotten spoils of a sexual war, a war apparently initiated by its victims, the males.   The continuation of such
a battle is blamed on its females, seen as mythic figures.
The witty confrontation of traditional (and ill-founded) categories by this sprightly persona declares that cant is cant,
in whatever time and place.   Should we, as readers, mis-
takenly suppose that either the persona or MacDonald is suggesting that women are whores, the second stanza makes
quite clear that it is the merchandizing of sex, capitalism,
the bartering of sex in the tawdry pawn shops of the soul,
all of these are what debase sex and not the woman, either
in her person or in her fantasies.   And it is here that Mac-
Donald is qualified to speak for humanity, male or female,
in the sexual war.   Her sympathy for the plight of the female
allows her to create a persona who understands and condemns
traditional categories.   This persona is not one for game-
playing, for she understands and condemns the general, cosmic disturbances of the American male psyche.

        What MacDonald is doing in "Objets d'Art," as she
does in others in the collection, is to refine notions of what
victim and castrator are.   It is customary for women, who
are dislocated subjects and secondary citizens in both America and Canada, to turn the violence inward, to go mad, to
commit suicide, to answer the indictment of females-as-people
or females-as-writers in personal terms.   Hence, the unbearable life of Sylvia Plath finds its resolution in a gas oven
in a cold winter in 1963.   Or Anne Sexton goes mad and is
hospitalized.   Or Margaret Atwood shows us the woman im-
paled on a fish hook in Power Politics[2] or presents her wan-
dering bleakly through the woods, away from civilization in
search of her father and her self, as in Surfacing. [3]   But
MacDonald shows us another kind of woman, one who confronts the horror of living and one who nevertheless shouts
with great courage that she will survive, even if to do so
means that she must pass herself off as a pawnbroker of
spirit, as in "Objets d'Art."

        In another poem, "Inventory," the first person nar-
rator is again used.   The first stanza tells us that she carries a suitcase everywhere with her and that the weight varies,
depending on its contents.   Counterpoised nicely against the
formless, colloquial language of the introductory three lines
is the following catalogue:

                A down-filled pillow, a gray Army
                blanket, a package of Droste bitter

> orange chocolate, my tape recorder
> with a tape of Der Freischütz, boots,
> sea-water from Vancouver Bay, next
> rooms opened by Nemerov, Lotte Lehmann's
> "Ich" and my Grandmother's trunk [ℓℓ. 4-10].

Here, the impedimentia and minutiae of daily living, which
is characterized by collecting goods by Americans, is satirized and defined for the rampant idiocy that it is.   A busi-
nessman's slim attache case, ever ready and ever practical,
cannot compare with the suitcase or emotional baggage that
a woman carries with her.   Its practicality, however, is
limited and illustrated by its ability to recapture remembrance
of things past, a time when this woman lived with zest, and
so lived because she connected her fantasy life with her cultural life and with her individual past.   Yet MacDonald's
persona also repudiates easy explanations for her memories.

The next stanza begins, "The case is useful, but
doesn't justify it; I can't/ Justify it. "   The pun on "case"
as suitcase and as circumstances of the persona's life is
necessary for the hard, dry integrity of the poem.   Not content to fill her present with trivialities of the past, she constructs a new catalogue, beginning with the same elements,
but taking new directions after the pillow and blanket:

> blanket, typewriter and Corrasable
> Bond, a bowl of agates from Saudi
> Arabia, popcorn, Buddenbrooks, pieces
> of a red glass DANGER sign on which
> I'd cut my knee when I was five
> and disobeyed and walked on Milton Road,
> three fur hats and my Grandmother's trunk [ℓℓ. 15-21].

Now the act of writing is itself important and made mock of;
the persona tempts us into an easy, Freudian reading:  look
at the scar I got as a child for Disobedience.   She uses the
implements of contemporary writing (paper and typewriter)
and its sources (Buddenbrooks, which symbolizes cultural
history rather than personal history), but as the catalogue
winds its way along, the focus is re-directed from girl child
to woman-as-accumulator of three fur hats.   Thus MacDonald
makes further irony of a circumstance in which the reader
is tempted to acknowledge the psychic scars of a nasty childhood on a sensitive and quivering babe; grandmother's trunk,
reappearing here, begins to sound like an albatross around
the neck of the fantasizing artist.

The third stanza changes focus from the persona as artist to a presentation of her as mad, beset by paranoia and egotism. Next she meets Gunther, and they decide to go to a show at the Whitney; she declares parenthetically that the suitcase must be what he remembers best about her. The narrator, obsessed with herself, her trivialities of memories and emotional clutter, condemns her acquaintances (personified by Gunther) to providing relief from the albatross as she obtrudes the baggage on to them. She forces Gunther into a conventional male response, that of gallantly offering to carry the suitcase, so that she can reject him and the offer.

The next image presented of the suitcase is that it is rather like her unborn baby, sticking between her and the dinner table, causing her to "look messy" (ℓ. 37). With some deliberate irony, the persona blames the case for interfering with personal relationships, but she continues to be unable to relinquish this suitcase.

As she and Gunther get into bed, the suitcase provides an impediment to successful or satisfactory intercourse and the phrasing is wittily poised against the arrangement of the lines on the page:

Making me look messy. When we got in bed it was
        the same old story:
Three of us. To spell it out: my case gets between me
And friends, especially
If they are not agile or are easily bruised [ℓℓ. 37-40].

She retreats to the bathtub, and in the verses preceding the last indented catalogue, shows us a handful of the images she will condense, compact, and circumscribe simply by the act of cataloguing them. Thus, the last catalogue is a wistful reprise, using the envelope technique of retaining the first two items and the familiar last one:

A down-filled pillow, a gray Army
blanket, a hate note to the editor
of a certain magazine, my radio,
an empty cordial cherry box, Beowulf,
a tube of Gunther's cobalt blue,
my left-handed father's left index
finger and my Grandmother's trunk [ℓℓ. 49-55].

So we see the persona in the act of process which is progress.

As she has learned to live with her suitcase and the structural elements which determine the suitcase's contents, those contents become capable of being changed. Although such change may be arbitrary and beyond the control of the persona, as in the second catalogue in "Inventory," by the time that she has adjusted herself to the vengeful rejection of Gunther (and there is no suggestion that Gunther did not deserve his fate), she is able to control some elements of what must be installed in the suitcase in the third catalogue. Her present life in the third listing finally seems to be controlling future developments in her psychic life, for things from the moment present are used to establish a catalogue which is a resolution of psychic trauma and torment. She tells us that she lies in the bathtub eating cordial cherries, while reading of heroic deeds in Beowulf, which typifies and symbolizes conflict between humans, rather than returning to Buddenbrooks and its depiction of dessicated human relationships, and does these things while listening to her radio of Pop Culture.

The concluding line of the poem, "It's true; it is really true; that is the case" ($\ell$. 56), makes clear the pun on suitcase and circumstances of the persona's life. Additionally, the line, if read meditatively, describes a process of coming to knowledge on the part of the persona. She has finally integrated the meanings of her past, is willing to be responsible for her actions of the present, and is certain that these two elements of experience, in examination and re-examination of the past and during integration of the present, will lead her to understanding the process of self-discovery. The suitcase's contents do not change in an arbitrary way; the persona has only thought that they have. Rather, she is capable of selecting, of abstracting, of holding up to the light of close scrutiny, those elements which are typical of aspects of her experiences. When she is able to control what appears in the catalogue, then she has attained the verbal and artistic control necessary to the word-taming artist. What appears to be yet another comment from a poet for a blessed rage for order now extends itself into demonstrating that such rage can be resolved in terms of knowledge. That order can be imposed is shown in the skillful development of the last catalogue. The persona, however, must come to terms with the knowledge that she has gained in the poem; the last line is necessary to prove to the reader that the persona has learned some lessons. Assertions of "it's true," are not mere childish fancy, but rather are philosophical verifications of her examination of the process she has undergone in making her inventory.

The reader also needs to consider how "Inventory" is
part of the pattern of Amputations. The only mention of a
severing of part of the human body comes in the last catalogue where the "left index finger" ($\ell$. 54) appears. The
second catalogue does show the poet cutting herself as a
child, but she does not undergo a physical amputation. Rather, it is her father who has suffered a physical cutting off.
The persona herself separates her senses of personal history
from the people able to hurt her in the present. It is only
through cutting herself from her father and grandmother that
she herself can live. Thus she neatly juxtaposes the real,
amputated finger to the Grandmother's trunk.

The third poem to deal with cutting as a metaphor
for breaking of bonds between people, especially members
of a family, is "Departure," in which a mother carefully
preserves the feet her son cuts off before leaving home.
The son, who is obviously more self-aware than the persona
at the beginning of "Inventory," knows that he must cut to
survive. He does so. And MacDonald picks up the poem
from that point, choosing to trace the maunderings of the
sentimental mother, who narrates. She keeps the feet in a
velvet-lined box and puts the son's occasional picture post
cards, which depict the Corn Palace, Mormon Tabernacle,
Astrodome, and Mt. Rainier, above the gilt table, which
holds the box of feet.

MacDonald again uses irony to great advantage in the
development of the poem. The first line says, "When he cut
off his feet I knew he was leaving ... " and the next begins
with the biting parody of conventional mothers' normal reactions, as this one sighs, "A mother's instinct." By using
the cliché and conventional phrase after the grotesque introductory line, MacDonald, by developing a conventional and
slightly stupid narrator, again shows up cant for cant. If
mothers are to be all-indulgent, no matter what the sons do,
then these women will be comfortable in their repudiations
of responsibility; if they assume that the actions of the children are predictable, knowable, and easily categorized, then
they deserve to be satirized, with the meaningless umbrella
of "mother's instinct" as a viable method of linguistic attack.

MacDonald goes on to develop the narrator as hopelessly sentimental in the first stanza; she presents a weak-
minded mother who relies on the comfortable "Everyone said
so" ($\ell$. 5), for corroboration of her belief that the son must
leave her. She cries over his corrugated toenails, calls

up the past in clichéd conventional phrasing and syntax:  "How
many times I had notched/ Those nails to ease a swollen
corner" (ℓℓ. 9-10).  And she tells us that she, "kissed the
heels" (ℓ. 11).  Rather than having given birth to and having
reared an Achilles, an Apollo, or a Mercury, this woman
has borne a normal human son, who responds to their separation in a normal way; he sends her post cards.  She makes
a normal response of putting a want ad in the newspaper,
with the clichéd and dull message, "Come back, Scott,/ Mother misses you" (ℓℓ. 18-19).  Because she has acceded to
his initial amputation and departure, her want ad is self-
indulgent; MacDonald underscores the idiocy of it by leaving
the exact content of the newspaper message unclear.  It may
end with "Mother misses you" or it may continue through
the rest of this concluding stanza:

> Mother misses you.  I will give you everything or
>     nothing,
> Whichever you need.  Your bed is freshly made
>     with striped sheets;
> Spaghetti sauce and pies are in the freezer.
> I love you.  I have kept the feet in perfect condition
>     [ℓℓ. 19-22].

If the message is the entire stanza, then the doltish mother
is shown to be desperate in her pulling in the apron strings.
If she has concluded the ad with "misses you," then the rest
of the stanza is an articulation of the madness latent in this
woman who has lost her son through overpossessiveness.
She promises him anything, so that he will come back to her
on her own terms.

    The amputated feet now take on an even more startling
aspect.  In the first and second stanzas, the feet are symbolic
of the growing son, a smaller human who is under the control
of an adult.  But in the last stanza, they become symbolic
of the frustrated desires and wishes of the mother to retain
the body of the child, even though he has become an adult.
The polymorphous perverseness of the childhood phase has
never been surrendered by the woman speaking the poem;
she focusses her uncontrolled desire on the feet of her son.
Through the ironic reversal, with the son/child as thinker
and the mother/adult as child and non-cognitive, MacDonald
underscores the dangers of a woman who devotes her life to
her children and then fails to acknowledge that the children
will grow and leave her nest.

    And MacDonald, in concluding the second stanza with

"He has left me alone/ With souvenirs and my spondees"
(ℓℓ. 16-17), moves the mother out of the conventional home-
body, home-making figure she apparently is.  If this persona
is a poet, then we must look for the spondees; they appear
in predictable places in the concluding stanza.  We find:
"back, Scott," "love you," "have kept," "the feet."  The
message in the spondees is the message in miniature which
the poem is intended to convey by the persona.  MacDonald's
message and meaning surely must be different.  If the narrator really is a poet, she should have more perceptions
about the reality of the mother-son relationship depicted in
"Departure" and should not retreat into conventional terms
and phrases in discussing amputation.  This poem fails, ultimately, because of the variance between the narrator's
comments and MacDonald's witty intrusions as a skillful poet,
who deliberately directs and controls the voice of the narrator.  MacDonald allows her reader to see that MacDonald
has put herself into the poem and the authorial intrusion is
troublesome.

These three poems, then, "Objets d'Art," "Inventory,"
and "Departure," are representative of the work of Cynthia
MacDonald.  She has a fine gift for the jugular, often attacks,
often satirizes, as the grotesque amputees of body and soul
are set before us.  MacDonald has a good gift for irony and
uses it forcefully in all three poems.  She is a powerful
poet, with intense promise and fine perceptions.


## REFERENCES

1.  Quotations are from Cynthia MacDonald, Amputations
        (New York: George Braziller, 1972).
2.  See Margaret Atwood, Power Politics (New York:  Harper
        & Row, 1971).
3.  See Margaret Atwood, Surfacing (New York:  Simon &
        Schuster, 1973).

Beth Miller

WOMEN AND FEMINISM
IN THE WORKS OF ROSARIO CASTELLANOS*

When discussing women writers in Mexico, it has
become customary to begin by mentioning Sor Juana Inés de
la Cruz, the seventeenth-century Jeronymite poetess. The
next most frequently mentioned Mexican woman writer is
Rosario Castellanos. Unlike the nun, who was markedly
individualistic, Castellanos developed a habit of mind which
permitted her to see her personal problems as social ones,
to identify her subjective experiences with those of women
historically, to understand sex roles as cultural and women's
struggles as political. A young Mexican critic, José Emilio
Pacheco wrote at Castellanos' death in August of 1974: "When
the commotion passes and people reread her works, what
will become evident is that nobody in her time has as clear
a consciousness as she did of the meaning of the double condition of woman and Mexican. And no one else has made
that consciousness the subject matter of a literary production,
the central line of a body of work. Of course we didn't know
how to read her."[1]

The "double condition" of woman and Mexican, as
Pacheco calls it, is something Castellanos understood from
earliest childhood: "I had a brother a year younger than I.
He was born with a privilege no one could dispute: he was
male. But in order to help maintain a certain equilibrium
in our relationship, our parents recognized that the right of
primogeniture had fallen to me. And that if he won people
over with his charm, intelligence, and easygoing nature, I,
however, had whiter skin."[2]

*A first version of this essay was presented at the Conference
on Latin American Women Writers, Carnegie-Mellon University, Pittsburgh, in March 1975. It appeared in Spanish in
the Revista de la Universidad de México 30, 4 (1975-1976),
33-38. It is printed here in English by permission of the
author.

In "Malinche," the embracing of literary tradition (pre-Columbian poetry, Greco-Roman drama) adds dimension to Castellanos' sketch of a woman and universalizes its cultural particulars--a matrilinear inheritance of rejection and covert competition, a paternal legacy of abandonment and alienation. Malinche's search for identity is not that of a divided self, but that of an outsider, a displaced person, attempting to understand her lost birthright, to recover a sense of roots in language and the past, and to find in these a source of courage and a path to the blurred world.

## MALINCHE

From the throne my mother announced: "He's
      dead."
And she let herself fall, without spirit,
into the arms of the other, the usurper, the
      stepfather
who kept her not with the respect
a servant owes the majesty of a queen,
but with that mutual depression
which humiliates lovers and accomplices.

From the Plaza of Interchanges
my mother said: "He's dead."

The balance
stayed still for a motionless second
and that grain of cacao silent in the chest
and the sun remained in the middle of the sky
as if waiting for a sign
which was, when it burst like an arrow,
the first sharp oh of the weepers.

"The many-petaled flower is stripped,
perfume evaporated,
torch flame consumed.

A young girl returns, scraping along, to a place
where a midwife discarded a placenta.

She returns to the Place of Those who Lived.

And recognizes her murdered father,
oh, oh, oh, by poison, dagger
snare at his feet, rope around his neck.

They take hands and they walk, walk, losing them-
      selves in the mist."

Thus they wept, thus lamented
over an anonymous corpse, a body

not mine since I was sold
to the merchants and went as a slave,
a nobody, into exile.

Dismissed, expelled
from the kingdom, from the palace, and from
      the warm insides
of the one who bore me in a legitimate bridal
      bed
and despised me for being her equal
in form and rank
and contemplated herself in me and hated her
      image
and destroyed the mirror against the ground

I advance enchained toward destiny
and leave behind the lingering,
funereal sounds of my burial.

And my mother's voice decreeing
with tears (with tears!) my death. [3]

      Castellanos is expert at conveying feminist statement
through literary allusion and dramatic monologue.    Malinche/
Electra is not Woman, but a woman, one with whose suffering
the poet identifies her own.    Similarly, Dido's memories of
her girlhood in "Lamentación de Dido" (Dido's Lament) are
abstract and impersonal enough to evoke the generalized
experience of time lost, capacities wasted, and boredom:

      The way I spent my youth:  performing
      small domestic chores,
      celebrating daily rites
      attending solemn civil ceremonies [p. 93].

Castellanos has said that this poem is "a kind of interior
biography transfigured by a great metaphor, Dido."[4]    Here
again her re-creation of literary, historical, and legendary
figures provides vehicles for connecting personal and social
experience.

      There are few aspects of life--childhood to childbirth,
puberty to divorce--not covered in Castellanos' poetry.    In
her choice of such themes she recalls Alfonsina Storni, an
Argentine poet who committed suicide in 1938, from whose
works Castellanos first learned how to use irony for social
protest and self-defense.    Her social concerns sometimes
lead necessarily to moral imagery and to political statement,
as in "Emblema de la virtuosa" (Emblem of a Virtuous Woman) and "Memorial de Tlatelolco" (about the student uprising

and slaughter in Mexico City in 1968). [5]

The image of woman in "Metamorfosis de la hechicera" (Metamorphosis of a Witch) is "obedient and sad" and full of wiles:

> A woman, she had her masks
> and played at deceiving herself
> and everyone else                    [p. 205].

In a militantly feminist essay, "La mujer y su imagen" (Woman and her Image), Castellanos analyzes this stereotype in political terms: "Women have been accused of being hypocrites, and the accusation is not without ground. But hypocrisy is the response of the oppressed to their oppressors, of weak persons to strong, of subordinates to a master. Hypocrisy is ... a self-defensive conditioned reflex--like a chameleon's protective change in color--when there are many dangers and not many options. "[6]

Another recurrent "feminine trait" in Castellanos' work, one which she explored obsessively, is patience. While deception may be considered a weapon, patience implies inaction, mere passivity:

> filling up the empty space
> with invented dialogues and men,
>
> the spinster waits and waits and waits. [7]

Both themes are significant because of the threat these traditional characteristics pose to personal authenticity (or psychological integration) and, therefore, to dynamic social and political participation. Castellanos credits women themselves with being the effective transmitters and most patient teachers of passivity:

> My mother used to say:
> Patience is precious as gold. [8]

For her character Hecuba, as for Castellanos herself, femininity becomes a hard act to swallow:

> Someone attends my dying, makes
> me sip a difficult docility. [9]

Castellanos puts it eloquently in an essay: "The audacity to investigate oneself, the need to make oneself conscious of

the meaning of one's own bodily existence or the unheard of
pretension of conferring meaning on one's own spiritual existence is severely repressed and punished by the social
apparatus.   Society has decreed ... that the only legitimately
feminine attitude is waiting. ...   Sacrificed, like Iphigenia on
the patriarchal altars, a woman doesn't die:   she just waits"
(Mujer, p. 14).

      Castellanos' women suffer, but often ironically.   Even
in her own case, suffering was learned ("I was taught to
cry").   In her poem entitled "Autorretrato" (Self-portrait),
she claims:

> I suffer more out of habit and by inheritance--
> so as not to be too different from my line--
> than from any concrete causes          [p.  298].

The "line" she speaks of is matrilinear.   A mother tells her
daughter in Castellanos' poetic drama "Salomé":

> ... My sisters
> have hells of their own.
> I was brought up to obey
> and suffer in silence. [10]

Little girls are brought up to be like their mothers, and
femininity is bestowed breast to breast:

> Instead of milk what my mother
> fed me was subjection. [11]

      In "Lecciones de cosas" (Lessons about Things) Cas-
tellanos blames the miseducation of women on the patriarchal
system:

> They taught me things mistakenly,
> the ones who teach about things:
> fathers and teachers and priests.
> For they told me, You have to be good.
> It's enough to be good.   The good
> receive medals, heaven, candy, love    [p.  307].

      Castellanos sees these feminine traits as a series of
constants in the feminine ideal of Western culture through
the centuries and traces them back to Christianity:   "The
strong woman who appears in the Holy Scriptures is strong
because of her prenuptial purity, her fidelity to her husband,
her devotion to her children, her laboriousness in the house,

her care and prudence in administering a patrimony which she wasn't able to possess or inherit. Her virtues are constancy, loyalty, patience, chastity, submission, humility, caution, abnegation, the spirit of sacrifice, the governing of all her acts by the evangelical precept that the meek will inherit the earth" (Mujer, p. 22). Those particular virtues have been used of course to restrict a woman's possibilities and keep her at home. The shrunken world-view is reflected in the famous lines of Emily Dickinson, which Castellanos translates:

> Jamás he visto un páramo
> y no conozco el mar
>
> (I never saw a Moor--
> I never saw the Sea--)[12]

Castellanos, with practiced understatement, is able to create tragedy out of soap-opera materials. In the following excerpt from "Monólogo de la extranjera" (Monologue of a Foreign Woman), the traditional verses (lines mainly of seven and eleven syllables) and religious vocabulary help make her case. Her intentionally hackneyed phrasing ("supreme pride," "supreme renunciation") make the painful turn of phrase at the end neatly effective:

> Supreme pride is found
> in supreme renunciation. I refused
> to be an extinguished star
> that comes alive by borrowed light.
> Without a name, without a memory,
> in spectral nudity I revolve
> in a brief domestic orbit. [13]

The "domestic orbit" of an Indian woman's experience is poignant in this monologue, one of Castellanos' earliest and best known. The poem dramatically combines Mexican social reality and myth:

> I came from far away. I forgot my country.
> I no longer understand the language
> they use there for coin and tool.
> I've achieved the mineral muteness of a statue. [14]

If Castellanos shows how women are turned into patient spinsters and silent statues, she also shows how their closed galleries nurture ignorance and triviality. Along with docility and goodness they are taught a sexist "golden rule":

> Here is the golden rule, the secret of order:
> have a place for everything
> and everything
> in its place.... 15

Much of Castellanos' later poetry is what has come
to be called "open," that is, not dependent on metaphor.
This trend, most evident in her last works, is historically
significant in that it represents the accomplishment of a
sought-after break with the dominant symbolist tradition--a
much discussed goal of her contemporaries in the Generation
of 1950 from the time they were schoolmates at the National
University. 16   Secondly, to the degree that it is true that a
poem may present "its case and its meaning by the very
form it assumes" (William Carlos Williams), the "social-
realist" mode is appropriate for Castellanos for much the
same reasons as the dramatic monologue form and the literary allusions to legendary women.   In "Kinsey Report,"
for example, the woman's tone of voice is confessional, but
Castellanos provides a necessary parody in order to state
her case:

> ... And one day I know
> my Blue Prince will come.   (I've
> prayed to Saint Anthony for a miracle.)   And
> then we'll be happy.   Forever in love [p. 330].

"Mirando a la Gioconda" (Looking at the Mona Lisa) is equally humorous, but more obviously self-conscious and more
overt as political satire:

> If I were Sor Juana
> or Malinche or--not to abandon folklore--
> some incarnation of the Güera Rodríguez17
> (as you can see, like Gide, I'm an extremist)
> you'd probably consider me
> a representative social specimen
> of some Third World country.        [p. 335].

A "Third World specimen," Castellanos explores the
root of machismo, which she believes has a double source.
Mexico, she writes in her essay, "The Participation of Mexican Women in Formal Education," is heir not only to the
European culture of the fifteenth and sixteenth centuries, but
to a series of severly patriarchal civilizations.   The Conquest
brought about a deeply divided culture in which "the violence
of the clash between conquerors and conquered came to pre-
side even over sexual unions" (Mujer, p. 25).

Castellanos was a woman who read women. She has acknowledged the early influence not only of Storni, but of Juana de Ibarbourou and, especially, of Gabriela Mistral, the 1945 Nobel prizewinner. 18 The anti-symbolist direction is already apparent as early as 1959 in poems such as "La velada del sapo" (The Toad's Watch) whose featured animal recalls Marianne Moore's "poetry garden" with "real frogs." In Al pie de la letra (Starting from Scratch, 1959) and Lívida luz (Livid Light, 1960), her poetry is less abstract and intellectual, increasingly socially committed. As she sees her own evolution: "Among slow echoes I began to recognize my own voice. ... Three threads to follow: humor, grave meditation, and contact with my rootedness in history and my body" (Mujer, p. 207). Her poetry of the fifties benefits from her intermediate experiments in prose writing and perhaps somewhat from her work experience at the Instituto de Ciencias y Artes de Chiapas (1952), the Centro Coordinador del Instituto Indigenista de San Cristóbal de las Casas (1956-57), the Instituto Indigenista de México (1958-61).

By 1960, her esthetic values have changed, and the world, as she sees it, is no longer "an object of contemplation, but ... a battle ground for the struggle we're engaged in." 19 The title of the 1960 volume (Lívida luz) is a reminder of death, emphasizing the necessity for choice and signaling acts of self-recognition through creation, as in "Destino" (Destiny):

> The deer goes for a drink. The water
> reflects the figure of a tiger [p. 171].

En la tierra de en medio (In No One's Land), published in the collected works of 1972, bears an epigraph from T. S. Eliot: "Human kind/ cannot bear very much reality." Laced with humor and confidence, the poetry is tough in its statement--as announced by the title of the opening poem, "Bella dama sin piedad" (Belle Dame Sans Merci). It is lucid and honest poetry, sometimes too simple, but often deceptively simple ("Malinche"). It is generally very open (e. g. , "Autorretrato") and contemporary (e. g. , "Valium 10"--the name of a tranquilizer). Many of the feminist monologues recall earlier poems such as "Emblema de la virtuosa," in Materia memorable (Memorable Materials, 1969), and "Jornada de la soltera," in Lívida luz. The tierra de en medio of the title is a no-place place which Castellanos uses mainly to describe her spiritual condition as a woman writer in contemporary Mexico. Her usage of the term in

an earlier autobiographical prose passage makes its tenor,
I think, clear (she is writing of her first difficult days at
the University): "But, oh, like Sor Juana, like the trans-
planted Spaniards, like so many Mexicans not yet recovered
from the Conquest, I was living [in a state of] nepantla."[20]
The feeling evoked is akin to the alienation described by
Storni and Sylvia Plath.

Castellanos' identification with other women, whether
illiterate Indian peasants or nineteenth-century noblewomen,
fictional heroines or historical villains, may be ascribed to
her radical feminism:[21]

> No, the solution is not
> to throw yourself before a train like
>       Tolstoi's Anna
> nor to swallow arsenic like Madame Bovary
> nor to wait on the plains of Avila
> for an angel's dart
> before you put your shawl on your head
> and begin to act.
>
> Nor to study geometric laws by counting
> the timbers of your prison cell
> as Sor Juana did.   The solution is not
> to write, while the visitors arrive,
> in the living room of the Austen family
> nor to lock yourself up in the attic
> of some New England residence
> and dream, with the Dickinson Bible
> under your spinster pillow.
>
> There has to be another way ...
>    . .
>
> Another way to be human and free.
>
> Another way of being. [22]

In her literary work as in her life, Castellanos went
far in search of "another way of being."   She is significant
as a prose writer, not only for her novels and short stories,
but as critic, essayist, and journalist.   It has been said that
Balún-Canán is the novel which opened the way for what was
to be called the "boom" of the contemporary novel and that
its success abroad, in translation, made the boom possible.
It has also been said that the articles Castellanos published
from 1964 to 1969 in Excelsior, the oldest and most prestigious Mexican daily, anticipated the journalism of the seven-

ties.[23]  These articles were later collected into two volumes,
Juicios sumarios (Summary Judgments, 1966) and Mujer que
sabe latín (Intellectual Woman, 1973).

The earlier collection includes two essays on Sor
Juana, one on Saint Teresa, three on Simone de Beauvoir,
and one on Virginia Woolf (and mentions of Ana María Matute,
Nathalie Sarraute, Simone Weil, and other women writers).
The 1972 collection contains essays on such writers as María
Luisa Bombal, Ivy Compton-Burnett, Isak Dinesen, Betty
Friedan, Penelope Gilliat, Natalie Ginzburg, Lillian Hellman,
Violette Leduc, Doris Lessing, Clarice Lispector, Mary Mc-
Carthy, Silvina Ocampo, Flannery O'Connor, Mercedes Ro-
doreda, Corín Tellado, Elsa Triolet, Simone Weil, Eudora
Welty, and Virginia Woolf.  Castellanos also includes little-
known nineteenth-century writers such as Fanny Calderón de
la Barca, internationally famous writers such as Katherine
Mansfield and Agatha Christie, contemporary writers in Mex-
ico such as Ulalume González de León and María Luisa de
Mendoza.

Although Castellanos writes that in Mexican literature
"the gallery of feminine portraits is not very abundant, very
varied, or very profound" (Mujer, p. 159), she does what
she can to correct the situation, examining a wide variety
of feminine literary images (Anna Karenina, Melibea, Hedda
Gabbler, Dorotea, Celestina), cultural ideals, archetypes
(Eve, Lucretia Borgia, the Virgin Mary) and stereotypes
(by class and geographic location in her fiction).  In one
brief essay Castellanos discusses the three major images of
women in Mexico and their significance:  the Virgin of Gua-
dalupe, Malinche, and Sor Juana.  The first is revered beyond religion, is all good; the second, all sexual, dangerous,
seductive, destructive of morality and culture; the third, an
unconventional woman (a female intellectual in the seventeenth
century), one whose femininity "was always an hypothesis"
and who would have liked to be beyond sex roles.  She is
to be admired, in Castellanos' view, especially because "in
spite of all the resistance and all the obstacles in her milieu,
she exercised her vocation as a writer and transformed it
into a body of work."[24]

According to Elena Poniatowska, the thesis Castellanos
wrote for her degree at the University of Mexico, Sobre cultura femenina (On Feminine Culture, 1950), which denied the
existence of a specifically feminine culture, represents "the
intellectual point of departure for Women's Liberation in

Mexico."[25]  Coming from Mexico's top woman journalist,
and a feminist one, that comment pays a more significant
homage to Rosario Castellanos--who died last August in Tel
Aviv where she was serving as Mexico's Ambassador to
Israel--than even her burial in the "Rotonda de los Hombres
Ilustres" (Rotunda of Illustrious Men), the first woman writer
to be so honored.   Yet, of course, there is a contradiction.
Why deny the existence of femininity and then devote hundreds
of pages to defining it, tracing it through biographies, writings, and literary images of women--except for feminist ends?
Obviously, it is useful to know the tradition, the terrain,
and the charges before setting out to build a case.

        Her voice, changing and tentative, questions and de-
clares.  Castellanos' broad preparation in history, anthropology, and literature provides her with perspectives from
which to judge the women writers she discusses.  She says,
for instance, of Silvina Ocampo: "neither psychological analysis nor local color, the Scylla and Charybdis of women's
writings, have tempted her" (Mujer, p. 150).  And, she explains, any woman can profit from some preparation if she
wishes to go against convention: "The feat of becoming what
you are (always an accomplishment of the privileged, of whatever sex and social conditions) demands not only the discovery
of your own underlying characteristics ... but, above all,
the rejection of those false images offered women by the
false mirrors in the closed galleries in which their lives
pass" (Mujer, p. 20).

        What Castellanos is talking about here is sex-role
stereotyping.  In her works she explores, describes, and
works against cultural patterns of dominance-submission--
between men and women, whites and Indians, Mexicans and
Europeans or North Americans, lower class and elite, parents and children.  What she sees as the goal for women is
liberation from deceptive, long-suffering femininity.  But she
believes that the "feat of becoming what you are" is always
problematical, a matter of mind as well as of political, social, and economic circumstances: "What we have to do,
then, is laugh.  We all know that laughter is the first testimony of freedom" (Mujer, p. 207).


REFERENCES

1.  José Emilio Pacheco, "Inventario," Diorama de la Cul-
        tura: Suplemento cultural de Excelsior, 11 Aug.

1974, p. 16.

2. Los narradores ante el público, Vol. I (México: Joaquín Mortiz, 1966), p. 89.

3. Malinche was the native interpreter and mistress of Cortez. "Malinche" appears here in my translation, as do all other excerpts. Since Rosario Castellanos' poetry is most accessible in the recent volume of collected works, Poesía no eres tú (México: Fondo de Cultura Económica, 1972), all page numbers in the text which accompany quotations of poetry will refer to this edition, hereafter abbreviated in my notes to Poesía.

4. Margarita García Flores, "Rosario Castellanos: La lucidez como forma de vida," La Onda: Novedades, 18 Aug. 1974, pp. 6-7.

5. "Emblema," pp. 209-10; "Tlatelolco," pp. 297-98, in Poesía.

6. Mujer que sabe latín (México: Secretaría de Educación Pública, 1973; Col. SepSetentas 83), p. 25. All further references to this work will be abbreviated to Mujer in my text. The title derives from a popular saying: "Mujer que sabe latín, ni tiene marido ni tiene buen fin" (literally, a woman who knows Latin will not get a husband and will come to no good end).

7. "Jornada de la soltera," Poesía, p. 175.

8. "Acción de gracias," Poesía, p. 217.

9. "Testamento de Hécuba," Poesía, p. 197.

10. Salomé y Judith: Poemas dramáticos (México: Editorial Jus, 1959), pp. 17-18; in Poesía, p. 126.

11. Salomé, p. 18; Poesía, p. 126.

12. "Versiones," Poesía, p. 226.

13. "Monólogo de la extranjera," Poesía, p. 113. This poem was first published in México en la Cultura: Novedades, 9 Mar. 1958.

14. "Monólogo de la extranjera," Poesía, p. 112.

15. "Economía doméstica," Poesía, p. 301.

16. The "Generation of 1950" was the name sometimes given to a group of Latin American writers (who published their works in América) which includes Emilio Carballido, Ernesto Cardenal, Dolores Castro, Rosario Castellanos, Sergio Galindo, Otto-Raúl González, Miguel Guardia, Luisa Josefina Hernández, Carlos Illescas, Sergio Magaña, Ernesto Mejía Sánchez, Augusto Monterroso, Jaime Sabines.

17. La Güera Rodríguez was celebrated by Humboldt as the most beautiful woman he had ever encountered any-

where in his travels. She is discussed by Fanny Calderón de la Barca in Life in Mexico, During a Residence of Two Years in That Country (London and Boston, 1843). For a complete study, with bibliography, see Artemio de Valle Arizpe, La Güera Rodríguez, 9th ed. (México: Porrúa, 1960; Col. Biblioteca Mexicana 2).

18. Los narradores ante el público, p. 93; Mujer, p. 206.

19. Emmanuel Carballo, Diecinueve protagonistas de la literatura mexicana del siglo XX (México: Empresas Editoriales, 1965), p. 451.

20. Los narradores ante el público, p. 93.

21. According to Shulamith Firestone, in "On American Feminism": "The contemporary radical feminist position is the direct descendent of the radical feminist line in the old movement ... [of the nineteenth century]. It sees feminist issues not only as women's first priority, but as central to any larger revolutionary analysis," Woman in Sexist Society, Ed. Vivian Gornick and Barbara K. Moran (New York: New American Library--Mentor, 1972), p. 684.

22. "Meditación en el umbral," Poesía, p. 326.

23. Pacheco, ibid., p. 16. Castellanos published two novels: Balún-Canán (1957; trans. Irene Nicholson, The Nine Guardians, London: Faber & Faber, 1958; New York: Vanguard Press, 1959) and Oficio de tinieblas (México: Joaquín Mortiz, 1962). Her short stories are collected in three volumes: Ciudad real (Xalapa: Edit. Veracruzana, 1960; Col. Ficción 17); Los convidados de agosto (México: Eds. Era, 1964; Col. Letras Latinoamericanas 4); Album de familia (México: Joaquín Mortiz, 1971).

24. Juicios sumarios (Xalapa: Universidad Veracruzana, 1966; Col. Cuadernos de la Facultad de Filosofía, Letras y Ciencias 35), p. 29.

25. Conversation with Poniatowska, Mexico City, 1 Aug. 1974. Also see Poniatowska's essay, "Evocaciones de Rosario Castellanos," La cultura en México: Suplemento de Siempre!, No. 1106, 4 Sept. 1974, pp. 6-8.

Ann Ronald

THE FEMALE FAUST

Virginia Woolf imagined the demise of Shakespeare's sister.  Undoubtedly a similar fate befell Homer's, Plato's, Aristotle's, and Milton's, since little valuable women's writing or thinking survives from their eras, and this suggests something important for the woman who wants to write today.  The essential foundations of English and American literature were created by men, not women; and so our myths--the ones which basically inform our writing--are male, not female.  This means women work in a predominantly male tradition, too often borrowing myths instead of creating their own.  It also means they must twist those myths in order to say something about the female condition rather than the male which, in turn, means they subvert them in the process because such patterns inherently are not theirs.  To show how this happens and what results from it, I want to look at a particular mythic pattern which I find recurs with disturbing regularity in women's literature, even though it first was originated by men writing about men.  It is a pattern both men and women adopt when writing about women; it is a pattern authors began using when the novel became a recognizable genre; but it is a pattern found in poetry as well as fiction.  From Moll Flanders to Fear of Flying and from Emily Dickinson to Sylvia Plath, it is possibly the most frequently-adapted pattern of all.

At its center stands Faust.  His story, now almost five hundred years old, grew from the level of truth (a sixteenth-century German necromancer) to the level of legend (a Renaissance scholar who, glutted with learning, sells his soul to the devil in exchange for twenty-four years of unabated power and pleasure) to the level of myth (man searching for universal knowledge and truth).  Although the tale changes through the centuries, its variations always deal with certain key questions:  who Faust is, who he sells his soul to, what he hopes to gain, and what he actually gains (or loses) upon completion of the contract.  We find answers to these questions couched in distinctly female terms when we magically transform Faust into a female protagonist. So imagine a Faustess, one who is ready and willing to make a private bargain with her own kind of devil.

Unlike her masculine counterparts, she possesses no special knowledge, holds no special position. She generally is sensitive, usually intelligent, often innocent; but then so are many other literary protagonists. She is young or old, virgin or lover, heroine or villain, success or failure. In fact, she appears in so many guises that it becomes impossible to pinpoint her characteristics other than to say she is a woman living in a man's world, a feminine protagonist ensconced in a masculine milieu. And specifically, that masculine milieu is personified by some kind of Mephistophelean figure with whom she can strike a bargain. He may be father, brother, son, lover, husband, friend, or foe, but he consistently occupies a position close enough to hers so that their relationship can lead to some kind of contractual agreement, whether explicit or implicit.

Few women openly call men devils, yet many writers do so. To go back several centuries, Richardson's Clarissa says Lovelace's "rattle warns me of the snake,"[1] while Lovelace directly compares himself to "the devil in Milton" and then suggests Clarissa "could not keep her eye from my foot; expecting, no doubt, every minute to see it discover itself to be cloven."[2] Granted, Richardson is writing from a man's point of view, but similar imagery appears frequently during the next century in novels written by women. The Brontë sisters, for example, created a variety of male devils--Charlotte's Mr. Rochester, Emily's Heathcliffe, Anne's Arthur Huntingdon--perhaps all growing from the image of their own brother, Branwell, fused with the ways they envisioned the Byronic hero of their childhood imaginations. The results are three very different diabolical men--but all depicted explicitly as dark, mysterious, tainted, and implicitly as emissaries from hell.

Women writing novels today continue suggesting men are devils. Listen to Margaret Drabble introduce James in The Waterfall: "he looked dangerous, he seemed to carry with him the yellow sulfurous clouds of some threatening imminent danger."[3] Certain poets are still more direct. H. D. insists "man is clumsy/ a devil"[4] because Odysseus, after accepting Callypso's gifts, has abandoned her to her song. Later she affirms "man is a devil," explaining Callypso has gotten the worst of a bargain made with a man who "never looked back." Powerful, too, are the images used by Sylvia Plath to picture "Daddy":

> A cleft in your chin instead of your foot
> But no less a devil for that, no not
> Any less the black man who
>
> Bit my pretty red heart in two. [5]

Since Plath not only calls Daddy a devil but also suggests a bargain struck at birth, the contextual implications of her imagery are significant for us. Her remaining stanzas pose the intellectual and emotional frustrations resulting from the agreement, as the poet first reaffirms the compact by crying, "I do, I do," then negates it by screaming, "Daddy, daddy, you bastard, I'm through." But despite her attempt to break away from constricting childhood ties by stabbing her father with "a stake in [his] fat black heart," the poet achieves only temporary purgations instead of true exorcism. She wavers, remains caught. Beyond the barriers of the lines of poetry, the father of her imagination remains very much alive, for their bargain cannot so easily be broken.

Plath talks about a similar kind of entrapment in another poem, "The Applicant," where she offers:

> A living doll, ...
> It can sew, it can cook,
> It can talk, talk, talk.
>
> It works, there is nothing wrong with it. [6]

Any man willing to marry it, to buy it, to strike a bargain with it, will find a hand "willing/ To bring teacups and roll away headaches/ And do whatever [he tells] it." This poem, with its ironic tone and bitter stance, dehumanizes the female and undermines the bargain, but I cite it because it clearly presents the parameters of the compact made by the typical female Faust. Plath knows such a deal would be empty, but a majority of women think it would be fine.

A Faustess expects her agreement to be a fortunate one wherein she gains marriage (or at least love), children (perhaps), peace, contentment, fulfillment, but most of all, security. In return, she gives up only her individuality. Sara Teasdale, writing half a century before Plath, sees this as good and literally begs her readers to strike a bargain:

> Spend all you have for loveliness,
>     Buy it and never count the cost:
> For one white singing hour of peace
>     Count many a year of strife well lost,
> And for a breath of ecstasy
> Give all you have been, or could be. 7

"Barter" pulls no punches.  Teasdale's women need only "give
all [they] have been, or could be" to gain "eyes that love
[them], arms that hold," to have "children's faces looking
up," to succeed with their femininity.  One could quibble
about whether or not this is a true Faustian bargain since it
says nothing very profound, but I think Teasdale intends it
as such.  Traditionally, the protection of a good man along
with the reputation of a good family are the highest goals a
woman can strive for, and the female Faust reaches for just
that.

    Many fictional heroines of the past two centuries have
delighted their readers with such Faust-like activities.  The
whole spectrum of Jane Austen's leading ladies, for example,
marry good men and live happily ever after.  I wonder, though,
whether they really got what they expected, since authors of
George Eliot's stature suggest the fairy-tale ending might be
flawed.  Dorothea Brooke makes two marriages in Middlemarch:  one with Mr. Casaubon which we know is a disaster
and one with Will Ladislaw, the success of which critics have
speculated about for years.  My feeling is that her most productive days were those between the two contracts when she
was free to be herself and do her good works, but of course
I read the book as a twentieth-century career woman, not as
a nineteenth-century wife and mother.  Anyway, Dorothea's
family sees her final bargain as her salvation, while her
creator implies otherwise.  After agreeing to marry Will,
Dorothea announces, "I will learn what everything costs. "8
She is speaking specifically about money, since she loses a
large portion of her income by becoming Mrs. Ladislaw, but
I think Eliot means much more.  For one thing, she strate-
gically placed the sentence at the end of a chapter where it
would catch the reader's eye.  For another, a few pages
later she wrote that Dorothea's peers "thought it a pity that
so substantive and rare a creature should have been absorbed
into the life of another, and be only known in a certain circle
as a wife and mother. "9  Although superficially Dorothea has
succeeded in the traditional woman's role, George Eliot's
diction--"being absorbed" and "being only known"--carries
sobering impact.  Dorothea has struck her bargain and will

live with it; she has gotten her "happy home," but she has
had to pay a price.

Many more female protagonists sell out for much less.
The list is endless.  It includes such different women as
Moll Flanders who, for financial security, gives her body
away at least fifteen times (maybe more, one loses count)
and Isadora Wing who returns to a lukewarm bath and a tepid
husband at the end of Fear of Flying.  Certainly, it includes
James' Isabel Archer and Hardy's Tess Durbeyfield.  It even
includes, I think, women like Mrs. Ramsey in To The Lighthouse.  Such characters as these give up a part or all of
themselves while hoping to find some magical reward for
their acquiescence.  Too often, though, they find something
quite different, something much more horrible than Dorothea's
gradual absorption.

Male authors have not given a uniform response to
the question of what happens to Faust after his contract has
been completed, so there is no reason to expect women to
be consistent either.  Marlowe's Dr. Faustus ends in hell,
Goethe's Faust in heaven, Mann's Adrian Leverkuhn in madness, and women's literature echoes the same three answers.
We have already seen how, until the present century, the
female Faust's bargain theoretically was supposed to result
in heaven.  Sara Teasdale, whose traditional thoughts make
such telling touchstones against which change can be measured,
insists "though love be heaven or love be hell" a woman
should always love "the voice and the eyes and the soul of
a man" for "only through love will [she] enter heaven."[10]
Teasdale's assertion is naive and shallow, and since the bargain she contemplates in no way measures up to the incisive
agreement made between Goethe's hero and his devil, the
outcome she imagines in no way can parallel the denouement
of that masterpiece.

The more sensitive writer recognizes the short-sight-
edness of her position and realizes that the price a woman
pays in a Faustian compact can be costly.  George Eliot said
as much in Middlemarch; Emily Dickinson argues from a
similar point of view:

> For each ecstatic instant
> We must an anguish pay
> In keen and quivering ratio
> To the ecstasy. [11]

She does not specify that ratio in her second stanza but merely

juxtaposes "sharp pittances" and "bitter farthings" against
"beloved hours." However, we can surmise how intensely
she would have disagreed with Teasdale and how sympathetic
she would be today with the ideas women authors are expressing, ideas like the one Joan Didion attributes to her main
character in Play It As It Lays: "Maria did not particularly
believe in rewards, only in punishments, swift and personal."[12]
During the last two decades, increasing numbers of women
have shown that the end result of the Faustian bargain is not
a reward but a punishment--not heaven, not even purgatory,
but hell or madness or a combination of the two. Hoping to
find peace, security, and love, the contemporary Faustess
finds instead only despair.

The twentieth-century female version of hell takes a
variety of forms both physical and mental. Generally it is
described through indirection rather than with the straight-
forward admission that this is hell because its forcefulness
comes from the subtlety of its presentation. For example,
nowhere in "Women" does May Swenson use the word "hell,"
but we cannot question that her toyroom world is one:

| Immobile | willing |
|---|---|
| sweetlipped | to be set |
| sturdy | into motion |
| and smiling | Women |
| women | should be |
| should always | pedestals |
| be waiting | to men[13] |

Swenson lets her readers stand outside and view her hell
dispassionately, whereas most authors drag us into the hell
they are making, expecting us to intuit the hellish positions
in which they are leaving their characters. For example,
Virginia Woolf closes her short story, "Lappin and Lapinova,"
with the line: "So that was the end of that marriage."[14] The
reader understands, given preceding characterizations and
events, that the marriage as fact probably will continue for
another forty years but that the marriage as relationship is
over. In other words, although Woolf does not say so directly, the marriage will be hell.

Such a hell, however, may be nearly as shallow as
Teasdale's heaven. Today, in order to intensify the outcome
of the woman's bargain, more and more writers are showing
hell as process rather than product. They see it organically,
as something that begins when the compact is made but con-

tinues to grow long after the agreement has been completed.
When his play is over Marlowe's hero disappears forever
amid thunder and lightning; the female Faust stays right where
she is.    Her hell is in her head, and from it there is no
escape.    Erica Jong describes it as intellectual self-flagel-
lation in "Alcestis on the Poetry Circuit":

> The best slave
> Does not need to be beaten.
> She beats herself.

And she does so

> ... with the fine whip
> of her own tongue
> & the subtle beating
> of her mind
> against her mind

because

> ... who can hate her half so well
> as she hates herself?
> & who can match the finesse
> of her self-abuse? [15]

The distance between this kind of hell and total madness is so little as to be indistinguishable.    Consider the
number of suicide attempts, the number of stream-of-consciousness babblings, the number of complete personality
disintegrations found in the fiction of recent women writers.
There is the intermittent agony of The Golden Notebook's
Anna Wulf and The Bell Jar's Esther Greenwood, the complete mental anguish of such diverse heroines as Joan Didion's
in Play It As It Lays and Shirley Jackson's in Hangsaman,
to name only a few.    In each case the protagonist tries un-
successfully to flee her bargain but finds she is fated to endure.    For the female Faust, finally, madness and hell are
practically synonymous.

Although each Faustess differs and her bargain and
its denouement vary from work to work, the basic pattern
remains the same.    A woman sells out to a man; she hopes
for love and security, but she gets something quite unexpected
instead.    The pattern is everywhere, pervading poetry as
well as fiction, nineteenth-century works as well as twentieth-,
high-quality literature as well as trash.    Recently, however,

it has been particularly prevalent in best-selling fiction (those
novels which, purporting to give a typical view of the modern
female and her crises, sell a million copies and then disappear from sight).   As one might surmise, using the Faust
myth as the informing principle behind such works has led
to less than profound results.   A look at one of them--<u>Mem-
oirs of an Ex-Prom Queen</u>--should tell why.

        Sasha Davis, the narrator-protagonist of Alix Kates
Shulman's novel, is a Faustess.   Elected Queen of the S. L.
T. Bunny Hop in high school, a potentially brilliant student
in both college and graduate school, married twice to apparently successful men, mother of two healthy and attractive
children, Sasha seems the all-American matron.   But from
her earliest childhood days, she has needed men to affirm
her worth.   She tells us, "In high school they called it 'boy
crazy'; in college, where everything accelerated, 'oversexed.'
To me it was life insurance."[16]   In exchange for positive
reinforcement to her constant question--"Do you think I'm
beautiful?" (p. 207)--Sasha gives body and soul.   To complete
the other half of the bargain, a number of Mephisthophelean
surrogates parade through her life:   Joey, Cookie, Dr. Alport, Franklin Raybel, Manolo, Leonard, various unnamed
businessmen, and finally, Willy Burke.   The list is exhaust-
ing if not exhaustive, but as Sasha says, "I knew I hadn't
the muscle for an independent life" (p. 212).   To each she
must sell herself in return for praise and admiration.   She
knows exactly what she is doing and why, since she admits,
"My mirror image always had to be interpreted.   And for
that I sought my reflection in someone else's eyes" (p. 16).
While in college, for example, she falls in love with philosophy.   Enamored, she spends every waking hour reading,
studying, thinking, assimilating; but she cannot trust her own
enthusiasm until philosophy responds to her, until Dr. Alport,
a surrogate for both the discipline and the devil, sleeps with
her.   Then, with philosophy's (and his) sanction, she can
trust her own worth.   The pattern, set early in her youth,
continues through the novel, covers twenty-four years in
fact, and is the familiar Faustian one.

        Familiar, too, is the Faustian intimation that her bar-
gaining may not bring all she hopes for.   When she was in
high school her sorority sisters cursed her beauty, and one
pronounced in a fit of jealousy:   "Someday it'll all catch up
with you and then you'll pay!   You'll pay for everything!"
(p. 58).   Like all other Fausts, Sasha does.   Through a series of flashbacks, <u>Memoirs of an Ex-Prom Queen</u> catalogues

the steps in her life that brought her to the present, then shows the bargain that cements her future and fulfills the high school curse. We see her at the novel's close with a new husband, two children, and a new haircut. Her mind is vacillating wearily between Dr. Spock, Beauty Bar face cream, and the horrible thought that "a thing of thirty is a bitch forever" (p. 288). Sasha knows, and we know, that this is the equivalent of hell on earth. She understands "that those very remedies I had come to count on--haircuts, diets, sun, lovers--would produce in time such terrible symptoms of their own that more cures, more tricks, more devices would be necessary to control them" (p. 284). Such superficiality merely confirms the shallowness she has been betraying throughout the book. Then she interprets the results of her bargaining:

> To find myself at thirty locked under a dryer eagerly studying ads in magazines while I worry about the sitter and my husband is away on a business trip; now, after my schemes and triumphs, my visions and dares, to be, without income or skill, dependent on a man and a fading skin--it can only be the fulfillment of a curse! [p. 285].

The fulfillment of a curse! Like all the Fausts who have gone before her, Sasha is doomed--a victim of her own dreams and desires.

But there is a significant difference between her fate and the fates of her masculine predecessors, a difference which is the key to the female use of the pattern. Marlowe metaphorically compared Dr. Faustus with Icarus, whose "waxen wings did mount above his reach,"[17] and suggested that both their falls came because they tried to soar too high. Sasha Davis never soars at all; in fact, she never even makes the attempt but sells out to find admiration, comfort, security. A shadow of the real Faust figure, she is constitutionally unable to achieve tragic stature. Here, then, is the female digression from, and de-fusion of, the essential Faust myth. Instead of creating female protagonists who soar, or who at least try to reach the heights, women writers draw shadow figures, protagonists who sell out to mediocrity and then find themselves either caught in a shallow version of hell or fleeing hastily into madness. Not one of them could carry the intellectual or philosophical burden of an Adrian Leverkuhn because their plights spring not from tragedy but from pathos. The voice of Plath's "Daddy" and "The Applicant," H. D.'s Callypso, Swenson's "Women," Drabble's Jane, Lessing's Anna

Wulf, Didion's Maria Wyeth, Shulman's Sasha Davis--to name
only some of many--have been inspired by a pathetic inversion of a male myth rather than by an imaginative vision of
a female one.   As a result, not one is a tragic figure nor
can she ever be.

Faust-based works have historically been written during
explosive intellectual eras, and since these are exciting days
for women, the preponderance of the pattern seems appropriate.   Contemporary women writers should be able to
achieve dramatic results by using Faust's story.   But as we
have seen, they do not.   First, they employ the myth incorrectly, subverting its basic thrust by drawing protagonists
with mundane aspirations.   Secondly, they are working with
a myth which belongs to a tradition other than their own.
Women writers must dream their own dreams before they
will succeed in creating a body of fully expressive literature.
So long as they do not, so long as they continue borrowing,
they will continue writing imitative and undistinguished works
like Memoirs of an Ex-Prom Queen.

Women writers must originate myths ending not in
pathos but in power, myths where women resolve their conflicts in terms of self rather than in terms of other.   Instead
of "Reader, I married him," they must conceptualize "I go
to encounter ... the reality of experience and to forge in the
smithy of my soul the uncreated conscience of my sex."   Then,
and only then, will women's literature reach beyond the grasp
of Faustess.


## REFERENCES

1.   Samuel Richardson, Clarissa, abridged by George Sher-
         burn (1747-48; reprinted Boston:   Houghton Mifflin,
         1962), p. 161.
2.   Richardson, p. 285.
3.   Margaret Drabble, The Waterfall (New York:   Signet,
         1969), p. 11.
4.   H. D. [Hilda Doolittle], "Callypso Speaks," in Rising
         Tides, ed. Laura Chester and Sharon Barba (New
         York:   Washington Square Press, 1973), pp. 13-15.
5.   Sylvia Plath, "Daddy," Ariel (New York:   Harper & Row,
         1961), pp. 49-51.
6.   Plath, "The Applicant," Ariel, pp. 4-5.
7.   Sara Teasdale, "Barter," Collected Poems of Sara Teas-
         dale (London:   Collier-Macmillan, 1966), p. 97.

8.  George Eliot, Middlemarch (1871-72; reprinted Boston: Houghton Mifflin, 1956), p. 594.
9.  Eliot, p. 611.
10. Teasdale, "Child, Child," Collected Poems, pp. 97-98.
11. Emily Dickinson, "No. 125," The Complete Poems of Emily Dickinson, ed. Thomas H. Johnson (Boston: Little, Brown and Co., 1960), p. 58.
12. Joan Didion, Play It As It Lays (New York: Bantam, 1971), p. 72.
13. May Swenson, "Women," Iconographs (New York: Charles Scribner's Sons, 1970), p. 14.
14. Virginia Woolf, "Lappin and Lapinova," A Haunted House and Other Stories (New York: Harcourt, Brace & Co., 1944), p. 78.
15. Erica Jong, "Alcestis on the Poetry Circuit," Half-Lives (New York: Holt, Rinehart and Winston, 1971), p. 25.
16. Alix Kates Shulman, Memoirs of an Ex-Prom Queen (New York: Bantam, 1972), pp. 14-15. Page numbers of other quotations from this book will be included in the text.
17. Christopher Marlowe, Doctor Faustus (1616; reprinted New York: Signet, 1969), p. 23.

Edna L. Steeves

## PRE-FEMINISM IN SOME
## EIGHTEENTH-CENTURY NOVELS*

Feminism as a movement appears barely before the
nineteenth century.  In fact, no record exists of the use of
the word before 1850.  In 1888 the New English Dictionary
defined feminism simply as "the qualities of female," and
lists it as rare.  Not until recent times has it been concerned
with women's rights, or the doctrine of equality of women
with men.  If today the word sounds like a war-cry--"Women's
Lib" having become a highly organized political movement--
nothing of that sort appears in the early history of feminism.
Individual women, militant or modest, fought their individual
battles to gain security and independence, but they did not
think of themselves as feminists in the present-day connota-
tion, nor had they conceived the idea of a political program
to secure their ends.

Discussion of the woman question, however, begins
long before 1800.  Sporadic interest in some aspects of woman's social and economic subjection appears before 1700,
witness Mary Astell's A Serious Proposal to the Ladies for
the Advancement of Their True and Greatest Interest (1694),
and Defoe's Essay on Projects (1697), both of which outlined
practical schemes for higher education for women.  Again,
in 1739-40 the "Sophia Pamphlets" touched off a flurry of
interest in the much-debated question of woman's inferiority.
In general, however, these early manifestations of what today
we would term feminist propaganda did not greatly arouse the
British--unlike France, where from the mid-eighteenth-century
intellectuals like Montesquieu, Diderot, Holbach, and Condor-
cet espoused the cause of women's rights as part of the lib-
erative philosophy of the Enlightenment.  On this controversial

*Reprinted by permission of the author and publisher from
The Texas Quarterly 3 (Autumn 1973), 48-57.  Copyright ©
1973 by The Texas Quarterly.

subject, French writers were very much further advanced than
English writers of the same period.

In England we can nevertheless discern in the course
of the eighteenth century a mild but increasing interest in
woman's situation in a man's world.   The attitudes toward
"the fair sex" set forth by Addison and Steele are at once
outside the scope of fiction and almost too familiar to call
for discussion.   But at the opening of the century they well
express the general view of woman.   "I have often wondered,"
writes Addison, "that learning is not thought a proper ingre-
dient in the education of a woman of quality or fortune.   Since
they have the same improvable minds as the male part of
the species, why should they not be cultivated by the same
methods?" (Guardian 155, September 8, 1713).   This indeed
sounds progressive.   But Addison reveals his true opinion of
the feminine mind in his description of Lady Lizard's family
engaged in simultaneously making jam and reading Fontenelle's
Plurality of Worlds: "It was very entertaining to me," he
writes, "to see them dividing their speculations between jel-
lies and stars and making a sudden transition from the sun
to an apricot or from the Copernican system to the figure
of a cheesecake" (Spectator 435, July 19, 1712).

Here is the light, satiric thrust, the attitude more
sentimental than practical, more patronizing than helpful.
This same view of woman as mental light-weight is pithily,
if not entirely politely, phrased by Balzac: "I could," he
comments, "more willingly tolerate a woman with a beard
than one who pretends to learning. "

Defoe's presentation of the feminine position is also
too well known to need elaboration here.   Moll Flanders is
a whore, a thief, and a transported felon; yet Defoe makes
her his heroine and treats her sympathetically.   Moll insists
on her right as a woman to make her way in the world; she
recognizes no obligation to contemporary mores; and she de-
plores the disadvantages of women.   Roxana, too, insists on
her right to choose her own mode of life; and on at least
two occasions she refuses marriage as the easy solution.   Of
course Defoe's concern in these she-rogue stories is only
incidentally with the woman problem.   One of the projects of
his Essay on Projects treats the question of women's education with proper seriousness.   He presents therein a draft
for an academy for women, which he introduces with the comment: "I have often thought of it as one of the most barbarous
customs in the world, considering us as a civilized and Christian country, that we deny the advantages of learning to women. "

But if we are earnestly searching for the first impulses
in England of what today we call feminism, we shall find
them mirrored in many of the novels of the century, particularly of the latter half of the century.  In such novels
the question is repeatedly raised:  How should men feel and
act toward women, and how should women interest men--
within the bounds, of course, of discretion and security?
That question comes sharply forward in the women novelists
of the last decades before 1800.  Needless to say, in this
brief paper I can consider only a few of those novelists who
set forth contemporary views on the position of women, their
duties, and their mentality.

The fiction of the century as a whole reflects two
social attitudes in two sharply contrasting modes of life:
first, and in the earlier half of the period, upper-class lib-
ertine society; and second, and later, middle-class pietistic
society.

Libertinism figures largely in the novels of Mrs. Manley and Mrs. Haywood.  Mary de la Riviere Manley (1672-
1724), who married unfortunately and was deserted by her
husband after the birth of her first child, began writing for
the stage in 1696 and became the mistress of Sir Thomas
Skipworth of Drury Lane, and later of John Barber, with
whom she was living at the time of her death.  After some
success in the theater, she turned to novel writing:  Queen
Zarah (1705), a fictional history of the "secret memoirs"
type, which involved her in a lawsuit; the New Atlantis (1709),
to which Steele gave a place in Leonora's library; Rivella
(1714) and The Power of Love (1720), both of which touched
lightly upon the ills of women.  Mrs. Manley is an example,
only one among many, who, without economic security or
assured social position and forced to live by her wits, found
it impossible to be both financially independent and respectable.

Eliza Haywood (1693-1756) made the headlines of her
day by eloping from her husband, the Reverend Mr. Valentine
Haywood.  This break with her husband launched her on a
career of play-writing, novel-writing, translating, and editing.
In 35 years she produced some 70 works, most of which
sold well.  Her best-known novels are Love in Excess (1719);
The Court of Caramania (1726); The History of Miss Betsy
Thoughtless (1751); and Jemmy and Jenny Jessamy (1753).
The last two owe something to Pamela and are aimed at the
chaste servant girl who hankers after uplift.

In the works of these two female authors we see the marriage de convenance as an anchorage for family fortunes: "arrangements" to the last detail of financial security for the two parties.   Affection is not only irrelevant, but often ridiculed.   The important determinant is the judgment of the parents, for aristocratic training and tradition tended to make girls compliant.   No young woman could casually oppose her parents' plans for her marriage, as Clarissa's predicament showed.

In practice, the marriage of convenience was regarded by the upper classes as a background for social and sexual liberty--often by a perfectly clear understanding between husband and wife.   The adulteress is therefore a familiar type in the fiction of the day:  Lady Bellaston in Tom Jones, the "Lady of Quality" in Peregrine Pickle, and Mrs. Hardy in Eliza Haywood's Betsy Thoughtless.   Absolute male freedom is taken for granted.   The heroes of Fielding and Smollet are at least sexual opportunists, at worst, ruthless young rakes.   The significant point is that in upper-class urban society the married woman had in actuality great liberty of action, and in many cases sexual liberty.   Yet in these same novels there is invariable insistence upon the purity and submissiveness of the heroine, who conducts herself in strict conformity with the best examples of romantic pietism.   Most fiction of the time pictures two orders of women for the young man's interest:  the "pure" and the accommodating.   He usually pays attention to both.

Sophia Western is a good example of the kind of heroine readers expected.   The argumentative background that gives us a character like Sophia can be found in such works as Mrs. Hester Chapone's Letters on the Improvement of the Mind (1773); the Rev. Dr. John Gregory's Legacy for His Daughters (1774); the Rev. Dr. Thomas Gisborne's An Inquiry into the Duties of the Female Sex (1797); and an early and very influential book on the subject of female conduct, the Marques of Halifax's Advice to a Daughter (1688), sixteen editions of which had appeared by 1765.   These were popular handbooks whose pronouncements upon the proper conduct of young ladies found complete acceptance in their day.   They assume a young lady's destiny to be marriage, her breeding and education to be directed accordingly.   In eighteenth-century society the single woman is a virtual anomaly, largely because of the absence of any opportunities for self-support on a respectable level.   A young woman's education, then, aimed only to prepare her for wifehood.   It consisted of the

"accomplishments"--dancing, singing, a superficial musical
training, drawing, needlework, perhaps a slight acquaintance
with French, plus (in more practical schools for females)
some acquaintance with domestic management--not cooking
(although an occasional pastry school is advertised), but care
of clothing and household linen, and some knowledge of ele-
mentary accounting, the assumption being that she would
spend her life managing a domestic establishment.    She was
generally denied the qualities of mind that would warrant
serious study.

    The prime example of cheerful womanly compliance
may be found in Pamela.    The setting, it may be recalled,
is Mr. B--'s wish to exhibit Pamela to his neighbors, dressed becomingly in her plain country fashion.    There is possible embarrassment here; for Pamela, a servant girl, though
now affianced to her master, cannot sit down with his guests.
As a favor to himself, he asks her to accept the situation,
which she does, in these words:

> 'Sir,' said I, 'after all that has passed I should
> be unworthy not to say that I can have no will but
> yours; and however awkwardly I shall behave in
> such company, weighed down by the sense of your
> obligations on one side, and my unworthiness on
> the other, I will not scruple to obey you.... I
> should be best pleased to wear this humble garb
> till you, for your own sake, shall order it other-
> wise; for,' said I, 'I hope it will be always my
> pride to glory most in your goodness, to show
> everyone that as to my happiness in this life, I am
> entirely the work of your bounty, and to let the
> world see from what a lowly original you have
> raised me to honor that the greatest ladies would
> rejoice in. '
>
> 'Admirable Pamela,' said he; 'excellent girl!--
> Surely thy sentiments are superior to those of all
> thy sex!    I might have addressed a hundred fine
> ladies, but never could have had reason to admire
> one as I do you. '

Pamela's concluding comment strikes exactly the right note
of humility and submissiveness expected of her:

> As, my dear father and mother [she writes], I
> repeat these sayings only because they are the ef-
> fect of my master's goodness, being far from pre-

suming to think I deserve them, so I hope you will
not attribute it to my vanity. For I do assure you,
I think I ought rather to be more humble, as I am
more obliged; for it must be always a sign of a
poor condition to receive obligations one cannot
repay, as it is of a rich mind when it can confer
them without accepting or needing a return. It is,
on the one side, the state of the human creature,
compared, on the other, to the Creator. And so,
with due deference, may his beneficence be said
to be god-like, and that is the highest that can be
said [Richardson, Pamela, or Virtue Rewarded,
ed. W. W. Sale, Jr. (New York, 1958), pp. 286-
87; first published 1740].

The general assumption in Richardson's novels--that
woman is by nature subordinate to man, submissive, domestic, limited in vision and in interests--prevails in fiction of
the century, even in fiction of the latter half of the century written by women. As a rule, this attitude side-steps the question
whether woman's subordinate position implies inferiority (as
Rousseau assumes in Émile). If there is anything resembling
what we call "evaluation" of the sexes, it is usually a balancing
of masculine intellectual strength against feminine delicacy and
emotional refinement. Did this imply "equality with difference"?
The question is never fairly faced.

Marriage is still the one career. Fanny Burney, Maria
Edgeworth, Jane Austen can see or imagine no other. In their
novels they create personalities in a traditional social situation,
but never examine the situation itself closely. Burney, Edgeworth, and Austen were not bold women; they are not critical
of institutions, nor even of men in their character as men. The
arguable issues connected with marriage at the time, as it affected women, were the inequities involved in marriage; man's
social freedom versus woman's domestic confinement, surrender
of control over property both real and personal, inability to ex-
tricate herself from an unhappy marriage or to bring an action
for divorce on any ground--all these in addition to the multitude
of problems of accommodation to a husband's habits and temper.
Furthermore--and this equally important--there was no attempt
to face the problems of the single woman in a man's world.

If there is one articulate complaint in the fictions of women writers of the period, it is that woman's education does not
prepare her for marriage--or for anything else. But there is
never a concrete suggestion as to the proper kind of education
for a woman--even though in Edgeworth's case her father was

an educationalist, and she wrote with him books concerned with the education of children. Mrs. Elizabeth Inchbald, in her novel A Simple Story (1790), approaches the question of education, but only to pronounce that Protestant education is less effective than Catholic because it does not enforce the idea of feminine subordination.

In the women novelists to whom we have been referring, their ingenues have good minds and good digestions, they are in the way of recovery from the sentimentalism of the early and middle century, and since they have been reared in the polite tradition, they accept society as it is, without criticism. Miss Burney's Camilla (1796) gives us a heroine of a more nervous constitution, and in The Wanderer, or Female Difficulties (1814) she introduces as a minor character a young woman whose emancipated mind leads her into merely bold and silly indiscretions. In fact, the attitude toward "advanced" young women is far from favorable--as is evident from the fact that the wise Jane Austen in Pride and Prejudice (1813) bestows some rough treatment upon Elizabeth's younger sister Mary, because Mary is a reader who likes to show off her learning. One almost hears an echo of Swift many years earlier, one of whose Thoughts on Various Subjects asserted: "A very little wit is valued in a woman as we are pleased with a few words spoken plain by a parrot." But of course this is not the serious Swift.

It is only in a secondary way that pre-feminist ideas are advanced by the fact that the fictional heroine's hesitant steps toward marriage show a steady increase in firm command of herself and her emotional needs. Fiction is, after all, little more than a tentative measurement of the ethos of a period. But it demonstrates something, speaking at large, as to the complexion of contemporary thought. And that thought was not then favorable to feminism, in part because of its identification in the general mind with French revolutionary philosophy, which was anathema to the conservative British viewpoint.

It must be noted particularly that in England the writer who foresaw and argued all the matters of contention that appeared in feminist propaganda after 1800 was Robert Bage (1728-1801), the stoutest defender in fiction of female liberty. A recent writer on the novel has called him "an eighteenth-century Shaw" (Harrison R. Steeves, Before Jane Austen [New York, 1965], p. 292). Between 1782 and 1796 Bage wrote six novels, in all of which his general position on the woman question anticipates strikingly Shaw's position in Candida, Man and Superman, and Getting Married. But Bage is not a radical activist,

only a mild and humorous observer of humanity.   His effec-
tiveness as a promulgator of rational doubts lies in large
part in collisions of strong-minded characters with sharply
opposed opinions.   The conflict of ideas is, naturally enough,
conservative with critical.   In his novel The Fair Syrian
(1787), a gravely virginal young Englishwoman gathers enlightenment, if not conviction, from a colloquy with a Levan-
tine slave who has been transferred as desirable and salable
property from one man to another, and has not found difficulty in adjusting her feelings and habits of life to a succession of Oriental lords and masters.   In the same novel
the same young woman has a revealing conversation with an
English gentlewoman who is not greatly disturbed that her
husband has "made improper advances" to the girl, and who
laughs at the phrase "moral sanctions. "   In James Wallace
(1788) there is a situation of tragic implications in which a
young woman, to her own distress as well as her lover's,
refuses to marry a man whose free way of life she is unwilling to take for granted.

These are not counsels of immorality--far from it--
but broad suggestions that different minds and tempers look
at these problems in different ways, and that chastity itself
may be viewed in a different light from the Puritan's.   With-
al, the moral effect of Bage's suggestions is strikingly unlike the flippant cynicism of a Fontenelle or a Restif de la
Bretonne.   Bage has the Englishman's underlying sobriety
that obliges us to take him seriously.   It is unfortunate that
he did not have enough artistic conscience to make his rather
random counsels stick.

The two women of the period with marked interest in
feminist issues were Charlotte Smith and Mary Wollstonecraft.   Married at sixteen to a man for whom she had no
inclination, Charlotte Smith (1749-1806) soon found herself
with a growing family and without means to support them.
For a time in 1782 she and her husband were in debtors'
prison.   After that experience she began to write actively
for a living, and to the end of her life produced a stream of
novels, poems, translations, and hack-work, managing by
her wits and her pen to support herself and her children.
Two of her novels in particular, Emmeline (1788) and Desmond
(1792), voice protest against woman's debarment from an
independent or even an active life, and blame the debased
position of woman upon the failure to provide her with a
large mental horizon.   But pre-feminist argument of this
kind is only incidental to Mrs. Smith's main purpose, which

was frankly and simply to write novels that would sell and would therefore provide a living for her.

Mary Wollstonecraft (1759-97), whom the general reader knows only as the author of the Vindication of the Rights of Woman (1792), wrote three fictions, all of them literarily awful, but significant in their contribution to pre-feminist sentiment. All three name their principal character Mary or Maria, and doubtless there is an autobiographical connection there.

The first of these fictions, Original Stories from Real Life (1788), is a "juvenile" that fairly reeks with propriety. It reveals the same reverent attitude toward goodness as her Thoughts on the Education of Daughters, written in the preceding year, 1787, and purveys the best schoolmarmly thought of the period. Her views on women appear to be unexceptionably sound and conventional, perhaps for the good reason that at the time she and her sister were conducting a school for girls.

Her second novel, Mary: A Fiction (1788), is a highly emotional attack on loveless marriage, no doubt reflecting the tragic experiences of her mother and her sister. But it is not directed especially at the "arranged marriage" of upper-class society, and it takes no position with regard to the fact (which is the focus of action in the story) that a motion for divorce was until the mid-nineteenth century legally impossible for a married woman. In a word, her novel projects the problem of marital incompatibility, but without a single effort at rational solution.

Her last fiction, The Wrongs of Woman: or, Maria (1798), was under her hand for some years, and was unfinished (with alternative endings noted) when she died. It is a cruel story, cruel and incredible, in which brutalities of husband toward wife take the taint of criminality, but with no possibility of escape or redress. Here again, the reader might properly have expected some intimation of a solution; but there is none. Her quarrel is obviously with the institution of marriage itself, which she pictures as a graceless and barbarous indignity. It is in this light that the story can be regarded as the rationalization of her unrewarded advances to the painter Fuseli and her liaisons with Imlay and Godwin before her marriage to Godwin. In all these cases, it must be noted and emphasized, she places her confidence unreservedly and profoundly in an attachment to which she was completely faithful and which she brought into con-

formity with deep religious convictions.    She deplored pro-
miscuity.

Her Vindication of the Rights of Woman, one of the
first truly feminist documents, if not actually the first, falls
outside the scope of our topic.    It is (unlike her fiction) not
only an attack upon woman's helpless position under the marriage laws, but an arraignment of her exclusion from political life, her effective debarment from respectable employment, and her handicaps if unmarried.    On this latter point
several writers of the period had touched:    Johnson in the
Rambler had described and deplored the relative helplessness
of spinsters and widows and the lack of decent employment
for single women as the prime causes of prostitution.    And
this situation was the subject of two books by women written
in the last decade of the century:    Mary Ann Radcliffe's The
Female Advocate (1799) and Priscilla Wakefield's Reflections
on the Present Condition of the Female Sex (1798).    But
Mary Wollstonecraft's views went much further than the mild
feminist sentiment espoused by certain women writers of her
time:    she was the first to take a stand against institutional
and sacramental marriage--the first, that is, in England,
for Montesquieu and Diderot had both taken the same position
much earlier in the century.    She would not have married
Godwin except in the expectation of the birth of their child;
and they both agreed that under the existing law and custom
it would be shameless to rear a child under the shadow of
illegitimacy.    But the influence of Mary Wollstonecraft on
feminism had to wait at least a half century for its proper
recognition.

To sum up:    although in the progress of the novel
from Defoe to Miss Austen we can discern a growing interest
in the improvement of woman's situation, yet fiction in this
period reflects little practical or organized effort by society
to better the position of women.    Considering the fact that
much of the later fiction was written by women, does this
indicate a lost opportunity?    Perhaps it does.    But one of
the reasons for this failure to show anything resembling an
organized woman's rights program is that in these fictions
the central feminine character is almost invariably a young
woman who has been carefully trained not for marriage, but
for getting married.    Before Charlotte Smith and Mary Wollstonecraft, most writers of fiction had skirted the problems
of marriage itself.    In fact there are almost no exceptions.
Mrs. Haywood's Betsy Thoughtless (1751) and Miss Edgeworth's A Modern Griselda (1804) are simply exceptions that
point up the rule.    The avoidance of discussion of the critical

problems met in marriage is due in part to the fact that most of the women writers in the later part of the century were, at least at the time of their writing, spinsters. But it is also due to the fact that upper- and middle-class young women were carefully trained to view marriage as a dispensation of Providence, and the only proper setting for a woman's life. Every purveyor of wisdom for the marriageable girl stressed that she must accept all her husband's pretensions to superiority and his absolute authority over her, even to the grossest personal indignities.

With the many opportunities that the novel offers for the presentation of human problems, why do we not find in this period any really serious and practical proposal for bettering woman's condition? Progress toward solution of this problem was hampered by a variety of internal conditions in England: the general conservatism of the English temper; the prevalence of Puritanism, particularly among dissenters, and the unquestioning acceptance of Biblical sanctions for woman's subjection; the preoccupation with foreign wars and with diplomatic involvements; the absence of organized protest as to social and economic issues; and the general feeling among the upper and middle classes that a woman--by the very nature of her womanhood--must depend for her welfare and happiness upon her family, her husband, and her friends. Certainly after the French Revolution, which had scared the British stiff, there was a long lapse of interest in the woman question, which after all had about it a whiff of radicalism. One recalls Horace Walpole's conviction that Mary Wollstonecraft was a hyena in petticoats.

Are we to conclude, then, that because pre-feminism makes but a mild showing in the fiction of the century, we are dealing not with the history of an idea, but with its non-history--like Sherlock Holmes's dog that did not bark in the night. That would be a faulty reading of the evidence. The seedbed of feminist propaganda was being prepared with patience and care, especially by certain women novelists of the later part of the century. But it was not harvest time yet. The unescapable conclusion is that the time was not ripe for rational and meaningful discussion of women's rights, which means no more than that women themselves, in the aggregate and before 1800, could not be made to feel an interest. That in turn meant that as feminism was a phase of the equalitarian movement, it had to wait until equalitarian sentiment became more widely diffused. That story belongs to another era.

Evelyn Thomas Helmick

CONSTANCE FENIMORE WOOLSON:
FIRST NOVELIST OF FLORIDA*

In the Atlantic Monthly of 1875 appeared a series of
papers called "An English Sportsman in Florida," describing
this exotic peninsula in precise detail.   Such description was
not a novelty, for men had written accounts of their journeys
into Florida from the beginning of its exploration:   the list
includes Sidney Lanier, John James Audubon, John Bartram,
Jonathan Dickinson; it reaches back to Cabeza de Vaca's Ad-
ventures in the Unknown Interior of America published in
1555.   But immediately preceding the English sportsman's
article in that March 13 issue of the Atlantic was something
truly new in literature--a short story with a Florida setting.
The significant fiction of the state, in fact, begins with the
author of that story, Constance Fenimore Woolson, who captured in novels, short stories, and poems the genius loci of
northern Florida. 1   The Florida fiction is the best work of
a writer highly praised in her day by such critics as Henry
James and William Dean Howells and judged as late as 1929
"one of the finest novelists that America thus far has produced. "2

Miss Woolson--or Fenimore, as her friend Henry
James called her and as her great-uncle, James Fenimore
Cooper had been called--began to publish in national periodicals in 1870 with stories of the Lake Country near Cleveland,
where her family had moved a few months after her birth in
New Hampshire in 1840.   Her first collection of stories (after
the prize-winning Old Stone House for children) was Castle
Nowhere:   Lake Country Sketches in 1875.   Before that time,
however, she and her mother and sister had begun to spend
much of each year in St. Augustine, with frequent visits to
the Carolinas, Tennessee, and Georgia.   From this experience
came her second collection, Rodman the Keeper:   Southern

*Reprinted by permission of the author and publisher from
The Carrell 10 (1969), 8-18.

<u>Sketches,</u> in 1880.   After her mother's death she sailed for
Europe, where she lived in Italy and England, producing an
astonishing number of books before she died in 1896.   These
works include the novels <u>Anne,</u> <u>East Angels,</u> <u>Jupiter Lights,</u>
and <u>Horace Chase;</u> a novelette, <u>For the Major;</u> two story
collections, <u>The Front Yard and Other Italian</u> Stories and
<u>Dorothy and Other Italian Stories;</u> and a book of travel sketch-
es, <u>Mentone, Cairo, and Corfu.</u>

As the titles of the story collections indicate and even
a cursory examination of the novels reveals, Miss Woolson
was fascinated with places.   And through the whole of her
life, the place that seemed to mean most to her was Florida.
Soon after she arrived in St. Augustine in 1873, she wrote
to a friend:

> The life here is so fresh, so new, so full of certain
> wild freedom.   I walk miles through the hummocks,
> where it looks as though no one had ever walked
> before, gathering wild flowers everywhere, or sit-
> ting down under the pine trees to rest in the shade
> ....   You know the ocean is new to me and I am
> so fond of it already that I feel as if I never cared
> to go inland any more. [3]

Her admiration for the area continued undiminished during
her residence there, so that she could write to her literary
mentor, Edmund Clarence Stedman, just a month after her
arrival in Europe that she wanted to return to Florida to
live as soon as possible:

> I am only waiting to store up a little more money;
> then I shall return; buy a wee cottage down there;
> set up a crane and three orange-trees; & never
> stir again. [4]

No wonder, then, that some of her most vital work sprang
from a Florida background.

Her earliest writing about the state appeared in verse
form in <u>Harper's Magazine,</u> <u>Galaxy,</u> and <u>Appleton's Journal</u>
soon after she settled in St. Augustine.   The poems, written
in careful rhythm and rhyme and full of inversion and nineteenth-century poetic diction, nevertheless evoke some remarkable pictures.   The fourth stanza of "Pine Barrens,"
is one example:

Abroad upon the Barrens the saw-palmetto reddens

The ground with arméd ranks that firm for centuries
   have stood;
They kneel and pray to Heaven that their sins may be
   forgiven,
Their long green knives in readiness, bold outlaws of
   the wood!

That the pine barrens were more than mere landscape to her
is apparent in the last stanza of "The Florida Beach":

Alone, alone, we wander through
   The southern winter day.
The ocean spreads his mighty blue,
   The world is far away:
The tide comes in,--the birds fly low,
   As if to catch our speech--
Ah Fate! why must we ever go
From the beautiful Florida Beach?

Other descriptive poems about the Florida landscape, all
published between 1874 and 1876, are "Yellow Jessamine,"
"The Ancient City," and "The Ocklawaha." "Dolores" is a
narrative poem about a Minorcan woman and a surgeon in
the Union Army who saves her child.[5]

   Miss Woolson soon turned to short stories as the way
to relate her Florida experience, a fortunate change because
of her greater skill and originality in prose than in poetry.
There are four stories with north Florida settings,[6] and they
grow progressively more permeated with a sense of the mystery of the natural surroundings and of the role of environment in men's lives. "Miss Elisabetha" is the story of a
proud northern spinster who rears her lover's son to be a
gentleman in the town of Beata along the Warra River. Two
other women challenge her for control of Theodore; Miss
Elisabetha is victorious over the prima donna who wants to
teach him opera in Europe but is defeated by the beautiful,
uneducated Minorcan girl who marries him, provides him
with a large brood of lazy, ignorant, happy children, and
sends him to an early death. They tolerantly regard Miss
Elisabetha, who tirelessly works in the household, as a "species differing from theirs, but good in its way, especially
for work." Here is Miss Woolson's constantly recurring
theme of the way in which men's origins confer certain life-
long character traits. The Minorcan character is treated
again in "Felipa," a story of a wild southern child who falls
in love with a northerner and tries to kill both herself and

him when she learns of his impending marriage to a northern
woman.   Contrast between the northern and southern temperaments is important in the next Florida story Miss Woolson
wrote, "Sister St. Luke."   Pedro, a lighthouse keeper, is
married to Malvyna, a New England woman, whom his Minorcan friends and relatives regard as a "woman of wonder--of
an energy unfathomable."   Even her seven-year-old New
England bonnet is trimmed with a "durable" green ribbon and
a "vigorous" wreath of artificial flowers.   The characterization of Pedro and Malvyna provides most of the interest in
the story, whose plot focuses on the heroism during a storm
of Sister Luke, a timid nun from a nearby convent who is
nursed by Malvyna during an illness.

The most powerful of the Florida short stories without
doubt is "The South Devil," which moves quickly toward the
skillfulness of the novels, and which contains the germs of
the themes developed more fully in them.   Contrast between
the northern and southern character is central to the plot.
Mark Deal, a northerner, works from daylight until dusk
("and was probably the only white man in the State who did")
to create order and beauty in his plaza and to care for his
southern step-brother Carl, whom he has only recently met.
Carl sleeps most of the day, works not at all, and gambles
away Mark's savings in one card game.   But his strongest
and strangest vice is an attraction to the evils of the South
Devil, the poisonous cypress swamp nearby.   Mark's two
excursions into the swamp to rescue Carl give Miss Woolson
an opportunity to display her powers of description:

> They passed under the gray and solemn cypresses,
> rising without branches to an enormous height, their
> far foliage hidden by the moss, which hung down
> thickly in long flakes, diffusing the sunshine and
> making it silvery like mist; in the silver swung
> the air-plants, great cream-colored disks, and
> wands of scarlet, crowded with little buds, blossoms
> that looked like butterflies, and blossoms that looked
> like humming-birds, and little dragonheads with
> grinning faces.   Then they came to the region of
> the palms; these shot up, slender and graceful,
> and leaned over the stream the great aureum ferns
> growing on their trunks high in the air.   Beneath
> was a firmer soil than in the domain of the cypres-
> ses, and here grew a mat of little flowers, each
> less than a quarter of an inch wide, close together,
> pink, blue, scarlet, yellow, purple, but never white,

producing a hue singularly rich, owing to the absence
of that colorless color which man ever mingles
with his floral combinations, and strangely makes
sacred alike to the bridal and to death. ... The
air was absolutely still; no breeze reached these
blossoming aisles; each leaf hung motionless. The
atmosphere was hot, and heavy with perfumes. It
was the heart of the swamp, a riot of intoxicating,
steaming, swarming, fragrant, beautiful, tropical
life, without man to make or mar it. All the
world was once so, before man was made [pp. 191-
192].

Her ambivalent feelings toward the tropical land, so prominent
in the novels, begin to become apparent in this tale, even
slightly in the description of the swamp. The end of the
passage quoted reveals another of Miss Woolson's themes:
the awareness of the long history of the Florida peninsula.
One paragraph of "The South Devil" prods the reader into
an immediate awareness of that history; as Mark notices
fifty-year-old furrows in his field, the author comments:

There are many such traces of former cultivation
in Florida; we come suddenly upon old tracks, furrows, and drains in what we thought primeval forest; rose-bushes run wild and distorted old fig-trees
meet us in a jungle where we supposed no white
man's foot had ever before penetrated; the ruins
of a chimney gleam whitely through a waste of
thorny chaparral. It is all natural enough, if one
stops to remember that fifty years before the first
settlement was made in Virginia, and sixty-three
before the Mayflower touched the shores of the New
World, there were flourishing Spanish plantations
on this Southern coast, --more flourishing apparently,
than any the indolent peninsula has since known.
But one does not stop to remember it; the belief
is imbedded in all our Northern hearts that because
the narrow, sun-bathed State is far away and wild
and empty, it is also new and virgin, like the lands
of the West; whereas it is old, --the only gray-haired
corner our country holds [p. 175].

The consciousness of the past and of the beauties of the un-
spoiled land are two ever-relevant themes for readers of
Miss Woolson's fiction. A final theme of "The South Devil,"
one recurring frequently in her stories, is consummately Vic-

torian and dates her work for the contemporary reader. The idea of sacrifice, often to no purpose, appears again and again. In this last Florida short story, Carl takes a fatal walk through the swamp to post a letter, thinking perhaps he can redeem his worthless life by informing his cousin that Mark loves her. Often such sacrifices seem to be made only to prove strength of character.

Such unattractive, if not improbable, martyrs are perhaps part of the reason Miss Woolson's work is seldom read today. The problems with her books are undoubtedly those characteristics which made them popular in her own day. Her characters, in exercising a restraint admirable to the Victorian mind, seem wooden and unreal; the endless feminine analysis of emotions and motivations becomes comic after a while; the plots become too circumstantial to bear. If, however, the reader is able to recognize and isolate the Victorian elements, as, for example, a playgoer might recognize the conventions of British comedy, he or she can still find much to enjoy and appreciate in a Woolson novel. The humor alone often makes her stories worth the reading. Much of her humor is very subtle, and mildly malicious, as in her description of Felicité, the French woman, who looked as though she would like to be wicked: "In reality, however, she was harmless, for one insatiable ambition within her swallowed up all else, namely, the ambition not to be middle-aged. As she was forty-eight, the struggle took all her time" (p. 228). Another example in the same novel, Horace Chase, is the party given by a local St. Augustine do-gooder for the Indians held prisoner at Fort St. Marco. The company commander has wisely chosen only six of the Indians for the party, and the hostess tries to convert them:

> 'If I could only speak to them in their own tongue!' she said, yearningly. And the long sentences, expressive of friendship, which she begged the interpreter to translate to them, would have filled a volume. The interpreter, a very intelligent young man, obeyed all her requests with much politeness. 'Tell them then we love them,' said Mrs. Kip. 'Tell them that we think of their souls.'
>
> The interpreter bowed; then he translated as follows: 'The white squaw says that you have had enough to eat, and more than enough; and she hopes that you won't make pigs of yourselves if anything else is offered--especially Drowning Raven!' [pp. 183-184].

The reader who values a subtle wit, or one frequently not so subtle, will find much in Woolson.

But her real accomplishment is in her evocation of that sense of place that is an accomplishment confined to a few:  Thomas Hardy with the heaths of England, Sarah Orne Jewett with Vermont, Willa Cather with Nebraska, and Marjorie Kinnan Rawlings with rural Florida.  Miss Woolson's ability to see and to describe brings early Florida to life. Such scenes as the annual search for the first jessamine in early St. Augustine not only add flavor to her novels, but serve to reinforce both character and structure, as Hardy's Egdon Heath so often does.  The Florida settings in two novels--East Angels entirely and Horace Chase in part--control the characters, the action, the morality, the tone of the stories.  Miss Woolson, so often labeled a local colorist, does much more than skilfully describe an unknown region. For her, a sense of place pervades every area of life.

True, by the time of East Angels of 1886 and Horace Chase of 1894, her powers of descriptive writing are developed fully enough to be pleasurable in themselves.  She can describe the movements of a character in East Angels:

> He went to look at some camellias, whose glossy leaves formed a thicket at a little distance; on the other side of this thicket he discovered a crape-myrtle avenue, the delicate trees so choked and hustled by the ruder foliage which had grown up about them that they stood like captives in the midst of a rabble, broken-hearted and dumb [pp. 48-49].

She is able to weave her descriptions into the very fabric of her story without intrusion upon the action or change in pace. A trip in a canoe from East Angels, for example, shows her skill:

> Lightly it sped out towards deep water, the slightest motion sent it forward; its sides were of such slender thickness that the two men could feel the breathing of the great soft stream, which had here a breadth of three miles, though in sight, both above and below, it widened into six.  These broad water stretches were tranquil; from shore to shore the slow, full current swept majestically on; and even to look across the wide, still reaches, with the

> tropical forests standing thickly on their low strands,
> was a vision of peace for the most troubled human
> soul.
>
> Kildee plover flew chattering before the canoe
> while they were still near land.　Far above in the
> blue a bald-headed eagle sailed along.　Lanse chose
> to go out to the centre of the stream--Lanse never
> skirted the edge of anything; reaching it, he turned
> southward, and they voyaged onward for nearly an
> hour [p. 410].

Such scenes interested northern readers of 1886, many of
whom, like one of the characters in East Angels, must have
supposed there was nothing worth their personal consideration
south of Philadelphia.

With her two Florida novels, both popularly and crit-
ically acclaimed, Miss Woolson was able to capture the interest of northerners in the state.　The novels, like the
stories, are conventional and somewhat sentimental in characterization and plot.　East Angels tells of the romances and
marriages of two women:　the shallow southerner Garda Thorne
who marries unthinkingly twice, the second time to a Spaniard
whom she respects little, and the patient, noble northerner
Margaret Harold who stands by a husband even after he has
deserted her twice, although she loves another man.　Horace
Chase, only partly set in Florida, is the story of a young
woman married to an older successful man.　When a younger
colleague encourages her infatuation, it is the husband who
sacrifices his pride after a near-indiscretion confessed by
his wife.　It would seem nearly impossible to make such
slim plots interest a reader in 1970; yet they do, chiefly
because Miss Woolson's appreciation of surroundings and her
insight into the relationship between place and character make
fascinating study.

Beyond her ability to describe clearly those exotic
sights and smells which intrigued her in Florida, she brings
to the novels careful observation of the groups of people she
found there.　The Minorcans appear as colorful embodiments
of an indolent, sunny landscape.　The southern Negroes, particularly in East Angels, are carefully and attractively drawn.
Their speech, at times as incomprehensible in Miss Woolson's
printed version as it is aurally, has been called a "careful
philological study."　She observed with care the new immi-
grants to Florida, sometimes with admiration, sometimes
with disdain, as in East Angels:

> This new class counted within its ranks at present
> the captains and crews of the northern schooners
> that were beginning to come into that port for lum-
> ber; the agents of land-companies looking after
> titles and the old Spanish grants; speculators with
> plans in their pockets for railways, with plans in
> their pockets for canals, with plans in their pockets
> (and sometimes very little else) for draining the
> swamps and dredging the Everglades, many of the
> schemes dependent upon aid from Congress, and
> mysteriously connected with the new negro vote.
> In addition there were the first projectors of health
> resorts, the first northern buyers of orange groves:
> in short, the pioneers of that busy, practical Amer-
> ican majority ... [p. 54].

Of special interest to the modern reader is Miss
Woolson's wide knowledge of Florida history.  Her awareness
of the region's past expressed in "The South Devil" pervades
most of her southern stories.  In "Sister St. Luke" the structure of a lighthouse affords the opportunity to tell the history
of Pelican Island as each alteration and addition to the lighthouse is analyzed.  In East Angels the tracing of a deed back
to the original Spanish settlers becomes an informative lesson.  Miss Woolson tries to make the reader as conscious
of Florida's history as is Evert Winthrop in that novel:

> There was--he could not deny it--a certain com-
> parative antiquity about this southern peninsula
> which had in it more richness of color and a deeper
> perspective than that possessed by any of the rather
> blank, near, little backgrounds of American history
> farther north.  This was a surprise to him.  Like
> most New Englanders, he had unconsciously cher-
> ished the belief that all there was of historical im-
> portance, of historical picturesqueness even, in
> the beginnings of the republic, was associated with
> the Puritans from whom he was on his father's
> side descended, was appended to their stately hats
> and ruffs, their wonderful perseverance, their dig-
> nified orthography, the solemnities of their speech
> and demeanor [p. 15].

In Horace Chase, the "ancient city," as Miss Woolson calls
St. Augustine, provides historical comment, with much focus
on Fort San Marco and the Indian past.

The Florida environment exerts its influence on the

present just as much in these novels.  Miss Woolson's major
theme in all her southern work is the contrast between the
northern and southern temperaments.  East Angels opens
with a contrast between the regions and soon adapts the doctor's point of view: "to him the difference between New England and the South was as wide, whether considered geograph-
ically, psychologically, or historically, as that between the
South and Japan."  The indolent, sweet-natured Garda Thorne
of that novel is a natural product of the pine-barrens who
lacks the fortitude to cope with adversity.  Her mother, described by Henry James, as "the little starved yet ardent
daughter of the Puritans, who has been condemned to spend
her life in the land of the relaxed," expends her dying breath
in an attack on the region:

> Oh!  I so hate and loathe it all--the idle, unreal-
> izing, contented life of this tiresome, idle coast.
> They amounted to something once, perhaps; but
> their day is over, and will never come back.  They
> don't know it; you couldn't make them believe it
> even if you should try.  That is what makes you
> rage--they're so completely mistaken and so com-
> pletely satisfied! [p. 219].

Florida is variously referred to in these stories as the land
of the lotus eaters, the land of the alligators, and "this
miserable little half-afloat land."  And its shortcomings affect its inhabitants.  In Horace Chase, the infatuation of the
young wife Ruth occurs in St. Augustine "by fatality."  Her
comment that the winter in that town was the happiest of her
life is ironic, since her infatuation destroys both her health
and her happiness.  In East Angels, Evert Winthrop behaves
impulsively during a ride through the Monnlungs swamp and
declares that a man is not responsible for his actions in
such a place.

Miss Woolson's ambivalence makes her observations
of Florida more interesting than unmitigated praise might.
Perhaps she was trying for the balance of a Thomas Hardy,
whom she admired as a writer and of whom she wrote, "his
landscapes have no moral meanings."  Her final personal
judgment appears in a letter to Stedman from Europe in 1877:

> I hardly appreciated myself, until I was separated
> from it, how much I loved that warm hazy peninsula
> where I spent five long happy winters. . . .

Her admiration was combined with her skill to capture a spirit of early Florida which we might otherwise never know.

## REFERENCES

1.  Two Florida novels by William Gilmore Sims (The Lily and the Totem and Vasconselos) and one by James Fenimore Cooper (Jack Tier: or the Florida Reef) preceded Miss Woolson's work, but Sims' books were historical romances and Cooper's was a sea story with little description of the state.
2.  John Hervey, Saturday Review of Literature (October 12, 1929).
3.  Clare Benedict, Voices out of the Past, vol. 1 of Five Generations (London, 1930), pp. 230-231.
4.  This letter is reprinted in Rayburn S. Moore, Constance F. Woolson (New York, 1963), p. 27.
5.  The Florida poems and the periodicals in which they originally appeared are: "Yellow Jessamine," Appleton's Journal, March 1874; "Dolores," Appleton's Journal, July 1874; "The Florida Beach," The Galaxy, October 1874; "Pine Barrens," Harper's Magazine, December 1874; "The Ancient City," Harper's Magazine, December 1874 and January 1875; "The Ocklawaha," Harper's Magazine, January 1876.
6.  The Florida stories and the periodicals in which they originally appeared are: "Miss Elisabetha," Appleton's Journal, September 1875; "Felipa," Lippincott's Magazine, June 1876; "Sister St. Luke," The Galaxy, April 1877; "The South Devil," The Atlantic Monthly, February 1880.

Judith Kegan Gardiner

## THE HEROINE AS HER AUTHOR'S DAUGHTER

The nineteenth-century novel often ended with the heroine's marriage. Many twentieth-century novels climax, instead, with the heroine's deciding to walk out on--or back in on--her husband. If she survived the marriage and had children, the nineteenth-century heroine was likely to die of one of them--pathetically, and often with great convenience to the plot. If the twentieth-century heroine has children at the novel's end, at least in several contemporary women's novels, she is seen as dying spiritually, giving over her possible freedom and independence for an old and ensnaring role. If the nineteenth-century heroine spends her time trying to find a suitable husband, the twentieth-century heroine spends hers trying to find a suitable identity.

Many recent women's novels are semiautobiographical or confessional; the author seems to identify with her heroine. I am interested in the nature of this identification between author and heroine and its connection with the formation of women's psychological identities. Relationships between mothers and daughters are central to the development of women's identities, and therefore, novels which kill the heroine's mother throw some light on these psychological connections. The nineteenth-century fictional mother often died in childbirth to insure her child an unencumbered ascent as a self-made person. The twentieth-century heroine's mother also dies-- in the birth of the heroine's identity.

Jean Rhys' After Leaving Mr. Mackenzie presents a difficult and painful woman's transformation, that of the crushed rebel who becomes first a humiliated victim and then an indifferent one. [1] Julia ran away from poverty and sought adventure, "Only in [her] adventure men were mixed up, because of course they had to be" (p. 51). Ten years later she is in Paris, her baby long dead, abandoned by her last, prosperous lover, and "free" in a social world where her only recognizable status is mistress or prostitute. She seeks

money and relief from loneliness from various men, drifting
downward as her looks fade.

At the center of this progress, Julia returns home to
England and visits her sister and dying mother. Her younger
sister, Norah, has devoted herself for years to caring for
their paralyzed mother. Her bitter respectability offers no
alternative to Julia. Norah thinks, "My life's like death.
It's like being buried alive. It isn't fair" (p. 103). The
impoverished mother represents death-in-life to Julia, too:

> She had been accustomed for years to the idea that
> her mother was an invalid, paralyzed, dead to all
> intents and purposes. Yet, when Norah said in
> that inexorable, matter-of-fact voice, 'she doesn't
> know anybody,' a cold weight descended on her
> heart, crushing it [p. 72].

Julia cries from pity when she sees her mother tortured in
each breath, despite the others' insistence that she isn't suffering because she isn't conscious. The women can give each
other nothing because they are the same; the mother's dying
mirrors Julia's living, the life of poor women helpless in a
hostile society. Sitting in her sick mother's room, Julia
remembers "when she was a very young child, she had loved
her mother" (p. 106). Her mother had come from South
America. She had once been a vivacious woman, but she
felt cold and isolated in London. At first she longed for the
orange trees, the brightness of her past life; then she became
cold and turned her discontent against her daughter:

> From being the warm centre of her world her moth-
> er had gradually become a dark, austere, rather
> plump woman, who because she was worried, slap-
> ped you for no reason you knew.... Then you stop-
> ped being afraid or disliking. You simply became
> indifferent [p. 107].

Julia's life constantly repeats this cycle; at her mother's
funeral she abandons herself to tears, thinking of the "long
succession of humiliations and mistakes" of her life. For a
moment she feels herself "shooting upwards" like a "defiant
flame." Then she again sinks, feeling useless, quenched,
as though she has "reached nothing" (p. 131).

Her mother's death is necessary to Julia. It cuts
the last tie; it also relaxes her and frees her to return to

her own death-in-life. She is miserable, yet like her mother, apparently unconscious of her suffering. Her mother's death is a release from the intolerable past for Julia, though her future is even less tolerable. And she gets her only moment of peace, her only release into the semblance of a dependency that is not exploitative, after standing by her mother's death-bed. Then she feels "all right. She was only very sleepy, horribly sleepy, as a child would be after a very exciting day" (p. 125). She wakes from this restored childhood to motherless maturity: "both the effort and the relief were over and she faced a certain blankness" (p. 132).

Julia has rebelled against her mother's lot, but because she is poor and a woman, she has not escaped it. Her demi-monde death-in-life, her sister's and her mother's tortured paralysis are all one. Her mother's death is central in the novel, then, but it gives Julia the power only to cease car-ing, freedom only to die herself.

Julia's mother symbolizes the powers that thwart the heroine's life. In Margaret Drabble's Jerusalem the Golden, Mrs. Maugham is cast more directly as the power that re-stricts and hardens her daughter. [2] Cold, nasty, anti-intel-lectual, and hypocritical, the mother represents a death-in-life that Clara escapes by using her intellect to gain school scholarships and, finally, freedom in London. There she meets a remarkable family, apparently the complete opposite of her own: a golden, privileged, much-loved daughter who becomes her friend; a rich, glamorous son; and a wonderful writer-mother, whose house is filled with books and plants and light. Clara is dazzled and deliberately starts an affair with her friend's brother, with whom she goes to France. She excused her absence by claiming that her mother was ill. On her return, she is shocked to find that her mother is ill:

> When Clara opened the telegram and saw the news
> about her mother, she trembled.... Her first
> thought was, I have killed my mother. By taking
> her name in vain, I have killed her [p. 208].

The mother is dying of cancer. Clara returns north to see her, and their last conversations are as cranky and irritable as they had been throughout Clara's childhood. At the end of the novel, Clara leaves her childhood home with her lover. No longer excessively impressed by him, she is still attract-ed to his world of sexual freedom and material success that she has so long been denied:

> Her mother was dying, but she herself would survive
> it, she would survive even the guilt and convenience
> and grief of her mother's death, she would survive
> because she had willed herself to survive [p. 224].

Before this moment, however, she had come across some
old notebooks of her mother's, written "before her mother's
marriage, before the end of her hopes" (p. 214).    At first
Clara shrinks from the evidence of the notebooks.    She had
wanted her mother to remain the pure force of hatred and
negation; she had wanted to be sure that her mother deserved
all the blame.    But Clara reads the notebooks and cries when
she thinks of "so much deception, of so much disappointment,
of a life so eked and spent and drawn and withered away" as
her mother's had been.    Yet, she falls asleep at last in relief, even in reconciliation, "for she was glad that she had
however miserably pre-existed, she felt, for the first time,
the satisfaction of her true descent" (p. 214).

In Agnes Smedley's Daughter of Earth, the heroine
also comes to view her mother as deeply oppressed by sexual
and economic conditions. 3   A victim herself, the mother has
victimized her daughter by transmitting to her a legacy of
harshness, lack of tenderness, and fear of sex.    Marie's
first understanding of parental sexual relations darkens her
attitude towards her mother:

> From that moment the mother who was above wrong
> disappeared, and henceforth I faced another woman.
> Strange emotions of love and disgust warred within
> me.    And now when she struck my body she aroused
> only primitive hatred.... For years afterwards
> she and I gazed at each other across a gulf of
> hostility [pp. 16-17].

Marie is an active, imaginative child who is misunderstood
by her mother.    Her mother beats her for starting fires,
for lying, and for being stubborn: "As the years of her unhappy married life increased, as more children arrived, she
whipped [Marie] more and more" (p. 11).    Like Drabble's
Clara, Marie is starved for affection: "it was difficult for
her to beat my need for her love out of me" (p. 12); yet,
she too prides herself on becoming hard as a result.    As
her mother becomes poorer and more broken by work, Marie
begins to sympathize with her and to act from an understanding of their common oppression.    When her drunk father tries
to beat her mother, Marie joins her mother in "a bond of

misery that was never broken" (p. 114). But mother and
daughter can show no affection towards each other until Marie
watches over her mother's death from starvation and over-
work.

After her mother's death, she tries briefly to take on
the burdens of her family but abruptly escapes, for years
remaining filled with self-hatred, hatred for her parents,
and fear of the love that enslaves women. Her mother's
death does not free Marie sexually; instead, she continues
to associate sex, her mother, and death. When she reluc-
tantly is persuaded to marry, she faces "a finality that [seems]
akin to the finality of [her] mother's death" (p. 196). Ultimately, her mother's death reinforces her dedication to freedom from oppression, the oppression that wasted her "mother
who lay under the earth" (p. 326). A "daughter of Earth,"
in her political goals Marie thus becomes her mother's daughter at last.

Other current women's novels treat the death of the
heroine's mother similarly; for example, there is the dead-
alive mother in Margaret Atwood's Surfacing and the com-
plaining, cancer-ridden mother in Marge Piercy's Small
Changes. 4 In these novels and in those we have already considered, the heroines' mothers die from "natural" causes.
They die slow, horrible, wasting deaths, often from cancer
or something connected with the stomach. The mothers who
fail to feed their daughters with adequate love and self-esteem
are themselves eaten up by disease.

In the novels of Rhys, Drabble, and Smedley, the
heroine, who originally expresses hatred and resentment
against her mother, achieves some kind of reconciliation
with her through the mother's death. Julia, Clara, and Marie
learn to understand their "rejecting" mothers in terms of the
mother's own thwarted lot in a patriarchy that bears down
hardest on poor women. However, we should not view the
mothers merely as edifying examples of social injustice:
their deaths are crucial to the heroines' formation of their
own identities. In Small Changes and Jerusalem the Golden,
the heroines' sexual experiences are concurrent with the
mothers' dying. The death of the mother thus becomes a
death of childhood repression. Yet, more centrally, the
mothers in these novels are what the daughters fear and must
kill in themselves in order to achieve a positive female identity.

The concept of identity is a complex and troubling one.

To some sociologists, it means identification or imitation based on sex-role socialization. In Freudian psychology, a child identifies with the parent of the appropriate sex, based on the successful resolution of the Oedipus complex, but the process is assymmetrical for the two sexes. The girl may retain a strong primary libidinal tie with her mother, but she does not form an impersonal or "abstract" identification with her, as the boy does with the father. [5] The ego psychologists, like Erik Erikson, have developed the concept of identity as fundamental to their approach to whole-life psychology, [6] but none of these theories have yet been persuasive to feminist scholars, who have sought recently to forge a more appropriate understanding of the formation of female identity.

According to Nancy Chodorow, in order to have a strong, healthy, sex-appropriate identity, the girl must model herself on her mother. In some societies, like the Javanese and the Mundurucú, female identity seems to form securely and easily. [7] Even under some forms of patriarchy, separate spheres for women may have the effect of secluding women in a women's realm within which they can achieve creativity, identity, and distinction. Carol Smith-Rosenberg has documented the existence of strong networks of affection and support and of a demiworld of private writing in diaries and letters for the segregated middle-class American women of the nineteenth century. In this world, she finds no evidence of the hostility between mothers and daughters we are taught to regard as universal. [8] For the twentieth-century English or American woman novelist, however, coming to independent power and creativity has meant competition with men in a patriarchal culture which until now has not recognized a supportive "sphere" of women. This exclusively male frame of reference causes difficulty for the girl who must shape her identity on a person who is culturally devalued and depreciated, who often regards herself as inferior and who is resented by her daughter for having produced her as a member of the less valued sex. As Chodorow writes, "Various kinds of evidence suggest that separation from the mother, the breaking of dependence, and the establishment and maintenance of a consistently individuated sense of self remain difficult psychological issues for Western, middle-class women" (p. 58).

The formation of a female identity is central to female personality, then, and the task of creating an identity seems to differ for men and women in Western society. Moreover, the creation of literary identities tends to reflect the psy-

chologies of their authors.    I think it likely, therefore, that
women novelists identify with their heroines.    For the woman
writer, her characters provide a way of creating and rejecting, of trying out, various identities, and the most important of these will be formed on the mother-daughter line:
"Mothering ... involves a double identification. ...    A woman
identifies with her own mother and reexperiences herself as
a cared-for child" (Chodorow, pp. 46-67).    The novelist can
thus "mother" or create a "daughter" identity for her heroine.
She experiences her heroine as a cared-for child, though,
as we have seen, she may need to create and kill the heroine's
devalued fictional mother in order to do so.

If fictional motherhood holds a possibility for the novelist establishing a positive identity for herself, she may
nonetheless continue to see biological motherhood as dangerous,
as an intrinsically suicidal role.    Having children may obliterate a woman's fragile identity and make her a conduit
for the life forces of others, rather than a person in her
own right.    Certainly, in most contemporary women's fiction,
motherhood is not the fulfillment and completion promised
by the Freudian paradigm and the feminine mystique.    If,
after freeing herself from her own mother, the heroine of
some current novels allows herself to have children, she
must give them up in order to establish her own identity.
Lessing's Martha Quest follows Ibsen's Nora in this respect.
In stories by Kate Chopin and Gail Godwin, the young wife
commits suicide as the only way to gain freedom from her
husband, her children, and her prescribed social roles. [9]

Mothering and daughtering, then, remain difficult in
twentieth-century women's fiction, and female problems of
identification, deeper and more complex than mere sex-role
socialization, recur repeatedly as the novelists try to forge
viable identities for their heroines.    As we have seen, the
novelists killed their heroines' mothers in After Leaving Mr.
Mackenzie, Jerusalem the Golden, and Daughter of Earth in
order to free them; yet, the daughters were still shadowed
by their mothers' inheritance, unable to love fully, not yet
strong enough to carry on the line by becoming mothers themselves.

Christina Stead, in The Man Who Loved Children,
handles the theme of female matricide with mythic clarity,
and it is the most direct of these novels in tracing the growth
of the heroine's identity as a writer. [10]    Henrietta Pollit is
a rebel against marriage and motherhood without seeing any

alternatives to them:

> About the girls she only thought of marriage, and
> about marriage she thought as an ignorant, dissat-
> isfied, but helpless slave did of slavery.... 'A
> mother! What are we worth really? They all grow
> up whether you look after them or not' [pp. 426-27].

She cannot see anything in her life except her children; "a
woman's children are all she has of her body and breath,"
she tells her stepdaughter Louie (p. 463).

The adolescent Louie plots to kill both her selfish,
infantile father and her stepmother, who has become more
and more witch-like and intolerable in reaction to her huge
family and its pressing financial problems. The parents
quarrel incessantly and violently, and Henny threatens to kill
herself, her husband, and the children. Louie decides,
"they're too cowardly to separate. If I killed them both we
would be free" (p. 467). But Louie poisons only one cup.
Henny realizes what Louie is doing and drinks from the cup.
She exonerates and salutes her stepdaughter and dies defying
her husband:

> 'You beast, you pair of beasts, my womb is torn
> to pieces with you.... And your dirty sheets fal-
> ling on to me to suffocate me with the sweat, I
> can't stand it any more--she's not to blame, she's
> got guts.... Damn you all' [p. 472].

Thus Louie succeeds in murdering the wicked stepmother of
fairy tale, and at the same time she is innocent because
Henny commits suicide. The desperate nexus between sexuality, motherhood, and death closes in again. Henny is not
the one Louie most hates, but she is the mirror of what
Louie must not become, and so she must be killed. After
Henny's death, Sam tries to make Louie into his ego-supporter
and housekeeper. "'It is a pity you never had a mother,'
he tells her sentimentally. 'Well, I'm my own mother,'
Louie says, without emotion. 'And I can look after myself'"
(p. 488). After assuming the power to kill her stepmother
and to "mother" herself, Louie is further empowered to leave
her father and to assert herself as a potential artist: "Why
didn't I run away before? she wondered.... They would
look everywhere and conclude she had gone for a walk. 'So
I have,' she thought, smiling secretly, 'I have gone for a
walk round the world'" (p. 491).

To speak of the heroine as her author's "daughter,"
then, is an oversimplification, but one which points to the
problematic and interesting connections between mother-daughter ties, the formation of female ego identity, and the identification of the author with her heroine. I speculate that
contemporary women writers typically identify with their heroines in a way congruent with the vicissitudes of female psychology in a patriarchal culture. Even now, creating her
own identity, mothering herself, is still so difficult that the
woman novelist kills her heroine's devalued mother so that
the heroine can achieve power over her own identity. "We
think back through our mothers," wrote Virginia Woolf. 11
We have yet to think forward through them.


REFERENCES

1.    Jean Rhys, After Leaving Mr. Mackenzie (New York:
        Harper & Row, 1931). Page references follow in
        text.
2.    Margaret Drabble, Jerusalem the Golden (London: Wei-
        denfeld and Nicolson, 1967). Page references fol-
        low in text.
3.    Agnes Smedley, Daughter of Earth (1927) (reprinted, Old
        Westbury, Conn.: Feminist Press, 1973). Page
        references follow in text.
4.    Margaret Atwood, Surfacing (New York: Popular Library,
        1972); Marge Piercy, Small Changes (Greenwich,
        Conn.: Fawcett, 1972).
5.    Christopher Lasch, "The Emotions of Family Life," New
        York Review of Books, Nov. 27, 1975, p. 39, crit-
        icizes the sociological conception of "identification"
        as shallow; Juliet Mitchell tries to interpret Freud
        as providing descriptions useful to the feminist,
        Psychoanalysis and Feminism (New York: Random
        House, Vintage Books, 1974).
6.    In a recent version, Erik H. Erikson, Dimensions of a
        New Identity, the 1973 Jefferson Lectures in the
        Humanities (New York: W. W. Norton, 1974).
7.    Nancy Chodorow, "Family Structure and Feminine Per-
        sonality," in Women, Culture, and Society, ed. by
        Michelle Zimbalist Rosáldo and Louise Lamphere
        (Stanford, Calif.: Stanford University Press, 1974),
        pp. 60-62. Later page references follow in text.
        The Mundurucú are described by Yolanda Murphy
        and Robert F. Murphy, Women of the Forest (New
        York: Columbia University Press, 1974).

8.  Carroll Smith-Rosenberg, "The Female World of Love
    and Ritual... ," Signs, 1 (Autumn 1975), 15.  The
    Mundurucú have such a separate sphere of women
    also.

9.  Kate Chopin, The Awakening (New York:  Capricorn,
    1964); "The Story of an Hour" in By a Woman
    Writt, ed. by Joan Goulianos (Baltimore:  Penguin,
    1973), pp. 249-52; Gail Godwin, "A Sorrowful Wo-
    man" and "Interstices" in Dream Children (New
    York:  Knopf, 1976), pp. 167-74; 99-114.

10. Christina Stead, The Man Who Loved Children (New York:
    Avon, Bard Books, 1966, c1940).  Page references
    follow in text.

11. Virginia Woolf, A Room of One's Own (New York:  Har-
    court, Brace & World, Harbinger Book, 1957,
    c1929), p. 79.

Evelyn Thomas Helmick

ZORA NEALE HURSTON*

Even as a young girl, Zora Neale Hurston remembered,
"I had the map of Dixie on my tongue." She was able to
draw that map in language of great vitality in her four novels,
an autobiography, and two books of folklore, all written during the thirties and forties. Interest in those books, which
won great critical acclaim at the time of their publication,
is reviving today; their author, as a fascinating personality,
an anthropologist, and an outspoken Negro observer of racial
problems, is due no less attention.

Zora Neale Hurston was born on January 7, 1901, in
Eatonville, Florida, an all-Negro town near Orlando.[1] Her
father was John Hurston, carpenter, minister, and mayor who
considered his younger daughter too full of spirit to survive
in a white-dominated world. Her mother was Lucy Ann Potts,
who married John Hurston at fourteen and bore him eight
children before she died when Zora Neale was nine, leaving
the child with no one to encourage her to "jump at de sun."

"Passed around like a bad penny" for the next several
years, Zora Neale became an introspective young lady. Her
closest friend was an elderly white man who had passed the
Hurston cottage at the moment of her birth and became responsible for her safe delivery. For a time, he tried to
guide her, but he too died when she was ten. Alone, she
retreated to a world of fantasy remarkable for its inventive-
ness and intensity. One passage in her autobiography, for
example, recounts her anguish at discovering that the moon
followed not only her, but the other children as well. She
created dolls of corn shucks and clear bars of soap and for
years imagined events in their lives. Very early she began
to make up stories to match those she heard the men tell in

*Reprinted by permission of the author and publisher from
The Carrell 11, 1 & 2 (June–December 1970), 1-19.

their "lying sessions" at the general store.   In her world of
constant fiction her imagination was so stirred that the trees
and animals seemed to talk to her; eventually she had visions
of her future which recurred frequently until each was fulfilled.

    Her inventive habits would seem good practice for a
future novelist, but Zora Neale discovered obstacles in the
way of her learning the more formal tools of the profession.
She attended school only sporadically and, worse, lived with
families who had no books for her to read.   The desolation
of those years can best be told in her own words:

> There is something about poverty that smells like
> death.   Dead dreams dropping off the heart like
> leaves in a dry season and rotting around the feet;
> impulses smothered too long in the fetid air of
> underground caves.   The soul lives in a sickly air.
> People can be slave-ships in shoes. [2]

Her hopes for school rose when her brother sent for her to
live with his family and were dashed when she discovered
she was to be a full-time unpaid maid.   With the help of
friends, she ran away to become a lady's maid to a singer,
who offered friendship, learning, and finally assistance with
Zora Neale's return to school.   When the singer left the
touring company, they were in Baltimore; there the lady's
maid became a student again.

    She attended night school for a few weeks, but was
encouraged by sympathetic teachers to enter the preparatory
division of Morgan College.   Both delighted and somewhat
awed by the good looks and manners of her classmates, who
were children of the members of a wealthy Negro community,
she became conscious of her own appearance, as this passage
in her autobiography reveals:

> And here I was, with my face looking like it had
> been chopped out of a knot of pine wood with a
> hatchet on somebody's off day, sitting up in the
> middle of all this pretty.   To make things worse,
> I had only one dress, a change of underwear and
> one pair of tan oxfords. [3]

But the young people were friendly and, more importantly,
her teachers were exciting.   "The atmosphere made me feel
right," she said.   "Every new thing I learned in school made

me happy. "  Her experience was so satisfying that she planned to stay at Morgan for her college work.   But an acquaintance, the daughter of a Howard University professor, made
her consider that school seriously.   She was able to earn
her tuition and board working as a waitress and later as a
manicurist in Washington.   In all, she did a year and a half
of work at Howard, losing some months because of illness.

Even holding a full-time job, she was able to take
part in all the literary activities on campus, and soon her
abilities earned her membership in The Stylus, a small literary society.   A short story which she wrote for the organization's journal brought her work to the attention of
Charles Johnson, founder of the Negro Renaissance taking
place at the time.   He published two of Zora Neale's short
stories, "Drenched in Light" and "Spunk," in his Opportunity
Magazine.   His encouragement took her to New York, even
though she had only $1.50 and no prospects for a job there.
The Johnsons helped with food, money, and friendship, and
through Dr. Johnson's admiration for her work came a prize
for a short story at the first award dinner of Opportunity
in 1925.   That prize led to further good fortune:   Fanny Hurst
offered her a job as secretary and a home; Annie Nathan
Meyer, a trustee of Barnard, obtained a scholarship to that
school for her.

Like all her other educational experiences, Barnard
brought great pleasure to her.   The Social Register crowd,
she said, soon took her up, and she became "Barnard's
sacred black cow.   If you had not had lunch with me, you
had not shot from taw. "   Academic life was as glorious as
social life.   She had planned to major in English, but showed
such promise in an anthropology course that her term paper
was shown to Dr. Franz Boas, the chairman of the department, who was to Zora Neale "the king of kings. "   She worked
under Gladys Reichert and Ruth Benedict as well, accomplish-
ing so much before she graduated in 1928--the second Negro
to be awarded a degree by Barnard--that Dr. Boas arranged
a Rosenwald graduate fellowship for her.

The results of the first six months of her project--
to collect folklore of the South--were disappointing.   Recog-
nizing that her approach in "Barnardese" was wrong, she
corrected it for her next field trip to her home country, and
thus was able to find many stories and work songs, particularly in the sawmills and phosphate mines of Polk County.
From there she traveled to New Orleans, where her interest

turned to Hoodoo, or "sympathetic magic" as she called it. She studied the lore with the Frizzly Rooster and other "two-headed doctors," each time submitting to elaborate initiation ceremonies.   Moving on to the Bahamas, then to the British West Indies and Haiti, she discovered other Hoodoo rites of the natives.   In Nassau she was enchanted by the subjects which the natives "put in sing" and by their "jumping dances." She attended every dance she could and learned to "jump." On her return to New York in 1932 she introduced these Bahamian folk songs and dances in order to "show what beauty and appeal there was in genuine Negro material, as against the Broadway concept."   Her production, called "From Sun to Sun," was successful, both in New York and in many other cities throughout the country.

In 1932 there was little money for research grants; Miss Hurston was forced, perhaps fortunately, to return to her native village of Eatonville to begin writing.   Her first project was to edit the material she had gathered in four years of field work in the southern states.   The resulting book, entitled Mules and Men, is comprised of an introduction by Franz Boas, a section on folk tales, one on Hoodoo, and an appendix containing Negro songs with music, formulae of Hoodoo doctors, a list of paraphernalia of conjure, prescriptions of root doctors, and a glossary.   The beginning is in the form of a first-person narrative of Miss Hurston's return to Eatonville with its "love of talk and song."   There follow many simple tales, often with little point, told merely for the joy of storytelling.   Some are the Brer Rabbit stories so popular in the South; others are tall tales of the lumber camp; many are stories in dialect filled with an ironic sense of the Negro's destiny in a white man's world. 4

One "lying session" of lumberjacks is a contest to describe an ugly man.   One speaker says, "Ah seen a man so ugly till they had to spread a sheet over his head so sleep could slip up on him."   Another counters, "Ah'm goin' to talk with my mouth wide open.   Those men y'all been talkin' 'bout wasn't ugly at all.   Those was pretty men.   Ah knowed one so ugly till you could throw him in the Mississippi River and skim ugly for six months."   When he is declared the winner of the contest, another man agrees, "He ain't lying. Ah knowed dat same man.   He didn't die--he jus' uglied away."

A constant subject in Miss Hurston's work is the language of the South; naturally, dialect figures prominently. One example in Mules and Men is a recording of her conversation with a lumber worker in the Everglades:

> "Ma'am, whut might be yo' entrimmins?"
>
> "My whut?"
>
> "Yo' entrimmins?  Yo' entitlums?"

The "entitlums," says Miss Hurston, gave her the cue.    "Oh,
my name is Zora Hurston.   And what may be yours?"  With
her gift for capturing authentic sounds and syntax, she can
write long passages in dialect without wearying her reader.

The introduction to part two of the book explains that
she had enjoyed gathering folktales in Florida, but had done
nothing about Hoodoo.   "So I slept a night, and the next
morning I headed my toe-nails toward Louisiana and New
Orleans in particular. "  In New Orleans, the Hoodoo capital
of America, her preparation to become a practitioner included
fasting, meditation, drinking of blood, and animal sacrifice.
Although the rituals of worship are bound in secrecy, Hoodoo
is not, she insists, drum-beating and dancing.   "Hoodoo, or
Voodoo, as pronounced by the whites, is burning with a flame
in America, with all the intensity of a suppressed religion. "

Although Mules and Men was the first book Miss Hurston wrote, the first published was a novel, Jonah's Gourd
Vine.   The idea had come to her, she said, in 1929, when
she was researching in the South, but she postponed writing
it because she was expected, as a black, to write about the
racial problem.   "My interest," she said,

> lies in what makes a man or woman do such-and-
> so, regardless of his color.   It seemed to me that
> the human beings I met reacted pretty much to the
> same stimuli.   Different idioms, yes.   Circum-
> stances and conditions having power to influence,
> yes.   Inherent difference, no. [5]

But the publication of a short story, "The Gilded Six-Bits,"
brought inquiries from several editors.   The gentlest of them,
from J. B. Lippincott, encouraged Miss Hurston to reply that
she was writing a book, even though the first page was not
written.   But as she said in her autobiography, "the story
told itself to me"; she completed the novel in three months
in the fall of 1933.

The most striking thing about Jonah's Gourd Vine is

the correlation between the novel and the young Zora's early years.    The protagonist is John Pearson, a man whose life parallels the life of John Hurston in every verifiable way. Both arrive from "over the creek" to court a girl named Lucy Potts, gravitate to Eatonville to become carpenter and minister, marry a predatory woman after Lucy dies, lose favor in the town, and die prematurely in an automobile accident.    Perhaps this story told itself to Miss Hurston because writing it was a way to rid herself of her ambivalent feelings toward her father.    From the beginning of Zora's life, her father had favored her older sister Sarah and had predicted a dire future for Zora; he had not allowed her to carry out her mother's dying wishes; he had married a woman whom she and her siblings hated.    When Miss Hurston, the Barnard graduate, was told of her father's death, she could say objectively, "With my mother gone and nobody to guide him, life had not hurt him, but it had turned him loose to hurt himself. "

The story of Jonah's Gourd Vine, then, is of a young bastard son born into a poor family in cotton country who courts a young girl on the right side of the creek.    The trials of even the most intelligent, energetic, and handsome of young blacks in the South are evident.    However, the couple prosper for a while when they help to settle Eatonville, and John's industry as a carpenter and his magnetism as a preacher make them prominent in the town.    But John is unable to resist the charms of other women.    When one entices him through Hoodoo, the neglected Lucy dies, deliberately, it seems to John.    The other woman, again with the aid of An' Dangie Dowie the Hoodoo woman, forces John to marry her. As a result John loses his power in Eatonville, where he can no longer earn a living as a carpenter.    He flees to Plant City, where he meets a wealthy widow who buys him a Cadillac which allows him to return to Eatonville to impress his former parishoners.    But while he is there, he dallies with a young girl for most of his last night and dies in an automobile crash because he is too sleepy to drive home. At the funeral service, his friends beat upon O-go-doe, the ancient drum: "O-go-doe, the voice of Death--that promises nothing, that speaks with tears only, and of the past. "    The final eulogy is spoken:  "He wuz uh man, and nobody knowed him but God. "

Much of Jonah's Gourd Vine is devoted to Miss Hurston's philosophy.    Her frequently-repeated phrase, "Ah ain't got to do but two things--stay black and die," appears here for the first time. The relationship between blacks and whites is explicit, as in this exchange between two Negroes:

> "What the news?"
>
> "Oh the white folks is still in the lead."

But the no less desperate struggle among the members of the Negro race, with envy impelling mass man of whatever race to destroy the man on top, is a dominant theme of this first novel, as well as her other works of fiction. Many of the superstitions, games, songs, mores of the Florida Negro are repeated here. Such customs as feeding sheep shadney-- tea made from sheep droppings--to infants who seem too weak to survive are recounted. (This seems only a little more horrifying than putting woodlice around the infants' necks to help them cut their first teeth--a practice mentioned in Miss Hurston's autobiography.) The picture of Negro life in Florida is full and rich in this novel. The New York Times reviewer praised especially "the excellent rendition of Negro dialect":

> Unlike the dialect in most novels about the American Negro, this does not seem to be merely the speech of white man with the spelling distorted. Its essence lies rather in the rhythm and balance of the sentences, in the warm artlessness of the phrasing.

The exceptional praise for a first novel by the Times indicates the general critical acclaim received by Jonah's Gourd Vine.

With the publication of Mules and Men in 1935, Miss Hurston renewed her interest in Hoodoo, returning to New York to apply for a Guggenheim fellowship to finance research in Haiti. Once in Haiti, however, she took seven weeks from that research to write a novel, one that she claimed had been dammed up inside her. Their Eyes Were Watching God was written as she fled from a stormy love affair that threatened to overwhelm her. 6 And the story is, from beginning to end, a love story of Janie, a romantic, sixteen-year-old quadroon, who dreams of marriage:

> She was stretched out on her back beneath the pear tree soaking in the alto chant of the visiting bees, the gold of the sun and the panting breath of the breeze when the inaudible voice of it all came to her. She saw a dust-bearing bee sink into the sanctum of a bloom; the thousand sister-calyxes arch

to meet the love embrace and the ecstatic shiver
of the tree from root to tiniest branch creaming
in every blossom and frothing with delight.   So
this was a marriage!   She had been summoned to
behold a revelation.   Then Janie felt a pain re-
morseless sweet that left her limp and languid. [7]

This bit of pathetic fallacy characterizes Janie's dreams and
at the same time contrasts brutally with the events of her
life.

Her grandmother, assuring her that love comes with
marriage, gives her to a farmer, middle-aged, dirty, un-
loving, who assigns her increasing amounts of farm work.
Before a year is up, she runs off with Joe Starks, on his
way from Georgia to Eatonville.   Joe provides the leader-
ship the people of the town have been looking for, as he buys
land, installs a street light, builds a general store, and is
elected mayor.   Janie, working long hours in the general
store and neglected by her husband, considers fleeing down
a country road again, but she realizes that she is thirty-
five--twice as old as last time.   She determines to pretend
that Joe is everything she wants.   But one day during an
argument in the store before many townspeople, her frustration impels her to strike such a humiliating blow at his manhood that he never recovers.   When he dies soon afterward,
Janie gives him a funeral that is "the finest thing Orange
County had ever seen with Negro eyes" and returns to run
the store.   The arrival in town of Tea Cup (whose real name
is Virigible Woods) brings her one more chance for fun and
love.   They move to the mucks--the Everglades near Clewis-
ton and Belle Glade--to plant and pick beans; there they find
a life of vigor and joy.   When a hurricane--graphically described in the book--drives them to Palm Beach, Tea Cup
is bitten by a rabid dog while protecting Janie, develops tet-
anus, and forces her to shoot him in his madness.

Although this novel is written about many of the same
people and places that appear in Jonah's Gourd Vine, Miss
Hurston's more poetic style, her fuller development of character, and her greater gift for description of setting all reveal a writer of increasing power.   Many of the themes
match those of Jonah's Gourd Vine, as well.   The struggle
for position among blacks is demonstrated by the high-yellow
barkeeper who wants to restrict her place to lighter blacks.
The struggle between whites and blacks appears after the
hurricane when the skin color of each corpse must be deter-

mined because whites, however unidentifiable, are placed in
separate coffins, while blacks are thrown into a common
burial hole.   And the struggle of the Negro woman, perhaps
the most desperate of all, is experienced by Janie and described by her grandmother:

> 'Honey, de white man is de ruler of everything as
> far as Ah been able to find out....   So de white
> man throw down de load and tell de nigger man
> tuh pick it up.   He pick it up because he have to,
> but he don't tote it.   He hand it to him womenfolks.
> De nigger woman is de mule of the world so far
> as Ah can see.   Ah been prayin' fuh it tuh be dif-
> ferent wid you.   Lawd, Lawd, Lawd!'8

These struggles are balanced by scenes of high comedy, such
as the funeral service of the town's favorite donkey with its
parody of many religious rites.   As always in Miss Hurston's
works, dialect adds its lighter moments.   Teacup, eating
Janie's mulatto rice, says, "Gal, it's too good!   You switches
a mean fanny around in a kitchen. "   And Janie's disdain for
gossipers is expressed in equally colorful language:   "If God
don't think no mo' 'bout them then Ah do, they's a lost ball
in de high grass. "   All the elements add up to what the New
York Times critic called "a well-nigh perfect story. "

     That second novel completed, Miss Hurston worked on
research for her authoritative book on Hoodoo, Tell My Horse,
published in England as Voodoo Gods:  An Inquiry into Native
Myths and Magic in Jamaica and Haiti.   (She spells the word
with a V throughout this book.)   Part I includes five essays
on Jamaica, most of them centering about problems of color
and racial lines.   She describes the Jamaican practice of
claiming percentage of white blood of one's father while ignoring the existence of a black mother.   But, then, she says,
the situation is improving, and we must allow time.   After
all, "Some Americans are still aping the English as best
they can even though they have had one hundred and fifty
years in which to recover. "   Another essay is a discussion
of the superstitions of Jamaica, in which Miss Hurston maintains a remarkable tone.   She tells of Brother Anansi, the
Spider, a culture hero who is personated in Haiti by Ti Malice and in the United States by Brer Rabbit.   One fascination is with duppies, those Spirits who live in trees.   Without
condescension, Miss Hurston discusses one man who "had a
covenant with a tree on the sunny side. "   She tells of the
preparation of the young Jamaican girl for marriage and of

the place of woman in a society in which her only function
is to afford pleasure to a man who can divorce her simply
by returning her to her parents. Of a woman in the Carib-
bean she writes:

> If she is of no particular family, poor and black,
> she is in a bad way indeed in that man's world.
> She had better pray to the Lord to turn her into a
> donkey and be done with the thing. It is assumed
> that God made poor black females for beasts of
> burden, and nobody is going to interfere with prov-
> idence. [9]

Part II of Tell My Horse is a series of essays on the
troubled political climate of Haiti, so apparent even thirty-
five years ago. Miss Hurston sees the problem in perspective: "In the past, as now, Haiti's curse has been her poli-
ticians." Here is the first indication of the preoccupation
with politics which would become so passionate in her later
years.

Part III delves into the study of Haitian Voodoo, again
with a tone both sympathetic and objective. At the same time
that Miss Hurston shows a feeling for and understanding of
Voodoo gods, she can compare their worship with that of
Greek, Roman, and Scandinavian gods. She gives a very
explicit explanation of the sexual basis of all Voodoo belief.
The important three-legged horse, for example, is a survival
of an African puberty rite for males. Girls are taught to
fear it; boys are not. Another of the investigations concerns
zombies. Miss Hurston was allowed to touch and even photo-
graph an authentic zombie: "I know that there are Zombies
in Haiti. People have been called back from the dead." Her
final judgment on Voodoo is found in her autobiography. Voodoo is as valid as any religion that satisfies, she says.

> If science ever gets to the bottom of Voodoo in
> Haiti and Africa, it will be found that some impor-
> tant medical secrets, still unknown to medical
> science, give it its power rather than the gestures
> of ceremony. [10]

The appendix to Tell My Horse prints some fascinating songs
of worship to Voodoo gods. This book and Mules and Men
have caused Miss Hurston's work to be called definitive in
the field of Voodoo.

The months in her life after the completion of Tell My

Horse are not very well documented.   She returned to New
York, went South for several months, then back to New York
to resume her love affair with a man identified only as A.
W. P.   During this interval she was undoubtedly working on
her next novel, Moses, Man of the Mountain, but strangely
she does not mention that book anywhere in her autobiography.
Moses is the story of Egyptian oppression of the Hebrews
told in modern Negro dialect, making clear a number of parallels.   The dominating one is between Moses--the serpent
god--and the most powerful god in any Negro culture.   Miss
Hurston indicates the widespread worship of Moses in an
introduction and makes the identification stronger when he
is called in the book "the finest Hoodoo man in the world."
In the scenes in which Moses demonstrates his magic tech-
niques, or climbs to a mountain top obscured by clouds, or
casts hypnotic spells, he is truly a shamanistic figure.   Many
of the incidents point up Miss Hurston's own view of religion,
a rather ambiguous judgment, finally.   Moses, as a witch-
doctor, is admirable in his strength and his devotion to his
people, but he is impatient with the knowledge without wisdom
of the priests.   He has learned all their lore until

> he knew all that there was to be known and still he
> found no doors that either hinged on hell nor heaven.
> He called the names a thousand times, but he saw
> no faces of gods.   But he learned many things to
> distract the minds of unthinking people from their
> real troubles, and to taint men with the fear of
> life.   In this he saw a certain mastery over people
> if one cared to use it or needed to use it. [11]

The power struggles between Moses and Aaron reveal the
conflict between the divinely inspired prophet and power-
seeking priest.   One of the few departures in plot from the
story of Exodus is the killing of Aaron by Moses on the
mountain top, a signal of the power of the witch-doctor, the
man of strength.

      If Miss Hurston's device of identifying the Israelite
with the Negro shows the universality of religious ideas, it
also provides for minute details, many of them made humorous by the Negro dialect.   Moses finds, for example, "a
little teenincy voice raised up in the back of his mind."   A
festival becomes "a big clothes-putting-on and eating down
the road a piece."   When Moses rids his father-in-law's
land of unwelcome relatives by raining frogs, Jethro sends
them a letter suggesting that Moses' greatest magic may have

been stopping them from eating somebody else's groceries.
But that may be wrong, he adds. "Have you ever seen his
sendings of snakes and lice?" Miss Hurston's version of
the Moses legend, then, is a combination of primitive, almost
childish, superstition and magic with a great spiritual experience. The final tone, however, is poetic and rather ma-
jestic, and it suggests the need of a god of force by any people struggling to maintain their humanity in the face of slavery
of any kind. Moses thinks as he looks over the tents of
Israel that he had meant to make a people

> free and just, noble and strong.... He had found
> out that no man may make another free. Freedom
> was something internal. The outside signs were
> just signs and symbols of the man inside. All
> you could do was to give the opportunity for free-
> dom and the man himself must make his own eman-
> cipation. He remembered how often he had had to
> fight Israel to halt a return to Egypt and slavery.
> Responsibility had seemed too awful to them time
> and time again. They had wanted to kill him sev-
> eral times for forcing them to be men. Only their
> awe and terror of his powers had saved his life. [12]

That force is necessary to religion is a conclusion she reaches
again in the chapter on religion in her autobiography. Con-
stantine, she says, "as pagan as he could lay in his hide,"
became after his vision a power for Christianity. Although
he could not sing, even as well as her father, "he had his
good points--one of them being a sword--and a seasoned
army." The anthropologist is at work in all of Miss Hurston's discussions of religion.

Her next book was her autobiography, Dust Tracks
on a Road, published in 1942. She had gone to California
the year before to visit friends and relax. Instead, she
worked for Paramount Studios and began her new book, which
would win the Anisfield Award for its contribution to better
race relations. Dust Tracks on a Road is a very informal
narrative about the people and places which form the background of Miss Hurston's life. The most prominent figure
is her father, whose attitude toward young Zora Neale seems
consistent from the moment he threatened to cut his throat
when he heard the news that he had a second daughter. (The
threat is presented as hearsay, not fact, but squares with
the father-daughter relationship that maintained until he died.)
Miss Hurston says, "Let me change words with him--and I

am of the word-changing kind--and he was ready to change
ends. " Fortunately her mother was gentle, loving, and in
her own way stronger than her husband.   Lucy managed to
save the child from the father's anger until her death when
John Hurston's new wife persuaded him to banish all the
children from the house.   This incident must have obsessed
Miss Hurston throughout her life; her frequent mention of
it is notable even in a book so generally unstructured.   The
scandalous second marriage is prominent in Jonah's Gourd
Vine, that biographical novel which is perhaps an attempt
at exorcism of the spectre of her father's dislike and her
own hatred of his second wife.

        The second half of Dust Tracks is brighter, as Zora
Neale finds delight in reading, studying, and finally writing
her own books.   Her success came partly through her own
enterprise, partly through the remarkable number of influential people who helped her.   When she had attained her Barnard degree and been given her research assignment, she
could finally talk of a happy interval which produced a "glow-
ing aura. "   That glow makes itself felt often in this book.
The section on her research in Florida, for example, turns
into a spirited, Whitmanesque celebration of the workers of
Polk County:

> These poets of the swinging blade!   The brief, but
> intensely graceful, dance of body and axe-head as
> it lifts over the head in a fluid arc, dances in air
> and rushes down to bite in the true, all in beauty
> ....   Sweating black bodies, muscled like gods,
> working to feed the hunger of the great tooth.   Polk
> County! [13]

Other chapters in this second half include a discussion of
love and the men in her life; an examination of religion, both
the evangelism of her childhood and the anthropological views
of her adult years; an appreciation of two women important
to her--Fanny Hurst and Ethel Waters.   Perhaps most significant, at least in terms of the Anisfield Award, is the
chapter entitled "My People!   My People!" in which Miss
Hurston catalogs many of the traits of her race she has written about in her novels: the class consciousness within the
race, the rivalries of women fighting over men, the Negro's
ambiguous evaluation of himself.   But she is proud to be
Negro: "Consider that with tolerance and patience, we godly
demons may breed a noble world in a few hundred generations
or so. "

This book is filled with the candor that marks all of
Miss Hurston's work.  Her sister Sarah, she writes, "was
struggling along with a husband for whom we all wished a
short sickness and a quick funeral."  She could say of her
father: "Old Maker had left out the steering gear when He
gave Papa his talents."  The autobiography well earned its
praise from the New York Times as being "saucy, defiant,
high-pressure ... as vivid as jasmine and as vulgar as a
well-liquored fish-fry."

Miss Hurston completed one more book, a novel of
social realism with Freudian overtones entitled Seraph on
the Suwanee.  It is the story of Arvay Henson, who, five
years past the marrying age of girls in town, thinks she
loves her older sister's minister husband, one reason she
has denounced the joys of the world and plans to become a
missionary.  But when Jim Meserve, a handsome young man
of a higher class than these poor whites of Sawley, appears
and decides he wants Arvay as his wife, she learns to respond
to his love after a period of uncertainty and a few attacks of
hysteria.  Their marriage is fulfilling, but Arvay's sense of
her inferiority combined with self-pity erodes the relationship through the years.  She is also too emotionally attached
to her first-born retarded son who threatens the lives and
security of the family and the help.  Jim, who has been successful in the lumber and shrimp businesses, decides to leave
her and live aboard one of his boats.  After a dramatic incident during which she is unable to help free him from a snake
threatening to crush him, Arvay comes eventually to an understanding of her own worth through a conflict with her sister's
family in her childhood home after their mother's death.
With a new awareness and self-valuation she returns to her
husband and a renewal of their love.

Much of the novel is devoted to the exploration of the
meaning of love.  And the relationship between Arvay and
Jim is tender and strong, sexual and alive, revealed in vigorous dialog and carefully chosen symbols.  Another theme,
but subordinate here, deals with racial attitudes.  The strongest of friendships are between Jim and a Negro friend who
saves his life and Jim and a Portuguese fisherman who builds
his fleet.  Arvay cannot accept these men and their wives
as her equals; her world, in fact, is so closed that she objects to her daughter's marriage to a Yankee.  Miss Hurston
shows the vitality in the lines of the minority groups, perhaps
epitomized in the words of a black man to a white: "If you
ever was to be a Negro just one Saturday night, you'd never
want to be white no more."  The author knew that her pow-

ers as a novelist were maturing during these years; the complexity and beauty of <u>Seraph on the Suwanee</u> justifies her confidence.

   Although she published no more books after this novel
of 1948, the later years were filled with activity of an almost
incredible variety.   She taught creative writing at Florida
Memorial College in St. Augustine, where she met Marjory
Kinnan Rawlings, who was to become a close friend.   (She
had taught before, or had at least held a post as chairman
of the drama department at North Carolina College for Negroes,
but the dates coincide with years she was in the field in
Haiti.)   She wrote radio scripts for her own sustaining program in Cincinnati.   She lived on a houseboat in Daytona
Beach for a while, but when her restless spirit rebelled, she
sold the boat to finance a mysterious expedition to Honduras.
When she returned she was without funds; so she went to
work as a maid in a Miami Beach household.   That job ended
when her employers discovered an article written by her in
a current issue of the <u>Saturday Evening Post;</u> it was impossible to employ as a maid one of the few Negroes listed in
<u>Who's Who</u>.   She then lived on a fishing boat for several
months, waiting for the owner to sail back to Honduras.
Learning that he had no intention of leaving Florida, she
moved into the Miami home of Judge Frank Smathers to help
him write his autobiography.   She served as librarian at
Patrick Air Force Base in 1956 and 1957, but was fired for
"being too well educated for the job."   The last two years of
her life were meagerly supported by her substitute teaching
in Fort Pierce.[14]

   Two interest gave her life coherence during these
frantic years.   One was politics, which became almost a
passion.   Miss Hurston made many radio speeches and public
appearances in support of her favorite candidates, but never
adhered to a party line.   The highlight of her political activity
was an outspoken article in the <u>Saturday Evening Post</u> entitled
"A Negro Voter Sizes Up Taft," in which she coined the
phrase "Mr. Republican."   Her second interest was her old
love, writing.   She was producing articles and stories for
<u>American Mercury</u>, the <u>Saturday Evening Post</u>, and other
prominent periodicals.   And through all of this period, she
was researching and writing what she expected to be her
most important book, a life of Herod the Great.   In 1955
she was two-thirds finished and had such great hopes that
she invited Winston Churchill to write a running comment on
the political implications of each chapter.   But she suffered

a stroke before she could complete her work and died a year
later on January 28, 1960, having spent the last months of
her life in the St. Lucie welfare home.

She left memories of a strong, colorful woman with
an immense capacity for affection.   Langston Hughes remembered her as the most amusing member of the literary members of the Negro Renaissance--the "niggerati," they called
themselves.   "Only to reach a wider audience, need she ever
write books--because she is a perfect book of entertainment
in herself."   She seemed to know everyone in New York, he
says, so many of them close friends that she was able to
move into an unfurnished apartment at a time when she had
no money (those times were frequent throughout her life) and
have it furnished in a few days with gifts from friends. [15]
In fact, she attracted so many friends who offered money,
fellowships, and other forms of help that Theodore Pratt
thought she had been spoiled.   But Pratt was angry because
of a mild altercation.   Miss Hurston had written him from
Miami to say that she had no money but did have an offer of
a job in New York if she could pay her fare.   When she
remained in Miami after he and other friends sent her money,
he wrote to her, he says, to scold her.   He was astounded
at her response:

> She wrote back that she had read, just at that time,
> that I was going through the trying process of hav-
> ing a book published.   Because of this she under-
> stood why I was being so testy, and she forgave
> me for being put out with her. [16]

Even in periods of bad fortune, she remained the spirited
Zora Neale of Eatonville.   Her appearance was flamboyant
as well: in 1942 Current Biography wrote of her: "Strikingly
attractive, she wears exotic clothing and affects bizarre
jewelry."   She was the personification of her own ideal: "I
love courage in any form.   I worship strength."

Yet she could be quite humble when the feelings of
her friends were involved.   Norton Baskin recalls Miss Hurston's visit to his late wife, Marjorie Kinnan Rawlings, at
their apartment in his hotel.   Knowing the racial climate of
St. Augustine in the forties, they were apprehensive of the
reception she might get from the townspeople and hotel guests,
so Mr. Baskin warned his help and waited at the door to
greet Miss Hurston.   When she did not arrive, he called his
wife to say he was sorry she had been stood up and was told

that their friend was there and he should join the fun.    Miss
Hurston, realizing the possibility of embarrassment to her
white friends, had entered through the kitchen door and climb-
ed the back stairs.    Pratt tells a similar story of her consideration of him and his wife.

Because her vibrant personality animates everything
she wrote, there are no stereotypes in her books, as there
were none in her life.    She rejected the kind of writing that
was being done by other members of her race:

> I saw that what was being written and declaimed
> was a pose.    A Negro writer or speaker was sup-
> posed to say those things.    It has such a definite
> pattern as to become approximately folklore.    So
> I made up my mind to write about my people as
> they are, and not to use the traditional lay figures. [17]

Thus she reveals her people in their infinite variety.    And
her readers know that her own variety is no less infinite.
When we encounter the listing in Who's Who of her religious
preference as "pagan," for example, we know from her work
that she really believed in Hoodoo, she really believed in
the religion of Moses, and she really believed in the Baptist
evangelism of her father's preaching.    Her soul was large
enough to embrace them all.

## REFERENCES

1.    Various sources give conflicting dates for the year of
      her birth--1901, 1903, 1907, 1908.    The earliest
      year tallies best with those few dates Miss Hurston
      mentions in her autobiography.
2.    Dust Tracks on a Road (New York, 1942), p. 124.
3.    Dust Tracks, pp. 158-159.
4.    George Rosner of the University of Miami Library recalls
      extraordinary interest in Mules and Men on the part
      of students because the book contains language not
      often found in print in that era.
5.    Dust Tracks, p. 214.
6.    She was still in love with the man, identified only as A.
      W. P., as she wrote her autobiography in 1942,
      but she never married him.    There was a brief
      marriage to Herbert Sheen just after she left Bar-
      nard; recognizing their mistake almost immediately,
      she returned to New York to continue her research,

and he went to Chicago to study medicine.    They were divorced four years later.

7. Their Eyes Were Watching God (New York, 1937), p. 24.    This novel has recently been reissued by Fawcett in paperback.    Anticipating a revival of interest in Miss Hurston's work, J. B. Lippincott [reissued] Jonah's Gourd Vine and Dust Tracks on a Road in 1971, and Harper and Row [and Negro Universities Press reissued] Mules and Men.

8. Their Eyes, p. 29.

9. Tell My Horse (New York, 1938), p. 76.

10. Dust Tracks, p. 213.

11. Moses, Man of the Mountain (New York, 1939), pp. 81-82.

12. Moses, pp. 344-45.

13. Dust Tracks, p. 187.

14. Much of the information about these later years is taken from Miss Hurston to Senator and Mrs. George Holland.

15. These reminiscences by Hughes appear in "Harlem Literati in the Twenties," Saturday Review of Literature, XVI (June 22, 1940) 13-15.

16. Theodore Pratt.    "Zora Neale Hurston," Florida Historical Quarterly, July, 1961.

17. Kunitz and Haycraft, Twentieth Century Authors (New York, 1942), p. 695.

Ellen Morgan

## HUMANBECOMING:
## FORM AND FOCUS IN THE NEO-FEMINIST NOVEL*

Woman as neo-feminism[1] conceives of her is a creature in the process of becoming.  She is struggling to throw
off her conditioning and the whole psychology of oppression.
She is pitting herself against her patriarchal culture and its
institutions.  She is teaching herself how to play the game
of sexual politics on her own terms, and the stakes are her
personhood and humanity.  In short, her story in this period
of transition is the story of an education, of a coming to
consciousness and a subsequent development of authentic selfhood.  It is rebellion and the dream of resolution.  Her task
is the integration of all of her parts, disconnected as they
have been by the socialization which has prepared her to play
the feminine role.

Neither the conventional psychological nor the sociological novel is a form adequate to express the neo-feminist
conception of woman.  She is not only a psyche but a political
being, not only a product and victim of her culture but also
a personal being who may transcend it.  For similar reasons
the stream-of-consciousness novel, with its tendency to equate
reality with consciousness, cannot sufficiently express her
experience; that experience is outward--political and social--
as well as inward--personal and psychological.

According to Thrall, Hibbard, and Holman the apprenticeship novel or Bildungsroman is

a novel which recounts the youth and young manhood

*Reprinted by permission of the author and publisher from
Images of Women in Fiction:  Feminist Perspectives, ed.
Susan Koppelman Cornillon (Bowling Green, Ohio:  Bowling
Green University, Popular Press, 1972), pp. 183-205.  Copy-
right © 1972 by the Bowling Green University Popular Press.

of a sensitive protagonist who is attempting to learn
the nature of the world, discover its meaning and
pattern, and acquire a philosophy of life and 'the
art of living.' Goethe's Wilhelm Meister is the
archetypal apprenticeship novel; noted examples in
English are Samuel Butler's The Way of All Flesh,
James Joyce's A Portrait of the Artist as a Young
Man, Somerset Maugham's Of Human Bondage, and
Thomas Wolfe's Look Homeward, Angel. [2]

As may be seen from this description, the Bildungsroman has traditionally been a male affair. For femaleness
has been defined as essential rather than existential. At
physical maturity, woman was treated as if she were at the
peak of her natural development because her potential for
growth, and her potential to be interesting, were construed
as physically sexual. When she entered physical adulthood,
she was loved. That was her story. As she aged, she
ceased to appear on the stage of the novel. Or else she
occupied a minor and/or a very negative place in the cast
of characters. This has been the pattern.

Prior to the neo-feminist movement, even the female
characters who did grow as selves were generally halted and
turned back before they reached authentic selfhood. They
committed suicide or obligingly died; they compromised by
marrying and devoting the whole of themselves to sympathetic
men; they went mad or into some kind of retreat and seclusion
from the world. They grew up to a point, and then, as I
heard one woman say at a Women and Literature section of
the 1970 meeting of the Modern Language Association, they
"grew down." Thus even the works which began as female
Bildungsromane usually ended otherwise. What the heroine
had learned about the nature of the world was pruned to fit
the confines of the social role which eventually circumscribed
her. Her efforts to acquire a philosophy of life and the art
of living were stunted when they began to imply real rebellion and social alienation. Peace to your proud truncated
shade, Dorothea Brooke. And to yours, Isabel Archer.

Neo-feminists do write stories of defeat, for the psychology of oppression is not conquered, and women are in a
period of transition in which the future is uncertain and largely unimaginable. There are still female protagonists who
"grow down." But then there are those "apprentices," like
Miriam Berg in Marge Piercy's Small Changes and Isadora
Wing in Erica Jong's Fear of Flying, whose stories end not

with outright defeat, but with the doubt, uncertainty, and
inconclusiveness which are the experience of many women
in this era.    Such books give evidence that the thrust of neo-
feminism is toward change and futurity.    The single most
absorbing consideration, the obsessive need of the neo-feminist woman, is to envision and approach authentic selfhood.
Because there is such yearning for potency, for the breaking
out into free selfhood, many neo-feminist artists are concerned
not only with documenting the effects of oppression and the
chaos of struggle, but with constructing images of transcendence and authenticity for women.

     For this reason, despite the male history of the
Bildungsroman, the female novel of apprenticeship and education seems to be a most natural form for literature influenced
by neo-feminism.    This type of novel is proving admirably
suited to express the emergence of women from cultural conditioning into confrontation with institutional forces and into
full personhood.

     But as black liberationists have said, without one's
history, one does not know one's name.    I think that like
blacks (consider Roots), neo-feminists will gravitate also
toward some species of the historical novel.    Neo-feminist
historians and essayists, as well as writers of short fiction,
are already engaged in mutually complementary attempts to
rescue and restore to woman her history.    They are interested
in the "common" woman, believing that a valid history is the
story of culture and not simply of power, and that woman
has never in fact stood, as non-feminist historians have implied, to one side of history.    Their aim is to convey the
quality of life lived by the average woman of the past, and
to identify and celebrate the strengths with which she met
oppression.    They demonstrate her ingenuity, her courage,
and her capacity to affirm her humanity over and against
the specifics of her condition as a woman.    Perhaps most
important, they present female culture as it has existed.
That is, they present it as an amalgam of art and metaphor,
skills and wit and wisdom, centered on the twin motifs of
survival and rebellion, that has given women relief from
and perspective on the dominant male culture.

     That this kind of interest in women's history is likely
to prove important for the neo-feminist novel is, I believe,
discernible in the effects it has been having on the short fiction in contemporary feminist journals.    First, in this fiction,
types of women who have heretofore been largely absent from

both history and fiction are not only appearing, but appearing as heroines. Before this development, one generally had to turn to the "local color" writers like Sarah Orne Jewett to find books in which a genuine heroine is neither conventionally beautiful nor, in the usual sense of the word, extraordinary.

Second, neo-feminist writers are telling the stories of the women in their own families. They are recreating the lives of their grandmothers and great-grandmothers from the memories of their grandmothers, their mothers, and themselves.

Third, neo-feminist writers are showing curiosity about some of the very talented but over-shadowed and sometimes maligned wives, mistresses, mothers, and sisters of men of historical prominence. Stories and some novels--like Zelda--have been arising in the context of the need to identify and take pride in these lost heroines, and to relate their failures to flower to their situations as women. (In passing, I note that I have been seeing indications that neo-feminists are interested also in women who have achieved historical prominence in their own right; there is an understandable suspicion that the existing portraits of such women are flawed by bias and unfaithful to the originals.)

The female historical novel offers to neo-feminist writer and reader alike the opportunity to reconstruct the lives of their female forebears and to avail themselves of their example and their strength. The importance of this historical legacy for the building of the contemporary woman's selfhood cannot be overestimated. As living women learn to view women's past in their own terms, that part of woman's conditioning which has resulted from the focus of history on exclusively male pursuits loses its power. Women are freed from the debilitation of believing their sex has been ancillary to the making of civilization.

A few words need to be said about the third form in which neo-feminist influence on the novel has been surfacing. The propaganda novel seems to be an unavoidable corollary to social movements of any scope. Neo-feminist journals contain some writing--poems and plays and short stories-- which is propagandistic: that is, writing in which message is more important than, and emphasized to the detriment of, form and/or language. Una Stannard's novel The New Pamela and other such works may be primarily valuable as message. But they function to encourage women to break out of their

conditioning.   They teach something valid about the human
condition.   Propagandistic writing can share with art what
is perhaps the most important characteristic of art--magnitude
of conception--even if it lacks magnitude of form and language.
The capacity to teach and to delight which some neo-feminist
work of this kind has would suggest that critical standards
which deny literary legitimacy and value to propagandistic
writing are inadequate tools for its evaluation.

While on the subject of the propaganda novel, I should
explain that I do not think neo-feminist writing is, or will be,
chiefly propagandistic.   Where there is passion for reform,
there is the desperate need for form.   It will be a long time
before women's sexual identities cease to be problematic and
painful to them, because it will take a long time to rid culture of sexism.   Neo-feminists have already often expressed
the need for both intellectual and emotional tools with which
to render their rage constructive and their yearnings bearable
in the wearing interim.   To ensure their own psychic survival
in the midst of psychic trauma and turmoil, they must produce both the intellectual framework and the artistic form to
shape and contain and finally redeem their experience.   We
have seen this process in action before.   To use Ellison's
Invisible Man as just one case in point, passionate consciousness of oppression not only does not preclude, but can well
call forth the creation of art.

But it is not a myth that artists frequently also antic-
ipate new sensibilities and are able to express, even if in
fragmentary form, the substance and mood of cultural change
before it comes into mass consciousness.   The central ideas
of the current women's movement are not new, even if they
have not always been at the center of mass consciousness.
Both these ideas and the feelings of rebellion which women
have had have always been available to some women writers.
So it is not surprising to find that prior to the current women's movement, some novels were written by women who
independently had come to many of the conclusions now openly
being expressed in works like Alix Kates Shulman's Memoirs
of an Ex-Prom Queen.   The surprise is that these women--
Kate Chopin for example--should have made public their perceptions at a time when they were virtually alone in their
willingness to challenge accepted mores and assumptions,
and at a time when they were subject to castigation for doing
so.   Among these earlier writings there have been tales both
realistic and fantastic.   We should not make the mistake of
omitting them from considerations of literary neo-feminism

just because they were, so to speak, prematurely born, or
because they do not look like the movement-inspired Bildungsromane, historical works, or polemics.   They belong fundamentally to the same category of writing and are similarly
discrete from other literature.   Moreover, in the case of
the novels of fantasy, earlier ones like Virginia Woolf's Orlando have been followed right into the present by recent
fantasies such as June Arnold's Applesauce and Brigid Bro-
phy's In Transit:  An Heroi-Cyclic Novel and by science fiction such as Joanna Russ' The Female Man.   These novels
are all responses to exactly the same fact.   That is, that
the social reality in which the realistic novel is grounded
has been, and is still, firmly patriarchal, and it still makes
the realistic novel about a liberated woman very nearly a
contradiction in terms.   The fantasy is still the only forum
for the depiction of women successfully breaching all the
barriers of sexual caste, and it serves the important function
of taking the reader where neither the realistic novel nor the
real woman has yet been able to go.   It expands our store
of images of what is possible.

      The neo-feminist novel of today--for example, Memoirs
of an Ex-Prom Queen, Fear of Flying, Small Changes--is
most often a realistic novel.   It portrays the condition of
women in transition between the old ways and the new, and
their responses to the shifting of their identities and aspirations.   It explores their possibilities for struggling to achieve
authentic selfhood.   Its heroine is not an exception to the rule
of her sex, not a typical heroine of stereotype, dissociated
from other women by beauty or superior endowments.   She
has no magic wand like the women of fantasy.   New-born to
her own personhood as her story closes, she embodies the
human potential of the real woman of our time who has not
yet established her new home in her new world.   We do not
know how she will survive or how she will conduct herself.
We have yet to see a realistic novel in which she shows us
what it is like to live as a free and fully human female being.
The heroine of that novel will be the final product of neo-
feminist influence on literature.   We will rejoice in her in
time to come.


### REFERENCES

1.   I use the word neo-feminism to distinguish the current
       feminist movement from its predecessors, and
       especially from the movement which led to American

woman suffrage.
2.  William Flint Thrall, Addison Hibbard, and C. Hugh Holman, A Handbook to Literature, rev. (New York: Odyssey Press, 1960), p. 31.

Agate Nesaule Krouse

# TOWARD A DEFINITION OF LITERARY FEMINISM*[1]

While writing a dissertation on the feminism of Doris
Lessing, I became acutely aware that little agreement existed
on the meaning of feminism and literary feminism.  Lessing
herself, her entire canon, individual works and characters
were labelled feminist by reviewers, critics and editors--
often much to my surprise.  Granted, none of them could be
aware of the scattered notecards marked "sexist," "misogynistic," or "anti-feminist" on my desk; I myself was only
gradually coming to a decision about their significance.  But
it was disconcerting to remember that Martha Quest had been
called "a feminist in the African veld" as I was thinking about
her passivity, her physical revulsion at sexual infidelity, and
her meek acceptance of Thomas Stern's blatantly repressive
view of monogamy for women. [2]  After I had decided that
The Golden Notebook was implicitly feminist in its attention
to the aesthetic, philosophical, and political concerns of women but quite traditional and sexist in the treatment of the
sexuality of women and the underlying definitions of "real
women" and "real men," I was uneasy to see it described
as "the well-known feminist novel" by editors with a recognized expertise in feminism. [3]

As I examined other implied definitions by feminists
themselves, I was occasionally puzzled as well.  For example, Robin Morgan, the editor of Sisterhood Is Powerful,
lists nine of Lessing's volumes in the "Literature and Literary Criticism" section of her Bibliography. [4]  Included is
even Retreat to Innocence, which might more properly belong
in the "Drop Dead List" of the same Bibliography:  Julia,
the protagonist, is neither admirable nor interesting in her
own right; she is clearly inferior to Jan, the major male

---

*This essay in somewhat different form was presented at the
Women's Caucus for the Modern Languages Workshop "Feminist Criticism," Midwest MLA, St. Louis, November 1974.

character; and her limitations are the result of too much, rather than too little, opportunity for women. On the other hand, novels I had always assumed to be feminist--such as Chopin's The Awakening, Wharton's The Custom of the Country, Stead's The Man Who Loved Children, Arnow's The Dollmaker, Drabble's The Garrick Year--were omitted altogether. Lucinda Cisler's Women: A Bibliography follows a similar pattern in the "Literature, Literary Criticism, and Essays" section. [5]  Eleven titles, including Retreat to Innocence, are listed for Lessing, who is also the only one designated "A key writer" (p. 25); Chopin, Wharton, Arnow, and Drabble are absent. In Female Studies, in syllabi used in women's studies courses, Lessing is especially prominent and even the questionable Retreat to Innocence appears with some regularity.

Two feminist critics have done valuable work toward defining feminism in fiction. Annis Pratt, in her important pioneering essay "The New Feminist Criticism," surveys a number of implied definitions of feminism in fiction and finds most of them too narrow since the critics formulating them were "themselves equipped with too stereotyped an understanding of feminism."[6] She suggests a distinction between feminist fiction "narrowly defined as works in which the author's explicit intention is to expose some aspect of sexism" and "novels which are unintentionally if implicitly feminist and of concern because of their place in the literature of women." The latter constitute "a fiction which includes a brilliant exploration of woman's existential situation within a carefully orchestrated treatment of other and broader human conflicts and relationships--a genre which I would define as encyclopedic feminism." Pratt's forthcoming book, Feminism in Fiction, will doubtless provide other much needed definitions, concepts, and patterns, as well as give additional answers to the question, What is feminist criticism?[7]

Ellen Morgan also discusses feminism in fiction in her essay "Humanbecoming: Form and Focus in the Neo-Feminist Novel." She finds that neo-feminism conceives woman as "a creature in the process of becoming ... struggling to throw off her conditioning and the whole psychology of oppression."[8] She argues that the psychological and sociological novel are inadequate forms to express this concept of woman and that the Bildungsroman, the historical novel, and the propaganda novel are three forms most influenced by neo-feminism. She looks forward to "a realistic novel, in which she [the heroine]

shows us what it is like to live as a free and fully human
female being.  The heroine of that novel will be the final
product of neo-feminist influence on literature. "

Morgan's categories are helpful for surveying contemporary writing by women.  In addition, she recognizes
precursors and sister works which will be seen to "belong
fundamentally to the same category of writing and are similarly discrete from other literature. "  She finds this fiction
"written by women who independently had come to many of
the conclusions now openly being expressed" to be "tales both
realistic and fantastic. "

Since influences and sources for literary works are
notoriously difficult to establish,[9] my purpose here is to
isolate some elements of literary feminism which will be
useful for analyzing and teaching novels written under various
influences, in different time periods, and even by male writers.  My discussion is intended as a possible beginning for
feminist critics reevaluating the work of neglected writers
as well as for feminist teachers, often bound by inflexible
reading lists, who nevertheless wish to discuss, however
briefly, feminism evident in widely different novels.  Morgan's
concept of neo-feminism in fiction, on the other hand, is
suggestive and should prove valuable for grouping and dis-
tinguishing novels of such different quality and form as Jong's
Fear of Flying, Piercy's Small Changes, Weldon's Female
Friends and Alther's Kinflicks in that large and ever growing
number of novels all having elements of literary feminism.

## II

In its general, non-literary applications, feminism has
a number of different meanings and connotations.  Thus, man-
haters, lesbians, believers in free love, nymphomaniacs,
and career women have occasionally been loosely described
as feminists because they reject, consciously or unconsciously,
the traditional definition of a woman as one who finds her
highest happiness in loving and being faithful to one man,
living through his achievements, having children, or making
a home.  All of the following have been more precisely described as feminists:  the great nineteenth-century advocates
of women's rights; suffragists; contemporary women interested
or active in the Women's Movement; members of one of the
liberal, socialist, or radical feminist groups; authors of
theoretical books or essays which expose sexism or injustices

to women, or which explore ways women can achieve justice
and full humanity.  A characteristic common to members of
this group is that they advocate or support greater freedom
or equal rights for women in politics, education, employment,
or personal life.  In so doing, they also question or reject
in various ways traditional definitions of the nature or roles
of women, but they differ considerably in several basic ways:
while they agree that women are oppressed and that a number
of their character traits are the result of cultural conditioning
rather than being inherent, they do not agree which traits,
if any, consistently distinguish women from men, which of
such distinctions are worth preserving, what changes in society are the most desirable, or what methods should be used
to achieve their goals.

    Literary feminism is indirectly of service to the fem-
inist cause because it provides documentation that the traditional definitions of women are inadequate or that women suffer injustices because of their sex.  It need not deal with
feminists themselves nor does it need to provide a positive
blueprint for the reform of society.  A simple, though limited
analogy may be helpful:  Owen's "Arms and the Boy" and
Heller's Catch-22 are indirectly of service to pacifism without
dealing directly with pacifists or showing how society may
be changed so that war would be obsolete.

    In describing literary feminism, I will concentrate on
such matters as characterization, point of view, selection of
details, and themes rather than on the intentions of the author, a far more complex problem.  My discussion will be
of little use to a bibliographer trying to compile lists of
"pure" feminist works--feminist and sexist elements can co-
exist happily, as they do in The Golden Notebook, for instance. 10  Consequently, it is much more precise and fair
to consider individual elements.  In addition, the author's
explicit intentions may be difficult to discover or are mis-
leading.  For instance, Lessing has tried to dissociate herself from feminism and has said The Golden Notebook has
been misunderstood by being regarded as a feminist manifesto. 11

    Elements of literary feminism may appear in the work
of both women and men.  Although the question whether a
man can write perceptively about women or be a good feminist critic sometimes threatens to replace the controversy
whether a bad man can write a good book, literary feminism
does not have an absolute relationship to the author's sex.

Thus, Angus Wilson's <u>Late Call</u> and <u>The Middle Age of Mrs.</u>
<u>Eliot</u> or John Gardner's <u>October Light</u> have some prominent
feminist characteristics, while Lessing's characters or themes
are sometimes anti-feminist.  It is very likely, of course,
that upon extensive analysis of individual works and writers
by feminist critics, we will find that certain feminist elements
occur much more frequently in the work of women. [12]

On the simplest level, a work with characteristics of
literary feminism will have either a female protagonist or
several female characters who are significant to the theme
or central action.  To take an extreme example, <u>Moby Dick</u>
can be dismissed automatically since even the most interesting whale is male.  But mere presence of women characters
is not enough.  Examination of the point of view can reveal
not only whether women form a significant part of the work,
but to what extent they are taken seriously.  Thus, Bellow's
novels refer to the wives, ex-wives, daughters, and sisters
of heroes undergoing serious crises.  However, because of
the restriction of the point of view to male protagonists, the
women either do not emerge clearly as individual characters
in their own right (e. g. , Lily in <u>Henderson)</u>, or, if they do,
the serious kind of attention given to the existential anguish
of the main character is not accorded them.  Thus, in spite
of Bellow's emphasis, any feminist reading <u>Herzog</u> can recognize Madelaine is having a serious identity crisis of her own:
she wants to be an intellectual, she wants sexual satisfaction--
more than she wants to be known as a good wife to Herzog.
She reads in the conjugal bed piled so high with books it
leaves no room for him, and she applies lipstick by looking
at her reflection in a knife--two rather spiteful images to
suggest she is not a "real" woman.  The suffering she causes
Herzog is real enough, but there is no indication her identity
crisis is as serious or important as or inherently or themat-
ically parallel to the man's.  Herzog suffers; Madelaine is
bitchy.

Even when a female character appears who is more
fully developed, who earns the reader's sympathy, and who
can be understood more fully by reference to some feminist
idea, point of view and emphasis must still be considered.
For example, the indecisive and destructive Jake Horner,
the narrator of Barth's <u>End of the Road</u>, has an affair with
Rennie which leads to her abortion and death.  Rennie is
clearly the victim of male possessiveness and a terrifying
example of the fate of a woman who has formed herself solely
on the ideas of a man:  after committing herself to Joe, she

has given up her friends, opinions, and even memories.    But
the novel focuses on Jake:   Rennie is primarily only a cause
for his final paralysis of will.    She is a man's problem rather
than important in her own right.    Similarly, Malamud solicits
most of our sympathy for Morris and Frank in The Assistant
rather than for Helen, whose rape, poverty, and lack of opportunity are treated as peripheral to the moral anguish of
the men.

    In addition to the inclusion of female characters whose
lives and fates are treated seriously, feminism in characterization may be distinguished by the author's avoidance of
stereotypes and stock characters of women.    Feminist critics
have isolated and discussed stereotypes of women in fiction
so entertainingly and so well, that this one area of feminist
criticism no longer needs much theoretical effort or explanation. [13]  I should only note that several methods of departing
from stereotypes exist.    Most frequently, complexity and
specificity save a character from being a stereotype.    For
example, Lessing's, Drabble's, and Ashton-Warner's women
often have fairly traditional responses to men and children--
they like them--but in addition they are also interested in
artistic, intellectual, political, or academic matters.    However, although their authors present them as intellectual,
they are neither vicious or cold creatures who deny life itself, as does Hermione in Women in Love or Miss Head in
Kinflicks, nor comic figures, as are so many bright women
(e. g. , Rose Lorimer in Wilson's Anglo-Saxon Attitudes, Dorothy Merlin in Hansford-Johnson's Skipton trilogy, Margaret
in Lucky Jim, etc.).    Another highly effective way of avoiding
stereotypes is multiplicity, so well practiced by Weldon in
the best of the neo-feminist novels, Down Among the Women
and Female Friends:  while individual responses by her numerous women characters often fit one stereotype or another,
taken together they develop no trite commonplace about women, suggest change and growth, and are rich in humor and
irony.    Simple reversal--i. e. , assigning a stereotypical characteristic of one sex to another--sometimes seems a forced
way out, as is the protagonist's view of men as sex objects
in Fear of Flying, but even this assault on the stereotype
may lead to more androgynous literature.

    Although feminist critics have been very properly an-
gered at the number of unpleasant, bitchy, and "castrating"
women created by American novelists, occasionally strikingly
unpleasant female characters can still be used to make a
feminist point.    For example, Undine Spragg in Wharton's

The Custom of the Country is shallow, vain, selfish, frivo-
lous, and dishonest.  But Wharton deliberately shows Undine
as a product of the status of women in American society
rather than innately evil or uniquely vicious.  As Bowen
points out in Chapter XV, Undine is "a monstrously perfect
result of the system," of "the custom of the country" which
keeps women from "the real business of life" and tries "to
trick out the leavings tossed them by the pre-occupied male--
the money and the motors and the clothes...."[14]  Wharton
underlines by her title that Undine has to be judged by reference to Bowen's analysis.  Likewise, Lessing's Mrs. Quest,
Martha's meddling, domineering, self-pitying, and downright
vicious mother, is made understandable and pitiable in Lessing's authorial indictments of society's unfair treatment of
women who find themselves unnecessary and useless after
their child-rearing days are over.  The necessity to reject
yet forgive mothers with traditional attitudes is often essential to understanding the protagonists of Atwood, Drabble,
Alther, and Weldon.  In other words, women characters who
are clearly similar to unpleasant and recurring stereotypes
can nevertheless be acceptable and even useful, depending on
the context in which they appear and the explanation for the
causes of their behavior.

In addition to the inclusion of significant female characters who are not subordinate to a male point of view, various departures from stereotypes, and a sensitivity to the
question whether women are inherently or uniformly vicious
or whether they are victims of society, literary feminism
may also be evident in the attention given to the details of
the lives of women, especially attention to areas ignored or
sentimentalized.

A qualification in evaluating such details is necessary,
however.  One obvious oversimplification in evaluating such
details is to assume that explicit references to women's sex-
uality--so obviously absent from the great nineteenth-century
novels--is a great advance.  Reduced to its absurd extreme,
such an assumption would make nymphomaniacs pandering to
male fantasies into feminist heroes and elevate Henry Miller
to a feminist.  Explicit details about sexuality are a result
of changing standards of "good taste" and restrictions of publication.  It is all too common an assumption that the Women's
Movement and the Sexual Revolution are the same thing anyway.  But far more significant in fiction are the author's
attitudes towards a character who chooses celibacy, who has
no interest in men at all, or who prefers the friendship or
love of women, and yet whose choice is not implicitly crit-

icized. In other words, attitudes to a character's sexual autonomy and freedom of choice are much more revealing than the specificity of the language.

A significant feminist element is the attention given to some areas of the lives of women which have been relatively unexplored or greatly sentimentalized. The development of the effects of children on mothers rather than the adverse effects of mothers on sons is implicitly feminist and especially well done in such novels as Drabble's The Millstone (American title, Thank You All Very Much) and The Garrick Year and Lessing's A Proper Marriage. Another frequently slighted area is the experience of old women. Of course, old people generally play a less significant part in modern fiction, possibly because to present full portraits of the old means to forego the popular themes of search for identity and awakening sexuality. Graham Greene's Travels with My Aunt is comic: it utilizes rather than questions the unfair notion that women are sexual beings but that past a certain age they should have learned better. Notable serious and powerful exceptions to the modern trend to ignore or laugh at old women may be found in Spark's Memento Mori, Sarton's Mrs. Stevens Hears the Mermaids Singing and As We Are Now, and Olsen's Tell Me a Riddle.

Women's friendships are yet another relatively unexplored area. Virginia Woolf, the earliest and most brilliant feminist critic, speaks in A Room of One's Own of "how immense a change" is evident in a novel by one of her contemporaries who has chosen to describe friendship between two women. [15] She finds that the "relationships between women ... in the splendid gallery of fictitious women, are too simple. So much has been left out, unattempted" (p. 86). Since women have been shown primarily in relationship to men, the writer who knows how to present friendships between women "will light a torch in that vast chamber where nobody has yet been" (p. 88). For Woolf, female friendships are the key to fully human and complex characters as well as a sign of a strikingly modern work. And although there have been notable exceptions--McCarthy, Lessing, Piercy, and Weldon--relatively few contemporary novelists have treated this subject either extensively or successfully.

Feminism is also evident in emphasizing, documenting, and exploring fully the injustices suffered by women either because of the sexist nature of society, or because of their relationships with individual men, or both. Christina Stead

shows in The Man Who Loved Children the way motherhood,
poverty, and powerlessness destroy Henny while Sam retains
his naive exuberance and optimism.    Harriet Arnow in The
Dollmaker details the effects of war and economics on women,
who also feel most acutely the disintegration of their families,
rather than devoting equal time to both sexes.    While women
suffer because they are human, and while they are affected
by politics and economics, feminism is evident if the writer
shows an awareness of the additional difficulties of being female.

Point of view, characterization, departures from stereotypes, examination of social causes for unpleasant characters,
and attention to the details of lives of women are all elements
of literary feminism.    They are just some of the elements  •
which need to be examined before we label an individual work
feminist, let alone a writer, a group of writers, or a whole
era.

### III

It is customary for feminist critics to conclude with
suggestions for future critical activity (helpful) or predictions
about the future of literature (risky).    I will live up to this
custom only in a limited way.

I have provided a definition of feminism generally and
of literary feminism specifically as distinguished by an examination of the traditional literary elements of point of view,
characterization, emphasis, and details.    Obviously literary
feminism could profitably be defined in other ways (e. g. , by
causes and effects) and my definition could be expanded and
refined to include structure, diction, or figurative language.
Additional definitions and concepts are still necessary.

I will conclude by indicating only three areas in which
definitions by feminist critics are helpful yet need further
discussion.    Early in this paper I referred to Ellen Morgan's
definition of neo-feminism evident in novels influenced by the
Women's Movement.    To describe and evaluate the novels of
this definition alone--a project I would not have considered
without Morgan's earlier attempts to define--we have to consider at least some of these characteristics:   the fragmentary, almost jerky form with its abrupt shifts in time, often
for no clearly discernible aesthetic reason (e. g. , Memoirs
of an Ex-Prom Queen, Fear of Flying); the reliance on paired

or multiple complementary characters (e. g. , <u>The Park</u>, <u>Small</u>
<u>Changes</u>, <u>Heat and Dust</u>); and feminist comedy, often so stren-
uously attempted by American novelists, but successfully executed by British and Canadian (e. g. , <u>Realms of Gold</u>, <u>Female</u>
<u>Friends</u>, <u>The Fire Dwellers</u>, <u>Lady Oracle</u>). These novels
all have characteristics of literary feminism as I have described it, of course, as well--a fact that immediately distinguishes them from the work of many other contemporary
novelists (e. g. , Vonnegut).

Second, I believe that distinctions currently used by
feminist critics can be made sharper--consider explicit and
implicit feminism alone. In addition, already existing concepts need to be popularized. Not even the discussion of
stereotypes has become popular enough to affect most reviewers: Durham's <u>The Man Who Loved Cat Dancing</u> and
Wells's <u>Jane</u>, for example, were repeatedly praised for their
feminist ("women's lib-type"), original, modern heroines.
Wider acceptance of concepts already almost too familiar to
us will in turn lead to other feminist critical methods being
used more widely, which should prove helpful to extended
serious feminist critical endeavors.

Finally, some new terms are obviously necessary as
well. Morgan in "Humanbecoming" finds most neo-feminist
novels to be realistic and looks forward to "a realistic novel
in which she shows us what it is like to live as a free and
fully human female being. " Like Morgan, I believe all of
us will rejoice at such a novel because it will show that significant changes have taken place in society. But meanwhile
most critics of contemporary fiction are lavishing attention
on novels departing from the conventions of realism: fabula-
tion as expressed in romance, satire rejecting ethical abso-
lutes, cruel picaresque, ambiguous allegory, and epic vision. 16
Feminist analyses of such fiction by males is increasingly
necessary but examination of stereotypes or the lack of authenticity of women characters are frail tools here. Many
of the terms and methods used by feminist critics of fiction
are as yet best suited for discussing realistic novels. New
concepts will be necessary for the "female fabulists and ex-
perimentalists ... being politely elbowed into obscurity right
in front of us. "17 It may well be that the new experimental
women writers or fabulists will ultimately produce the most
profoundly feminist works precisely because they are not
bound by the conventions of realism. Thus, the development
of new concepts and methods will be useful both for contemporary fiction but also for further analysis of earlier women
writers like Stein who encoded perceptions of male culture

in highly experimental style.

A final example of the necessity for new terms and concepts will suffice. Confronted by such different works as Glasgow's Barren Ground and Didion's Play It As It Lays, I am certain we need to explore the distinctions between positive and negative feminism (cf. Morse Peckham's definition of romanticism), a project beyond the scope of this paper.18

I hope that literary feminism is discussed further in a systematic and thorough way so that we eventually mean roughly the same thing when we label a particular work feminist, have additional tools to discover and describe similarities in widely different works, develop necessary new concepts, and have a solid basis for discussing the significance of feminism in determining aesthetic or literary value.

REFERENCES

1. This paper in its original form received an honorable mention in the Women's Caucus for the Modern Languages Florence Howe Essay Contest of 1975.
2. Anon. , "Martha's Quest," Newsweek, 64 (December 7, 1964), p. 106.
3. Editorial comment after Lessing's "Not a Very Nice Story," Ms. , 1 (August, 1972), p. 123.
4. Sisterhood Is Powerful: An Anthology of Writings from the Women's Liberation Movement (New York: Vintage Books, 1970), pp. 578-79.
5. 6th ed. (New York: Lucinda Cissler, 1970), pp. 24-27.
6. In A Case for Equity: Women in English Departments, ed. Susan McAllester (Urbana, Ill. : National Council of Teachers of English, 1971), p. 29. Reprinted in the present anthology, beginning on page 11.
7. Useful recent surveys of feminist criticism are: Cheri Register, "American Feminist Literary Criticism: A Bibliographical Introduction," in Feminist Literary Criticism: Explorations in Theory, ed. Josephine Donovan (Lexington: University Press of Kentucky, 1975), pp. 1-28; and Elaine Showalter, "Literary Criticism," Signs, 1 (Winter 1975), 435-460.
8. This essay is reprinted in the present anthology, beginning on page 272.
9. See, for example, Richard D. Altick, The Art of Literary Research, rev. ed. (New York: W. W. Norton, 1975), pp. 90-113, passim.

10. For a full discussion of feminist and sexist elements, see my dissertation, "The Feminism of Doris Lessing," University of Wisconsin-Madison, 1972.

11. "A Talk with Doris Lessing," interview by Florence Howe, The Nation, 204 (March 6, 1967), p. 312.

12. A seminal work in this area is Ellen Moers's Literary Women (Garden City, N. Y.: Doubleday, 1976).

13. For an important, early, and thorough discussion, see Mary Ellmann, "Feminine Stereotypes," Thinking About Women (New York: Harcourt, Brace, Jovanovich, 1968). For examples of specific applications as well as some interesting speculations about causes of stereotypes, see Mary Anne Ferguson, "Sexist Images of Women in Literature," in Female Studies V: Proceedings of the Conference, Women and Education, ed. Rae Lee Siporin (Pittsburgh: KNOW, Inc., 1972), pp. 77-83; Dolores Barracano Schmidt, "The Great American Bitch," A Case for Equity, pp. 54-59; and Phyllis R. Kotman, "The White Bitch Archetype in Contemporary Black Fiction," Bulletin of the MMLA, 6 (Spring, 1973), pp. 96-110. For opposing views whether stereotypes need further exploration, see Wendy Martin and Mary Louise Briscoe, "Women's Studies: Problems in Research," Women's Studies: An Interdisciplinary Journal, 2, No. 2 (1974), pp. 249, 253-55.

14. 1913 (reprinted, New York: Scribner's 1941), pp. 205-08.

15. 1929 (reprinted, New York: Harcourt, Brace & World, 1957), p. 86.

16. Robert Scholes, The Fabulators (New York: Oxford University Press, 1967). For an opposing view about the death of the realistic novel, see David Lodge, The Novelist at the Crossroads and Other Essays on Fiction and Criticism (Ithaca, N. Y.: Cornell University Press, 1971). The influence of Scholes' clear and persuasive arguments can be seen, for example, in the selection of writers and issues discussed in Joe David Bellamy, The New Fiction: Interviews with Innovative American Writers (Urbana: University of Illinois Press, 1974).

17. Showalter, pp. 459-60.

18. "Toward a Theory of Romanticism," PMLA, 66 (1951), 5-23.

Cheryl L. Brown

## JEAN RHYS' RECENT FICTION:
## HUMANE DEVELOPMENTS IN WIDE SARGASSO SEA

Before World War II, Jean Rhys published a collection of short stories--The Left Bank (1927)--and four novels: Quartet (1928), After Leaving Mr. MacKenzie (1931), Voyage in the Dark (1934), and Good Morning, Midnight (1939). Since then, she has published two more collections of short stories-- Tigers Are Better-Looking (1976) and Sleep It Off, Lady (1976)--in addition to a novel: Wide Sargasso Sea (1966). Among the novels, Wide Sargasso Sea is singular because Rhys exploits an alien setting, the West Indies, and because she develops a unique heroine, Charlotte Brontë's Mrs. Bertha Rochester.

Although Rhys documents Bertha's life up to and including her confinement in Thornfield Hall, Wide Sargasso Sea is not simply a re-dress of Jane Eyre. As Francis Wyndham argues, "it is in no sense a pastiche of Charlotte Brontë and exists in its own right, quite independent of Jane Eyre."[1] What complicates Wide Sargasso Sea, then, is not its relationship to Brontë's earlier work but, rather, how Rhys chooses to tell Bertha's story. Rhys experiments with multiple first person narrators so that the world as perceived is never quite the same; different intelligences constantly re-shape environmental data. One way to approach an otherwise slippery novel is through point of view. Attention to inside views and distance will prevent misreadings such as Elgin W. Mellown's.

Although I do not believe in setting up critical straw persons, Mellown's "Characters and Themes in the Novels of Jean Rhys" should not go uncorrected. It is the only full-scale treatment of Jean Rhys in print, albeit dated, and it raises questions about male critics writing feminist criticism. Certainly, male critics can and do write sensitive feminist criticism; however, male critics are handicapped because they have not encountered the female experience firsthand.

Such is the case with Mellown.   Many of his conclusions
about Rhys' heroines are misdirected, and they mar his reading of Wide Sargasso Sea. [2]

Mellown provides much useful information in his essay.
He includes a brief biography, summarizes Rhys' work, documents the influences of Ford Maddox Ford, attempts to
place Rhys in an historical and literary tradition, and supplies essential bibliographic data.   When he attempts to define what he terms the archetypal "Rhys woman," though, he
errs:

> The most basic experience treated by Rhys concerns
> the woman's childhood.  Its peace and security are
> associated with a warm climate, in contrast to her
> adult insecurity in a cold northern world. ...   This
> archetypal woman never finds a man who will faith-
> fully continue to fulfil her needs. ...   The Rhys
> woman may be a mistress in name, but in fact
> she is always a victim of love because she is at
> the mercy of her uncontrollable desires. [3]

The archetypal heroine in Rhys' fiction does possess the
initial characteristics Mellown attributes to her, but she is
not "at the mercy of her uncontrollable desires"; she is not
a slave to an insatiable sexual appetite. [4]   What Mellown
misses is that Rhys' novelistic heroines are at the mercy of
men because they control the money.   Men control the money;
women require money to survive; therefore, women require
men.   Sexual attraction often exists, but the primary need
is economic--not sexual.

Money, or the lack of it, is a recurrent theme in
Rhys' fiction, but nowhere is it better tied to men than in
Good Morning, Midnight.   Here, Sasha Jansen muses on Mr.
Blank and, in doing so, clarifies the economic hierarchy:

> Well, let's argue this out, Mr. Blank.   You, who
> represent Society, have the right to pay me four
> hundred francs a month.   That's my market value,
> for I am an inefficient member of Society, slow in
> the uptake, uncertain, slightly damaged in the fray,
> there's no denying it.   So you have the right to
> pay me four hundred francs a month, to lodge me
> in a small, dark room, to clothe me shabbily, to
> harass me with worry and monotony and unsatisfied
> longings till you get me to the point when I blush

at a look, cry at a word.... Let's say that you
have this mystical right to cut my legs off. But
the right to ridicule me afterwards because I am
a cripple--no, that I think you haven't got. And
that's the right you hold most dearly, isn't it? [5]

The debasement Mellown notes does exist, but it is a debasement that occurs because of economic not sexual enthrallment.
Sasha knows what it means to be without money: "If you
have money and friends, houses are just houses with steps
and a front door.... [If you don't] they step forward, the
waiting houses, to frown and crush" (p. 32). She must try
to secure some money, whatever the result.

Mellown's misconception of the economic hierarchy
flaws his argument when he moves from a discussion of the
archetypal woman to a discussion of adjunct themes. He
notes, for example, that "Woman as creator and sustainer
of life has no part in this archetypal figure," and he even
cites an economic reason:

having no husbands to provide for them and with
no way of earning a living other than by selling
their bodies (which must thus be kept free of a
dependent child) they must abort any life that may
spring in their wombs [p. 464].

While this is certainly true in Voyage in the Dark, Mellown
overlooks a larger issue. Woman as creator and sustainer
of life has no part in any of Rhys' early novels because men
monopolize the role of sustainer, and women are relegated
to the role of children. It is not, as Mellown suggests,
that "these tortured women" are not able to "reach maturity
by giving birth to a child" (p. 464). It is, rather, a matter
of these oppressed women's not being able to reach maturity
in a world that allows them little freedom.

Similarly, when Mellown explores the link between
personal identity and economic wealth, he is so busy attempting to reconcile Rhys with Defoe and Richardson that he blurs
the economic situation. Rhys' novelistic heroines do not, as
he argues, "disdain ... the money upon which society is
based" (p. 465); they see it as a welcome remedy to their
present state:

Then I start thinking about the black dress, longing
for it, madly, furiously. If I could get it every-

thing would be different.   Supposing I ask So-and-
so to ask So-and-so to ask Madame Perron to keep
it for me?...   I'll get the money.   I'll get it...
[Good Morning, Midnight, pp. 31-32; Rhys' el-
lipses].

Likewise, when in After Leaving Mr. Mackenzie "Julia Martin throws away the check and ... spends her last shillings
on roses for her mother's cremation" and in Quartet "Marya
and Stephen recklessly spend their last francs on an unneeded,
luxurious meal," they are not rejecting the money-based society.   They can opt for defiant, necessary actions and still
wish they could afford a "devil may care attitude to money"
(Mellown, p. 465).   In fairness to Mellown, it should be
noted that here, as well as elsewhere in his essay, he mentions all of the crucial elements; however, he does not seem
to fit the pieces together properly.

These issues--the archetypal heroine, men and money--
figure in Wide Sargasso Sea.   Antoinette Cosway Mason Rochester, called Bertha only by Rochester, fits the archetype.
She moves from a warm to a cold climate and "never finds
a man who will faithfully continue to fulfil her needs."   Moreover, her plight is marked by economic servitude to Rochester.   At their marriage her entire inheritance is turned over
to him, despite Aunt Cora's objections.   Although Wide Sargasso Sea shares these characteristics with Rhys' earlier
novels, an important development distinguishes it, and this
shift in focus is the result of Rhys' experimentation with
multiple first person narrators.

Rhys' novelistic world is deterministic.   Her novels
are peppered with words like "predestined" and "fate."   As
Mellown argues, Rhys "develops her single vision of a world
in which free will is a myth and the individual has no power
to control his destiny" (p. 474).   Usually, the narrative focus
is on the female protagonist, so it is with her that sympathy
resides, not with male counterparts who share her hostile
world; however, since the male antagonist, Rochester, is
allowed to narrate part of Wide Sargasso Sea, the narrative
focus is, for the first time in Rhys' novels, divided almost
equally between female and male.   The result is a more fully
drawn male character who is capable of compelling sympathy
and a shift in culpability.   The villain is now distinguishable
as the world, not simply as men and money.   Rochester's
thoughts reveal him as no less a victim than Antoinette, even
if he does control the money.   By manipulating first-person

points of view, Rhys expands her humanistic vision and, therefore, makes an even stronger statement about the nature of the world.6

Antoinette narrates Part One, devoted to her childhood, and Part Three, devoted to her stay in Thornfield Hall. Rochester narrates all of Part Two, a history of their married life in the West Indies, with the exception of a short narrative by Antoinette that occurs midway:

Part One: Antoinette, 45 pages

Part Two: Rochester, 43 pages
Antoinette, 11 pages
Rochester, 55 pages

Part Three: Antoinette, 11 pages

Although Rochester actually narrates approximately a third as much as Antoinette, Wide Sargasso Sea is Antoinette's story. The book begins and ends with her. What the story traces, though, is not only her plight, but also Rochester's. Their extensive inside views reveal the moral, emotional, and intellectual distance that separates them. This distance is the basis of their troubles, but the nature of their universe precludes lessening it.

Part One establishes sympathy for Antoinette because it documents her responses to the forces that shape her. The dramatic highpoint is the burning of Coulibri, the family estate, and Antoinette's confrontation with Tia, her native friend, illustrates the malevolence of the world. When the natives set fire to Coulibri, Antoinette spots Tia in the crowd and runs towards her, but Tia throws a "jagged stone" at Antoinette and immediately begins to cry (p. 46). Both children are victims of racial tension and compel sympathy because the current situation is controlled by pre-emancipation hatred. They are simply pawns. Part One also introduces a larger determinism and, in doing so, prepares for Rochester's entrance into the narrative. The persistent clash between the Creoles and the English dooms Antoinette and Rochester's relationship before it even starts. The union of Antoinette's mother and Mr. Mason prefigures the outcome of Antoinette and Rochester's marriage.

The first half of Part Two, up to the insertion of Antoinette's narrative, develops sympathy for Rochester by tracing his increasing alienation from the environment. He

fulfils the prophecy of Mr. Mason.   He does not understand
the country or its people.   On his way to Granbois, Antoinette's inherited estate, he notes that "everything is too
much. ...   Too much blue, too much purple, too much green.
The flowers too red, the mountains too high, the hills too
near" (p. 70).   And, when he arrives at Granbois, the already
hostile environment threatens to obliterate his identity just
as it ate away the name on one of the family books:   "<u>Life
and Letters of ...</u>" (p. 75).   The locale stifles communication with Antoinette--"I wanted to say something reassuring
but the scent of the river flowers was overpoweringly strong.
I felt giddy" (p. 83)--and it deprives Rochester of his freedom:   "She [Antoinette] said, 'Here I can do as I like', not
I, and then I said it too.   It seemed right in that lonely
place.   'Here I can do as I like'" (pp. 92-93).   After establishing Rochester's doubts and fears, the first half of Part
Two climaxes in three confrontations between Rochester and
the antagonistic environment.   He receives Daniel Cosway's
letter; he gets lost in the "hostile" forest; he reads about
Obeah.   At the height of Rochester's alienation the narration
passes to Antoinette.   This is a necessary switch in point
of view because the moral, emotional, and intellectual distance between Antoinette and Rochester due to their disparate
backgrounds begins to take its toll.   Antoinette flees Granbois
in search of Christophine, an old family servant, and an
inside view of how Rochester's distance affects Antoinette
follows.

     Antoinette is miserable and asks Christophine to use
magic to make Rochester love her.   In the course of their
discussion, Christophine affirms the basic good nature of
Rochester:

     ... the man not bad-hearted [p. 110].

     The man not a bad man, even if he love money,
     but he hear so many stories he don't know what
     to believe [p. 114].

Christophine's testimony is important because, as the distance
between Rochester and Antoinette increases and their actions
towards one another become more strained and cruel, Rhys
must prevent either partner from becoming a cardboard monster out to destroy the weaker partner.   Moreover, neither
Antoinette nor Rochester should be faulted.   They are victims
of cultural distance, which is amplified in a world that precludes communication.   Christophine addresses this problem
when she tells Antoinette how to strengthen her relationship

with Rochester:

> Speak to your husband calm and cool, tell him about
> your mother and all what happened at Coulibri and
> why she get sick and what they do to her.   Don't
> bawl at the man and don't make crazy faces.   Don't
> cry either.   Crying no good with him.   Speak nice
> and make him understand [p. 116].

A knowledge of Antoinette's past would help Rochester understand both Antoinette and the locale.   The distance between
all three, then, would decrease.   Unfortunately, communication is again ruined by the environment.   Antoinette relies
on Christophine's black magic, and Rochester turns on her.

In the remainder of Part Two, Rochester becomes
increasingly more violent and vicious, until his frenzied
thoughts on himself, the environment, and Antoinette peak:
"All the mad conflicting emotions had gone and left me wea-
ried and empty.   Sane" (p. 172).   Along the way, though,
Rochester reveals two important facts about himself.   First,
he has arrived at his present state through little fault of
his own, as documented by a letter he intends to write to
his father:

> 'I know now that you planned this because you wanted
> to be rid of me.   You had no love at all for me.
> Nor had my brother.   Your plan succeeded because
> I was young, conceited, foolish, trusting.   Above
> all because I was young. '   ...   But I am not young
> now, I thought, stopped pacing and drank [pp. 162-
> 63].

Secondly, Rochester is hurt by the situation and lashes out
at Antoinette because he is confused and poorly informed.
He did not set out to destroy her.   Both Antoinette and Rochester talk about betrayal (pp. 118, 163, and 171), but the
real betrayer is the world, which fixes people's destinies
and then thwarts any attempts to transcend.

Rochester takes Antoinette to England, and Grace
Poole's preface to Part Three reaffirms sympathy for all
characters.   When she speaks or thinks about Thornfield Hall,
she recalls the threat of the world:

> 'After all the house is big and safe, a shelter from
> the world outside which, say what you like, can be

> a black and cruel world to a woman.' ... The
> thick walls, she thought.... But above all the
> thick walls, keeping away all the things that you
> have fought till you can fight no more [p. 178].

Grace Poole specifies how cruel the world can be to a woman,
but when Mrs. Eff defends Rochester to Grace, she illustrates
the effect of the world on a man as well:

> I knew him as a boy. I knew him as a young man.
> He was gentle, generous, brave. His stay in the
> West Indies has changed him out of all knowledge.
> He has grey in his hair and misery in his eyes
> [p. 178].

Antoinette, now insane, narrates the remainder of Part Three.
Her mental destruction highlights the savage force of the
world.

When Mellown begins to summarize his thoughts on
Wide Sargasso Sea, he argues:

> Here, then, spelled out clearer than in any of the
> previous novels, are the details of the life of the
> now familiar Rhys heroine: a happy childhood in
> a tropical state of nature, growth into adolescence
> without the presence of a father, a complete sub-
> mission to physical love, the inevitable loss of that
> love, and the consequent misery [p. 472].

Although the specifics of Mellown's argument are slanted, he
is correct in isolating the female archetype; however, implicit
in his study and explicit in Rhys' fiction is also a male archetype, who complements the heroine's characteristics. He is
associated with a cold climate; he is usually financially secure;
and he invariably becomes disillusioned with the heroine.
Granted, the male archetype is less distinctive than the female
archetype, and the details of his life are more varied; however, just as the female archetype becomes sharper in Wide
Sargasso Sea, the male archetype begins to take shape. Mellown suggests that external points of view help to distinguish
Antoinette from previous heroines, who are seen "always from
the inside, so to speak" and who are "shadows of an archetypal figure" (p. 472). 7 Certainly, multiple points of view
contribute to the conformation of both the female and the male
archetype. Antoinette's and Rochester's inside views counter
one another nicely and assure a clear sense of the individual
in conflict.

For the first time in her novels, Rhys has attempted to portray a sensitive and complete male character, by allowing him to describe his own insecurities and vulnerability. I find it odd that Mellown can categorize Rochester with the rest of "Rhys's men" and argue that he is little more than a creature "with physical desires who [has] the power of simple, logical thinking" (p. 472). Rochester has many desires, only some of which are physical, and they surface with such intensity that I would hardly call his thinking "simple" and "logical." I hope that critics do not view the male portraits in Rhys' recent collection of short stories, Sleep It Off, Lady, as harshly, for there she continues her attempt to give her male characters more depth. Mr. Ramage, in "Pioneers, Oh Pioneers," and Captain Cardew, in "Goodbye Marcus, Goodbye Rose," are every bit as captivating as the best of Rhys' heroines.

Recently, feminist critics have suggested that the critical goals feminist criticism "encompasses should finally reach way beyond the gender denomination" and that "it would be a sad comment on humanist studies in general were feminist criticism not permitted to so enlarge the boundaries of all literary criticism that we finally achieved a full 'humane' literary criticism."[8] Surely, Rhys' more recent works are ripe for such "humane" endeavors. She is expanding her vision to include the plight of men, as well as women, in a difficult world. Granted, her portraits of women are essential contributions to twentieth-century literature; however, they are not lessened because Rhys has proven herself capable of compelling sympathy regardless of gender.

## REFERENCES

1. "Introduction," Wide Sargasso Sea (New York: Popular Library, 1966), p. 11. For an earlier version of this essay, see Wyndham's "Introduction to Jean Rhys," The London Magazine, 7 (1960), 15-18. Further references to Wide Sargasso Sea will be noted in the text.

2. It should be noted that Mellown published his article at a time when feminist criticism was beginning to take shape and may not have realized what he was taking on. Only one year before, Annis Pratt and Lillian S. Robinson had published their seminal articles: "The New Feminist Criticism" and "Dwelling in Decencies: Radical Criticism and the

Feminist Perspective," in <u>College English</u>, 32 (19-
71),    872-78 and 879-89  respectively;   both of
these essays are reprinted in this anthology.

3.    <u>Contemporary Literature</u>, 13 (1972), 463-64.    Further
references will be noted in the text.

4.    Thinking along these lines caused Mellown to make a
critical blunder.    He described Bertha as a "frustrated nymphomaniac" (p. 464).

5.    (New York:   Vintage Books, 1974), p. 29.    Further references will be noted in the text.

6.    Bear in mind that in <u>Good Morning, Midnight</u> Sasha alludes to the culpability of the world--"You, who
represent society" (p. 29)--but a balance is never
struck and men carry the blame.

7.    Mellown knows that two of Rhys' early novels are written in the third person.    He feels, however, that
"Rhys's point of view is ... patently that of the
female character" (p. 470).

8.    Annette Kolodny expresses this sentiment in "Some Notes
on Defining a 'Feminist Literary Criticism,'" <u>Crit-
ical Inquiry</u>, 2 (1975), 92; reprinted in this anthology.

Ellen Morgan

ALIENATION OF THE WOMAN WRITER
IN THE GOLDEN NOTEBOOK*

In her interview at Stony Brook (1969), Doris Lessing said, "I'm impatient with people who emphasize sexual revolution. I say we should all go to bed, shut up about sexual liberation, and go on with the important matters."[1] But looking at the text of The Golden Notebook--which is, after all, on one important level about the female-male relationship in the middle of the twentieth century and about the meaning of femaleness in contemporary Western culture--one cannot help being aware of the tension that exists between Lessing's sensitive observations of the malaise between the sexes and such denials of the importance of discomfort with the sexual status quo.

In the course of The Golden Notebook, Lessing writes in the persona of Anna: "the quality a novel should have to make it a novel [is] the quality of philosophy.... Yet I am incapable of writing the only kind of novel which interests me: a book powered with an intellectual or moral passion strong enough to create order, to create a new way of looking at life."[2] This statement is a good entrance into The Golden Notebook, for the novel contains all the perceptions necessary to create a radical transforming and ordering vision of the relationship between women and men. These perceptions, however, are not gathered into the philosophical form proper to and inherent in them. Reading The Golden Notebook carefully forces one to realize how women writers can be, and have been, alienated from their own authentic, sensitive, and accurate perceptions of sexual politics. This alienation is very common in eras in which feminism is kept quiescent and latent. For in such eras, women writers do not see

*Reprinted by permission of the author and publisher from Contemporary Literature, XIV, 4 (1973), 471-80. Copyright © 1973 by the Regents of the University of Wisconsin.

their perceptions corroborated anywhere in their culture; they
see them instead made targets of antifeminist disparagement
and ridicule.

The world of The Golden Notebook consists, in addition
to its crucial artistic, racial, social, and political dimensions,
of Anna Wulf's closely rendered experiences with a number
of acquaintances and lovers, sometimes told through Ella,
her alter-ego and literary creation. But more significantly,
the book consists of Anna-Ella's interpretations of these experiences, her judgments and evaluations of them and of herself. Repeatedly, as I shall attempt to show, her judgments
belittle, deny, or distort her experiences and censor her
spontaneous responses to them. The difference between Anna-
Ella's actual attitudes and responses and those she does not
permit herself is the measure of her alienation from her own
perceptions and, I believe, the extent of Lessing's failure to
come to terms with female authenticity.

Ella and her friend Julia quite obviously feel, on the
one hand, an instinctive human need to respect themselves
as people and, on the other, a conditioned contempt for themselves as women. Spontaneously they trust one another and
are very close, but they judge this trust to be less valuable
than they feel it to be, less valuable than their far less trust-
ing relationships with men. As Anna says of herself and
Molly, no matter how close they are on the basis of shared
understanding, experience, and life style, their "real loyalties
are always to men, and not to women" (p. 48). Anna-Ella
feels strongly inclined to discuss with Molly-Julia her problems
with men, but she judges that all the "complaints and the
reproaches and the betrayals" (p. 48) ought not to be voiced.
These judgments, which undermine the solidarity between the
two women, are the result of their conviction that men are
superior to women and that their own self-interest lies in
relationships with men, however damaging their individual relationships with men may be. The two women share a mi-
nority-group psychological orientation which compels them to
depreciate their femaleness and their friendship with each
other and seek approval from and identification with men.
This fact becomes clear when Ella describes the contempt
she feels for the magazine for which she works (p. 178) and
even for the stories she writes because they are "feminine"
(p. 170). The two women also reveal this self-deprecatory
orientation by blaming only themselves for troubles to which
men have contributed, as Julia wryly recognizes (p. 458).

Ella judges that the future without a man is unimagin-

able.  But she hates the parties she has to go to in order to
meet men because the parties make her aware of the fact
that she is "on the market again" (p. 171).  Neither Ella
nor Julia, however, thinks that there is any use indulging in
complaint over this fact.  Julia says, "It's no good taking
that attitude--that's how everything is run, isn't it?" (p. 171).
The two women thus dismiss their feelings, convinced that
they have no legitimate grounds for complaint and that com-
plaining would only be self-pity.

        The pattern of opposition between feelings and judgment
is shown in particularly high relief when Dr. West, Ella's
employer, tries to start an affair with her while his wife is
away.  When she refuses, he turns to the other women in
his office and finally to the eldest, who is grateful and flat-
tered.  Ella's spontaneous reaction is to become "angry on
behalf of her sex," but she quickly turns away this feeling,
telling herself that the emotion really is "rooted in a resentment that has nothing to do with Dr. West" (p. 450), a resentment which she sees as shameful.  Ella retreats from
sympathizing with the older woman for fear of "cutting off
some possibility for herself" (p. 203).  She feels a natural
bond with other women but judges solidarity with them dangerous because it is to men that women, she believes, must
turn for any advantages which they may gain.

        "Sometimes," says Julia, "I think we're all in a sort
of sexual mad house" (p. 458).  But Ella tries to quash this
rebellious reaction in her friend and in herself: "My dear
Julia, we've chosen to be free women, and this is the price
we pay, that's all" (p. 458).  Neither woman considers actually fighting back; there is no visible solidarity among women which would sanction and support such rebellion.  Moreover, their analysis of the situation is fundamentally apolitical.  For example, Ella says that unlike men, women cannot
obtain sexual satisfaction without love, and that therefore the
inequality in sexual relations is inherent.  Neither woman
sees that the vulnerability she feels may be caused not by
some kind of fixed biological or psychological difference between the sexes, but by the fact that in a culture in which
sex is still apt to be viewed as a kind of conquest for the
man, the psychologically healthy woman cannot afford to experience sexual relations without asking love in return to even
the bargain.  Ella and Julia know that the kind of sex offered
them is a threat to their dignity and self-respect.  They cannot act directly while holding the apolitical view they do of
female-male relations, but neither is willing simply to capit-

ulate--hence their bickering and criticism of men and Ella's
inability to function sexually unless she is in love.

Most of Ella's keenest observations are followed by
turnings away, efforts to escape the essentially political consequences of their logic.   She is very much afraid that her
perceptions, because they are feminist, are illegitimate and
inconsistent with the broader humanism to which she is committed.   But the woman who has permitted herself to consider
the real extent of her oppression as a woman, and has stopped being ashamed of her anger and bitterness before asking
of herself the humanism to view men as co-victims of the
cultural web of power patterns, is one phenomenon.   Quite
another is the Lessing woman, who consistently tells herself
that her oppression is her own fault or an unchangeable condition to which one must gracefully resign oneself.   She refuses to face and deal with the anger always just under the
surface and forces herself not only to regard men as co-
victims, but to sympathize with them against the healthy interests of her own sex.

It is only in the vignettes Ella writes that she shows
the willingness to describe, albeit indirectly, the reality of
female-male relations as she has experienced them.   The
vignettes are about Ella's openness to men as persons, her
desire to communicate with them as people both sexually and
emotionally, and their refusal to relate on this personal basis
to her and to love her.   Ella grasps the fact that this refusal
in the men to connect sex and love (and thus integrate the
emotional and sexual components of personality) is a sickness.
But she fails to make the connection between the fact that
society teaches men not to allow themselves to be fully trust-
ing, open, and involved emotionally with women, and her
observation that the men she knows ask women for refuge,
strength, commitment, and loyal support while withholding
these things from them.   Neither of the women in The Golden
Notebook connects this male fear of reciprocity to prevailing
concepts of masculinity.   Neither does either woman see that
healthy men may retreat from women rather than try to fill
the emptiness and assuage the self-contempt women often
feel because, having internalized the prevailing social estimate
of femaleness, women feel incomplete and inferior as persons.

Ella's relationship with Paul gives the reader even
more convincing proof that the pattern of her psychic life is
withdrawal from and censorship of her perceptions, and failure to live an authentic existence.   Believing that female-

male relationships are inherently unequal and therefore not
susceptible of transformation, she seeks to justify the in-
equalities so that she may convince herself to accept them
without the resentment and rebellion she constantly feels.

She senses and resents, for instance, Paul's will to
dominate her.  But Ella, like the other women in this book
who are confronted with the choice of taking a man on terms
which are less than egalitarian or of turning away from him
to uphold their own terms, chooses the man on his own
terms.  When a sexual relationship is offered, she is unable
to refuse because the terms available are the only ones imag-
inable to her.  She does not make any attempt to change the
basis of relating from exploitation to genuine egalitarian
friendship and love.  The idea that she could refuse to deal
with men in the style suggested by their behavior does not
occur to her.  Rebellion and self-assertion are present in
her propensities for condemning men with Julia and for feeling mistreated and hurt, but she tries to hide from herself
the kinds of thoughts which encourage these propensities.
Thus Ella perceives that part of Paul's personality is rakish,
corrupting, and detrimental to her dignity, but she refuses
to connect this part of him with the rest, which she calls
his true self.  His rakishness, she tells herself, "was on
a level that not only had nothing to do with the simplicity
and ease of their being together; but betrayed it so completely
that she had no alternative but to ignore it.  Otherwise she
would have had to break with him" (p. 197).  She is happy
only when she does not think about the ugly aspects of their
relationship.  Anna writes of her, "she drifted along on a
soft tide of not-thinking" (p. 199).  At one point Paul's behavior makes her envision his paying her money as if she
were a prostitute: "It was somewhere implicit in his attitude."  But Ella pushes the thought away: "What's that got
to do with all these hours we've been together, when every
look and move he's made told me he loved me?" (p. 202).

After five years as Paul's mistress, Ella begins to be
disturbed by thoughts about his wife and not only stops feeling
triumph over her for having captured her husband, but envies
her.  Ella builds up a picture of the other woman as a "se-
rene, calm, unjealous, unenvious, undemanding woman, full
of resources of happiness inside herself, self-sufficient, yet
always ready to give happiness when it is asked for" (p. 207).
She realizes that this picture is not derived from what Paul
says about his wife, but that this is the kind of woman she
herself would like to be, especially since she has grown aware

and afraid of the extent of her dependence upon Paul.    It is
interesting to note that Ella's idea of a defense against her
own dependency is selflessness, the old ideal of the woman
as giver who does not require gifts for herself.    She is incapable of thinking of less self-damaging ways than self-
abnegation to reduce her vulnerability.    Significantly it is
not because Ella wishes to respect herself more for being
a complete, self-sufficient, self-motivated person that she
admires and envies this figure; it is because she envisions
such a woman as relatively invulnerable to being hurt by
people like Paul.    The attraction to the figure has a negative
motive, as all of Ella's emotional life is negative, because
she does not allow her spontaneous reactions to her experience
to govern her behavior and shape her values.

When Paul finally leaves Ella, she is devastated.    She
feels "as if a skin had been peeled off her" (p. 312) and
realizes that the relationship was not free for her, as she
had thought, simply because she had remained unmarried;
nor was it really a love relationship, since it pulled her out
of herself, unbalanced and diminished her, and proved altogether a destructive experience with regard to her self-respect and firmness of identity.    Openly she admits, "I am
unhappy because I have lost some kind of independence, some
freedom," and she acknowledges that her attitude toward Paul
has been "dishonest" (p. 314).    But then Ella turns away from
this realization.    She concludes that it is not Paul, or society's sexual mores and views, but she herself who is to
blame for the failure she feels.

Ella's life is a long series of encounters with the unhappy dislocation between the sexes, the implications of which
neither Ella nor her creator Anna can face.    The extraordinary amount of energy Ella expends in interpreting her relationships with men and compartmentalizing, disapproving of,
and suppressing her feelings is a good indication of the seriousness of the discrepancy between what Ella is capable of
perceiving and what she can afford to admit to herself, and
therefore of her alienation from her perceptions and distance
from personal authenticity.

The pattern of alienation, of withdrawal from authenticity, is also apparent in the Anna-Molly spectrum of The
Golden Notebook.    The two women allow Molly's ex-husband
and son to bully them despite the fact that they are aware
that the two men are hurting them.    They extend friendship
to other men who also mistreat them, such as the sadistic

and misogynistic Nelson, de Silva, Willi, George, and Paul.
In connection with one of these relationships Anna comments,
"Sometimes I dislike women, I dislike us all, because of our
capacity for not-thinking when it suits us; we choose not to
think when we are reaching out for happiness" (p. 485).
Again one sees Anna turning the anger she feels at being ill-
used against herself and other women and refusing to curtail
relationships with men who damage her.   One could interpret
her responses to these men as humanistic in the profoundest
sense--as evidence of a mature ability to see that no human
being is all good or bad, that most have something to offer
which redeems at least in part that which is ugly in them.
But such a view misses the crucial point here, which is that
Anna and Molly have legitimate cause for anger, and that they
feel the anger but believe it to be an illegitimate reaction to
their experiences.   Their behavior is inconsistent with their
real self-interest and shows them once again to be alienated
from themselves.

With her two male homosexual tenants, both of whom
happen to be rabidly anti-woman, Anna permits some of her
anger to surface and she links their attitudes toward women
with those of heterosexual men.   "The mockery," she says,
"the defence of the homosexual, was nothing more than the
polite over-gallantry of a 'real' man, the 'normal' man who
intends to set bounds to his relationship with a woman, consciously or not." She continues, "It was the same cold,
evasive emotion, taken a step further; there was a difference
in degree but not in kind" (p. 393).   But Anna, true to form,
then criticizes herself for her anger.   She feels unfree to
oust the tenants simply because they are so disagreeable to
her.   Finally she also rejects her perception of the similarity
between the tenants' attitudes toward women and those of
heterosexual men who wish to remain emotionally detached
in their relationships with women.   Deciding to throw one
tenant out so her daughter will not be hurt by his misogyny,
she declares that her daughter is someday to have a "real"
man, implying that the evasive attitudes toward women of
"real" men are not, after all, damaging as she had spontaneously remarked.

The discrepancy between Anna's spontaneous perceptions and superimposed judgments is even clearer with regard
to two men at a further remove from her:   one who follows
her out of the subway and another who exposes himself to
her.   Her immediate reaction to both is, naturally, fright.
On second thought she tells herself that something is abnormal

about her. "This happens every day, this is living in the
city," she says (p. 390), refusing to indict a society in which
such treatment of women is to be expected.

The discrepancy is most obvious, however, in Anna's
major relationships with men. With Michael, she is period-
ically happy and resentful. She resents his inability to accept her as a writer and a responsible mother and his refusal
to give her the kind of unmeasured love and support he asks
of her. She also resents the fact that because he is a man,
the petty details of his life are taken care of for him by women, whereas because she is a woman, her life is composed
largely of seeing to the details of others' needs. Anna calls
this resentment the "housewife's disease" (p. 333). But instead of facing squarely the fact that she resents Michael
because he is a holder of the privileges which accrue to
males in a patriarchal society and is taking advantage of
this fact and of her, she turns her anger away, depersonal-
izing and depoliticizing it. She tells herself the anger has
nothing to do with Michael. It is "impersonal," the disease
"of women in our time" which is evident in their faces and
voices, a protest against injustice, but nevertheless a protest
which should be fought down and not on any account turned
against men (p. 333). The idea is that one must adjust
rather than act in one's own self-interest to change the system.

With Saul the relationship is more complex because
he alternates communicating with Anna on a very high level
with misogynistic, hostile withdrawal from her. But the pattern still holds. For example, at one point she gets angry
enough to explode at him for referring to women and sex in
demeaning terms. But predictably there follows the retrac-
tion, the denial of legitimacy of her own spontaneous emotion.
She feels "ridiculous" (p. 560) and softens toward Saul. As
with Michael, Anna is ambivalent, but she only accepts her
positive feelings for him.

Anna sees that any relationship structured along the
lines of the heterosexual model of our culture, as are the
female-male relationships in The Golden Notebook, pits the
interests of women and men against each other, women being
driven to need and grasp for security and protection and men
resisting being drawn into the restrictive role of provider.
This is the meaning of her statement, "I am the position of
women in our time" (p. 579). But although she is aware of
this separation of interests, and also of the rhythm of alter-

nating love and hate in her relationships with men, she never connects these two phenomena. And because she does not make this connection, the sexual pain which she experiences never is recognized as a problem susceptible of solution, a problem calling for remedial action. Thus when Saul vents hatred upon her, Anna does not act to alter the situation. Instead she follows her preëstablished pattern, turning her anger and frustration in upon herself. Instead of defending herself from his attacks, she disparages herself for the very strength with which she meets them. "I longed," she writes, "to be free of my own ordering, commenting memory" (p. 585). Her stomach clenches and her back hurts, but she does not connect these details with the fact that her refusal to act in her own self-interest hurts her and is making her lose her sense of personal worth and identity. She relates the physical ills rather to Saul's hostility. The solution to the pain is thus made to lie with him and not with herself; she adopts the posture of a helpless victim instead of acting to bring herself relief.

Anna is aware that what is wrong between her and Saul is a problem common to women. She wonders to herself what it is that women need and are not getting from men and senses that perhaps this unfulfilled need is the cause of the note of betrayal that women strike in this era. But predictably, instead of permitting herself to conclude that this "note" is legitimate, she disparages women by describing it as self-pity, a "hateful emotion" which is "solemn" and "wet" (p. 597). She never really stands up for herself as a woman and never opts out of the self-damaging collusion of tolerating and playing a role in the submission-dominance syndrome which is the leitmotiv of female-male relations in patriarchal societies. The only approach to the problem which she feels legitimate is contained in her dream about Saul as a tiger. The tiger claws her and she sympathizes with it instead of with herself; then comes an image of her flying above the tiger's cage. Apparently it is legitimate to try to "rise above" the situation, but not to change it.

As she views the imaginary movie composed of scenes from her past life, Anna realizes that the meaning with which she has endowed each scene has been "all false" (p. 620). She finds that the judgments she has been making have ordered the material "to fit what I knew" (p. 620) rather than emerging in a direct response to her experience. But she never escapes her pattern of self-punishment and alienation. The novel ends with Molly's getting married although she

knows "the exact dimensions of the bed" (p. 666) and with
Anna's entering marriage counseling work and the teaching
of delinquent children.   There is a "small silence" as the
two women together contemplate their capitulation, their integration "with British life at its roots" (p. 666).

The Golden Notebook reveals through its main female
characters the peculiar problem of the woman writer working
in a climate of assumptions and sympathies about women and
sex roles which does not support female authenticity.   The
woman writer in this situation is unlikely to conceive of the
relative status of women and men in political terms; prevailing opinion convinces her that the condition of women in
society is rooted in biological and psychological immutables.
She may, nevertheless, be acutely sensitive to and resentful
of the power dynamics which characterize female-male relations, aware to a large extent of what we have come to
call sexual politics.   If so, she finds herself on the horns
of a dilemma:   she cannot completely deny her awareness,
but, unencouraged by any cultural sanction for those of her
perceptions which are, at the deepest level, feminist and
potentially political, she doubts these perceptions and feels
they are indicative of some abberation or defect in herself.

The overriding weakness of The Golden Notebook is
alienation from the authentic female perspective, a perspective which repeatedly is clearly sketched in and then smeared
by the censor in Lessing, who so conceived this book that
nowhere within it are Anna's and Ella's final censoring judgments of their experiences permitted to seem anything but
unavoidable.   The discrepancy between the perceptions and
the alien standards imposed upon them seriously flaws the
novel.   But at the same time, the tension produced by this
discrepancy makes the book a superb rendering of that state
of alienation from themselves, from authentic selfhood, to
which women, like blacks and members of other minority
groups, are subject until they find solidarity and begin to
confirm and legitimize their experience.   In addition, Lessing's study of the malaise and dislocation between the sexes
in Western society does set a very important precedent in
literature because it examines the relationship between women
and men so humanistically and analytically, in such great
detail and variety, and with a good faith which never permits
a descent into vituperation or abuse.

REFERENCES

1. Jonah Raskin, "Doris Lessing at Stony Brook: An Interview," New American Review 8 (New York: New American Library, 1969), p. 175.
2. Doris Lessing, The Golden Notebook (New York: Ballantine Books, 1962), p. 61. All subsequent references in the text are to this edition.

Estelle C. Jelinek

## ANAÏS NIN: A CRITICAL EVALUATION*

It must have been early in 1971 that I began hearing
Anaïs Nin's name put forth by my friends in the women's
liberation movement.  I couldn't pin them down when I asked
why they adored her; they said I had to read her to understand.  So I read A Spy in the House of Love first, and I
found its style impressionistic, its content repetitive, and
its heroine unsympathetic.  She is in a constant state of flux,
living now in one role, now in another, play-acting, fantasizing, going from one man to another for her identity, but
returning like a child, always to a husband who was like a
father to her.  Ladders to Fire was my second attempt at
a Nin "novel"; I wanted so much to "catch fire" as my friends
had.  I was disappointed again.  Ladders was no more than
a variation of the theme and plot of Spy--another actress
playing roles, lying, and taking her identity from men.

But I didn't give up.  I began reading Nin's diaries.
Although I appreciated her honesty and her struggle for a
personal identity, I was bored by her vanity and her endless
descriptions of adoring and adored men.  These early diaries
seemed to me merely the sourcebooks for her rather inept
and inane novels.  Nonetheless, I kept looking for the real
Nin.  When an "Anaïs Nin Celebration" was held at the
University of California, Berkeley, in December 1971, I
paid my $15, convinced that I could not help but be turned
on by her if only I saw and heard her "in the flesh."  During
that weekend, my initial reaction to Nin shifted from a tentative disapproval to outright rage.  Now, three years later,
having seen Nin in the flesh again, I realize that my anger
has diminished, but my disapproval of her is just as keen.

In the years that have passed, Nin has traveled across
the country speaking at colleges and feminist events, some-

---

*This essay was written prior to Anaïs Nin's death on Jan-
uary 14, 1977.

times solo, sometimes in conjunction with other women.
Always it is she, however, who is billed as the main attraction; it is her picture that accompanies announcements of the
events in local newspapers. And it is her performance that
the thousands of women, overwhelmingly white and middle
class, wait for in awed expectation. Radicals, conservatives,
feminists, Marxists, librarians, teachers, housewives, students, poets--all come to celebrate an idol. When Nin appears on stage, the audience seems to gasp in unison and
pay homage to her with "Ooh" and "Aah" and "Isn't she
lovely!"

The response to her was the same in 1974 as it was
in 1971. And her style and message have not altered either.
She reads from her diaries--now her fifth one, whose contents are hardly distinguishable from the previous four. Her
heroes and mentors are always men: D. H. Lawrence, Henry
Miller, Ingmar Bergman, Otto Rank, Picasso, Casals, Dalí,
Antonin Artaud, André Breton, Max Ernst, and others. At
some celebrations the audience is treated to a video portion
as well. It may be slides of the architecture of Lloyd Wright,
the "master builder," who, Nin says, has been overshadowed
unduly by his famous father; or perhaps a film on Jean Varda,
the Sausalito painter and "poet of collages," who adored women and "turned them into myths of all kinds"; or it may
be that film of unmistakable adoration, Anaïs Observed, by
Robert Snyder.

In the slides designed to show the architecture of
Wright's Wayfarers' Chapel in Southern California, we see
Nin strolling through the chapel wearing a flowing white gown,
then draped in a white cape, posing under the medieval arch
that marks the entrance to the chapel. In Snyder's film we
see her posing seductively in a field or sitting in her (now
familiar) long red velvet dress, serenely reclining on a couch
under a collage by Varda. Snyder often says, I am told, as
he did at that 1971 celebration I attended: "I guess we're
here to celebrate her sweet sixteen."

Between Nin's readings from her diaries about her
male heroes and scenes of "Nin the Hero," we may be fortunate enough to hear contributions from other women, some
reading critical interpretations of Nin's writings, others reading their own creative efforts. The women are talented and
deserve recognition; Nin herself deserves credit for encouraging them. But when Nin introduces one woman as "a critic,
unusual in women--she has her own point of view, she is

sensitive, and she is feminine and still objective," I must
then question Nin's feminism.   From reading her diaries
and novels and now having heard her in person, I can see,
despite what I have been told, that she holds views that are
anathema to me and the women's liberation movement.

As long as she continues to read from her diaries
and speak of her male heroes and to tell us that her heroes
today are Daniel Ellsberg and Ralph Nader (and, by the way,
that she is looking for women to worship as well), any woman who takes her feminism seriously must at least question
Nin's attitudes.   Equally to the point I am making is Nin's
belief that women have a special and unique nature, one that
will transform the world.   In 1971, one poet, reiterating
Nin's own views in the diaries, spoke of her as validating
the "female principle" in society:   fusion, anti-war, earth-
mother, gentleness.   Nin herself said that women "should
dominate, and men should let them because she has something special to give."   The future of our society, Nin declared, depends on women's finding themselves, being free,
for only by finding the truly feminine in themselves can they
"give rebirth to everything that is divided."   In 1974 her
message had not changed; in speaking of the woman of the
future, her theme, Nin said that she would be a "better fusion," she would make a "totally better world"; she will
combine the "intellectual with intuition and a sense of personal intimacy."   Woman, she said, has developed the intimacy quality, which she should keep, and man will have that
quality too when he recognizes the femininity in himself.   But
woman must not neglect the intellectual in herself, Nin said,
which, by implication, is man's realm.

In her diaries, especially, Nin speaks to these sexist
notions, which are offshoots of her mentors Lawrence and
Jung:

> It is feminine to be oblique.   It is not trickery [I,
> 58].

Or   When man lies in her womb, she is fulfilled, each
        act of love is a taking man within her, an act of
        birth and rebirth, of child-bearing and man-bearing.
        Man lies in her womb and is reborn each time anew
        with a desire to act, to BE.   But for woman, the
        climax is not in the birth, but in the moment when
        man rests inside her [I, 106].

Or        The territory of woman´ is that which lies untouched

by the direct desire of man.   Man attacks the vital
center.   Woman fills out the circumference [I, 184].

Or      Feminine vision is usually myopic.   I do not think
         mine is.   But I do not understand abstract ideas
         [I, 190].

Nin's concept of woman is really an alternate form of
sexism.   Where usually men have used the traits she celebrates against women, Nin puts women on a pedestal because
they (seemingly) possess these traits, as though they were
innate in women and absent in men.   I don't find it at all
justifiable to call women better than men because their thinking is intuitive and not logical, or that they are earth-mothers
and creators (which perhaps men envy), or that they are more
sensitive and compassionate.   This kind of sexism makes
logical women "masculine" and intuitive men "feminine,"
women who do not want to have children "unnatural," men
who are compassionate and sensitive "effeminate."

Even the women in her novels are not models for feminists.   We may identify with their search for an individual
identity, but ultimately these protagonists are searching for
their identity through men.   They go from one man to another,
looking for the hero who will fill all their needs.   Each is
helpless, lost, and playing a part.   Their roles become
second nature to them, so much so that they are never sure
who they really are without this external, male validation of
themselves.   In the last analysis, Nin's protagonists are
variations of Nin herself.   When one sees her performing
today, whether reading from her diaries or posing in films,
the theatrical effect is dominant.   Even she has questioned
her authenticity, her need to play roles:

> ... I begin to imagine that I am also a fake--that
> maybe all my journals, books, and personality are
> fakes.   When I'm admired I think I am duping the
> world.   ...   And I see the question of my sincerity
> could easily drive me insane if I studied it con-
> tinuously.   My imagination entangles me hopelessly.
> I lose myself.   What distresses me is that I seem
> to play on the feelings of people [I, 205].

Artaud felt her insincerity acutely: "You give everyone the
illusion of maximum love" (I, 245).   I, too, question Nin's
sincerity acutely; she is still playing roles.   Currently, it
is that of a feminist.

In her diaries, Nin has also written of her distaste
for anything but the extraordinary life:

> Ordinary life does not interest me.  I seek only
> the high moments [I, 5].

And she is not interested in politics:

> I don't rave against politics.  I ignore it [I, 12].
>
> ... politics to me, all of them, seem rotten to the
> core and all based on economics, not humanitari-
> anism [II, viii].

In seeking her own individual solution, she is revolted by
"realism"--the concern with externals, the world around us:
things, the world of science, facts, and so on.   The literature of realism, to her, is crude and absurd; why write
about opening doors, she says, refrigerators, the "ugly" in
life?   There is no room for despair, only joy.   As she
globalized her position in her diary, if everyone were like
her, there would be no wars, no poverty.

In "Notes on Feminism" (1972), Nin writes:

> Poverty and injustice and prejudice are not
> solved by any man-made system.   I want them to
> be solved by a higher quality of human being who,
> by his own law of valuation upon human life will
> not permit such inequalities [Woman:  An Issue,
> ed. by Edwards, Heath, and Bahin; Boston:  Little,
> Brown, 1972].

And that human being must struggle individually, from within,
to change the world.   The group solution is out as far as
Nin is concerned.   Tillie Olsen asks her students how many
servants go into making Nin's life possible: in her villas in
France, in her bohemian salons in New York, and now on
the West Coast?   Naturally, anyone who cannot tolerate ugliness, who lives in a world of admirers, who is a goddess
courting her worshippers, who lives for individual solutions,
is not going to believe in any form of collective action.   In
one interview she said:

> This is sometimes the only difficult thing I have to
> bridge when I speak to women's liberation:  That
> having been made responsible for their situation,
> they refuse the idea that we can help ourselves

individually [Everywoman, 1972].

For Nin, politics deal with external realities, whereas she is interested only in the internal, creative ones.   This makes her selective in her choice of friends, in the women she encourages, in the males she worships, in the privileged world she not only lives in but approves of to the exclusion of all others.   She doesn't really care about anyone but artists.   Somehow, she feels she can affect the whole world with her personalized aesthetics:

> I am not committed to any of the political move-
> ments which I find full of fanaticism and injustice,
> but in the face of each human being, I act demo-
> cratically and humanly.   I give each human being
> his due.   I disregard class and possessions.   It
> is the value of their spirit, of their human qualities
> I pay my respect to ... [I, vii].

But in "Notes on Feminism" Nin attacks the women's libera-
tion movement for being negative, for attacking male writers and male-dominated films or for "group thinking":

> I see so many women in the movement thinking in
> obsessional circles about problems which are solv-
> able when one is emotionally free to think and act
> clearly.

She sees women's "undirected, blind anger and hostility" as ineffective weapons.   "Slogans," she writes,

> do not give strength because generalizations are
> untrue. ....   The group does not always give strength
> because it moves only according to the lowest de-
> nominator of understanding.   The group weakens
> the individual will and annihilates the individual
> contribution.

Ayn Rand upheld this personal vision of the creative artist as a superior human being and, concomitantly the in-
feriority of the masses in The Fountainhead.   One could see Nin's individualism carried to the fascistic extremes that Ayn Rand articulated in her later books and in her philosophy of objectivism.   How can feminists and radicals of all types accept uncritically this elitism and miss the incompatibility with the rest of their lives?   To Nin, realism is distasteful: that means the poverty in ghettoes and barrios; that means

the inhumanity in prisons; that means the day-to-day practical
efforts to get equal pay for equal work or, even more difficult, getting welfare or foodstamps when one has no permanent address.    Nin is appealing to middle-class women
who have the leisure to lavish attention upon their creative
talents.    Nin is not essentially interested in the struggle of
poor women or women who haven't her talents.

But, one may say, there are other women doing that
and her interests are different.    Granted.    But Nin would be
repelled by that kind of work; she would feel above these un-
creative, untalented, "ugly" people for whom the "ugly" is
their everyday reality.    That is the difference between Nin
and other women artists who work in their chosen profession
exclusively.    It's the snobbish and elitist attitude that dif-
ferentiates her from these others.    Nonetheless, women who
call themselves feminists or Marxists swoon at her words
and applaud her "feminine" virtues.    These women seem incapable of discerning the inherent contradictions between their
sexual and/or radical politics and her views:  her emphasis
on, and embodiment of, conventional femininity, her hatred
of the ugly and ordinary, her touting of the individual solution, and her disdain of collective endeavors.

It took me a long time to understand my rejection of
Anaïs Nin and to analyze the reactions of my friends to her
writings.    In recent months, I've been getting support from
some women whose reactions to her are similar to mine,
but I am still meeting women who either give a long sigh at
the sound of her name or react defensively to my tentative
questioning of the implications of her views.    Some women's
reactions to my ideas on Nin's sexism are quite dramatic,
as though I were, by attacking Nin, attacking their own femininity.    This must be, at least partially, at the root of the
adoration for Nin:  the burden women still feel to prove their
"femininity" in spite of their individuality.

I can understand the model Nin herself presents to
other women who are struggling to realize a creative identity.
The validation she gives to the personal growth process, to
using the material of one's own life and one's own self in
creative expression is certainly reason for admiring her and
her diaries.    But admiration is a far cry from adulation.
We may admire Zelda Fitzgerald for her struggle to realize
her artistic potential or Isadora Duncan for her pioneer work
in liberating the human body through dance.    But we must
certainly not distort a woman's contribution to the arts just

because she is a woman.

The blindness I see in Nin's readers and audiences is also evident in the many articles written about her.  I have yet to read an article that questions her place in the women's movement, her feminism, or the relevance (or irrelevance) of the politics of her aesthetics.  In a New York Times guest editorial on the women's movement, it is Nin who is called on to define our origins.  She writes: "Several developments accelerated the growth and expansion of woman.  One was psychoanalysis which gave her self-confidence and guidance in the creation of herself as an individual.  ... The second development was political; women working in groups and organized efforts to change laws detrimental to the equality of woman, her economic independence, her happiness.  The third was the formation of consciousness-raising groups. Women gathered to discuss their problems openly, to discuss solutions, to strengthen each other's confidence, to establish solidarity" (January 14, 1972).

Nin's Times article points up two significant factors. The first is that she knows very little about the women's movement.  Anyone who has had any involvement in it knows that consciousness-raising groups were the first and basic foundation of the current movement; that political organizing and efforts to change laws have been going on for decades on a small scale, often hidden from the public eye, until their emergence on a large scale because of the thousands of women who joined the movement through consciousness-raising groups.  As for psychoanalysis, the women's movement has had to work doubly hard, in fact, to try to erase the damage that has been done by psychiatrists, predominantly influenced by Freud's often harsh and belittling judgments of women.  The fact that Nin, who was told by one psychiatrist (Allendy) that she was trying to "surpass men in their own work, to have more success" and by another (Rank) that she must discover which she wants to be, either "a woman or an artist," can still extol psychoanalysis shows how dated and unfeminist she really is.  Certainly analysis never made her a feminist, for she still needs her male heroes and her identification with them--even those she had forty years ago. She still needs to present herself as almost professionally seductive.  She has not overcome her adoration of her father, her need for men to define and to worship her.

The second significant factor concerning the Times article is that the press has been hoodwinked, just as her

readers have been, into thinking Nin is a feminist; and the
nation's most prestigious establishment newspaper prints her
opinions on the women's liberation movement as though she
represents that movement.   Both the feminist and straight
press have responded to her in much the same way that her
naive readers have:  with awe and with blindness to the facts
of her sexism and elitism.

    In all the articles I have read about her, I see three
distinct approaches to Nin.   The most typical is that represented by an adoring article in the November 1971 issue of
Off Our Backs, "Anaïs Nin:  Two Women React," by Linda
M. McGonigal and Sheri A. Maeda.   These women approached
their interview with the venerable Nin with the "anxiety of
meeting someone your gut already knows," hoping "for a
miraculous flow."  When they left Nin, they "walked further
into the reality, into the dream, and the becoming awareness
of being Woman."  In between, Nin expressed views that her
interviewers were obviously in too much of a daze to realize
were sexist:  "Woman perceives reality via her emotions,
spirit and mind, while man abstracts realism from reality,
a process limited to the mind.   Woman's closer contact with
and belief in the unconscious and emotional has produced a
different view of reality, one more real than that of man,
who goes about setting things in logical, rational schemes."
This article, coming as it did from a feminist newspaper,
most accurately typifies the blind reaction of Nin's readers.

    In the second type of article, which appears in both
movement and establishment publications, the authors may
raise questions rhetorically about Nin's views, but they do
not explore them, out of fear, perhaps, of incurring the wrath
of the Nin cult.   In her article in Notes from the Third Year,
Ann Snitow does mention that "it's fairly plain [that] Anaïs Nin
isn't a conscious feminist as we understand the term now,"
but Snitow never speaks to that point; instead she praises the
diaries for telling us the "painful truth."  Nin's honesty becomes the criterion for acceptance, no matter what views
are expressed.   The diary becomes for Nin "the place where
a woman can speak the truth without hurting all those people
she is supposed to protect and support."  Therefore, how
can we scoff, when Nin truthfully tells us that she feels for-
giving and compassionate toward Henry Miller when he sells
the typewriter she had given him for his writing in order to
buy some wine.   The question is:  truth about what?

    Others like Snitow handle a negative appraisal of Nin

by merely raising the issue, then dropping it. In the San Francisco Chronicle article (December 6, 1971) covering the first celebration I attended, the headline read "A Heroine for Feminists." Beverly Stephen led off her report with this statement:

> Who could have guessed that many new feminists
> would find a heroine in a soft-spoken 68-year-old
> woman who refuses to generalize about men as
> 'oppressors.' Who doesn't have much sympathy
> for slogans like 'male chauvinist pig.' Who feels
> no need for drugs. Who can wear a long black
> dress in the middle of the afternoon. Who can be-
> friend a man like Henry Miller.

But Stephen never pursues the point; the rest of the article is merely a factual account of the celebration.

In a feature story on January 16, 1972, about the same event, Jean Dickinson notes, in "Celebrating Anaïs Nin" (San Francisco Examiner and Chronicle): "So, no one asks about her husband and how she integrated him into a life filled with writing and Henry Miller. No one asks about her relationship to the Women's Movement, or about her attitude towards Kate Millett and other militant voices. No one questions her belief that women are more intuitive than men. No one challenges her 'Everywhere I look I am living in a world made by man as he wants it, and I am being what man wants ...' (I, page 46), [her] rejection of political solutions or her conviction that it is enough to build 'private shelters.'" But Dickinson does not pursue these points either. Again I suspect it is out of fear of antagonizing such a popular figure and her admirers.

In an Everywoman interview in 1972, Karla Jay did have the courage to question Nin on some of her views on psychoanalysis and individual solutions as opposed to the group process of consciousness raising. Nin's reaction was, "we can help ourselves individually," but then she deftly concedes that "we need both because there are some cases where the social has so twisted an individual that all he can bring is already a damaged human being, and a damaged human being doesn't get repaired by political methods." I wonder who she would consider damaged--anyone who was not creative? anyone who did not dream?--for certainly these are the only qualities in people to which she seems to relate. Jay's format is a question-and-answer interview so that the intention may have been to let readers draw their own conclusions.

But the fact that Jay does not follow up some of Nin's obviously elitist responses is further evidence of how tenderly
women treat this delicate "feminine" object.    Hidden among
the routine questions and answers, Jay's probing is lost in
the final positive impression left of Nin.

The third type of response to Nin by the press is
represented by Anna Balakian's review of the fourth diary
(New York Times Book Review, January 16, 1972).    This
type is actually rare, but it does exist.    What Balakian does
is deny that Nin possesses those traits of sexism or elitism,
without investigating them:  "Though she was placed by birth
in an international milieu, made up mainly of musicians,
artists and writers, there is no elitism in the world of Anaïs
Nin."    In the fourth diary, there is room for unknowns, as
well as people like "Gore Vidal, Edmund Wilson, Truman
Capote, Richard Wright, Salvador Dali, Martha Graham and
the surrealist Andre Breton,... "!

Balakian describes Nin as "Ariadne leading man through
the labyrinth....    She belongs to that almost extinct breed
that still espouses the doctrine:  'I am my brother's keeper.'"
Balakian does not question Nin's status in the women's movement:  "Is she a symbol of the liberated woman?    She has
been for so long a free spirit that it is hard to think of her
as 'liberated.'    Her so-called feminine intuition is really a
combination of poetic perception, acumen and the wisdom
gained from a wealth of encounters."

What we have in the cult surrounding Anaïs Nin is a
regressive aspect of the women's liberation movement.    I
am not impressed with her appearances at fund-raising events
for women's centers or her promotion of women's journals
because I see these, just as I view those "celebrations," as
opportunistic efforts to spread her name and sell her books.
At her appearance in San Francisco in the spring of 1974,
she asked to be introduced with the announcement of the publication of the fifth volume of her diaries, and she offered to
sign this book afterward in the lobby where her works were
the only ones on display (at a feminist event attended by
1000 women!).

I believe Nin's involvement in the women's movement
is insincere because she is not a feminist.    She holds views
that are contrary to those held by true feminists:  the glo-
rification of male heroes, the belief in the special nature of
women that makes them superior to men, her repulsion to

the ordinary, everyday struggles of oppressed peoples, her reliance on the individual solution, and her own self-glorification. Women will be poets and free thinkers without the Anaïs Nins. I think it is time women began to look at Anaïs Nin with some objectivity. She may be an inspiration and model for the struggling creative artist, but she is not a feminist; in fact, some of her views are outright sexist. She sees little if any value to collective efforts and is blind to the economic realities of most of society. Nin is using the women's movement for her own ends--to sell her books. We must not weaken our cause by nearsightedness; hero-worshipping should be anathema to all serious radicals and feminists.

Lynn Z. Bloom

PROMISES FULFILLED:
POSITIVE IMAGES OF WOMEN
IN TWENTIETH-CENTURY AUTOBIOGRAPHY*

Creative. Intellectual. Innovative. Self-reliant.
Dynamic. Self-confident. Strongly positive. So twentieth-
century women autobiographers knew themselves, sometimes
from very young ages. So the world knows them now. That
their images possess many significant characteristics in common is remarkable, considering the diverse backgrounds,
upbringings, interests, and careers of the women whose lives
were studied in this survey of twentieth-century autobiographies of quality, [1] including those of Gertrude Stein, Margaret
Sanger, Margaret Mead, Lillian Hellman, Simone de Beauvoir, Mary McCarthy, Maya Angelou, and Nikki Giovanni.

The conventional positive norm vs. the autobiographical variation: a new definition of "positive"

The conventional positive images and norms for women
of the twentieth century before the 1960s are represented by
the Freudian and feminine mystiques, which view woman as
a creature of her biological and social roles, a submissive,
long-suffering, unintellectual, intuitive wife, mother, home-
maker, the purveyor of "togetherness" at all costs to herself,
who "lives" through the accomplishments of her husband and
children. [2] In this view, characterized by Freudian psycho-
analyst Helene Deutsch in The Psychology of Women, the
"essential traits of femininity are narcissism, passivity, and
masochism"; masculine women are active, intellectual, aggressive witches or bitches in whom "warm intuitive knowledge
has yielded to cold unproductive thinking. "[3]

Manuals on marriage, homemaking, child rearing, and

---

*This essay was first presented in the "Women and Litera-
ture" section of the Midwest MLA meeting, Chicago, 1975.

etiquette, indicative of the prevailing culture of the time, generally regard these feminine characteristics as both the norm and the ideal.   To an extent even in the seventies this is still true, as attested by the enormous popularity of Total Woman and Fascinating Womanhood courses and books that promote "femininity."   This consists of incompetence, inefficiency, fearfulness, weakness, submissiveness, dependency, and childishness--in clothing, speech, and manner.   Thus the angry wife is advised to beat her fists on her husband's chest, pouting, "You hairy beast....   How can a great big man like you pick on a poor little helpless girl?   I'll tell your mother on you. "[4]

In contrast, each of the women autobiographers studied here has seen herself from childhood to maturity in a light that is very positive to her, though very different from the prevailing views of society, and sometimes at variance with the perspectives of her parents, spouse, and friends, as well.   The twentieth-century woman autobiographer has a strong counter-normative sense of herself as an intellectually, sexually, economically, strong, independent, unique person. Like dynamic, productive men (who represent the twentieth-century masculine norm and positive ideal), the woman autobiographer recognizes her own integrity of self, her intelligence and abilities.   As Gertrude Stein has her created Alice B. Toklas ventriloquize: "Gertrude Stein realizes that in English literature in her time she is the only one.   She has always known it and now she says it.   She understands very well the basis of creation and therefore her advice and criticism is invaluable to all her friends. "[5]

All of the women studied here have enormous vitality, and expend much of their abundant energy to fulfill the goals that their talents, interests, and convictions dictate.   As Margaret Sanger says, "I had practically reached the exploding point.   I could not contain my ideas.   I wanted to get on with what I had to do in the world"[6] by spreading birth control information throughout the United States.

The autobiographers' sense of professional mission, and desire for self-fulfillment therein, dominate much of their adult lives, and sometimes their later childhood.   Simone de Beauvoir describes the recognition at nineteen of her vocation as a philosopher: "I had pursued my own [ambitions to be a philosopher] with tenacious zeal.   I passed [my Sorbonne exams] in general philosophy ... and Greek.   These successes confirmed the good opinion I had of myself, they

assured me a brilliant future, I attached great importance to
them, and not for anything in the world would I have thrown
them away."[7]

Such autobiographers seem only peripherally concerned,
if at all, with marriage, maternity, and housekeeping.   None
of them have "given up" aspirations or promising careers
for the conventional alternatives.   These women control their
own biology (as Sanger would have others do), treat sex
(which they enjoy) as independent of marriage, and are self-
assertive (some would say dominant) in marriage or in other
long-term liaisons with either men or women.   Of the eight,
three were not married during the time their books cover.
One was a lesbian, though Stein does not discuss this at all
in any of her autobiographical volumes.   Hellman and de
Beauvoir had lifelong relationships with men they chose not
to marry; Angelou and Giovanni had children out of wedlock.
Only Mead and Sanger discuss their marriages and child
bearing and rearing in any detail--and both Mr. Sanger and
Mead's third (and last) husband fade out of their autobiograph-
ies--and lives?--with scarcely a ripple.

Most of these women delight in looking attractive,
from an early age.   Maya Angelou anticipates her eighth-
grade graduation in beautiful "butter-yellow piqué" dress hand-
embroidered by her grandmother:   "I was going to be lovely
.... My hair pleased me too.   Gradually the black mass
had lengthened and thickened, so that it kept at last to its
braided pattern, and I didn't have to yank my scalp off when
I tried to comb it."[8]   But, unlike the "total" or "fascinating"
women, these autobiographers disdain to use sex or other
"feminine wiles" as weapons or manipulative devices.   Hellman
has an abortion, even though she is "probably going to marry
the man anyway, but won't when she's pregnant."[9]   De Beauvoir regards the matrimonial bond as bondage, and prefers
to live with Sartre from continual free choice.

These autobiographers find fun less in flirtation than
in work (Mead, Sanger), in professional or social gatherings
of intellectually stimulating persons (Stein's Paris salon, for
example), and sometimes in the natural world (Hellman) and
in their children (Giovanni, Mead).   They are comfortable
with their scale of priorities ("I valued my independence; I
would have a profession"--de Beauvoir, p. 142).   And they
are pleased when they accomplish goals that they consider
enormously demanding and unequivocally worthwhile; they are,
in Abraham Maslow's term, "self-actualized" people, whose

lives reflect the power of their self-determination.

    The medium of autobiography contains a built-in con-
flict between the desire to avoid insufferable egotism and the
need to give credit even when it's due to oneself.    In women's
autobiographies this conflict may be somewhat subdued by
culturally inbred modesty; there are not many boastful Cel-
linis or Norma Mailers among women autobiographers.    But
prideful pleasure nevertheless permeates the autobiographers'
narration and honest assessment of various accomplishments.
As Margaret Mead says in an understatement of her nine-
month pioneering study in Samoa: "By studying pre-adolescent girls I also invented a cross-sectional method that can
be used when one cannot stay many years in the field but
wants to give a dynamic picture of how human beings develop.
In Samoa I went back only one step.    Later I went back to
small children and then to infancy, realizing that I needed
to include all the stages of growth. ...    I used case histories
and tests that I invented, such as a picture-naming test. ... "[10]

Sources of the positive self-images

    There is, obviously, considerable self-selection among
women autobiographers of quality works, an unusual group
with unusual accomplishments and extraordinary public recognition.    One would expect to find more "positive" images--
and more autobiographies--among such "successful" and jus-
tifiably egotistical people, in whose lives others, including
potential readers, would be interested.    Yet except for some
actresses, positive self-images are not nearly as common
in autobiographies of women who matured in the later nineteenth century as they are among women of the twentieth
century.

    The positive images of twentieth-century women may
result from the various social and political factors (such as
the women's suffrage movement) operating in Western cultures
during the first quarter of this century to raise women's
consciousness of themselves as individuals and as social and
political forces--phase II of women's liberation. [11]   Phase III
might be said to have begun in the early 1970s, following in
the wake of the civil rights movement--the effect of which
pervades contemporary autobiographies of black men and women, such as Nikki Giovanni's Gemini:    An Extended Autobiographical Statement of My First Twenty-Five Years of
Being a Black Poet: "We Black women are the single group

in the West intact.   And anybody can see we're pretty shaky.
We are, however (all praises), the only group that derives
its identity from itself....   We measure ourselves by ourselves, and I think that's a practice we can ill afford to
lose. "12

Often, too, the maturing young woman identified strongly with her father or mother or grandparent who was sympathetic to such social or political movements, as did Mead
and Sanger.   Or others encouraged her toward creative or
intellectual self-fulfillment: "I decided to be a writer because
people said I was a genius and then would ask what I would
become.   And I couldn't see anywhere to go intellectually
and thought I'd take a chance on feeling" (Giovanni, p. 148).
In other instances, the maturing person rebelled against representatives of a disliked status quo, as did de Beauvoir and
Hellman: "By seventeen, I was openly rebellious against
almost everything.   I knew that the seeds of the rebellion
were scattered and aimless in a nature that was wild to be
finished with something-or-other and to find something-else-
or-other, and I had sense enough to know that I was over-
proud, oversensitive, overdaring because I was shy and frightened" (Hellman, p. 26).

But whether her models were positive or negative,
individual or collective, the woman was aware of the objects
of and reasons for her identification, even as a child.   For
example Mead, in characteristic anthropological fashion, as-
sesses her father's influence on her, positive and negative:
"He loved to hold my hands and comment on their shape and
how they felt, and all my life I have enjoyed using my hands
for activity and for communication.   He taught me the importance of thinking clearly and of keeping one's premises
clear.   I learned to value male skills as something he did
not have and was somehow diminished by not having.   From
the beginning I certainly repudiated his fearfulness and de-
terminedly allowed my adventurous, but properly cautious,
young daughter to climb the tallest pine" (p. 140).

Likewise, the woman autobiographer was clearly aware
of her long-range goals that required her talents more than
her biology or social status to accomplish.   Thus at eighteen
de Beauvoir rejected the "luxury and easy living," the bourgeois status implied by possible marriage to her cousin
Jacques, and stated her goals: "I want my life to be an
all-consuming passion.   I need to act ... to bring plans to
fruition:  I need an object in life, I want to overcome dif-

ficulties and succeed in writing a book" (p. 213).

Often, the person whose adult image was very positive
felt different from most of her childhood peers, for indeed,
she was outstanding, even as a child.  Only the orphaned
Mary McCarthy continually strove for acceptance, "a walking
mass of lies, pretending to be a Catholic and going to confession while really I had lost my faith, and pretending to have
monthly periods by cutting myself with nail scissors....."[13]
The others were either pleased to be both set apart and chosen, or they had the stamina to endure such separateness--
even ostracism, in Mead's freshman year at DePauw--and to
turn it to creative advantage.  De Beauvoir explains that during her middle years at the Sorbonne, in spite of friendships
and an "uncertain love affair" she still felt that "there was
no one who knew or loved me completely for myself alone
....  I again took refuge in pride.  My isolation was a sign
of my superiority: ... I was somebody, and I would do great
things.  ...  As I was living in a world of [philosophical]
abstractions I believed that I had discovered, once and for
all, the truth of life....  My superiority over other people
came precisely from the fact that I didn't let anything escape
me: the peculiar value of my work would be the result of
this exceptional privilege" (p. 236).

Early on, as we have seen, such women received
encouragement either at home, or in school, or from social
or professional friends or groups to be innovative, independent, and goal oriented.  From these same sources, as well
as through their own determined efforts, they gained the education, economic support, and freedom to pursue their goals.
As Mead says: "We belonged to a generation of young women
who felt extraordinarily free--free from the demand to marry
unless we chose to do so, free to postpone marriage while
we did other things, free from the need to bargain and hedge
that burdened and restricted women of earlier generations....
We did not bargain with men" (p. 108).  That these women
accomplished the professional goals permitted by their freedom
and their abilities is evident from their eminence as well
as from their autobiographies.

Issues and implications of positive autobiographical images

Although these twentieth-century autobiographers would
seem to be ideal "liberated women," they are not liberated
from the human problems that are part of the human condi-

tion.   They experience orphanhood (McCarthy), running away
(Hellman, Angelou), disease (Sanger), discrimination (Angelou,
McCarthy), dissolution of marriage (Sanger, Mead) or meaningful friendship (Hellman, de Beauvoir), estrangement (Stein),
alcoholism (Hellman), rape (Angelou), rivalries (Mead), injustice (McCarthy), absence of professional recognition (Stein).
While popular autobiographies, like popular fiction--and even
quality fiction of the sort discussed below--exploit these personal problems, quality autobiographies more often tend to
objectify, subdue, or ignore them altogether.

Stein, for instance, simply writes her brother Leo
out of her autobiography after their estrangement, but she
never discusses their breach in print, nor does she refer to
Leo (or anyone else in her family, for that matter) by name,
only by their relationship to her: "Gertrude Stein's brother."
Likewise, she notes her lack of professional success at the
age of forty-six, after a quarter century of writing, with
characteristically objective understatement: "Gertrude Stein
was in those days a little bitter, all her unpublished manu-
scripts, and no hope of publication or serious recognition"
(p. 197).

Likewise, Hellman tersely mentions her own drinking:
"I was learning [at twenty-five] to drink hard.   I was out of
place [in "Hollywoodland"] and drinking made uninteresting
people matter less and, late at night, matter not at all" (p.
47).   In her extremely moving account of her thirty-year
liaison with Dashiell Hammett, she says essentially this--and
only this--of his eighteen years of intermittent alcoholism:
"But as the years passed from 1930 to 1948, he wrote only
one novel and a few short stories.   By 1945 the drinking was
no longer gay, the drinking bouts were longer and the moods
darker.   I was there off and on for most of those years, but
in 1948 I didn't want to see the drinking anymore" (p. 228).

These autobiographers also minimize the tension that
might occur in attempts to fulfill conflicting demands, such
as between those of a wife/mother as opposed to those of a
career.   One fifth of the way through her Autobiography (but
about halfway through the chronological period the volume
covers), Sanger dismisses her husband ("unaware the parting
was to be final," p. 105) and shifts her focus almost completely to birth control.   Not until 250 pages later do we
learn that she's been divorced for ten years, and then only
in connection with her second marriage, which she introduces
by saying, "It is as foolish to promise to love forever as to

promise to live forever" (p. 355).    She alludes only once
thereafter to her second husband, staid, male chauvinist "pil-
lar of finance," J. N. Slee, though the marriage was evidently
happy.

Such blandness and reticence about issues that are
problematic, at least to most of us mortals, raise the question of whether the autobiographers' positive images are genuine or hypocritical.    Might they be produced at the expense
of candor?    Could they be the creations of self-servingly
selective memories, insufferable egos, myopic perspectives,
or overriding desires to impose art--or "managed news"--
on life?

Allowing for some human fallibility, other writings
(novels, essays, treatises, biographies, diaries, letters) by
and about these autobiographers basically validate the perspectives in these autobiographies by corroborating these women's positive self-images, as strong, creative, productive,
independent people with a healthy sense of self.    For instance,
Alice B. Toklas's What Is Remembered (New York:    Holt,
Rinehart, and Winston, 1963) is an unabashedly biased, loving
corroboration of Stein's autobiographical writings.    Even if
one wishes to discount Toklas's partisanship, her views of
a strong, positive Stein are corroborated by the more objective, scholarly works of Donald Sutherland, Elizabeth Sprigge,
John Malcolm Brinnin, and Richard Bridgman, among others. [14]

## Images of women in autobiography compared to those in fiction

In general, these autobiographies, even if their authors
do not identify themselves as feminists, present much more
consistently positive images of women than does twentieth-
century fiction by women writers, feminist or not. [15]    The
most economical and appropriate comparisons, for similarities of mode, form, and intelligent, educated, middle-class
protagonists, may be made between these autobiographies and
feminist, [16] first-person novels in an autobiographical mode,
such as Alix Kates Shulman's Memoirs of an Ex-Prom Queen
and Erica Jong's Fear of Flying. [17]

Although one might expect the heroines[18] of feminist
fiction to be strong, positive, mentally and physically resil-
ient, productive or creative role models for aspiring women
readers, as are the autobiographers, such is not necessarily
the case.

In various ways the protagonists of these and comparable novels search for a positive, self-reliant identity.  Isadora Wing, twenty-nine (Fear of Flying), wants to be a re-
nowned, respected writer; Sasha Davis Burke (Memoirs) had
wanted to earn a doctorate in philosophy, and at thirty,
after two marriages and two children, appears (but am-
biguously) to be seeking an intellectually stimulating profession.

Yet each has to cope with her biologically and socially
imposed identity--to be a beautiful, feminine woman, dependent on a man.  So Sasha and Isadora spend disproportionate
amounts of their abundant energy and intellect in making themselves beautiful or in worrying about their departures (real
or imagined) from the feminine ideal--concerns of much lower
priority for the women autobiographers.  Isadora observes,
"Growing up female in America.  What a liability!...  If only
you took proper care of your smells, your hair, your boobs
... you would meet a beautiful, powerful, potent, and rich
man who would satisfy every longing ... with whom you
would live totally satisfied forever" (p. 9).  At twenty-four
Sasha believes, "Looks were everything, my only asset....
My mirror image always had to be interpreted [by a man]"
(pp. 15-16).

Thus brainwashed, Isadora and Sasha believe they cannot live--happily or otherwise--without men.  Sasha says,
"From the eighth grade on, no matter how I talked up freedom,
I had never managed to spend more than four consecutive
months without at least one man to count on, and frequently
two, in case one ran out.  In high school they called it 'boy
crazy'; in college ... 'oversexed.'  To me it was life insurance" (pp. 14-15).  Likewise for Isadora: "All my fantasies
included marriage.  No sooner did I imagine myself running
away from one man than I envisioned myself tying up with
another....  I simply couldn't imagine myself without a man.
Without one, I felt lost as a dog without a master; rootless,
faceless, undefined" (pp. 79-80).

So Sasha and Isadora are attracted by the magnetism
of two worlds: the powerful, conventional feminine environment of beauty, submissiveness, and socially-imposed dependence on men; and the active world of creativity and self-
expression, the realm of the women autobiographers.  These
heroines find it impossible to occupy both realms simultaneously.  Sasha concluded at twenty, "I hadn't really wanted

to marry at all.  I wanted to make something of myself, not
just give it away.  But I knew if I didn't marry I would be
sorry.  Only freaks didn't.  I had to do it quickly, too,
while there was still a decent selection of men....  The
heavy pressure was on" (p. 174).  And when Isadora's lover
says, "'I've never met an ass to rival yours'," she thinks,
"That remark makes me feel better than if I'd just won the
National Book Award.  The National Ass Award--that's what
I want" (p. 78).

Throughout most of these novels, and similar fiction,
the principal women characters experience considerable conflict between these worlds.  The choices they make, in favor
of conventional marriage (and for Sasha, children) are neither
satisfying nor fulfilling.  Perhaps this is because the choices
are not real options, but the blind conformance to social pro-
gramming in which these women either lack control over
their own lives or abdicate it to men.  The women autobiographers, whose adult lives seem to be within their own
control most of the time, are influenced (usually for their
own growth and betterment) equally by men and women,
whether relatives, friends, or professional peers.  Unlike
these real women, the fictional "heroines" relinquish to their
husbands, lovers, and significantly, psychiatrists--the control
of their psyches, destinies, senses of self, even creative
powers. [19]  Not only do these women admit that they are
"sick" when they feel stultified, unhappy, or otherwise unable
to cope, but they defer to the male chauvinistic standards
for both diagnosis and cure.  Sasha seeks psychiatric help
for "frigidity" (for which read "professional frustration") and
believes that her psychiatrist, whose ultimate advice is to
"accept yourself as a male-dominated childbearing woman,"
sees her as "a crazy nymphomaniacal penis-envying castrating
masochistic narcissistic infantile fucked-up frigid bitch [who]
was lucky to have hooked any man at all" (p. 205).  Isadora
has been treated by six male psychiatrists, is married to a
seventh to whom she returns by the novel's end, after a passionate affair with yet another psychiatrist, who uses and
deceives her.

In the endings of Memoirs and Fear of Flying Sasha
and Isadora make tentative and ambiguous attempts to "fly,"
to lead the lives of self-determination and power that are
customary for the women autobiographers.  But whether they
will succeed is uncertain.  Although these fictional women
are of ages comparable to some of their autobiographical
counterparts, they seem much younger because, unlike the

autobiographers, they are uncertain of who they are and dependent on others for their identities. Although both have
professional aspirations and talent, they are not firmly goal-
oriented, as are the autobiographers, whose zest and purpose-
ful determination they lack. At the age of twenty-four, shortly after her second marriage because she was "terrified of
being alone" (p. 55), Isadora observes, "I had no sense of
myself as a writer and no faith in my ability to write.…
Despite the obvious fact that I was obsessed with writing,
despite publications and despite letters from literary agents
asking whether I was 'working on a novel,' I didn't really
believe in the seriousness of my commitment at all" (p. 57).
Creative work for these women is subordinate to their feminine problems. They cannot cope as happily or as produc-
tively with their feelings of being different as the autobiographers can, who are characterized by de Beauvoir's attitude, "I sometimes used to tell myself proudly: 'I am different.' But I seemed to see in my difference the proof of
a natural superiority which would one day be acknowledged
by everybody.… I wanted to be someone, to do something,
to go on progressing …" (p. 183). Sasha, Isadora, and
their sisters are girls; the autobiographers are women.


Conclusion

        Thus the autobiographies of these positive, liberated
women, whose maturity fulfills the promises of both their
youth and their adulthood, embody the ideals of the mainstream
of the contemporary women's liberation movement. To date,
the protagonists of feminist fiction in the autobiographical
mode generally do not. Consequently, today such autobiographies, rather than fiction, not only explain and interpret
images of positive lives, but inspire and redefine positive
images for the lives of innumerable women seeking what
their notable predecessors have already found.


REFERENCES

1.  Popular autobiographies, such as many ghost-written vol-
        umes about film stars, tend to fit the stereotypes
        of women in popular novels, films (and to a lesser
        extent, soap operas) of the same period; particu-
        larly rags-to-riches or saint-to-sinner and vice
        versa; or woman-as-voluptuous-sex-object. Unlike
        the almost consistently positive self-images among

autobiographers of quality works, many of the self-images in popular autobiography are negative--to the reader if not to the autobiographer--whore, bitch, smother-mother, seductress, gold-digger-- or ambiguous, at best. See Lynn Z. Bloom, "Tramps, Sheiks, and Femmes Fatales: On- and Off-Screen Images of '20s Film Stars in Popular Biographies and Autobiographies," Midwest Modern Language Association, 1974.

2. See Betty Friedan, The Feminine Mystique (New York: W. W. Norton, 1963), passim.

3. (1944; reprinted, New York: Bantam, 1973), I, first quotation XV, second quotation, 298; and see Chapter 8, "The Active Woman: The Masculinity Complex."

4. Helen Andelin, Fascinating Womanhood (1965; revised and reprinted, New York: Bantam, 1975), p. 295. See also Marabel Morgan, The Total Woman (Old Tappan, N. J.: Fleming H. Revell, 1973). A counter thrust may be seen in the current appeal of assertiveness training for women--and for men-- in courses, and in such books as Manuel Smith, When I Say No I Feel Guilty (New York: Dial Press, 1975) and Lynn Z. Bloom, Karen Coburn, and Joan Pearlman, The New Assertive Woman (New York: Delacorte Press, 1975).

5. The Autobiography of Alice B. Toklas. (1933; reprinted, New York: Vintage, 1960), p. 77.

6. An Autobiography. (1938; reprinted, New York: Dover, 1971), pp. 104-105.

7. Memoirs of a Dutiful Daughter. (1959; reprinted, New York: Popular Library, 1963), pp. 236, 239.

8. I Know Why the Caged Bird Sings. (1970; reprinted, New York: Bantam, 1971), pp. 144, 145.

9. An Unfinished Woman: A Memoir. (1969; reprinted, New York: Bantam, 1970), p. 34.

10. Blackberry Winter: My Earlier Years. (1972; reprinted, New York: Simon & Schuster, 1972), p. 154.

11. Phase I peaked in the 1850s. See Alice Rossi, "Feminism and Intellectual Complexity," in The Feminist Papers: From Adams to de Beauvoir, ed. Alice Rossi (New York: Columbia University Press, 1973), p. 616.

12. (1971; reprinted, New York: Viking, 1973), p. 144. See also Anne Moody, Coming of Age in Mississippi (New York: Dial Press, 1968).

13. Memories of a Catholic Girlhood. (New York: Harcourt,

Brace, 1957), p. 136.

14. See Sutherland, <u>Gertrude Stein: A Biography of Her Work</u> (New Haven, Conn.: Yale University Press, <u>1951</u>); Sprigge, <u>Gertrude Stein: Her Life and Her Work</u> (New York: Harper & Row, 1957); Brinnin, <u>The Third Rose: Gertrude Stein and Her World</u> (Boston: Little, Brown, 1959); Bridgman, <u>Gertrude Stein in Pieces</u> (New York: Oxford University Press, 1971).

Of course, as an antidote there are Hemingway's increasingly savage attacks on Gertrude Stein, whom he had once admired sufficiently to make her the godmother to his son: "Homme des lettres. Woman of Letters. Salon woman. What a lousy stinking life," in which Stein's former talent had degenerated to "malice and nonsense and selfpraise." (Holograph MS of Hemingway's letters, p. 87; later revised in <u>The Green Hills of Africa</u> (New York: Scribner's, <u>1935</u>), pp. 65-66; quoted in Carlos Baker, <u>Ernest Hemingway: A Life Story</u> (1969; reprinted, New York: Bantam, 1970), pp. 341, 816.)

See also Hemingway's ambivalent "Miss Stein Instructs" and "Une Generation Perdue," in <u>A Moveable Feast</u> (New York: Scribner's, 1964), pp. 11-31.

15. I am not referring here to the positive images of women in fantasy or feminist science fiction, which are separate, not-so-realistic genres.

16. For a most interesting and useful exploration of this concept see Agate Nesaule Krouse, "Toward a Definition of Literary Feminism," which appears in the present anthology.

17. <u>Memoirs</u> (1972; reprinted, New York: Bantam, 1973); <u>Fear of Flying</u> (1973; reprinted, New York: Signet, <u>1974</u>).

18. "Heroines" is a problematic label both because of the sexism implicit in the term and because although these characters allegedly have the potential for being heroic they generally do not act that way.

19. For corroboration and amplification of these views, see Jane Larkin Crain, "Feminist Fiction," <u>Commentary</u>, 58 (Dec. 1974), 58-62.

## BIBLIOGRAPHY

Andelin, Helen. <u>Fascinating Womanhood.</u> Santa Barbara,

Calif. : Pacific Press, 1965.

Angelou, Maya. I Know Why the Caged Bird Sings. 1970;
    reprinted, New York: Bantam, 1971.

Baker, Carlos. Ernest Hemingway: A Life Story. 1969;
    reprinted, New York: Bantam, 1970.

de Beauvoir, Simone. Memoirs of a Dutiful Daughter. 1959;
    reprinted, New York: Popular Library, 1963.

Bloom, Lynn Z. , Karen Coburn, and Joan Pearlman. The
    New Assertive Woman. New York: Delacorte
    Press, 1975.

Bloom, Lynn Z. "Tramps, Sheiks, and Femmes Fatales:
    On- and Off-Screen Images of '20s Film Stars in
    Popular Biographies and Autobiographies," Midwest
    Modern Language Association, 1974.

Bridgman, Richard. Gertrude Stein in Pieces. New York:
    Oxford University Press, 1971.

Brinnin, John Malcolm. The Third Rose: Gertrude Stein
    and Her World. Boston: Little, Brown, 1959.

Crain, Jane Larkin. "Feminist Fiction," Commentary, 58
    (Dec. 1974), 58-62.

Giovanni, Nikki. Gemini: An Extended Autobiographical
    Statement on My First Twenty-Five Years of Being
    a Black Poet. 1971; reprinted, New York: Viking,
    1973.

Hellman, Lillian. An Unfinished Woman: A Memoir. 1969;
    reprinted, New York: Bantam, 1970.

Hemingway, Ernest. A Moveable Feast. New York: Scrib-
    ner's, 1964.

Jong, Erica. Fear of Flying. 1973; reprinted, New York:
    Signet, 1974.

Krouse, Agate Nesaule. "Toward a Definition of Literary
    Feminism," Midwest Modern Language Association,
    1974.

McCarthy, Mary. Memories of a Catholic Girlhood. New

York:  Harcourt,  Brace,  1957.

Mead, Margaret.   Blackberry Winter:  My Earlier Years.
      1972; reprinted, New York:  Simon & Schuster,
      1972.

Moody, Anne.   Coming of Age in Mississippi.   New York:
      Dial, 1968.

Morgan, Marabel.   The Total Woman.   Old Tappan, N. J. :
      Fleming H. Revell, 1973.

Rossi, Alice.   "Feminism and Intellectual Complexity,"  The
      Feminist Papers:  From Adams to de Beauvoir,
      ed. Alice Rossi.   New York:  Columbia University
      Press, 1973, p. 616.

Sanger, Margaret.   An Autobiography.   1938; reprinted, New
      York, Dover, 1971.

Shulman, Alix Kates.   Memoirs of an Ex-Prom Queen.   1972;
      reprinted, New York:  Bantam, 1973.

Smith, Manuel J.   When I Say No I Feel Guilty.   New York:
      Dial, 1975.

Sprigge, Elizabeth.   Gertrude Stein:  Her Life and Her Work.
      New York:  Harper & Row, 1957.

Stein, Gertrude.   The Autobiography of Alice B. Toklas.
      1933; reprinted, New York:  Vintage, 1960.

Sutherland, Donald.   Gertrude Stein:  A Biography of Her
      Work.   New Haven, Conn. :  Yale University Press,
      1951.

Toklas, Alice B.   What Is Remembered.   New York:  Holt,
      Rinehart, and Winston, 1963.

Kathleen Dehler

## THE NEED TO TELL ALL:
## A COMPARISON OF HISTORICAL AND MODERN
## FEMINIST "CONFESSIONAL" WRITING

Confessions have always been appealing. What is curious about recent feminist autobiographical and confessional books is that they have received such a large amount of serious thought and have sparked so many discussions. Recall the reaction to The Three Marias, Kate Millett's Flying, Ingrid Bengis's Combat in the Erogenous Zone, Jane Howard's A Different Woman, and Gabrielle Burton's I'm Running Away from Home, But I'm Not Allowed to Cross the Street. These books ask the reader to be not only a critic while reading them, but also a human being; they require the reader to feel, to be sensitive to the author's experiences. Consequently, the complaint has often been voiced that these books don't fit into any accepted category: autobiography, confession, or fiction. Furthermore, the critical reaction to these books has been mixed, and the women's movement has been chided for encouraging "confessional" writing, and more importantly, for heralding it as a new literary genre.

But is confessional writing a product of the New Feminism, or is it a style which has developed with the movement from the nineteenth-century suffrage writers such as Abigail Scott Duniway, Jane Grey Swisshelm, Elizabeth Cady Stanton, and Emmeline Pankhurst? A closer look at confessional writing, inspired by both the suffrage movement and the New Feminism, will not only reveal interesting similarities concerning the basic content and style of these books, but will also present the authors as having parallel motivating forces. Furthermore, answers will be suggested for questions concerning the popularity of, need for, and the effect upon the reader of modern, feminist confessional writing.

Since there is so much discussion about the use of the term "confessional," it warrants clarification. Kate Millett strenuously objects to application of the term "confession" to these works since inherent in the word "confession" is the acceptance of sin, an unnatural, wrong action for which the writer wishes atonement. She does admit, though, that the word becomes softened with Rousseau: "'Confessions' here is closer to confidences, intimacy, the experiences (some of them even sexually exceptional) which he [Rousseau] shared with his mistresses."[1] Millett goes on to discuss how certain women writers have converted "autobiography into fiction by changing the central character's name as well as those of others."[2] A writer ought to be "shameless," Miller maintains, making the fictionalizing of her autobiography unnecessary. A woman should not feel contrite because of her past actions; rather, she should want to proudly present her life and thoughts as a model worthy of study.

Northrop Frye makes the distinction that

> Most autobiographies are inspired by a creative, and therefore fictional, impulse to select only those events and experiences in the writer's life that go to build up an integrated pattern. This pattern may be something larger than himself with which he has come to identify himself.[3]

Confession, Frye continues, is "simply the coherence of his character and attitudes."[4] In the writings of some historical and modern feminists, these two forms--confession and auto-biography--come very close, and the distinction is almost impossible to make. Many of the women suffrage writers began by writing autobiography, but their lives became more a history of the movement with interspersed comments about their emotions and objectives. Within this "integrated pattern," however, the reader is confronted with their strong personalities and attitudes. These writers seemed more interested in selecting events which would expose their philosophy than in just revealing their actions. This leads to many modern revelatory works in which the reader hardly knows any incidents from the writers' past, can make no judgments about their future, but knows the authors intimately during the present.

Confessional writing can be divided into two major areas. First, there is autobiographical writing which takes on larger implications because it not only uncovers the individual's life, but also encourages the movement by exposing the beneficial effects which the ideas of the movement have had on the author. Modern examples of this writing are

Bengis's Combat in the Erogenous Zone, Millett's Flying,
Howard's A Different Woman, or Brown's Rubyfruit Jungle.
Older writings are Duniway's Path Breaking, Swisshelm's
Half a Century, Pankhurst's My Own Story, and Stanton's
Eighty Years and More.  The second type of confessional
writing is sociological studies of society, especially of woman's role, in which the author is ever present either by
exemplifying facts through examples from her own life or by
presenting theories in an admittedly opinionated manner:  almost a "thinking about" approach.  Modern examples are
Elizabeth Janeway's Man's World Woman's Place, Mary Ell-
man's Thinking About Women, Betty Friedan's The Feminine
Mystique, and Germaine Greer's The Female Eunuch.  Suffrage period examples are Charlotte Perkins Gilman's Women
and Economics, Sarah M. Grimké's Letters on the Equality
of the Sexes and the Condition of Women, Ellen Key's Love
and Marriage, and Margaret Fuller's Woman in the Nineteenth
Century.

It is the former type of confession, the autobiographical, which causes the most critical reaction, and which will
be emphasized in this paper.  A popular example of autobiographical confession is Millett's Flying, in which she relates her life after the publication of Sexual Politics.  Characteristically, Millett agrees with Doris Lessing's idea that
the feelings and actions which are most private to the writer
are actually those which are most universal and should be
the subject of books.  Lessing states:  "That's the moment
when I was speaking for others. "5  The reader's immediate
reaction to Millett's book, which often touches immensely
personal topics, is first to totally empathize, then to feel
embarrassed for her, then to become critical, and finally to
be overwhelmed with the power of this book.

Rita Mae Brown, in Rubyfruit Jungle, creates a similar experience by writing what it is like to grow up a lesbian
in America.  She not only describes the feeling, but forces
the reader to experience it.  Ingrid Bengis, in Combat in the
Erogenous Zone, adds a bit of humor, a bit of warmth; she
writes as a friend telling her tale of hitchhiking around the
world and living as she likes.  Similarly, Jane Howard's A
Different Woman presents a sensitive woman who, after fifteen years with Life magazine, decides to hit the road and
find out what women are really thinking.  The result is that
she reveals many more of her own thoughts than others'.
Looking at Gabrielle Burton's I'm Running Away from Home,
one finds underneath this down-to-earth gem a woman who

is carefully revealing herself, disguised under many laughs, to the reader. Moreover, the United States is not the only country where modern confessional writing has attracted attention. The Three Marias: New Portuguese Letters created worldwide publicity for its writers. The three Marias write intensely personal letters and poems to each other about life, interspersed with hypothetical letters an historical Maria could have written to her lover.

Similarly, the nineteenth-century suffrage movement has also produced its autobiographical confessional writers. Abigail Scott Duniway subtitles her book, Path Breaking; An Autobiographical History of the Equal Suffrage Movement in Pacific Coast States. In relating her own life, Duniway tells the story behind the suffrage fight; she reveals intensely personal feelings about powerlessness, especially in her work with other women. The acuteness of her feelings is underlined in her novel, From the West to the West, where she dwells on the crimes committed against women by selfish husbands.

Emmeline Pankhurst's My Own Story was written in 1914 while World War I was in progress, when she believed her goal, votes for women, was soon to be granted. She presents events in this autobiography not merely because of their importance in history, but because of their effect on her feminist ideas. She realizes the violence she has condoned; thus, she must explain her motivations. In a subtle manner, she expresses the motivations behind her relentless struggle for suffrage, and though she does not expressly state her willingness to give up such things as her family, her actions reveal it. Moreover, Jane Grey Swisshelm's autobiography, Half a Century, presents a classic example of the woman who realizes that, after she marries, she'll be living off her own ability, even though society is telling her that that is not so. She candidly states in her preface that one of the reasons she wrote her autobiography was

> to illustrate the force of education and the mutability of human character, by a personal narrative of one who, in 1836, would have broken an engagement rather than permit her name to appear in print, even in the announcement of marriage; and who, in 1850, had as much newspaper notoriety as any man of that time, and was singularly indifferent to the praise or blame of the Press;--of one who, in 1837, could not break the seal of silence

set upon her lips by 'Inspiration,' even so far as
to pray with a man dying of intemperance, and who
yet, in 1862, addressed the Minnesota Senate in
session, and as many others as could be packed
in the hall, with no more embarrassment than though
talking with a friend in a chimney corner.6

In so many ways this sounds like the story of a modern confessional writer who is finally seeing herself for all she is.
Similarly, Eighty Years and More, by Stanton, is definitely
an autobiography:  she even states in her preface that this
is the story of her private life, and if readers wish to find
out about her work with suffrage, they should turn to History
of Woman Suffrage.  However, many of the events that she
relates in Eighty Years and More take on importance only
because of her life work; furthermore, like many confessional
writers, Stanton concentrates on incidents that helped form
her philosophy and continually interjects her opinion about
important events.

Questions come to mind about the structure and im-
pulsion to write these confessional works.  Are they just re-
worked and published journals, a genre women have been
attracted to for a long time?  Stanton admits in her preface
that her work was not written for literary value, since much
of it was taken from her journals.  Ordinarily, journals are
private writing, notes one scribbles for one's personal use.
Moreover, one tends to write a journal entry either when
one is still in the midst of the incident, or soon after, when
one still feels its effects.  In confessional writing, however,
feminists tell of events with the full knowledge of how they
tried to improve the situation.  For example, Stanton relates
the story of how she was refused admittance to Union College
on the grounds of her sex when she was a young woman; however, part of the frustration is mitigated because Stanton
knows how she worked to change the situation in later life.
Similarly, Rita Mae Brown's feelings about her lesbian experience with Leota are muted by her later understanding of
it.

Interestingly enough, the reader will find the authors
of these works consistently refusing to feel sorrow or guilt
for the changes they have caused.  They are boldly presenting
facts about their lives and refuse to give excuses for their
actions.  This causes trouble with critics.  Repeatedly, critics
maintain that behind a confessional there should be an author
asking for absolution.  When the critics find something else,

their reaction becomes biting.  Jane Wilson writes of Flying
that Millett "is after absolution as well, empathy, approval
and admiration, and her demanding neediness hounds the
reader from the beginning to the end of the marathon essay
in self-absorption."[7]  Similarly, Elinor Langer warns Millett
that "Not all confessions end in absolution."[8]  Mary Ellmann
complains that Bengis's book is a frank "introductory admission of coyness."[9]  Jessie Bernard, in her thoughtful book
The Sex Game, states that confessional writers

> gladly tell all, and even more than all, if the lis-
> tener seems interested.  Their likes and dislikes,
> their sins of omission and of commission, their
> successes and their failures are all happily exposed.
> Some people do not even wait to be asked before
> they reveal themselves.  Confession is reputedly
> good for the soul.  But people who must bare it,
> who cannot keep any of their sins to themselves,
> who are, so to speak, compulsive confessors, who
> have to tell all, are viewed by clinicians as not
> really well.[10]

In a similar vein, a 1914 reviewer in The Nation senses,
in My Own Story, pride in Pankhurst's actions and is most
annoyed that she will not show contrition for the violence she
has condoned:  "All that she thinks is necessary for the jus-
tification of violence is (when she conveniently can) to find
a precedent."[11]  This same reviewer ends the article with
a bombastic moral statement:  "there can be little doubt that
they [the suffragettes] have served to discredit the cause of
suffrage in the eyes of many thoughtful men and women."[12]
One is reminded of Millett's comment about Langer's ruthless
criticism of Flying in Ms. magazine:  "by virtue of what
power does Ms. Langer withhold the sacrament?"[13]

These authors, however, do not see wrong in writing
about their controversial lives; paradoxically, it is the realization that more people should refuse to follow societal rules
that makes these feminists want to write their stories.  More
importantly, since they refuse to reveal guilt for their actions,
these authors are presenting a new morality of personal honesty.  What are these authors of confessional books really
talking about?  Are they trying to force society to acknowledge
aloud what it does privately?  In one sense, by revealing
intensely personal thoughts and actions, which they have thoroughly examined, these authors encourage others to analyze
their lives.  Furthermore, these books are usually very pos-

itive; the authors, simply because they are willing to confess,
show that they believe individuals and society can accept positive change.   Duniway writes that she "can foresee a time
when free enfranchised women will be wise enough, and morally strong enough to quit the business of marrying inebriates,
or mothering drunkards or criminals."[14] Duniway asks that
people accept their moral obligation to see society as it is
and change it accordingly.   Behind all the personal struggles
revealed in these writings, there is confidence in a new
found freedom, and confidence that society can be helped
through honesty and actions.

At this point another question arises:   why did these
authors write?   There is an awareness of their own worth,
an awareness that their lives and what they have to say is
valuable.   They want to communicate and share their insights
with other people experiencing similar circumstances.   They
also see value in showing why they decided to support either
suffrage or modern feminism.   Curiously, early feminists
see the suffrage movement as parallel to the story of their
lives.   As one reviewer, in a 1911 New York Times, says
of Emmeline Pankhurst:   "There have been few great reform-
ers who have so thoroughly identified themselves with the
gospel they proclaimed."[15]   Pankhurst, however, was not
alone in totally accepting suffrage as part of her life.   Emma
Goldman wrote, three years after publishing her autobiography,
Living My Life, an article in Harper's, "Was My Life Worth
Living?"   In it, Goldman wonders if her life was worth living,
since the value of her life was based upon the acceptance and
development of her ideals, and so few of her goals were
achieved.

Another reason these women wrote was to voice an
opinion against the traditional roles for women.   Stanton
thought seriously on this matter since, after the death of
her brother, her father told her he wished she were a boy;
consequently, she wanted to be free to do things both men
and women could do.   On the other hand, after realizing that
they didn't want to live these traditional female roles, these
confessional writers often found out that even if they did want
to, it would be impossible and impractical.   For example,
Swisshelm realized soon after her marriage that she would
have to financially support her family.

There is also an acceptance among confessional writers
that the ordinary, everyday events of their lives are important, as important as law, war, politics, or whatever else

is generally considered newsworthy.  Langer writes:  "In
the exploration and elevation of the 'personal,' sanctioned by
the Women's Movement, what on earth has happened to pro-
portion?"[16]  Perhaps these writers are setting up a new pro-
portion based on the premise that daily, personal activities
do effect larger world problems.  These women have realized
that the artificial standards which have made women's traditional domain secondary are not secure or permanent; tradition can be changed.

Another factor influencing women to write is the realization that they have accomplished something in their lives,
something which is important.  And there is no reason to
hide it.  Rita Mae Brown is proud of her life, and if there
are problems, she'll fight them even if it takes until she's
fifty.  As she adds, "if it does take that long then watch
out world because I'm going to be the hottest fifty-year old
this side of the Mississippi."[17]  Similarly, Pankhurst so
believes in her life work that she ends her book, which was
published five years before English women got suffrage, with
this statement:

> None will be willing to undertake the impossible
> task of crushing or even delaying the march of wo-
> men towards their rightful heritage of political lib-
> erty and social and industrial freedom.[18]

No longer are these women ashamed of their lives; they realize that their activities are interesting.

But is there a political side to these books?  The
suffragists were working for the vote; many New Feminists
are working for equality.  Therefore, some of these authors
wanted a personal reaction to their works, in hopes of causing
change.  Jane Kramer realized this when she reviewed The
Three Marias:

> There is no doubt that 'The Three Marias' was a
> political event in Portugal.  It raised challenges
> that were not political in the ordinary sense of
> challenges to the state, the wars in Africa, the
> notion of colonial empire, but political nonetheless
> and in a more profound sense, being challenges to
> a repression rooted in the sexual and social fabric
> of Portugal and to the willful Latin puritanism which
> had sanctioned and rewarded that repression.[19]

On another level, Bengis writes:  "if you see something of

yourself in me, I have seen something of myself in you, if my distortions are yours as well, then maybe we can begin to reexamine our ideas about distortion."[20] Similarly, Burton writes: "My gropings will not exactly parallel anyone else's, but hopefully they will encompass enough similarities to ease a reader's struggles and provide a base from which to start her own gropings."[21] Realizing this, Library Journal calls Burton's book "a down-to-earth piece of consciousness-raising literature, written in a plain and nonpolitical style."[22]

With something similar in mind, Pankhurst writes in her forward: "the struggle for full enfranchisement of women has not been abandoned; it has simply, for the moment, been placed in abeyance."[23] Obviously, Pankhurst wants people to keep the struggle alive. Likewise, Swisshelm states that one of the reasons she wrote Half a Century was to show that the Emancipation Proclamation of 1862 was not a "triumph of Skepticism over Christianity.... In no way can this error be so well corrected as by the personal history of those who took part in that struggle."[24] She is suggesting that individuals cause change; therefore, a study of the lives of women who have brought about advancements is worthwhile. Obviously, these women feel a certain bond between their lives and those of other women just awakening to their conditions. By sharing their experiences, the authors hope that the readers will react on a personal level and come to an understanding of themselves.

The success of the "personal" response of these books is hard to judge, though Millett does reveal receiving "envelopes from strangers funneled through the publisher, notes of thanks, notes that make one feel one has helped someone to live."[25] Understandably, the bulk of the personal response to these books has been quiet, though the critical response has been loud and varied. Moreover, the majority of the authors discussed have had professional writing experience. Howard had worked for Life magazine, Millett had written Sexual Politics, and the three Marias were all writers. Furthermore, Stanton had written a considerable number of articles and books, and had worked on The History of Woman Suffrage. Swisshelm had experience writing for her Pittsburgh paper, Saturday Visitor, and her St. Cloud Democrat. Duniway was a published novelist. These women knew the effect of different styles of writing on the reader and chose an autobiographical confession as the most potent means of achieving their goals.

The difficulties which critics have had when dealing

with confessional writing are varied. Langer found a major problem in Millett's work: "By pretending we are presenting 'life,' not art, we avoid criticism."[26] Langer continues, arguing that Millett

> has made criticism of the book's contents nearly impossible. Everything one might think of saying about it, she has said herself. Any negative comment, she has anticipated in her own fantasies. Though she says she wants to be seen as vulnerable, she has created a kind of armor: no one can lacerate her any more than she has lacerated herself.[27]

Obviously, Langer doesn't appreciate or accept as valid the personal and political effect of these books. Furthermore, since she has difficulty discussing the book as literature, she attacks the contents of the book, and since the book is about Millett, she attacks Millett personally.

Langer's approach typifies that of many critics of confessional writing. One hardly knows, from reading a review in The Nation in 1914, that Pankhurst, in My Own Story, discusses what caused her interest in women's suffrage and her early years of peaceful militancy. Since this reviewer has had a problem accepting the fact that Pankhurst condoned violence, he spends most of the article questioning her use of violence and her justifications, totally ignoring the major thrust of the book. He then makes belittling comments about Pankhurst: "The reader who proposes to take her argument seriously is likely to be exasperated by the constant evidence of a feline sophistry.... At times she becomes sweetly reasonable."[28] Similarly, Mary Ellmann succumbs to this type of criticism by making value judgments more about Bengis's life than about her book, Combat in the Erogenous Zone:

> This is a good and profitable time to have a sexual history, and Ms. Bengis is determined to have one .... That is why she worries about her interest in women (nonexistent).... Her [Jill Johnston's] opposite is Ingrid Bengis, pretending to homosexuality, brooding on the choice, undergoing self-scrutiny-like cleaning out one's navel.[29]

Again, Jane Wilson, in her review of Flying, is more interested in what caused Millett to write a "marathon essay in self-absorption" than in the actual contents and purpose of Millett's book.[30] Wilson further states: "From the moment that Millett decided on the 'documentary' form of 'Flying,' she must have lived her life in order to write about it. "31 Since this statement could have been made about any writer of autobiography, it doesn't follow why it is a particular criticism of Millett. From these reviews, one learns more about the reviewer than about the book under discussion.

There are, of course, alternate ways to review a confessional; one doesn't have to attack the author personally. A 1914 reviewer, in the New York Times, realizes that My Own Story is "rather a history of the suffrage movement from the late sixties to 1914 than Mrs. Pankhurst's autobiography. "32 This reviewer, then, does not attack Pankhurst; rather, he discusses the contents of her book as part of a movement. Similarly, Stanton's New York Times reviewer describes how the events in Stanton's life contributed to her philosophy and how her personality and philosophy motivated her actions. The personal reservations the reviewer may have had about Stanton are not discussed; this remains a review of Eighty Years and More.

Feminist confessional writing is obviously not a new genre, a product of the 1960's and 70's; it was a popular medium during the women's suffrage period. The writers of these works are women caught up in some form of self-liberation, which they feel can be of help to others, and they want to share their knowledge. After going through a major change in life, they no longer believe or follow some tenets they were brought up with. They are generally satisfied with their new life and want to cause change by spreading their new found truths. These books, therefore, reveal the individual author's beliefs and her actions which necessarily follow. The popularity of each of these books is due to the author's knowledge of where society's sensitive nerve is and her ability to touch it. People react to these books; they can't just impersonally digest them. Consequently, critical reaction to these books has usually been mixed. When individuals are deeply committed to a particular change, they want to write about it, and as these writers have learned from experience, the autobiographical confession is an effective approach.

## REFERENCES

1. Kate Millett, "The Shame Is Over," Ms. , January 1975, p. 27.
2. Millett, p. 2.

350          Feminist Prose Criticism

3.  Northrop Frye, Anatomy of Criticism (Princeton, N. J.:
    Princeton University Press, 1957), p. 307.
4.  Frye, p. 307.
5.  Millett, p. 27.
6.  Jane Grey Swisshelm, Half a Century (1880; reprinted,
    New·York: Source Book Press, 1970), p. 4.
7.  Jane Wilson, review of Flying, by Kate Millett, New
    York Times Book Review, June 23, 1974, p. 2.
8.  Elinor Langer, "Confessing," Ms., December 1974,
    p. 108.
9.  Mary Ellmann, review of Combat in the Erogenous Zone,
    by Ingrid Bengis, New York Review of Books, 2
    (February 1, 1973), 18.
10. Jessie Bernard, The Sex Game (New York: Atheneum,
    1973), pp. 172-3.
11. "The Arch-Priestess of Militancy," review of My Own
    Story, by Emmeline Pankhurst, The Nation, 10
    December 1914, p. 688.
12. "The Arch-Priestess of Militancy," p. 689.
13. Millett, p. 27.
14. Abigail Scott Duniway, Path Breaking (1914; reprinted,
    New York: Source Book Press, 1970), p. xiv.
15. "Her Autobiography in 'My Own Story,'" review of My
    Own Story, by Emmeline Pankhurst, New York
    Times Book Review, October 25, 1914, p. 468.
16. Langer, p. 71.
17. Rita Mae Brown, Rubyfruit Jungle (Plainfield, Vt.:
    Daughters, Inc., 1973), p. 217.
18. Emmeline Pankhurst, My Own Story (1914; reprinted,
    New York: Source Book Press, 1970), p. 364.
19. Jane Kramer, review of The Three Marias, by Maria
    Isabel Barreno, Maria Teresa Horta, and Maria
    Velho da Costa, New York Times Book Review,
    February 2, 1972, p. 1.
20. Ingrid Bengis, Combat in the Erogenous Zone (New York:
    Bantam Books, 1973), p. xiv.
21. Gabrielle Burton, I'm Running Away from Home, But
    I'm Not Allowed to Cross the Street (New York:
    Avon Books, 1972), p. 14.
22. "Social Sciences," review of I'm Running Away from
    Home, But I'm Not Allowed to Cross the Street,
    by Gabrielle Burton, Library Journal, February 1
    1973, p. 429.
23. Pankhurst, foreword (no page given).
24. Swisshelm, p. 3.
25. Millett, p. 26.
26. Langer, p. 71.

27. Langer, p. 70.
28. "The Arch-Priestess of Militancy," p. 688.
29. Ellmann, p. 18.
30. Wilson, p. 2.
31. Wilson, p. 3.
32. "Her Autobiography in 'My Own Story,'" p. 468.

WORKS CONSULTED

Barreno, Maria Isabel; Horta, Maria Theresa; and Costa, Maria Velho da. The Three Marias, tr. Helen R. Lane. New York: Doubleday, 1975.

Bengis, Ingrid. Combat in the Erogenous Zone. New York: Bantam Books, 1973.

Bernard, Jessie. The Sex Game. New York: Atheneum, 1973.

Brown, Rita Mae. Rubyfruit Jungle. Plainfield, Vt.: Daughters, Inc., 1973.

Burton, Gabrielle. I'm Running Away from Home, But I'm Not Allowed to Cross the Street. New York: Avon Books, 1972.

Duniway, Abigail Scott. Path Breaking. New York: Source Book Press, 1970.

Frye, Northrop. Anatomy of Criticism. Princeton, N. J.: Princeton University Press, 1957.

Fuller, Margaret. Woman in the Nineteenth Century. New York: W. W. Norton, 1971.

Gilman, Charlotte Perkins. Women and Economics. New York: Harper & Row, 1966.

Grimke, Sarah M. Letters on the Equality of the Sexes and the Condition of Women. New York: Source Book Press, 1970.

Howard, Jane. A Different Woman. New York: Avon Books, 1974.

Key, Ellen. Love and Marriage. New York: Source Book Press, 1970.

352        Feminist Prose Criticism

Millett, Kate. Flying. New York: Knopf, 1974.

Pankhurst, Emmeline. My Own Story. New York: Source
    Book Press, 1970.

Stanton, Elizabeth Cady. Eighty Years and More. New York:
    Schocken Press, 1971.

Swisshelm, Jane Grey. Half a Century. New York: Source
    Book Press, 1970.

ARTICLES AND REVIEWS

Ellmann, Mary. [Review of Combat in the Erogenous Zone,
    by Ingrid Bengis.] New York Review of Books,
    February 1, 1973, pp. 18-9.

Goldman, Emma. "Was My Life Worth Living?" Harper's
    Magazine, December 1934.

Kramer, Jane. [Review of The Three Marias, by Maria
    Isabel Barreno, et al.] New York Times Book Re-
    view, February 2, 1972, pp. 1-2.

Langer, Elinor. "Confessing." Ms., December 1974, pp.
    69-71.

Millett, Kate. "The Shame Is Over." Ms., January 1975,
    pp. 26-9.

[Review of I'm Running Away from Home, But I'm Not Al-
    lowed to Cross the Street, by Gabrielle Burton.]
    Library Journal, February 1, 1973, p. 429.

[Review of My Own Story, by Emmeline Pankhurst.] The
    Nation, December 10, 1914, pp. 688-9.

[Review of My Own Story, by Emmeline Pankhurst.] New
    York Times Book Review, October 25, 1914, p.
    468.

Wilson, Jane. [Review of Flying, by Kate Millett.] New
    York Times Book Review, June 23, 1974, pp. 2-3.

BIOGRAPHICAL SKETCHES

MARGRET ANDERSEN is a professor of French literature and chairman of the Department of Languages at the University of Guelph. Her mundane phase found its expression in a master's thesis on Marcel Proust; her religious phase demonstrated itself in a thesis and book on Claudel et l'Allemagne (Université d'Ottawa); her feminist commitment led to the book Mother Was Not a Person (second edition; Montreal: Black Rose, 1975), of which 4000 copies have sold across Canada. Margret Andersen also writes poetry and is deeply interested in Quebec literature, having lived and studied in Quebec for about ten years. She has lived in Germany, England, France, the United States, Tunisia and Ethiopia and is a Canadian.

RISE B. AXELROD teaches English at the University of Colorado, Boulder, where she also heads the College Expository Writing Program. Her article on John Stuart Mill's Subjection of Women appeared in Victorian Newsletter. Ms. Axelrod is working on a booklength study of the city in Victorian and modern literature.

LYNN Z. BLOOM is an associate professor of English at the University of New Mexico, where she teaches courses on women in literature, biography and autobiography, and composition. These interests are combined in various publications: Doctor Spock: Biography of a Conservative Radical (Indianapolis: Bobbs-Merrill, 1972); The New Assertive Woman, with K. Coburn and J. Pearlman (New York: Delacorte, 1975); Strategies for Composition (forthcoming, 1979); and various articles, poetry, and reviews.

KATHLEEN DEHLER attended the College of New Rochelle and did graduate work at the University of Wisconsin-Madison. Presently she teaches English and women's studies on both the college and secondary school levels. She writes for Women's Studies Abstracts and is doing research in minor literary genres such as letters, diaries, self-help works, and confessionals--all of which are repositories for many of women's thoughts.

PAMELA DIPESA was born in Massachusetts in 1946 and lived there until the age of 18. After receiving a B. A. degree in 1968 from Sarah Lawrence College, she completed a Ph. D. degree in English at the City University of New York. Between 1970 and 1976, she taught English and did educational research in New York City. She is currently assistant professor of English at Gettysburg College in Pennsylvania.

SUSAN STANFORD FRIEDMAN: assistant professor in the English Department and the Women's Studies Program at the University of Wisconsin-Madison. Her work in the interdisciplinary field of women's studies includes an article on H. D. 's Helen in Egypt and a co-authored book, A Women's Guide to Therapy. A book on H. D. and a co-authored feminist anthology called Androgyny as Literary Vision and Living Myth are in the works.

JUDITH KEGAN GARDINER: an associate professor of English and a teacher of women's studies at the University of Illinois at Chicago Circle, she has written Craftsmanship in Context: The Development of Ben Jonson's Poetry (The Hague: Mouton, 1975) and articles on Ben Jonson, Renaissance literature and psychology, mothers and daughters, and contemporary women's fiction. Her degrees are from Radcliffe College and Columbia University. Her mother and two daughters are among her heroines, she states.

EVELYN THOMAS HELMICK was an associate professor of English at the University of Miami when she wrote the articles included in this anthology. She is currently Academic Dean at Salem College.

ESTELLE C. JELINEK teaches women's literature at San Francisco State University. She obtained her M. A. from the University of Pennsylvania and her Ph. D. from the State University of New York, Buffalo. In 1975 she was a resident NEH "fellow" at Dartmouth College studying men's autobiographies, and in 1976 her article "Teaching Women's Autobiographies" appeared in College English. She is presently preparing a book on the tradition of women's autobiography.

SUZANNE JUHASZ is assistant professor of English at the University of Colorado, Boulder, where she teaches American literature, women's studies, and creative writing. She is the author of Naked and Fiery Forms: Modern American Poetry by Women; A New Tradition (New York: Harper

& Row, 1976), Metaphor and the Poetry of Williams, Pound, and Stevens (Lewisburg, Pa.: Bucknell University Press, 1974), and articles on women's poetry and women's studies. Her poems appear in various anthologies and journals.

ANNETTE KOLODNY, after receiving her Ph. D. from the University of California at Berkeley in 1969, taught at Yale and then at the University of British Columbia in Canada, where she helped initiate and direct the first credited women's studies program in western Canada; she is now an associate professor of English at the University of New Hampshire. Her publications include numerous articles on American literature, feminist literary criticism, and the tribulations of litigating a sex discrimination complaint. Her first book, a feminist study of the American pastoral genre, appeared in 1975: The Lay of the Land: Metaphor as Experience and History in American Life and Letters (Chapel Hill: University of North Carolina Press). She is presently at work on a follow-up study, concentrating on the writings of pioneer women.

AGATE N. KROUSE is professor of English and co-ordinator of women's studies at the University of Wisconsin-Whitewater. Her work on women writers, feminist criticism, and women's studies has appeared in Contemporary Literature, Critique, Female Studies, Journal of Communication, Southwest Review, Women's Studies Newsletter, and World Literature Written in English.

BETH MILLER completed her Ph. D. in Romance languages and literatures at the University of California, Berkeley, and is currently associate professor and chairman of the Department of Spanish and Portuguese at the University of Southern California. She has published two books on the Mexican poet Jaime Torres Bodet and a variety of articles on women writers. Miller has a volume of feminist essays (Mujeres en la literatura) in press and is at work on a book on Rosario Castellanos.

ELLEN MORGAN coordinated one of the early women's studies courses, chaired the NOW national Task Force on University Compliance, serves as head of the Women's Studies Program at the University of Delaware, and won a Florence Howe Award for literary criticism. She holds a doctorate from the University of Pennsylvania, has taught literature, writing, and women's studies in a variety of academic institutions, and has published sixteen academic and other articles in addition to poetry.

ANNIS PRATT is a feminist archetypal critic, currently working on a book to be entitled Archetypal Patterns in
Women's Fiction. The article that appears here consists of
a brief preliminary note; a fuller discussion of the subject
of archetypalism and feminism appeared in the spring 1973
Bucknell Review. She is also researching the pre-literary
symbols and narratives to be found in women's needlework.

LILLIAN S. ROBINSON is "36, a poet, long active in
the women's movement and on the left." Indiana University
Press will publish a collection of her essays, Sex, Class
and Culture early in 1978, as well as her next book, a study
of television, for which she has been awarded a Rockefeller
Humanities Fellowship. She is associate professor of American studies and women's studies at the State University of
New York, Buffalo, and for 1977-78 is visiting professor of
American studies at the University of Paris.

ANN RONALD is an associate professor of English at
the University of Nevada, Reno where she has taught for seven
years. She has published a monograph, Zane Grey (1975),
for the Boise State University Western Writers Series, and
articles on Dickens, George Eliot, and some obscure women
writers of Nevada. Her current project "involves further
investigation of obscure women writers, specifically to discover what women thought about and wrote about as they helped
to settle the American West."

DIANNE F. SADOFF got her Ph. D. at the University of
Rochester and has been teaching literature at Antioch College
in Yellow Springs, Ohio, since 1971. Her primary teaching
at Antioch is in nineteenth-century British literature and women's studies--"now flourishing because of renewed faculty-
student interest and political action." She has published
articles on Dickens, Morris, Mailer, and contemporary women poets in critical journals and anthologies. She says,
"My husband, Ira, and I are working on the delicate balance
of a two-career marriage."

EDNA L. STEEVES, professor of English, University
of Rhode Island, Kingston, R. I., obtained her A. B. degree
from the University of California at Los Angeles in 1932,
her M. A. from the University of Chicago in 1936, and her
Ph. D. from Columbia University in 1948. Her publications
include authoring Art of Sinking in Poetry (1953; reprinted,
New York: Atheneum, 1968), and co-editing Friedrich Ger-
stäcker's Wild Sports in the Far West (Durham, N. C.: Duke
University Press, 1968). She has also written numerous

articles on eighteenth-century writers and women writers. She is currently editor of <u>Modern Language Studies</u>; member, Board of Editors, <u>Abstracts of English Studies</u>; member, NEMLA Executive Council; and a member of MLA, ASECS and AAUP. Research-in-progress: a history of feminism.

R L WIDMANN, associate professor of English at the University of Colorado, Boulder, teaches and publishes in Shakespeare, Renaissance literature, bibliography, modern and contemporary novel and poetry, and computer applications to literature. She has been book review editor of <u>Computers and the Humanities</u> since 1971. She is editor of <u>the New Variorum Midsummer Night's Dream.</u> She has taught at the University of Illinois and at the University of Pennsylvania before coming to Colorado. She has also held visiting appointments at the University of Maryland and LaSalle College. She travels in Western Europe frequently to lecture and to do research.

# NAME AND TITLE INDEX